SAVING NATURE U

When East Germany collapsed in 1989–1990, outside observers were shocked to learn the extent of environmental devastation that existed there. The communist dictatorship, however, had sought to confront environmental issues since at least the 1960s. Through an analysis of official and oppositional sources, *Saving Nature Under Socialism* complicates attitudes toward the environment in East Germany by tracing both domestic and transnational engagement with nature and pollution. The communist dictatorship limited opportunities for protest, so officials and activists looked abroad to countries such as Poland and West Germany for inspiration and support. Julia Ault outlines the evolution of environmental policy and protest in East Germany and shows how East Germans responded to local degradation as well as to an international moment of environmental reckoning in the 1970s and 1980s. The example of East Germany thus challenges and broadens our understanding of the "greening" of postwar Europe, and illuminates a history of central European connection across the Iron Curtain.

JULIA E. AULT is Assistant Professor in the Department of History, University of Utah.

NEW STUDIES IN EUROPEAN HISTORY

Edited by

PETER BALDWIN, University of California, Los Angeles
CHRISTOPHER CLARK, University of Cambridge
JAMES B. COLLINS, Georgetown University
MIA RODRÍGUEZ-SALGADO, London School of Economics and Political Science
LYNDAL ROPER, University of Oxford
TIMOTHY SNYDER, Yale University

The aim of this series in early modern and modern European history is to publish outstanding works of research, addressed to important themes across a wide geographical range, from southern and central Europe, to Scandinavia and Russia, from the time of the Renaissance to the present. As it develops the series will comprise focused works of wide contextual range and intellectual ambition.

A full list of titles published in the series can be found at: www.cambridge.org/newstudiesineuropeanhistory

SAVING NATURE UNDER SOCIALISM

Transnational Environmentalism in East Germany, 1968–1990

JULIA E. AULT

University of Utah

CAMBRIDGE
UNIVERSITY PRESS

Shaftesbury Road, Cambridge CB2 8EA, United Kingdom

One Liberty Plaza, 20th Floor, New York, NY 10006, USA

477 Williamstown Road, Port Melbourne, VIC 3207, Australia

314–321, 3rd Floor, Plot 3, Splendor Forum, Jasola District Centre, New Delhi – 110025, India

103 Penang Road, #05–06/07, Visioncrest Commercial, Singapore 238467

Cambridge University Press is part of Cambridge University Press & Assessment,
a department of the University of Cambridge.

We share the University's mission to contribute to society through the pursuit of
education, learning and research at the highest international levels of excellence.

www.cambridge.org
Information on this title: www.cambridge.org/9781009001656

DOI: 10.1017/9781009003810

First published 2021
First paperback edition 2022

A catalogue record for this publication is available from the British Library

ISBN   978-1-316-51914-1   Hardback
ISBN   978-1-009-00165-6   Paperback

To my parents Bruce and Helene

Contents

Figures

Acknowledgments

This book is many years in the making and owes an enormous debt of gratitude to the many institutions, mentors, colleagues, friends, and family who made it possible. The first inklings of this project were rooted in a semester abroad in Freiburg, Germany, and then became clearer while on a Fulbright English Teaching Assistantship after college. Placed in Jena, a smallish university town in the former East Germany, the relationships and experiences I had there opened my eyes to the many legacies – environmental and otherwise – of communist dictatorship.

At the University of North Carolina, the notions took clearer form in a dissertation under the guidance and encouragement of Konrad Jarausch. His ability to see the whole machine of the project, as well as each of the moving parts within it made the project, and ultimately, the book that much better. My thanks also to my dissertation committee members, Chris Browning, Chad Bryant, Susan Pennybacker, and Donald J. Raleigh for their input. Chad in particular has been a source of calm and steadfast reassurance during grad school and in the years since. In Chapel Hill, innumerable friends and fellow grad students made the time there intellectually stimulating and certainly more enjoyable. Derek Holmgren and Sarah Lowry plied me with excellent food on many occasions while Laura Brade, Adam Domby, Aaron Hale-Dorrell, Jennifer Kosmin, Caroline Nilsen, and Lars Stiglich all accommodated my desire to kick a soccer ball, go for a run, or chat over a beer. Also, thanks to fellow Germanists Friederike Brühöfener, Tom Goldstein, Max Lazar, Steve Milder, Ned Richardson-Little, Michael Skalski, and Sarah Vierra for lending an ear and offering useful advice.

Numerous grants and fellowships enabled the completion of this project. FLAS grants from Indiana University, the University of Pittsburgh, and UNC provided me with the language skills to make my first forays east of the Oder, while Columbia's Council for European Studies offered the means to conduct research in Germany and Poland. The Free University's

Berlin Program supported a year of dissertation research, during which Karin Goihl's knowledge, care, and concern were invaluable in navigating German archives and academic culture. While in Berlin, Paul Nolte's and Martin Sabrow's research colloquia as well as the Berlin-Brandenburg Environmental History Colloquium offered insights into the project's potential. The Central European History Society also provided funds for additional dissertation research. Since coming to the University of Utah, I have received support at every level. A University Research Council grant along with College of Humanities International Travel Grants and Department of History funds all sponsored follow-up research and conference presentations in Germany.

The research behind this book would not have been possible without numerous archives and archivists. At the Archive of the Opposition, Petra Söllner kindly welcomed me every day. The Federal Archive in Berlin-Lichterfelde and the Federal Commission for the Records of the State Security Service (BStU) also provided a wealth of sources about the functioning of the GDR and SED. In particular, Julia Spohr at the BStU helped me to explore the many different ways the Stasi viewed the environment. At the Böll Foundation's Green Memory Archive, Robert Camp and Christoph Becker-Schaum guided me in finding material about the Greens' stance on the GDR and eastern Europe. Saskia Paul at the *Archiv Bürgerwegung Leipzig* kindly aided my regional research. In the Lusatian hinterland, at Großhennersdorf's Environmental Library, I had the opportunity to access rarely read files as well as to meet and talk with locals who had been active in the environmental movement. Andreas Schönfelder generously spent hours relating his experiences and connecting dots of the former opposition movement. Regional archives in Halle, Magdeburg, and Merseburg as well as the Evangelical Archives and the Political Archive of the German Foreign Office in Berlin provided invaluable sources for the book. The Ossolineum Library in Wrocław and the Open Society Archive were crucial in developing the Polish and eastern European aspects of this book.

I have been incredibly fortunate to have friends and colleagues who helped with the dissertation and then the transition to a book manuscript. In Berlin, Adam Blackler, Stefanie Eisenhuth, Monika Freier, Andrew Kloiber, Scott Krause, Allison and Andrea Schmidt, and Sean Wempe devoted countless hours listening to half-baked concepts and greatly improved them in the process. Scott Harrison and Laura Yacovone were critical to making Berlin – and a month-long stint in Leipzig – a positive and productive experience. Since then, Kathryn Julian and Alex Ruble have graciously gone down many a rabbit hole on East German history and read chapters as I revised them. A special thanks goes to Deb Barton, Jen Lynn, Willeke Sandler, Lauren Stokes, and Kira Thurman for providing essential feedback on the manuscript – and emotional support – throughout the book writing process. I also owe Astrid Eckert a debt of gratitude for her advice and mentorship. At the University of Utah, my fellow historians have offered a welcoming environment and stimulating hallway conversations over the last six years. I must especially thank Nadja Durbach, who has been an excellent mentor and crucially read the entire manuscript as it neared completion.

At Cambridge University Press, Liz Friend-Smith and the series editors for New Studies in Modern European History saw potential in this manuscript and expertly guided me through the revision process. Atifa Jiwa has also been incredibly helpful in innumerable ways. Liz and Atifa more than deserve to be thanked for their calm and professional handling of my many frantic emails. I would be remiss if I did not express my gratitude for CUP's production team in making this book a reality. The two anonymous readers of this manuscript provided thoughtful and extensive feedback. This book has greatly benefited from their insights, and any shortcomings are my own.

Thank you to my gaggle of giggling Grinnellians and to my family, who have been there through every step of this endeavor. Amanda Lewis, Marta Grabowski, Anne Eaton, and Brenna Curley have cheered on their sole nonquantitative friend, offering wisdom, perspective, and of course, cheese. Andy, Kerri, and Oskar Ault have kept me grounded and made sure I maintained my Midwestern roots. I could not have completed this book without the unstinting love and support of my parents, Bruce and Helene. They have been all that is encouraging while making countless trips to Chapel Hill, Kraków, Berlin, and Salt Lake City. As I was finishing this book, Oliver entered the world and made it so much brighter. Finally, to my husband and partner in all things, Joshua Knudsen, life is unimaginable without you. Ich liebe dich.

Abbreviations

AGU – Working Group for Environmental Protection, *Arbeitsgruppe Umweltschutz* (Leipzig)

BBU – Federal Alliance of Citizens' Initiatives, Environmental Protection, *Bundesverband Bürgerinitiativ Umweltschutz*

BEK – Alliance of Protestant Churches in the GDR, *Bund der Evangelischen Kirchen in der DDR*

BUND – German Federation for the Environment and Nature Conservation, *Bund für Umwelt- und Naturschutz Deutschland*

BNU – League for Nature and the Environment, *Bund für Natur und Umwelt*

CDU – Christian Democratic Union

CUR – Christian Environmental Seminar Rötha, *Christliches Umweltseminar Rötha*

EC – European Community

FOE – Friends of the Earth

FRG – Federal Republic of Germany, *Bundesrepublik Deutschland*

GDR – German Democratic Republic, *Deutsche Demokratische Republik*

GNU – Society for Nature and the Environment, *Gesellschaft für Natur und Umwelt*

IUCN – International Union for Conservation of Nature

KFH – Ecclesiastical Research Center, *Kirchliches Forschungsheim* (Wittenberg)

LOP – Nature Conservation League, *Liga Ochrona Przyrody*

MUW – Ministry for Environmental Protection and Water Management, *Ministerium für Umweltschutz und Wasserwirtschaft*

NKCh – Chemists' Scientific Club, *Naukowe Koło Chemików*

NSMs – New Social Movements

NHF – Friends of Nature and Heimat, *Natur- und Heimatfreunde*

PKE – Polish Ecological Club, *Polski Klub Ekologiczny*

PZPR – Polish United Workers' Party, *Polska Zjednoczona Partia Robotnicza*

RPEI – residual pollution exemption for investors
SED – Socialist Unity Party, *Sozialistische Einheitspartei Deutschlands*
SERO– secondary resource acquisition, *Sekundärrohstofferfassung*
SU – State Environmental Inspection, *Staatliche Umweltinspektion*
URG – Environmental Framework Law, *Umweltrahmengesetz*
WCC – World Council of Churches
WiP – Freedom and Peace, *Wolność i Pokój*
ZUG – Center for Environmental Development, *Zentrum für Umweltgestaltung*

Introduction

When Monika Maron published *Flight of Ashes* in 1981, she shocked readers with stark images of Bitterfeld, one of Europe's most polluted cities in the heart of the East German Chemical Triangle. Considered the first book about environmental degradation in East Germany (German Democratic Republic, GDR), Maron had to publish the novel abroad in West Germany (Federal Republic of Germany, FRG). Maron exposed the environmental devastation of Soviet-style economies: "And these fumes could serve as road signs. Please go straight ahead to the ammonia, then turn left at the nitric acid. When you feel a stabbing pain in your throat and bronchial tubes, turn around and call a doctor, that was sulfur dioxide."[1] Maron's work not only graphically portrays the pollution but also illustrates the GDR's unique position between eastern and western Europe during the Cold War. A West German press published the novel for a West German audience, revealing the conditions in Bitterfeld as well as conveying the uncomfortable feeling of constant secret police, or Stasi, surveillance. Moreover, East Germans clamored to have copies of the book smuggled into the GDR, underscoring the connection between the two Germanys.[2] East German environmental issues stemmed from a distinctive domestic situation. Nevertheless, they had impacts on environments, pollution, politics, and social movements beyond the GDR's borders, just as the GDR was influenced by forces abroad.

The GDR was the product of the Cold War in Europe, but from the beginning, the small central European state held practical and symbolic meaning disproportionate to its size. The communist dictatorship, founded amid heightening US–Soviet tensions in 1949, was hived off from West Germany and incorporated into the Soviet sphere of influence.

---

[1] Monika Maron, *Flight of Ashes*, trans. David Newton Marinelli (New York: Readers International, 1986), 8.
[2] Robert Havemann Gesellschaft (RHG) OWK 07, "Bücherliste Teil 2," undated.

I

With German lands east of the Oder–Neisse Line ceded to Poland after the World War II, the GDR was a strange fragment in the east tied to the "other Germany" through national and historical connections.[3] Within the Soviet bloc, the GDR was also the most industrialized state outside of the Soviet Union and proudly proclaimed the largest per capita income of all communist states in the Cold War.[4] The ruling Socialist Unity Party (SED) touted the GDR as a "display window" of socialism to the west and a model for other Soviet bloc states, establishing the country as an important pivot between east and west in central Europe.[5] The GDR's accomplishments, however, came at the expense of the physical environment, public health, and quality of life as pollution from East German industries, such as chemicals, plastics, and coalmining, wrecked the air, water, and soil.

Saving Nature argues that the GDR's engagement with nature reconfigures our understanding of environmentalism in postwar Europe, situating it behind and across the Iron Curtain. The GDR was inevitably entangled with environments, pollution, movements, economies, policies, and diplomacy that transcended its seemingly impenetrable borders. Despite obvious environmental failures later in the GDR's existence, the communist dictatorship embraced environmental protection at home and abroad in the 1960s and 1970s. The SED contended that only capitalism exploited both people and nature.[6] Over time, the degradation became a security risk

[3] Christoph Kleßmann, "Introduction," in *The Divided Past: Rewriting Post-War German History*, ed. Christoph Kleßmann (New York: Berghahn, 2001), 1. Frank Bösch, "Introduction," in *History Shared and Divided: East and West Germany since the 1970s*, ed. Frank Bösch, trans. Jennifer Walcoff Neuheiser (New York: Berghahn Books, 2018), 1–2.

[4] Charles S. Maier, *Dissolution: The Crisis of Communism and the End of East Germany* (Princeton, NJ: Princeton University Press, 1997), 82.

[5] Hermann Wentker, *Außenpolitik in engen Grenzen: Die DDR im internationalen System, 1949–1989* (Munich: Oldenbourg, 2007), 188. For a discussion of central Europe during the Cold War, see Yuliya Komska, *The Icon Curtain: The Cold War's Quiet Border* (Chicago, IL: University of Chicago Press, 2015), 12–13; Michael Kraus et al., "The Cold War and East-Central Europe, 1945–1989," *Journal of Cold War Studies* 19, no. 2 (Spring 2017), 169. For more on central European borders and nationality in the nineteenth and early twentieth centuries, see James E. Bjork, *Neither German nor Pole: Catholicism and National Indifference in a Central European Borderland* (Ann Arbor, MI: University of Michigan Press, 2008); David Blackbourn and James Retallack, eds., *Localism, Landscape, and the Ambiguities of Place: German-Speaking Central Europe, 1860–1930* (Toronto: University of Toronto Press, 2016); Brendan Karch, *Nation and Loyalty in a German-Polish Borderland: Upper Silesia 1848–1960* (New York: Cambridge University Press, 2018); Caitlin Murdock, *Changing Places: Society, Culture, and Territory in the Saxon-Bohemian Borderlands, 1870–1946* (Ann Arbor, MI: University of Michigan Press, 2010); Tara Zahra, *Kidnapped Souls: National Indifference and the Battle for Children in the Bohemian Lands, 1900–1948* (Ithaca, NY: Cornell University Press, 2008).

[6] Umweltbibliothek Großhennersdorf (UBG) 80–113, Klaus Kluge in *Mensch und Umwelt: Aus dem Protokoll eines Kolloquiums des Kulturbundes der DDR* (Berlin: Kulturbund der DDR, 1975), 51.

when regulation failed to reduce the pollution. Frustrated with official inaction, various structures and groups in the Protestant Church, which was the only semi-independent institution in the GDR, unmasked the weaknesses of communist responses. East German contact with media, information, and activists outside of the GDR – especially in the FRG and the People's Republic of Poland – further added to the SED's sense of fear and situates the pollution crisis in a larger context. Shared physical environments and concerns on the part of both states and individuals ensured the GDR's responses had implications beyond its borders.[7] Pollution, policy, and activism intimately tied the GDR to its neighbors and them to the GDR, transforming the small state into a crucial focal point in central Europe.

The Environment in Democracy and Dictatorship

With the collapse of communism in 1989–1990, environmental degradation in the GDR shocked audiences around the world, and the FRG shouldered the burden of cleaning it up. Because the West (now unified) German government successfully took up that task, scholarship often assumes that environmentalism was only possible in the "democratic west," reflective of lingering Cold War triumphalism.[8] The rights to assembly and press, much less the expectation of privacy, so common to democracies, were not guaranteed in communist states. Nevertheless, opportunities for responding to environmental degradation existed both in democracy and under dictatorship.[9] Environmentalism under communism stemmed from multiple sources, including the party and state's official channels, and ultimately posed a challenge to the SED's legitimacy. East Germans engaged in environmental activities for numerous reasons, including supporting the official conservation and anti-pollution measures, which stresses that the environment was not explicitly an oppositional issue. It became an effective

---

[7] Astrid M. Eckert, *West Germany and the Iron Curtain: Environment, Economy, and Culture in the Borderland* (New York: Oxford University Press, 2019) examines environmental and economic connections and disconnects along the German–German border. Frank Uekötter, "Entangled Ecologies: Outlines of a Green History of Two or More Germanys," in *History Shared and Divided*, ed. Bosch, 147–190. Uekötter sketches parallels and disconnects in East and West German approaches to the environment from the 1970s to the present.

[8] Katherine Pence and Paul Betts, "Introduction," in *Socialist Modern: East German Everyday Culture and Politics*, eds. Katherine Pence and Paul Betts (Ann Arbor, MI: University of Michigan Press, 2008), 4.

[9] Raymond Dominick, "Capitalism, Communism, and Environmental Protection: Lessons from the German Experience," *Environmental History* 3, no. 3 (July 1998), 326.

weapon against the SED and the state when they fell short of expectations.[10] The resonance of the environment across various sectors of East German society helps explain its role in the collapse of communism in 1989. Though environmentalism in Soviet-style communism presented a distinct set of domestic and systemic considerations, it sheds light on how such movements gained a foothold and developed *outside* of a democracy.[11]

Green politics in the democratic FRG provide the standard against which others are measured, reinforcing a narrative of (West) Germany as the "greenest nation."[12] While the FRG hesitated to regulate polluters in the 1960s and 1970s, many West Germans embraced environmental protection, reflecting a transition away from conservation and toward a more expansive understanding of ecological interconnectedness.[13] Activists organized citizens' initiatives (*Bürgeinitiative*), staged demonstrations, and occupied construction sites for airport runways, nuclear power plants, and other projects.[14] These efforts were not always successful and even turned violent at times, as in the occupation of a planned nuclear reactor at Brokdorf in 1976, but activists succeeded in shaping public opinion and pressuring the government into better regulation.[15] In this democracy, the state, market economy, and citizen represented at least relatively independent entities in conversation with one another. Ultimately, the green movement changed democracy in the FRG, introducing new topics and broadening the scope of legitimate politics to include environmental, peace, and other concerns.[16]

In contrast, environmentalism in the GDR illuminates how a communist dictatorship both supported and constrained responses to pollution. The one-party state controlled or attempted to control all aspects of the economy, politics, and society to take care of its citizens, the workers in a workers' state.[17]

---

[10] Christian Möller, *Umwelt und Herrschaft in der DDR: Politik, Protest und die Grenzen der Partizipation in der Diktatur* (Göttingen: Vanderhoeck & Ruprecht, 2020).

[11] For scholarship on green movements in a democracy, namely the FRG (and France), see Dolores Augustine, *Taking on Technocracy: Nuclear Power in Germany, 1945 to the Present* (New York: Berghahn Press, 2018); Stephen Milder, *Greening Democracy: The Anti-Nuclear Movement and Political Environmentalism in West Germany and Beyond, 1968–1983* (New York: Cambridge University Press, 2017); Andrew S. Tompkins, *Better Active than Radioactive! Anti-Nuclear Protest in 1970s France and West Germany* (New York: Oxford University Press, 2016).

[12] Frank Uekötter, *The Greenest Nation? A New History of German Environmentalism* (Cambridge, MA: MIT Press, 2014).

[13] Jens Ivo Engels, *Naturpolitik in der Bundesrepublik: Ideenwelt und politische Verhaltensstile in Naturschutz und Umweltbewegung, 1950–1980* (Paderborn: Ferdinand Schöningh, 2006), 307.

[14] Augustine, *Taking on Technocracy*, 98.   [15] Milder, *Greening Democracy*, 6–7.

[16] Uekötter, *The Greenest Nation?*, 2–3, 91.

[17] Konrad H. Jarausch, "Care and Coercion: The GDR as Welfare Dictatorship," in *Dictatorship as Experience: Towards a Socio-Cultural History of the GDR*, ed. Konrad H. Jarausch (New York: Berghahn Books, 1999), 47–49.

In this totalizing constellation, the state was both regulator and polluter.[18] It was not an independent actor apart from economic agents, nor was it accountable to an electorate in any real way. The GDR strictly controlled the dissemination of information, the formation of associations, the ability to publicly protest, and access to environmental data. Questions of degradation and public health were carefully managed and framed to put the SED in the best possible light, often at the expense of experts and activists who held contradictory evidence. These restrictions created a set of dynamics unlike those in a liberal democratic society. Any environmental issue was not only politically charged but a challenge to the SED and its legitimacy. Focusing on repression in the GDR does not diminish the police violence that environmental movements in the FRG or other democracies faced but underscores differences in how the two systems reacted to environmental problems.[19] The environment – and responses to its treatment – exposes the complex relationship between state, economy, society, and nature in a dictatorship.

The rise of environmentalism in the GDR illustrates the constant struggle between economy and ecology in the twentieth century from a different perspective than in western democracies.[20] Tensions between materialism, production, and quality of life posed challenges for states around the world after the World War II. In the postwar period, eastern and western European economies competed for superiority, changing dramatically over the course of the Cold War. Increased rates of production, consumption, and globalization reflected that rivalry, though these developments occurred unevenly. Communist economies, in particular, remained committed to heavy industry and reluctant to transition from

---

[18] I argue that the SED never reached its ambitions of totally controlling all aspects of life in the dictatorship, and use the term "totalizing" in recognition of the ambition but do not agree with the scholarship that labeled the GDR "totalitarian." See, for example, Sigrid Meuschel, *Legitimation und Parteiherrschaft: Zum Paradox von Stabilität und Revolution in der DDR, 1945–1989* (Frankfurt am Main: Suhrkamp, 1992).

[19] Milder, *Greening Democracy*, 138–141. Augustine, *Taking on Technocracy*, 150–151.

[20] Both environmental histories of Germany, such as Uekötter's *The Greenest Nation?* and David Blackbourn's *The Conquest of Nature: Water, Landscape, and the Making of Modern Germany* (New York: W. W. Norton & Company, 2006), and environmental histories of communism, such as Paul Josephson's "War on Nature as Part of the Cold War: The Strategic and Ideological Roots of Environmental Degradation in the Soviet Union," in *Environmental Histories of the Cold War*, eds. J. R. McNeill and Corinna R. Unger (New York: Cambridge University Press, 2010), tend to write off environmental efforts under communism. For more on modernity, materialism, and the GDR, see Pence and Betts, "Introduction," 11–21. Thomas Fleischman's *Communist Pigs: An Animal History of the East Germany's Rise and Fall* (Seattle, WA: University of Washington Press, 2020) further reminds us that capitalist and communist economies were intimately connected, especially from the 1970s onward, and not discrete entities.

coal to oil, even as planners devoted more attention to consumer goods.[21] Nevertheless, population growth and skyrocketing consumption forced capitalist and communist states and citizens alike to reconsider their relationship with natural resources and the impact that their habits had on the environment.[22] These conversations flourished in international venues such as the 1972 Environmental Conference in Stockholm as well as in local parish meetings and in living rooms.[23] In confronting the toll that natural resource extraction and consumption took on the environment, East Germans were at the center of global discourses from the late 1960s through the 1980s.

Officials and activists on both sides of the Iron Curtain embraced local and global trends during the Cold War. They recognized the challenges that inaction had caused, and therefore the importance of taking concrete steps to change the future. The Cold War added urgency to environmental questions as technology and consumption became battlegrounds between competing superpowers. These challenges extended beyond the United States and the Soviet Union to their blocs, and even to nonaligned countries.[24] East German environmental consciousness responded to a specific set of domestic and international impulses, but the issues raised there resonated across political and economic structures. Still, interactions were not always smooth. Activists and officials unintentionally and at times willfully interpreted information differently for cultural or political purposes.[25] Borders and limitations on interactions mattered, particularly for dictatorships and citizens of them, but neither environmental policy nor protest evolved in a vacuum.

[21] Eli Rubin, *Synthetic Socialism: Plastics and Dictatorship in the German Democratic Republic* (Chapel Hill, NC: University of North Carolina Press, 2008), 11.

[22] Eli Rubin and Scott Moranda, "Introduction," in *Ecologies of Socialisms: Germany, Nature, and the Left in History, Politics, and Culture*, eds. Sabine Moedersheim, Scott Moranda, and Eli Rubin (New York: Peter Lang Press, 2019), 3–4.

[23] BArch DC 20-I/3/948, "Vertrauliche Ministerratssache: Beschluß über eine Erklärung der Regierung der Deutschen Demokratischen Republik zur Stockholmer Umweltkonferenz vom 13. März 1972." RHG TH 02/01, "Woanders Gelesen – *Horizont* Nr. 8/1988, 'Brundtland Bericht: Umwelt und Entwicklung'."

[24] J. R. McNeill and Corinna R. Unger, "Introduction: The Big Picture," in *Environmental Histories of the Cold War*, eds. McNeill and Unger, 16. Simo Laakkonen, Viktor Pal, and Richard Tucker, "The Cold War and Environmental History: Complementary Fields," *Cold War History* 16, no. 4 (Fall 2016), 377–394.

[25] Andrew S. Tompkins, "Grassroots Transnationalism(s): Franco-German Opposition to Nuclear Energy in the 1970s," *Contemporary European History* 25, no. 1 (February 2016), 118.

The Environment in the GDR

Since the GDR's inception, the Soviet model of intensive industrial production resulted in extensive pollution that plagued the regime, deteriorating the environment and its citizens' health. The Soviet Union compelled its satellite states to specialize in certain economic sectors in order to compete with western European countries.[26] Coal, steel, and the chemical industry featured prominently in the GDR's economy, which quickly became the strongest in the bloc (aside from the Soviet Union itself).[27] The state's scarce natural resources were imbued with national significance for a better future, though Soviet directives and geographic limitations forced the GDR to rely on antiquated technologies and noxious energy sources.[28] The GDR's primary energy source, lignite, released high levels of particulate matter that polluted the air and led to staggering rates of respiratory illness.[29] Additionally, the presence of sulfur in the coal precipitated acid rain when burned, killing forests in the GDR as well as in neighboring countries.[30] This emphasis on heavy industry resulted in the extreme pollution and public health crisis of towns like Bitterfeld. In a system in which the state was both the polluter and the regulator, the responsibility of balancing political realities, economic needs, and nature conservation weighed heavily on the SED.

Party and state officials quickly recognized that pollution had social and cultural consequences that complicated their pursuit of unchecked economic growth. In a dictatorship, social and cultural matters were inherently political, and as a workers' state, the GDR felt obligated to shape and control them in the workers' interest.[31] Starting in the 1950s, the SED established environmental associations in its tightly controlled mass social organization, the Cultural League, as a sign of the party and state's commitment to nature. In particular, the Cultural League's Friends of Nature and *Heimat* – later reinvented as the Society for Nature and the Environment – carried out these objectives.[32] The SED drew on German

---

[26] André Steiner, *The Plans that Failed: An Economic History of the GDR* (New York: Berghahn Books, 2010), 71.

[27] Ibid., 12.   [28] Maier, *Dissolution*, 82.

[29] RHG Th 02/08, "PSEUDOKRUPP – Krankheitsverlauf und Therapie," undated.

[30] *Waldsterben* or "dying of the forests" did not come into common usage until roughly 1980, and then primarily in the West German context as a plank in the Green Party's platform. Into the late 1980s, East German officials denied that Waldsterben existed in the GDR. Uekötter, *The Greenest Nation?*, 113ff. BArch 5/5829, "Informacja o stanie środowiska naturalnego na terenach Dolnego Śląska, a w tym głównie w rejonach graniczących bezpośrednio z NRD i CSRS," March 1–3, 1988.

[31] Jarausch, "Care and Coercion," 59–60.

[32] Alon Confino, *The Nation as a Local Metaphor: Württemberg, Imperial Germany, and National Memory, 1871–1918* (Chapel Hill, NC: University of North Carolina Press, 1997), 125–126.

traditions of popular engagement with nature that dated back to the nineteenth century.[33] It encouraged conservation, landscape preservation, and hiking among other activities as a means of embracing Heimat, a German concept linking a sense of national identity to nature. Officials specifically sought to cultivate an East German Heimat that would bolster the fledgling socialist nation.[34] They relied on these traditions to publicize that they were confronting environmental degradation. Together, these measures raised East Germans' awareness of the natural world and signaled that the state prioritized its wellbeing.

The environment became a front in the Cold War for the East German leadership, which competed with the capitalist west to "outperform" in terms of conservation and consciousness.[35] For both domestic and diplomatic purposes, the GDR claimed to be at the forefront of the global debate over the dangers of economic growth, consumption, and their impact on the planet.[36] The GDR consequently vied for prestige abroad and popular support at home through its awareness of environmental concerns.[37] In the 1968 version of the constitution, the SED declared citizens' right and responsibility to a clean environment, claiming a commitment to providing for workers' cultural and spiritual wellbeing in a workers' state.[38] The SED further declared "socialist environmentalism" an essential component of East German society at the VIII Party Congress in 1972 and subsequently established the Ministry for Environmental Protection and Water Management (MUW).[39]

Over the course of the 1970s, the state built up a cohort of scientists and experts to specialize in environmental research and to implement

[33] Thomas M. Lekan, *Imagining the Nation in Nature: Landscape Preservation and German Identity, 1885–1945* (Cambridge, MA: Harvard University Press, 2004); John Alexander Williams, *Turning to Nature in Germany: Hiking, Nudism and Conservation, 1900–1940* (Stanford, CA: Stanford University Press, 2007); Jan Palmowski, *Inventing a Socialist Nation: Heimat and the Politics of Everyday Life in the GDR, 1945–1990* (New York: Cambridge University Press, 2009).

[34] Palmowski, *Inventing a Socialist Nation.*

[35] McNeill and Unger, eds., *Environmental Histories of the Cold War*; Astrid Mignon Kirchhof and J. R. McNeill, eds., *Nature and the Iron Curtain: Environmental Policy and Social Movements in Communist and Capitalist Countries, 1945–1990* (Pittsburgh, PA: University of Pittsburgh Press, 2019).

[36] Joachim Radkau, *The Age of Ecology: A Global History*, trans. Patrick Camiller (Malden, MA: Polity Press, 2014), 92.

[37] Laakkonen, Pal, and Tucker, "The Cold War and Environmental History".

[38] Artikel 15, Absatz 2, Verfassung der Deutschen Demokratischen Republik, 1968. Konrad H. Jarausch, "Introduction," in *Dictatorship as Experience*, ed. Jarausch, 6.

[39] BArch DK 5/4454, "Entwurf: Prognostische Grundlagen über die Entwicklung von Hauptrichtungen des Umweltschutzes," November 1973, Zeitweilige Arbeitsgruppe "Zur Entwicklung des Umweltschutzes."

regulation in the newly formed ministry. In the Academy of Sciences, experts theorized about the importance of the environment to socialism, generating an entire body of literature on the subject.[40] Universities introduced new fields of study relating to ecology, biology, and environmental protection, and the graduates of those programs entered into state-run research institutes or the MUW. Scientists recorded pollution levels, invented new technologies, and proposed and applied solutions, such as installing filters in smokestacks, ameliorating chemical spills into waterways, and recycling water more efficiently. At the ministry, they also addressed petitions (*Eingaben*) from frustrated citizens who sought relief from a range of environmental problems.[41] Scientists and experts, moreover, often took part in party-sponsored clubs to disseminate appropriate information to the public.[42] A generation of experts, then, became caught between furthering environmental protection within the party and state apparatuses, on the one hand, and being required, from 1982, to maintain secrecy regarding all environmental data, on the other.

The SED's stance on environmentalism created a conundrum; the party raised environmental expectations without committing the resources necessary to execute them. The GDR and socialist states more generally considered themselves immune to environmental issues because they worked in the name of the people without profit motive. The SED believed this position provided them a moral high ground in contrast to capitalist countries. Still, socialist solutions put forward through policy and mass social engagement did not dramatically improve environmental conditions. In the second half of the GDR's existence, pollution levels plateaued, and in some instances, worsened without investment in new technologies or structural change.[43] More and more, the GDR turned inward, restricting access to data for domestic and international audiences, which tacitly admitted the SED's failure. East Germans operated on the principle – underdelivered by

---

[40] Horst Paucke and Adolf Bauer, *Umweltprobleme: Herausforderung der Menschheit* (Dietz Verlag: Berlin, 1979). Umweltbibliothek Großhennersdorf (UBG) 80–113, Klaus Kluge in *Mensch und Umwelt: Aus dem Protokoll eines Kolloquiums des Kulturbundes der DDR* (Berlin: Kulturbund der DDR, 1975).

[41] Stadtarchiv Halle A. 40 Nummer 19, Band 1, "Konzeption zur Entwicklung der Umweltbedingungen in der Stadt Halle bis 1990," 1987 and Nr. 41, Bd. 5, "Zuarbeiten der Abteilung Umweltschutz und Wasserwirtschaft, 1973/74."

[42] Evangelisches Zentralarchiv (EZA) 101/633, Dr. Sabine Rackow, "Stellungnahme zur Vorlage des Johann-Gerhard-Institutes zum Thema 'Christ und Umweltverschmutzung'," February 4–5, 1972. BArch DK 5/1982, "Bericht über Probleme des Geheimnisschutzes bei Informationen zum Umweltschutz," October 25, 1982.

[43] *Umweltbericht der DDR: Information zur Analyse der Umweltbedingungen in der DDR und zu weiteren Maßnahmen* (West Berlin: Institut für Umweltschutz, 1990), 7.

their own government – that an active citizen and good socialist should both know the importance of the environment and demand its protection.

In response to degradation, and taking seriously the state's environmental imperative, a second strain of environmentalism unfolded in the Protestant Church. The Church presented an alternative to the socialist interpretation, shaping ordinary East Germans' understanding of nature.[44] Through institutions, such as the Ecclesiastical Research Center in Wittenberg and parish-based groups, engaged individuals took part in protecting and saving God's creation. Clergy attended the World Council of Churches' conventions on science and technology, while supporting activists in the parishes and taking up the state's offer to join party or state environmental organizations. East Germans engaged in both Church and official organizations and became "dual participants," breaking down traditional divisions between the two sets of actors.[45] Moreover, parish-based groups sprang up all over the country from the Baltic Sea to the Erzgebirge to the Thuringian Forest, decentering a Berlin-based narrative of opposition and dissent.[46] Activists organized workshops, seminars, tree planting campaigns, and bicycle demonstrations.[47] They further recorded their impressions in Church-sponsored publications and self-published underground, or "samizdat," newsletters and pamphlets.[48] Religious organizations supported East Germans' awareness of pollution

---

[44] Mary Fulbrook, *The People's State: East German Society from Hitler to Honecker* (New Haven, CT: Yale University Press, 2005), 251.

[45] BArch DO 4/800, Hans-Peter Gensichen, "Eine neue Phase des Umweltengagements in den Kirchen," *Die Zeichen der Zeit* 7/88, Heinz Blauer, ed., Berlin (Ost), Evangelische Verlagsanstalt. BArch DO 4/801, "Zu den staatlichen, gesellschaftlichen und kirchlichen Aktivitäten zur Realisierung einer sachlichen und sachbezogenen Zusammenarbeit beim Schutz und der Erhaltung von Natur und Umwelt seit dem 20.8.84," April 24, 1985.

[46] RHG Ki 18/02, "Die Karteibroschüre der kirchlichen Umweltgruppen in der DDR: Stand vom November 1988." East Berlin was a hotspot of opposition, and much of the scholarship has noted that fact, but environmental activism is exceptional in that it resonated in so many parts of the GDR, both in and beyond East Berlin: Gareth Dale, *Popular Protest in East Germany, 1945–1989* (New York: Routledge, 2005), 125–131; Carlo Jordan and Hans Michael Kloth, eds., *Arche Nova: Opposition in der DDR, "Das Grün-ökologische Netzwerk Arche," 1988–90* (Berlin: BasisDruck, 1995); Wolfgang Rüddenklau, ed., *Störenfried: DDR-Opposition 1986–1989, mit Texten aus den "Umweltblättern"* (Berlin: BasisDruck, 1992).

[47] Uwe Zuppke, "Aus der Tätigkeit des Zentrums für Umweltgestaltung," in *Umweltschutz in der DDR: Analysen und Zeitzeugenberichte, Band 3: Beruflicher, ehrenamtlicher und freiwilliger Umweltschutz*, eds. Hermann Behrens and Jens Hoffmann (Munich: Oekom, 2008), 73.

[48] Mary Fulbrook, "Putting the People Back in: The Contentious State of GDR History," *German History* 24, no. 4 (October 2006), 613; Dale, *Popular Protest*, 124–125; Nathan Stoltzfus, "Public Space and the Dynamics of Environmental Action: Green Protest in the GDR," *Archiv für Sozialgeschichte* 43 (2003), 399; Dieter Rink, "Environmental Policy and the Environmental Movement in East Germany," *Capitalism, Nature, and Socialism* 13, no. 3 (September 2002), 79–81.

and environmentalism. Thus, in the 1980s, as the SED diverged from international trends, East Germans came more into line with them.

Through exploring individual priorities and subjectivities, *Saving Nature* draws out intersections and interactions within East German society. It examines state experts and bureaucrats, party-controlled voluntary associations, and Church-based and independent activists, as well as the interactions between these actors, to produce a more nuanced understanding of who engaged with the environment.[49] Party and state officials cooperated and engaged with activists in the Church on environmental issues, illuminating multiple – and at times conflicting – motivations for engagement.[50] Nature enthusiasts, scientific experts, Christians, and oppositional figures contributed to East Germans' thinking about the natural world. The challenges of dictatorship disrupted but never fully eradicated the flow of information. The Ministry of State Security, or Stasi, worried so much about the impact of these contacts on the regime's stability that the state classified all environmental data in 1982, after earlier restrictions.[51] Despite those measures, information flowed across traditional divisions between state and society as East Germans participated in both Church and official organizations, intertwining what scholars often treat as discrete or adversarial spheres.

Frustration intensified after 1982 and increasingly found public expression after Chernobyl in 1986, coalescing environmental themes before the mass demonstrations of 1989.[52] New Church-based and independent groups sprang up in the wake of Chernobyl as the SED bungled the media response to the nuclear disaster. As environmental awareness grew, East Germans turned to transnational connections for inspiration, resources, and support. They also aimed to make others, especially West Germans, familiar with pollution and the suppression of data in the GDR.

[49] Andrew I. Port, "Introduction," in *Becoming East German: Socialist Structures and Sensibilities after Hitler*, eds. Andrew I. Port and Mary Fulbrook (New York: Berghahn Books, 2013), 9. Ilko-Sascha Kowalczuk creates a typology of attitudes in "Gegenkräfte: Opposition und Widerstand in der DDR – Begriffliche und methodische Probleme," in *Opposition der DDR von den 70er Jahren bis zum Zusammenbruch der SED Herrschaft*, ed. Eberhard Kuhrt (Opladen: Leske + Budrich, 1999), 63.

[50] Kowalczuk, "Gegenkräfte," 63.

[51] BArch DK 5/1982, "Bericht über Probleme des Geheimnisschutzes bei Informationen zum Umweltschutz," October 25, 1982.

[52] Works on the end of communism in eastern Europe tend to devote less attention to the growing environmental crisis, focusing instead on the political and economic challenges. Stephen Kotkin, *Uncivil Society: 1989 and the Implosion of the Communist Establishment* (Chapel Hill, NC: University of North Carolina Press, 2009); Padraic Kenney, *A Carnival of Revolution: Central Europe, 1989* (Princeton, NJ: Princeton University Press, 2002). Others see a distinct break between earlier "political alternative" groups and the mass demonstrations of 1989. Detlef Pollack, *Politischer Protest: Politisch alternative Gruppen in der DDR* (Opladen: Leske + Budrich, 2000).

The East German movement benefited from Poland's relatively relaxed political atmosphere, which enabled it to become a site of exchange and interaction for environmentalists from eastern and western Europe. The success of this movement became apparent in 1989 as communism unraveled. The vast majority of oppositional figures incorporated pollution and ecological transformation into their calls for reform. Given the universal recognition of degradation behind the Iron Curtain, in the 1990s, the FRG and other western European states prioritized environmental cleanup in the former communist bloc. The constellations of the Cold War disappeared, but the entanglement of central European environments did not.

Circuits of Knowledge and Transnational Interactions

Starting in the 1960s, East Germans sought to better understand and protect the environment, constructing and participating in circuits of environmental knowledge.[53] From the local to the national to the international level, they developed a common awareness, exchanged information and data, and pursued joint undertakings. Individuals in the GDR and outside of it established and strengthened these circuits through numerous forms of direct and indirect contact. Domestically, East Germans shared observations about pollution, connected with other Church-based environmental groups, met with and confronted officials about environmental conditions, and in some cases participated in party-run organizations. Through these networks and opportunities, East Germans accumulated information about specific sources of degradation in addition to developing a broader conception of environmentalism. Activists illicitly read western news and listened to the radio and television about the GDR's pollution to obtain data that was not readily accessible. They wrote about their impressions and experiences in religious publications and samizdat newsletters, circulating knowledge among activists. Yet, the SED and the state continued to promote environmental regulation and party-sanctioned engagement, adding overlapping and sometimes contradictory interpretations of the East German environmental situation. State officials and Church-based, or

---

[53] I adapt Ann Laura Stoler's term "circuits of knowledge" in order to highlight the flow of people, information, and pollution across borders. Ann Laura Stoler, "Introduction," in *Haunted by Empire: Geographies of Intimacy in North American History*, ed. Ann Laura Stoler (Durham, NC: Duke University Press), 6.

independent, activists pushed and challenged one another as they contributed to a larger corpus of environmental knowledge.

These circuits defied political boundaries as actors explicitly engaged with environments and discourses beyond their own borders. East Germans were transnational in their thinking, acting, and being as they placed themselves in a central European, and ultimately, global conservation. Information flowed between locations and countries, creating linkages that changed environmentalism in the GDR.[54] In turn, the GDR's neighbors were influenced by the East German environment and the associated activism, forming multidirectional learning processes that folded the GDR into the greening of postwar Europe. Though travel outside of the Soviet bloc was difficult for East Germans, experts and activists positioned themselves in a larger framework through their writings, protests, and attempts to sway policy. They built networks of contacts and information across the Iron Curtain and between Soviet bloc countries to contextualize domestic East German problems.

The multiple strains of East German environmentalism that emerged were thus inherently regional and transnational as pollution, people, ideas, and data flowed through central Europe.[55] To the west, the GDR was never completely severed from the FRG, as a shared history, cultural assumptions, and language obviously linked the two Germanys.[56] Their shared

---

[54] Tompkins, "Grassroots Transnationalism(s)." Tompkins also uses "transnationalism" to examine anti-nuclear protest in a regional, western European context, namely in France and West Germany. Tompkins, *Better Active than Radioactive!.* Isabel Hofmeyr in "AHR Conversation: On Transnational History; Participants: C.A. Bayly, Sven Beckert, Matthew Connelly, Isabel Hofmyer, Wendy Kozol, and Patricia Seed," *American Historical Review* 111, no. 5 (December 2006), 1443–1445.

[55] Many works focus specifically on the German or East German context without spending much attention on regional or global influences. Hermann Behrens and Jens Hoffmann, eds., *Umweltschutz in der DDR: Analysen und Zeitzeugen, Band 1–3* (Munich: Oekom, 2008); Martin Stief, *"Stellt die Bürger ruhig": Staatssicherheit und Umweltzerstörung im Chemierevier Halle-Bitterfeld* (Göttingen: Vanderhoeck & Ruprecht, 2019). In other cases, the scholarship revolves primarily around western-oriented debates, such as nuclear energy and *Waldsterben.* Augustine, *Taking on Technocracy;* Blackbourn, *The Conquest of Nature,* 311–335; Tobias Huff, *Natur und Industrie im Sozialismus: Eine Umweltgeschichte der DDR* (Göttingen: Vandenhoeck & Ruprecht, 2015); Uekötter, *The Greenest Nation?.* Christian Möller's recent monograph intentionally contextualizes the GDR by looking to the east and the west, a trend on which I expand. Möller, *Umwelt und Herrschaft in der DDR.*

[56] Christoph Kleßmann, "Introduction," 5; Tobias Hochscherf, Christoph Laucht, and Andrew Plowman, eds., *Divided but not Disconnected: German Experiences in the Cold War* (New York: Berghahn Press, 2005); Christoph Kleßmann, *Die doppelte Staatsgründung: Deutsche Geschichte, 1945–1955* (Göttingen: Vandenhoeck & Ruprecht, 1991); Simon Mikkonen and Pia Koivunen, eds., *Beyond the Divide: Entangled Histories of Cold War Europe* (New York: Berghahn Books, 2015); Bösch, ed., *History Shared and Divided.*

past allowed both countries to draw on longstanding traditions of German conservation that established a mutual sense of attachment to nature.[57] East and West Germans maintained contact through visits, correspondence, and media throughout the Cold War, despite growing economic and political disparities.[58] These ties fostered similar sensibilities, such as the importance of nature conservation, and directly influenced perceptions of shared pollution, such as pollution in the Elbe River.[59] West German environmentalism, and especially the Green Party, aided the independent movement in the GDR, which materially and intellectually benefited from the "greening of democracy" in the FRG.[60]

To the east, the GDR's relationship with its Soviet bloc neighbors illuminates important but understudied aspects of the environmental protection in central Europe.[61] East Germans and the SED government not only looked west to the FRG but were also influenced by and conversely influenced fellow communist states, especially Poland. The GDR shared its second longest border with Poland, forcing the two states to navigate common physical environments along the Oder and Neisse Rivers (which constituted the border) and in the Baltic Sea. Until 1945, large portions of western Poland had been German territory with mixed German and Polish populations, in some cases during World War II, and in others, for much longer. Poland's newly incorporated "wild west" or "recovered territories" included eastern Brandenburg and Pomerania as well as Lower Silesia. The latter, along with Upper Silesia, was one of Poland's most industrialized regions.[62] As Germans were expelled from these territories after the war, many ended up in the GDR and retained local knowledge as well as a sense of connection to

---

[57] Sandra Chaney, *Nature of the Miracle Years: Conservation in West Germany, 1945–1975* (New York: Berghahn Books, 2008).

[58] Edith Sheffer, *Burned Bridge: How East and West Germans Made the Iron Curtain* (New York: Oxford University Press, 2011).

[59] Tim Grady, "A Shared Environment: German–German Relations along the Border, 1945–1972," *Journal of Contemporary History* 50, no. 3 (July 2015), 660–679.

[60] Milder, *Greening Democracy*.

[61] Much of the literature to date has examined the East German dictatorship in isolation from the FRG or other Soviet bloc countries. Fulbrook, *The People's State*; Jarausch, ed., *Dictatorship as Experience*; Jürgen Kocka, *Civil Society and Dictatorship in Modern Germany* (Hanover, NH: University Press of New England, 2010); Thomas Lindenberger, ed., *Herrschaft und Eigen-Sinn in der Diktatur: Studien zur Gesellschaftsgeschichte der DDR* (Cologne: Böhlau, 1999); Meuschel, *Legitimation und Parteiherrschaft*; Port and Fulbrook, eds., *Becoming East German*.

[62] Beata Halicka, *Polens Wilder Westen: Erzwungene Migration und die kulturelle Aneignung des Oderraums, 1945–1948* (Paderborn: Ferdinand Schöningh, 2013), 7–10. Peter Polak-Springer, *Recovered Territory: A German–Polish Conflict over Land and Culture, 1919–1989* (New York: Berghahn Books, 2015), 185–186.

those areas.[63] Moreover, transboundary pollution in the Black Triangle at the juncture of the postwar East German, Polish, and Czechoslovakian borders emerged as a major source of contention in the 1970s and 1980s. These physical and historical ties complicated relations between the GDR and Poland (and Czechoslovakia) but also underscore interconnectedness.

East German interactions with Poland also situate the GDR in the Soviet bloc and decenter national (German) narratives in central Europe. East German–Polish relations instead depict a larger, regional understanding of environmental protection and activism that looks to the east as well as to the west.[64] From the 1960s, Soviet leader Leonid Brezhnev recognized the challenges pollution posed, encouraging environmental collaboration and cleanup throughout the bloc, though the Soviet Union rarely supported that rhetoric with significant financial resources.[65] Economic coordination, pollution, networks, policy, and news intimately linked East German policies to other Soviet bloc countries, especially Poland. Connections between the GDR and Poland underscore the similarities in Soviet-style communism as well as cooperation and competition among satellite states.[66] By the 1980s, Poland's relative openness with the west and mass opposition to communism inspired East Germans and further promoted environmental networks behind and across the Iron Curtain. After the rise of the independent trade union Solidarność (Solidarity), Poland became a site of contact and exchange that East Germans relied on to gain

[63] Andrew Demshuk, *The Lost German East: Forced Migration and the Politics of Memory, 1945–1970* (New York: Cambridge University Press, 2012), 28.

[64] Philipp Ther, "Beyond the Nation: The Relational Basis of a Comparative History of Germany and Europe," *Central European History* 36, no. 1 (March 2003), 46. Environmental histories, too, fall into this model. Eagle Glassheim, *Cleansing the Czechoslovak Borderlands: Migration, Environment, and Health in the Former Sudetenland* (Pittsburgh, PA: University of Pittsburgh Press, 2016); Edward Snajder, *Nature Protests: The End of Ecology in Slovakia* (Seattle, WA: University of Washington Press, 2008); Douglas R. Weiner, *A Little Corner of Freedom: Russian Nature Protection from Stalin to Gorbachev* (Berkeley and Los Angeles, CA: University of California Press, 1999).

[65] Joan DeBardeleben, *The Environment and Marxism-Leninism: The Soviet and East German Experience* (Boulder, CO: Westview Press, 1985); Open Society Archive (OSA), "Steps Towards Pollution Control in the USSR," Radio Free Europe, April 6, 1972.

[66] Comparative work from the 1980s onward already exists. I build on this body of literature to better understand connections alongside structural similarities. DeBardeleben, *The Environment and Marxism-Leninism*; Barbara Hicks, *Environmental Politics in Poland: A Social Movement between Regime and Opposition* (New York: Columbia University Press, 1996); Barbara Jancar-Webster, ed., *Environmental Action in Eastern Europe: Responses to Crisis* (Armonk, NY: M.E. Sharpe, 1993); Petr Pavlínek and John Pickles, *Environmental Transitions: Transformation and Ecological Defence in Central and Eastern Europe* (New York: Routledge, 2000).

access to western information and activists. Information flowed through –
and around – the GDR to create regional networks and a shared sense of
purpose.

Organization

To interrogate the evolution of East German environmentalism and its
relationship to developments in neighboring states, *Saving Nature* pro-
ceeds primarily chronologically. Chapter 1 investigates how the SED used
nature conservation and environmental protection to strengthen its socialist state, domestically and internationally. The chapter traces communist
economic and nature conservation practices after World War II and the
problems they generated. The GDR claimed science and technology would
forge a rational, technocratic future that both employed and protected
nature in the service of socialism and the East German people in a "People's
State."[67] This chapter situates the SED's actions in the context of an
environmental awareness emerging on both sides of the Iron Curtain in
the late 1960s and early 1970s. The SED harnessed the popular and
seemingly innocuous matter of the environment to leverage its position
at a moment when questions about consumption and the future gripped
leaders and citizens around the world. The GDR merged German traditions and Soviet-style communism in an attempt to balance the needs of
the economy with a deepening commitment to environment protection.

Chapter 2 shows how the SED institutionalized environmental protection in the 1970s based on the conviction that socialism provided solutions
to pollution. The SED succeeded in creating a more environmentally
minded population, and at least initially, the East German state tried to
address concerns within existing structures. The SED used mass social
campaigns to unite East Germans around the issue of environmentalism
and practiced protection through policy and negotiating petitions. The
GDR simultaneously reached out to other socialist countries to build
coalitions around its brand of environmentalism in contrast to the one
taking off in western Europe. This positioning intentionally placed the
GDR in the middle of a regional and global phenomenon that spanned the
Iron Curtain. Despite minor improvements, however, the discrepancy
between rhetoric and lived reality produced an untenable situation for
the SED. It relied more heavily on the Stasi to make decisions and police

---

[67] Dolores Augustine, *Red Prometheus: Engineering and Dictatorship in East Germany, 1945–1990*
(Cambridge, MA: MIT Press, 2007), xi–xii; Fulbrook, *The People's State*.

the population, and ultimately opted to classify all environmental data in 1982 when the SED recognized that conditions had not – and would not – improve. At this moment of internal turmoil and amid the international tension of the Second Cold War, the GDR turned inward, isolating itself from global trends.

The third chapter transitions to focusing on how non-party or state actors countered official claims, developed alternative narratives, and challenged the SED's authority. In the GDR, Church-based environmentalism evolved on the fringes of society and in a transnational context. Environmental engagement, its impetuses, and its forms led to a critique with theological underpinnings as well as practical frustration about degradation. Church-based activists fostered contacts with independent actors to the east and west, establishing networks across central Europe. In the FRG, the environmental movement became formalized in the Green Party, which underscored the SED's inability to adapt. In the Soviet bloc, Poland modeled a less repressive attitude toward society that opened opportunities for independent actors, especially Solidarność, which the SED feared undermined the entire bloc's security. These impulses encouraged East Germans to pursue activism outside of official channels, namely through the Church. The SED increasingly distrusted neighboring countries and the potential impact of their reforms at home. In response, the party obsessed over state security. The GDR's position as hinge between east and west became a liability for domestic stability.

Chapter 4 emphasizes the GDR's position as an ecological link as well as an environmental hazard to its neighbors. Moving geographically from west to east, this chapter traces the entangled evolution of policies in the GDR and with its neighbors after 1982. The chapter investigates growing dismay in the FRG and redoubled West German efforts to negotiate with the GDR. The chapter then turns to responses to pollution and the classification of data in the GDR, both from official channels and in Church-based circles. It argues that outcries over the environmental situation were not limited to the dissident hotspot of Berlin but emerged across the country and from an array of individuals. Lastly, environmental protest reawakened in Poland as the Polish United Workers' Party (*Polska Zjednoczona Partia Robotnicza*, PZPR) embraced Soviet reforms after 1985, making it an obvious node for activism in the Soviet bloc. These phenomena in turn put pressure on the GDR. Denunciations of pollution from within and outside of communist states heightened a sense of crisis that defied political divisions and revealed ecological interdependence.

Chapter 5 analyzes the expansion of environmental protest after Chernobyl in 1986. The environmental movement became more public in eastern Europe in general, and the GDR in particular. Bolstered by western support, unrest grew swiftly in an uncertain political context. Though Chernobyl offered a rallying point, the broader base generated new friction among participants. The Stasi's efforts to sow discord among uneasily allied environmentalists succeeded in curbing their potential impact. Moreover, the relative openness in Poland permitted outrage over Chernobyl and further fueled discussion of other environmental problems, making it an ideal location for exchange across borders within the region. Finally, the chapter turns to deepened West German inter-actions with eastern European pollution and protest, teasing out moments of cooperation and misunderstanding. Responses to Chernobyl reshaped environmental movements, anti-communist rhetoric, and connections. Nevertheless, the nuclear disaster and its fallout undermined a system already on shaky ground.

Chapter 6 interrogates the place of the environment and environmental movements in the end of communism and then in the double transitions to democracy and capitalism. The chapter first charts the end of communism in Poland – where the dismantling of the Soviet bloc began – and considers how the environment fit into these transformations there and across eastern Europe. Next, the chapter shifts to the GDR, demonstrating the environment's position as a source of protest and then mutually agreed upon tenet of unification. Participation in that environmental decision-making was uneven, however, often minimizing East German activists as West German influence waxed. The spread of environmental consciousness desta-bilized communism, but capitalism and democracy introduced powerful new actors that sidelined many of the groups and individuals that had shaped the environmental movement before 1989. The 1990s saw cleaner environ-mental landscapes in the former Soviet bloc, but decisions and investment often came from the outside and excluded local involvement.

The trajectory of environmentalism in the GDR reveals a complicated relationship between nature, communism, and global social and eco-nomic impulses. Soviet-style communism engaged with environmental-ism and promoted protection for pragmatic economic and domestic security reasons. Such communist states also sought to achieve geopolit-ical objectives in reaction to capitalism and democracy. The many different strands of East German environmentalism, including socialist materialist and religious (alongside others), expose a multitude of atti-tudes toward the environment and the SED that resist easy categoriza-tion. The SED's official environmental efforts were ultimately a paradox of success; the party raised awareness but could not follow through on its promises. Moreover, the GDR – a Cold War construct that no longer exists – highlights the importance of border-crossing pollution and activism, placing East German environmentalism in a regional movement and a global moment. Concerns over the balance between economy and ecology emerged around the world after the World War II. The GDR's unique position as a hinge between east and west reveals deeply interconnected environments and environmentalisms in central Europe that transcended the seemingly impermeable divisions of the Cold War.

CHAPTER I

Balancing Economy and Ecology: Building toward Environmental Protection, 1945–1970

From the GDR's founding in 1949, the tension between economy and ecology was an inescapable conundrum for the ruling Socialist Unity Party (SED). A product of Cold War hostility between the Soviet Union and the western Allies, the GDR's right to exist was uncertain and the SED's domestic legitimacy in question. The East German leadership therefore worked to build credibility at home and abroad by rebuilding industry that had been destroyed in the Second World War. As a result, nature – and making use of limited natural resources – figured centrally in plans for communists to consolidate power in eastern Europe, and especially in the GDR. The SED determined that a strong economy was necessary to win over reluctant East Germans who could readily observe a liberal democratic model of government and reconstruction to the west. The East German economy did experience significant growth (though it fell short of the FRG's) in its first few decades, a success that drove planners to set higher production norms.[1] Not everyone agreed with this exploitation of nature for the sake of industry, but such arguments gained little resonance in the first postwar decades as the GDR emerged from the ashes.[2]

Nevertheless, by the 1960s, this "smokestack industrialization" model for rebuilding also undeniably devastated the environment, leading to a reckoning in the GDR.[3] Pollution from heavy industries, such as mining, industrial agriculture, and chemicals along with other branches of the economy ravaged the environment, productivity, and workers' health. The SED realized the urgency of tackling the pollution and began to

---

[1] Charles S. Maier, *Dissolution: The Crisis of Communism and the End of East Germany* (Princeton, NJ: Princeton University Press, 1997), 83. André Steiner, *The Plans that Failed: An Economic History of the GDR* (New York: Berghahn Books, 2010), 70–74.

[2] Andreas Dix and Rita Gudermann, "Naturschutz in der DDR: Idealisiert, ideologisiert, instrumentalisiert?," in *Natur und Staat. Staatlicher Naturschutz in Deutschland, 1906–2006*, eds. Hans-Werner Frohn and Friedemann Schmoll (Bonn: Bundesamt für Naturschutz, 2006), 572–573.

[3] Konrad H. Jarausch and Michael Geyer, *Shattered Past: Reconstructing German Histories* (Princeton, NJ: Princeton University Press, 2003), 161.

place more emphasis on the idea that socialism encompassed the workers' physical and *geistig*, or spiritual, as well as material wellbeing. These ideas had their roots in nineteenth-century German movements.[4] The SED endeavored to enlist East Germans in this project by drawing on conservation, landscape preservation, and nature recreation.[5] Party leaders demonstrated their commitment in laws, a new ministry, and mass social organizations. The SED claimed "socialist environmentalism" trusted in rationality, science, and technology to improve nature as well as workers' lives.

Demonstrating a responsibility for the environment was to showcase the GDR's progressiveness, drawing on German traditions of engaging with nature as well as Soviet-style communism. The SED treated the GDR as a "display window" to the west that would also help the embattled state gain diplomatic recognition.[6] The SED supported increased participation within international conservation organizations, and the state made a number of assurances in pursuit of this objective. At the same time, the GDR sought to distinguish "socialist environmental protection" from similar trends in the west, allegedly offering a superior alternative.[7] Alongside international work, the GDR deepened relations with other Soviet bloc states to further expert and technological exchanges for economic and environmental purposes. Poland and the GDR faced similar structural pressures and transboundary pollution that motivated the states to collaborate in the 1960s and 1970s.[8] Through these many efforts, the East German leadership sought to depict the GDR as being on the front lines of environmentalism within the Soviet bloc and beyond.

This chapter argues that the SED embraced nature protection for domestic legitimacy and international recognition, though dedication to economic growth consistently complicated this endeavor. The chapter first traces communist economic policies and nature conservation practices as

---

[4] Thomas M. Lekan, *Imagining the Nation in Nature: Landscape Preservation and German Identity, 1885–1945* (Cambridge, MA: Harvard University Press, 2004), 7. John Alexander Williams, *Turning to Nature in Germany: Hiking, Nudism and Conservation, 1900–1940* (Stanford, CA: Stanford University Press, 2007).

[5] Jan Palmowski, *Inventing a Socialist Nation: Heimat and the Politics of Everyday Life in the GDR, 1945–1990* (New York: Cambridge University Press, 2009).

[6] Edith Sheffer, *Burned Bridge: How East and West Germans Made the Iron Curtain* (New York: Oxford University Press, 2011), 64.

[7] Sandra Chaney and Rita Gudermann, "The East's Contribution to International Conservation Part 1," *Environmental Policy and Law* 40, no. 2–3 (April 2010), 121.

[8] Romuald Olaczek, "Konserwatorska Ochrona Przyrody w Polsce – Osiągnięcia, rozczarowania, oczekiwania," in *Problemy Ochrony Polskie Przyrody*, eds. Romuald Olaczek and Kazimierz Zarzycki (Warsaw: Polish Scientific Publishers, 1988), 87.

well as the tensions between them after the Second World War, placing the GDR in a common central European context of rebuilding. The GDR claimed using science and technology could create a rational, technocratic future that both relied on and protected nature to construct socialism for the East German people.[9] Next, the chapter examines the sources and effects of pollution, much of which was documented in a comprehensive prognosis report in 1968 that forced the SED to confront the disaster. The SED importantly reached a turning point that year when it codified the right environmental protection in the new constitution. Finally, this chapter situates the SED's actions amid growing environmental awareness on both sides of the Iron Curtain in the late 1960s and early 1970s, revealing entanglements across central Europe and beyond. The SED espoused environmental protection at a moment when fears about pollution, consumption, and the future gripped leaders and citizens around the world. The GDR therefore attempted to construct a distinct approach to nature that balanced economic priorities with environmental protection under socialism.

Constructing Socialism, Conscripting Nature

After the Second World War, Germany was divided into four zones of occupation, with the Soviets controlling the zone that became the GDR in 1949. The Soviet-backed SED knew from its founding in 1946 that its most pressing tasks were to win over a reluctant population, and after 1949, to legitimize the GDR's existence.[10] As with other Soviet satellite states, rebuilding the economy to keep up with western European recovery proved critical to pacifying discontented peoples. To do so, the Soviet bloc states heavily relied on a smokestack industrial model that intensively used limited natural resources to increase its production, leading to extensive pollution. Yet nature served more than one purpose under communism. Both East German and Polish authorities used mass social organizations to engage with their populations, and later to strengthen ties between them. The SED in particular relied on voluntary associations, such as the Cultural League and National Front, to foster traditions of Heimat preservation and nature conservation to inculcate a new sense of national identity.[11] From the GDR's outset, the SED struggled to navigate employing nature for economic purposes while also practicing conservation for the benefit of the people.

---

[9] Dolores Augustine, *Red Prometheus: Engineering and Dictatorship in East Germany, 1945–1990* (Cambridge, MA: MIT Press, 2007), xi–xii.
[10] Palmowski, *Inventing a Socialist Nation*, 1–4.   [11] Ibid., 149–153.

Constructing socialism on a Stalinist model meant transferring the ownership of resources and means of production to the state and centrally planning the economy based on heavy industry. In the GDR, nationalization began under Soviet occupation, expropriating land from former Nazis, and intensified in the 1950s as the SED consolidated power.[12] The Soviets directly and indirectly dictated a smokestack industrialization or socialism to mine coal and produce steel in large quantities for rebuilding infrastructure and general industry.[13] The SED also expanded the chemical industry, which produced fertilizers and pesticides that were crucial to the industrialization and mechanization of East German agriculture. These industries witnessed unexpected successes and production grew tremendously in the first years.[14] By the end of the 1950s, wages had risen by more than seventy percent, too.[15] Yet economic growth came at the expense of the natural environment. The SED paid little attention to how these products were made or the impact they had on nature. Concerns primarily surfaced in the context of planning the use of resources to fulfill the Plan, and ideologically to serve the construction of socialism.

Across the Soviet bloc, satellite states also worked to construct smokestack industrial economies to rebuild after the Second World War. Poland, having been decimated over the course of six years of German and Soviet occupation, experienced similar pressure for economic growth after the War.[16] Warsaw lay in rubble, while other industrial cities like Wrocław (Breslau) fared nominally better.[17] Stalinist policies in the immediate postwar years sparked the rapid expansion of heavy industry with a focus on energy-intensive plants and massive coal-burning facilities, but little room was left for other products such as consumer goods. The coalmining region of Silesia provided the cheap energy required for massive steel production. Poland simultaneously encountered difficulties associated with urbanization, such as housing shortages, insufficient water supply, and issues with sewage treatment.[18] Even as the

---

[12] Steiner, *The Plans that Failed*, 26–28.

[13] Konrad H. Jarausch, "Beyond Uniformity: The Challenge of Historicizing the GDR," in *Dictatorship as Experience: Towards a Socio-Cultural History of the GDR*, ed. Konrad H. Jarausch (New York: Berghahn Books, 1999), 11.

[14] Maier, *Dissolution*, 83–85.   [15] Steiner, *The Plans that Failed*, 90.

[16] Padraic Kenney, *Rebuilding Poland: Workers and Communists, 1945–1950* (Ithaca, NY: Cornell University Press, 1997), 245. Antoni Z. Kaminski and Bartłowmiej Kaminski, "Road to 'People's Poland': Stalin's Conquest Revisited," in *Stalinism Revisited: The Establishment of Communist Regimes in East-Central Europe*, ed. Vladimir Tiseameanu (New York: Central European University Press, 2009), 196–198.

[17] Kenney, *Rebuilding Poland*, 14.

[18] Barbara Hicks, *Environmental Politics in Poland: A Social Movement between Regime and Opposition* (New York: Columbia University Press, 1996), 37–38.

Polish authorities prioritized coal and steel, the plants and machinery were aging, or in other instances, dismantled and taken back to the Soviet Union.[19] The absence of new technology or emissions controls set the stage for economic – and environmental – challenges moving forward.[20]

The GDR's lack of significant reserves and battered infrastructure led to a strict regulation of natural resources in addition to reliance on other Soviet bloc states. Postwar borders meant that Silesia's rich coal deposits that had been part of Germany now belonged to Poland, while Germany's major coalmining region, the Ruhr, lay in the western zones.[21] These border changes left Soviet and East German authorities with a less efficient and highly polluting type of coal known as lignite, or brown coal, as the only domestically available form of energy. This situation obliged the East German state to both extensively mine lignite as well as to rely on Polish coal deliveries through the 1950s and 1960s. Frequent delays in Polish coal production then reverberated throughout the Soviet bloc as importing countries, such as the GDR, faced shortages.[22] East German officials also frequently lamented that the GDR was one of the water-poorest countries in the world, which hindered economic growth.[23] The need to secure water for industrial production and domestic consumption led East German officials to adopt numerous conservation measures.[24] The GDR's physical constraints, mode of rebuilding, and dependence on other communist states placed many demands on East German nature.

Despite economic necessities, the SED nodded at preserving nature in the 1949 constitution and in the GDR's ministries and in party organizations. By the 1950s, the GDR's policies rested on three pillars: state nature conservation, party-controlled voluntary organizations, and scientific research.[25] This tactic drew on a German tradition of scientifically observing and altering nature,

---

[19] Peter Polak-Springer, *Recovered Territory: A German–Polish Conflict over Land and Culture, 1919–1989* (New York: Berghahn Books, 2015), 185–186.

[20] BStU MfS ZKG/14310, Helmut Schreiber, "Umweltschutz in sozialistischen Ländern: Das Beispiel des oberschlesischen Industriegebietes in der Volksrepublik Polen," (Berlin: Internationales Institut für Umwelt und Gesellschaft, September 1984), 27.

[21] Norman Naimark, *The Russians in Germany: A History of the Soviet Zone of Occupation, 1945–1949* (Cambridge, MA: Harvard University Press, 1995), 10.

[22] Open Society Archive (OSA), Item No. 10308/56, "Lack of Polish Coke Threatens East German Production Plans," November 10, 1956.

[23] Robert Haveman Gesellschaft (RHG) SWV 02/02, "Möglichkeiten einer ökologischen Modernisierung des Energiesektors der DDR."

[24] Hermann Behrens, "Rückblicke auf den Umweltschutz in der DDR seit 1990," in *Umweltschutz in der DDR: Analysen und Zeitzeugenberichte, Band 1: Rahmenbedingungen*, eds. Hermann Behrens and Jens Hoffmann (Munich: Oekom, 2008), 15. Formally, the "Law for the Protection, Use, and Maintenance of Water and Protection against Flooding," passed on April 17, 1963.

[25] Dix and Gudermann, "Naturschutz in der DDR," 546–547.

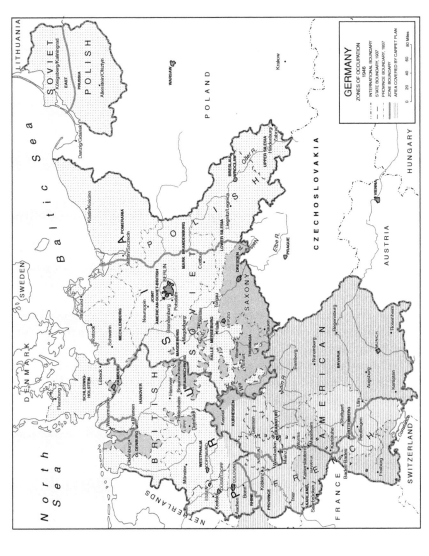

Figure 1 Central European Borders, 1946. The Soviet Zone of Occupation became the GDR in 1949 while the American, British, and French zones became the FRG. (Photo by ullstein bild/ullstein bild via Getty Images)

such as through forest management, while also romanticizing the landscape and imbuing it with cultural and national significance.[26] The constitution turned over ownership of natural resources and products of mining, iron and steel manufacturing, and the energy industry to the state, which was to oversee them in the interest of all East Germans.[27] The constitution also safeguarded against abuse in distributing and using the land, which the SED institutionalized through placing nature protection in the hands of the Ministries for Agriculture and Forestry as well as People's Education.[28]

The SED further engaged with nature through the party-controlled mass social organization called the Cultural League and a research institute. The Cultural League incorporated already existing voluntary conservation associations and channeled them in approved directions. The Cultural League relied on established ideas about nature and Heimat. In Germany, outdoor pastimes, such as hiking, maintaining natural landscapes and monuments, and nudism, coevolved with these notions, and the SED mobilized them to gain popularity.[29] Moreover, the state founded the Institute for Landscape Research and Nature Conservation (ILN) in Halle. Under the direction of Hermann Meusel, the institute adopted the conception of "landscape organism," which viewed species' health in connection to both their surroundings and their genetics.[30] This more integrated approach stood in contrast to economic planners' view of nature as primarily a means of supporting industry.

Conservation and Heimat organizations under the SED's control were crucial to boosting credibility, and the party sought to control them in the name of building socialism. The SED relied on the National Front, which was the umbrella for all mass organizations, including political parties and the trade union. The National Front presented a façade of democracy and a pluralistic society, but in reality the SED held the reins. In terms of nature protection, the National Front coordinated small-scale campaigns, mostly local beautification and cleanup projects. East Germans were encouraged to join these activities out of love for their homeland and construct a socialist Heimat.[31] This new understanding of Heimat was to be distinct from the Nazi and bourgeois pasts as well as from the FRG, which the SED

---

[26] Lekan, *Imagining the Nation in Nature*, 7.
[27] Verfassung der Deutschen Demokratischen Republik vom 7. Oktober 1949, Artikel 25.
[28] Ibid., Artikel 26.
[29] Williams, *Turning to Nature in Germany*; Palmowski, *Inventing a Socialist Nation*.
[30] Scott Moranda, *The People's Own Landscape: Nature, Tourism, and Dictatorship in East Germany* (Ann Arbor, MI: University of Michigan Press, 2014), 59.
[31] Palmowski, *Inventing a Socialist Nation*, 17, 149–150.

considered a continuation of fascism. A socialist Heimat embraced the SED's ideals of anti-fascism, social unity, socialism, and a planned economy. East German Heimat enthusiasts believed educational and cultural self-improvement were at the heart of both Heimat preservation and socialism.[32]

Within the National Front in the 1950s, the Cultural League more specifically took up nature conservation, having purview over technical-oriented groups. In general, the Cultural League was a collection of associations within the National Front that aimed to reach members of the intelligentsia who might not otherwise identify with working class, communist traditions.[33] The Friends of Nature and Heimat (*Natur- und Heimatfreunde*, NHF) was the Cultural League association that promoted conservation-related and often specialized subgroups, such as ornithology, botany, geology, and nature conservation.[34] Members of the NHF maintained protected lands, monitored the implementation of regulations, and mapped plants and animals. NHF subgroups exchanged information and interests across the Iron Curtain, which the SED nominally permitted.[35] Cultural League officials complained about ideological indifference on the part of NHF members, and increasing pressure to conform to the ideals of "socialist democracy" broke down those contacts over time.

In Poland, the Polish United Workers' Party's (*Polska Zjednoczona Partia Robotnicza*, PZPR) similarly supported nature conservation as a mass social effort in the early postwar years, albeit with less enthusiasm than the SED. In 1946, the party swiftly reestablished the Nature Conservation League (*Liga Ochrony Przyrody*, LOP), which had existed in the interwar period, under communist control. The organization boasted branches in Warsaw, Lublin, and Gdynia (near Gdańsk).[36] Like the NHF, the LOP attracted scholars, foresters, farmers, and teachers, among others, to its ranks. Yet, in the 1950s, nature conservation remained limited to a relatively small set of experts, scientists, and specialists rather than enjoying widespread interest. A decade later that changed as the PZPR intentionally targeted youth to join the LOP as part of larger,

---

[32] Ibid., 26–32. For more on continuity with and rupture from the Third Reich, see Moranda, *The People's Own Landscape*, 52–59.

[33] Mary Fulbrook, *Anatomy of a Dictatorship: Inside the GDR, 1949–1989* (New York: Oxford University Press, 1995), 60–61.

[34] Willi Oberkrome, *"Deutsche Heimat": Nationale Konzeption und regionale Praxis von Naturschutz, Landschaftsgestaltung und Kulturpolitik in Westfalen-Lippe und Thüringen (1900–1960)* (Paderborn: Ferdinand Schöningh, 2004), 282–283.

[35] Dix and Gudermann, "Naturschutz in der DDR," 554–555.

[36] "Historia Ligi Ochrony Przyrody," www.lop.org.pl/O_nas, accessed May 3, 2021.

bloc-wide initiatives to engage with nature. In the initial years of the People's Republic of Poland, though, economic rebuilding and industrialization remained the PZPR's primary objective.[37]

From a legal perspective, the SED adopted the 1954 Nature Conservation Law and distanced the GDR – on paper if not in personnel or substance – from the Nazi past. Eliminating the earlier law that the Third Reich had passed in 1935, the new one focused on using nature to build socialism.[38] In practice, the law was nearly identical to the 1935 version, admitting the economy required invasions into nature's bounty.[39] The preamble made clear that the preservation of conservation areas and indigenous plants and animals only guarded against the "unwarranted" removal of resources and cautioned that nature should be "destroyed no more than absolutely necessary."[40] Despite privileging economic concerns, the 1954 law still claimed that soil, water, plants, and animals were invaluable to the GDR and that current and future generations of East Germans must protect them. The law also set aside spaces for recreation and reserves for preservation, though it did not treat the whole of the land as something to be protected. Many of the law's more conservationist paragraphs and ideas came from Hermann Meusel, the director of the ILN.[41] While conservationists thought otherwise, nature as an interconnected system within and outside of conservation areas, however, did not feature prominently in the SED's understanding, especially before 1968. Nevertheless, the SED touted the 1954 law as progressive while the FRG continued to rely on the Nazi-era law well into the 1960s.[42]

Many experts were convinced that scientific and technological innovation would reconcile the "joy and recuperation of all friends of nature" with economic growth.[43] As in many areas of socialist thought, the SED believed rational solutions could fix all seemingly complicated problems. To this end, officials employed the concept of Landeskultur, which encompassed both improving or molding the land for a specific purpose, such as economic prosperity, and fostering national identity. The GDR

---

[37] Stanley J. Kabala, "The History of Environmental Protection in Poland and the Growth of Awareness and Activism," in *Environmental Action in Eastern Europe: Responses to Crisis*, ed. Barbara Jancar-Webster (Armonk, NY: M.E. Sharpe, 1993), 117–118.

[38] Oberkrome, *"Deutsche Heimat,"* 20.   [39] Moranda, *The People's Own Landscape*, 56.

[40] BArch DC 20/I/3/230, "Gesetz zur Erhaltung und Pflege der heimatlichen Natur vom 1954," July 8, 1954.

[41] Oberkrome, *"Deutsche Heimat,"* 329.

[42] Dix and Gudermann, "Naturschutz in der DDR," 552.

[43] Ibid. BArch DC 20-I/3/715, "Prognose: Industrielle Abprodukte und planmäßige Gestaltung einer sozialistischen Landeskultur in der DDR," 1968, 66.

sought to formulate a uniquely socialist version of Landeskultur that incorporated both resource management and nature conservation.[44] The SED planned on technology that would allow the GDR to use resources ever more efficiently, focusing on the "extraction and cultivation of reusable materials in waste products." The GDR's limited supply of fresh water made purifying runoff for reuse crucial, especially for desalinating rivers in the Harz where extensive potash mining made water saltier than the North Sea.[45] With the goal of advancing technology to overcome physical strictures, the relevant ministries anticipated fulfilling lofty economic goals and at the same time protecting nature for the workers' relaxation and enjoyment.

Landeskultur remained part of planners' mindset as they shifted away from Stalinist practices that emphasized heavy industry and rebuilding in the 1960s. This change in economic structuring and priorities offered both opportunities and challenges for environmental practices. In 1963, General Secretary of the SED and leader of the GDR Walter Ulbricht introduced the New Economic System (NES), which decentralized economic planning and management.[46] The NES initiated industry-based organizations collaborating on major decisions and stressed investment in technologies.[47] This flexibility focused on "progressive," or high tech, industries and renewed attention to conserving natural resources. Some SED officials, including Erich Honecker, who would oust Ulbricht in 1971, viewed the NES reforms as "unstable," and the SED abandoned it in the aftermath of the Prague Spring.[48] When the NES failed to perform, Ulbricht shifted to the "Economic System of Socialism" (ESS) in 1967–1968. In it, he aimed to "overtake without catching up" with the west, doubling down on a "scientific-technological revolution" that invested in the chemical industry, engineering, electronics, and automation of the economy to reduce dependence on western goods and imports.[49] As part of those measures, the SED instigated a different set of environmental hazards, namely intensive industrialization of agriculture, which relied on monoculture farming, fertilizers, and pesticides that changed the rural landscape.

[44] Landeskultur can be translated in a number of ways, including "land stewardship" and "national culture." It built on the longer German tradition of a constructed, cultivated nature as represented in the term Heimat. Moranda, *The People's Own Landscape*, 63.

[45] BArch DC 20/I/3/716, "Nachtrag zur Prognose: Industrielle Abprodukte und planmäßige Gestaltung, einer sozialistischen Landeskultur in der DDR," January 1969. Astrid M. Eckert, "Geteilt aber nicht unverbunden: Grenzgewässer als deutsch-deutsches Umweltproblem," *Vierteljahrshefte für Zeitgeschichte* 62, no. 1 (January 2014), 83.

[46] Mary Fulbrook, *The People's State: East German Society from Hitler to Honecker* (New Haven, CT: Yale University Press, 2005), 37.

[47] Augustine, *Red Prometheus*, 244–245.   [48] Steiner, *The Plans that Failed*, 110.

[49] Ibid., 119–120.

New regulations and negotiations with neighboring countries reflected the SED's ongoing attempt to balance inadequate resources for the desired economic growth amid the reforms. In 1963, the GDR introduced a law that centralized water management, weighted domestic water supplies above industry, and required industries to use water more efficiently and reduce runoff. The state eventually added fines for exceeding permitted levels.[50] A year later, the GDR also passed a regulation protecting the soil from agricultural and forestry-related runoff.[51] In the same period, the GDR signed agreements with Poland and Czechoslovakia about water levels and pollution in shared waterways. The GDR faced downstream pollution from Czechoslovakia and shared water in the Oder River with Poland, which had an impact on East German industry and agriculture.[52] Thus, the East German leadership acknowledged that environmental issues affected East Germans but constantly worried about their economic impact.

Poland's similar tension in balancing nature and economy underscores commonalities of Soviet-style communism in eastern Europe. Poland's 1949 law on the protection of nature changed the organization and administration, but it did not provide a concrete statement on the "content and implementation of nature conservation."[53] The law also failed to foresee the surge in air and water pollution that Poland's industry would spawn in the following decades, or the effect it would have on the environment.[54] In 1950, Poland passed its first law creating nature protection areas in industrial regions – including Silesia – but it omitted specific emissions levels.[55] The PZPR wrote environmental laws in the late 1960s that expanded on early conservation and health-based laws, including air quality laws in 1961 and 1966, that provincial (*województwo*) water management offices administered.[56] Still, officials regulated water and air quality in a piecemeal fashion with laws of dubious quality. One expert later stated that Poland's problem was "an excess of laws rather than a scarcity."[57]

---

[50] BArch DK 5/540, "Gesamtüberblick über die Vereinigung der Gewässer durch Mineralöle und deren Nebenprodukte und Massnahmen zur Verhütung derartiger Verunreinigungen in der DDR," undated.

[51] BArch DC 20/19102, "Grundgedanken für den Diskussionsbeitrag der DDR auf der XXIII. Generalversammlung in Luxemburg," January 20, 1971.

[52] BArch DK 4/427, "Vorläufige Tagesordnung der 4. Verhandlung der Regierungsbevollmächtigten DDR/VRP," January 30, 1970; "Direktive für das Auftreten des Regierungsbevollmächtigten der DDR und CSSR für die Regelung technischer und wirtschaftlicher Fragen an Grenzwasserläufen," January 30, 1970.

[53] Olaczek, "Konserwatorska Ochrona Przyrody w Polsce," 89.

[54] Hicks, *Environmental Politics in Poland*, 55.

[55] BStU MfS ZKG/14310, Schreiber, "Umweltschutz in sozialistischen Ländern," 7.   [56] Ibid., 7.

[57] Michał Kulesza, "Efektywność prawa i administracji w zakresie ochrony przyrody i środowiska, Fragment Raportu KOP PAN na III Kongres Nauki Polskiej," in *Problemy Ochrony Polskiej Przyrody*, eds. Olaczek and Zarzycki, 23–24.

The legislation existed on paper but lacked coherence and accountability. As in the GDR, the tension between production, resource conservation, and environmental protection restricted the PZPR's actions.

In the first decades after the Second World War, communist leaders pursued rapid industrialization while also accepting the importance of nature for their citizens. Economic concerns – and the domestic and international legitimacy a strong economy was supposed to ensure – typically took precedence over nature conservation. Nevertheless, the two were intrinsically linked. Smokestack socialism relied heavily on intensive extraction of natural resources as well as large amounts of water, compelling economic planners to constantly negotiate between using and conserving them. Moreover, East German leadership in particular recognized the centrality of nature to culture, namely, that preserving it and spending time out of doors held meaning for East Germans. As evidence of pollution from this Stalinist model mounted, these pressures would force the state to reevaluate its relationship with the natural world.

Confronting the Pollution

By the late 1960s, the SED's struggle between "economy and ecology" was obvious; pollution levels were rising in the GDR and spreading beyond the state's borders.[58] Moreover, East German citizens regarded their conditions, materially and environmentally, with increasing dissatisfaction. Sacrifices that had been tolerated in the name of building socialism in the immediate postwar years now wore on the population. The GDR lagged in comparison to western standards of living, while pollution from fast-paced smokestack industrialization inhibited East Germans' quality of life.[59] By 1968, the SED held significant and condemnatory data about the crisis. Experts had consolidated their findings in a "prognosis report" that was the thirteenth contribution to Walter Ulbricht's effort to examine the development of all aspects of society.[60] The pollution cut across all milieus of East German society, eroding health, working, and living conditions, blackening the sky, killing plants and trees, and poisoning the water. This ubiquity drove the SED to confront the escalating predicament and begin shifting its attitude on the environment.

---

[58] Maier, *Dissolution*, 91.   [59] Steiner, *The Plans that Failed*, 126.
[60] Tobias Huff, *Natur und Industrie im Sozialismus: Eine Umweltgeschichte der DDR* (Göttingen: Vandenhoeck & Ruprecht, 2015), 169.

The SED's economic planning prioritized the energy and fuel industries, which made up roughly forty percent of industrial investment at the beginning of the 1960s.[61] The pollution from energy production highlighted the drawbacks of the GDR's only viable energy source, low-grade lignite, which left an indelible mark on the natural and social landscape. The coal was (and is) most easily accessed via open-pit mines, which quickly became an established fixture of the landscape. In the GDR era, the size and scale of the mining eclipsed earlier periods. The enormous mines were physically many times bigger than nearby villages, destabilized the ground, and lowered the local water table. Outside of Leipzig, officials evacuated approximately fifteen villages between 1951 and 1988 and resettled their 7,800 residents. More than 3,000 of those were moved between 1977 and 1988.[62] The removal of inhabitants had social consequences, too, uprooting families and communities that had lived there for

Figure 2 View of the Welzow-Süd open-pit lignite mine in the Cottbus District (Brandenburg) in 1974. (Photo by Erich Schutt/ullstein bild via Getty Images)

---

[61] Steiner, *The Plans that Failed*, 73.
[62] Lausitzer und Mitteldeutsche Bergbau-Verwaltungsgesellschaft mbH, "10 Jahre Sanierungsbergbau mit Tagebaugroßgeräten" (2000), 196.

centuries and settling them in the new, prefabricated apartment blocks of Leipzig and Halle.[63]

Emissions from the coal beneficiation – or refining – plants harmed local populations by making the air nearly impossible to breathe. Respiratory illnesses such as bronchitis and asthmas plagued residents, especially children and the elderly. The plant in Espenhain (near Leipzig), for example, was originally built during the Third Reich and continued to function – with ever higher production levels – well into the 1980s without renovations or even repairs. According to engineers working there, the operators used two-thirds more coal in the plant's ovens than they had been designed to handle.[64] The air quality was nearly unbearable. As one report detailed, "These towns are falling apart, drab, and gray, creating an oppressive impression of filth in this poisoned atmosphere. The buildings are black with smoke and soot, and crumbling plaster on the facades ... shows the clear signs of thick layers of dust."[65] Residents could not leave windows open or hang laundry outside for fear that everything would turn a filthy brown-black color from the soot.

Though beneficiation plants were generally located in coalmining regions, such as Leipzig, Halle and Cottbus, lignite fueled power plants and factories all over the country. Complaints about air pollution stemming from them persisted throughout the GDR's existence. As early as 1968, future environmental minister, Dr. Werner Titel, and other experts acknowledged that coal-related air pollution had "deep and many-sided detrimental effects" on "humans, animals and plants, and the economy."[66] The prognosis report estimated that the total economic cost already amounted to more than a billion Marks per annum, which the authors assumed would rise with growing production.[67] The SED attempted to transition to oil and natural gas at various points during the GDR's existence, but the oil shocks of the 1970s and the logistical difficulties of converting to natural gas resulted in a renaissance for lignite that started in 1979 and lasted until the state's collapse.[68]

---

[63] BArch DK 5/4509, "Eingabe – Gisela Merkel, 1974," Eingaben 1974–1975.

[64] RHG ÜG 03, "Eine Reise nach Mölbis, Rötha und Espenheim: Erlebnisse, Fakten und ein Aufruf!" undated.

[65] Ibid.

[66] The report was the thirteenth contribution to an order from Walter Ulbricht to examine the development of all aspects of society. Huff, *Natur und Industrie im Sozialismus*, 169. BArch DC 20/19122, "Versuche einer Definition 'Sozialistische Landeskultur' sowie 'Natürlicher Lebensraum,'" Prognosegruppe "Abprodukte und sozialstiche Landeskultur," March 4, 1968.

[67] BArch DC 20-I/3/715, "Prognose: Industrielle Abprodukte und planmäßige Gestaltung einer sozialistischen Landeskultur in der DDR," 1968, 11. Moranda, *The People's Own Landscape*, 118–119.

[68] RHG Th 02/08, "Aus *Umwelt*, 4/83, Dr. Cord Schwartau, 'Umweltschutz in der DDR. Zunehmende Luftverschmutzung durch Renaissance der Braunkohle?' Fassung des DIW Wochenberichte, 4/1983."

The air pollution that Titel and his team identified in the 1960s continued and worsened over the next two decades.

Emissions from power plants, industrial production, and domestic consumption also damaged or killed large tracts of forest across the GDR and in neighboring countries. Sulfur laced the East German lignite and refining processes merely partially removed it. When burned, the sulfur produced acid rain that then devastated urban areas, corroding buildings, monuments, and cars as well as leading to an ecological crisis in the forest. Officials innocuously referred to this phenomenon as "forest damage" (*Forstschäden*), though in the FRG it was referred to as *Waldsterben*, or dying of the forest.[69] Its effects left visible scars in the mountainous Erzgebirge region, along the border to Czechoslovakia. Corpse-like tree trunks and broken-off branches devoid of needles covered entire hillsides and mountain ridges in an area known for its resorts and outdoor recreation.

The Erzgebirge's Waldsterben was intimately tied to transborder pollution between the GDR, Poland, and Czechoslovakia. The acid rain came not only from the GDR but also Czechoslovakia, leading to an agreement between the two countries in the 1970s. Seventy-four percent of Czechoslovakia's electro-energy was produced in northern Bohemia, near the East German border, and given prevailing weather patterns, was responsible for a significant portion of the Erzgebirge's acid rain.[70] Despite being affected by Czechoslovak industry, the GDR's emissions were far higher than the levels of neighboring countries, of which Poland bore the brunt.[71] By the 1980s, reports estimated that nearly half of Poland's air pollution came from the GDR and Czechoslovakia and became a point of diplomatic contention.[72] The Soviet bloc's heavy reliance on coal caused a myriad of transboundary pollution problems in a closely connected central European context.

---

[69] The more common term for this phenomenon today is *Waldsterben*, or forest death, but it did not come into common usage until roughly 1980, and then primarily in the West German context. Waldsterben became an important plank in the West German Green Party's platform in the 1980s. Even into the late 1980s, officials denied that Waldsterben existed in the GDR. For more on the Waldsterben debate in the FRG, see Birgit Metzger, *"Erst stirbt der Wald, dann Du!" Das Waldsterben als westdeutsches Politikum (1978–1968)* (Frankfurt am Main: Campus Verlag, 2015).

[70] Huff, *Natur und Industrie im Sozialismus*, 226–229.

[71] RHG Th 02/06, Untitled Pamphlet, 1983. BArch DC 20-I/3/715, "Prognose: Industrielle Abprodukte und planmäßige Gestaltung einer sozialistischen Landeskultur in der DDR," 1968, 11.

[72] Open Society Archive (OSA), Jacek Rostowski, "Environmental Deterioration in Poland," RAD Background Report/169, September 5, 1984.

In the GDR, the chemical industry, particularly prevalent in the area around Bitterfeld, Halle, and Merseburg known as the Chemical Triangle, further deteriorated the environment. Because the GDR had limited natural resources, SED officials sought to make up for shortages through science and technology to use materials more efficiently and to produce synthetic ones when necessary. This faith in science and technology prevailed in the chemical industry to such an extent that it even had its own ministry and produced everything from photo-processing chemicals to fertilizer and pesticides to household cleaning agents. One of the GDR's most prized chemical projects was plastics, which the SED viewed as an ersatz material for almost anything, including wood in furniture and pottery for tableware.[73] In the late 1960s, a report announced that the plastics and elastics division of the chemical industry grew at an incredible rate, especially for a planned economy, of fifteen to twenty percent per annum .[74]

The methods used to produce these goods, however, ravaged the natural environment and were hazardous in the home. Byproducts and waste were released into the air and into local bodies of water. The air quality deteriorated so badly in the Chemical Triangle that by 1968 experts estimated the GDR lost six million Marks per year from damage caused by emissions.[75] In these industrialized areas with high concentrations of particulate matter and sulfur dioxide, residents were prone to croup, laryngitis, and other respiratory illnesses. While lay people observed these symptoms anecdotally to their friends and family, officials from the Ministry for Public Health recorded them faithfully in reports.[76] The air pollution from industrial production compounded two connected sets of issues. First, coal burned to produce the goods generated pollution, and second, byproducts and waste from production degraded the environment. Together, they resulted in widespread health problems, acid rain, corrosion of buildings, and dying vegetation.

Alongside plastics, dyes also posed a range of dangers to consumers and the environment. East German dyes used dangerous heavy metals, such as cadmium, as stabilizers, endangering workers producing the goods and the

[73] Rubin, *Synthetic Socialism*, 10–11.

[74] BArch DC 20-I/3/715, "Prognose: Industrielle Abprodukte und planmäßige Gestaltung einer sozialistischen Landeskultur in der DDR," 1968.

[75] Ibid. The value of East German currency is difficult to calculate, because, as Steiner puts it, "They were politically distorted by state-set (and corrected) rates of exchange." Steiner, *The Plans that Failed*, 120. In this context, however, it is more important that the SED was attempting to understand the financial and economic impact of environmental degradation.

[76] RHG Th 02/08, "PSEUDOKRUPP – Krankheitsverlauf und Therapie," undated.

consumers. Despite being well aware that neighboring Poland and Czechoslovakia banned heavy metals in production, the GDR continued the practice.[77] The plastics industry also faced a range of alarming problems with many of the goods it produced. For example, after receiving reports of plastic furniture that melted when hot dishes were placed on them, the chemical industry began adding asbestos to improve the heat resistance of these products. Quick fixes, like using asbestos in plastics, meant that East Germans received more consumer goods, as the SED attempted to keep up with rising standards of living in the FRG. Yet these solutions illustrated that the SED's decision-making process hid such difficulties instead of correcting them.[78]

After producing problematic goods, waste from the GDR's many industries flowed unchecked into local water supplies. In 1968, sixty-six percent of the GDR's waterways were "inadmissibly polluted" in industrial centers.[79] Water became undrinkable in many districts, though most especially in Halle, and officials privately admitted that they had failed to properly care for its citizens' wellbeing. By 1980, classified reports from scientists warned that one-and-a-half million East Germans consumed drinking water that had an "impermissibly high level of nitrates" and which could have dangerous effects on the health of over 30,000 pregnant women and children. The administrative areas with the worst water quality (Potsdam, Dresden, Leipzig Erfurt and Karl-Marx-Stadt) comprised nearly a third of the districts in the GDR and well over a third of the population.[80] This strong reproach was removed from the final draft of the report, which merely commented on unacceptably high nitrate levels.

Chemical fertilizers posed yet another set of water pollution problems with wide-ranging implications. Used in high volumes in industrial agriculture, run-off from fertilizers dumped nitrates into the ground and water supply. As with other products of the chemical industry, it made the water undrinkable. The Office for Water Management, and later the environmental ministry, admitted that its water purification plants were incapable of cleaning water sufficiently to make it potable.[81] These fertilizers also

---

[77] BArch DK 5/5111, "Ergebnisse und Probleme beim Umweltschutz 1984."
[78] Rubin, *Synthetic Socialism*, 87.
[79] BArch DC 20-I/3/715, "Prognose: Industrielle Abprodukte und planmäßige Gestaltung einer sozialistischen Landeskultur in der DDR," 1968.
[80] BArch DK 5/2145, "Bericht über Ergebnisse des Umweltschutzes in der Deutschen Demokratischen Republik, 1981."
[81] BArch DK 5/5155, "Information über die Durchführung eines RGW-Symposiums zu theoretischen und technisch-ökonomischen Fragen abproduktarmer und abproduktfreier Technologien vom 15. bis 19. März 1976 in Dresden."

leached the soil of its nutrients, making the soil less fertile and less productive over time, and even poisoning pig and livestock populations.[82] Rivers and lakes became so polluted that officials forbade swimming even in nature preserves. In many places where it was not forbidden, East Germans simply considered it dangerous.[83] The industrial agriculture that fed the East German people in turn poisoned them with highly salinized water. These forms of contamination and more frustrated the general population, casting a pall on overall quality of life in the GDR just as western standards of living took off in comparison.

Given the GDR's small size, it is unsurprising that water pollution transcended borders, connecting the two Germanys. In central Europe, rivers disproportionately flow from east to west, which carried East German water pollution into the FRG. Fifty-two waterways crossed the German–German border, connecting the rival states even as they sought to politically distance themselves.[84] From the 1950s onward, pollution from the GDR – and in some cases even Czechoslovakia – caused an outcry on the other side of the Iron Curtain. Swimming in the Elbe River in and around Hamburg was inadvisable, while dead fish regularly floated to the top after East German chemical spills.[85] As the GDR confronted the challenges of industrial production, it was intimately tied to neighboring countries through environmental problems that necessitated negotiations and agreements.

Early on, East German officials recognized the transboundary character of their industrial pollution, and in order to resolve it, experts created a common set of environmental knowledge. Scientists and diplomats worked to reduce air pollution in the tri-border region known as the Black Triangle, where the GDR, Poland, and Czechoslovakia met.[86] Emissions far exceeded legal caps there, precipitating a host of health problems for residents as well as damaging forests in all three countries. Especially lignite mining and power plants in East German Lusatia and

---

[82] Thomas Fleischman, *Communist Pigs: An Animal History of East Germany's Rise and Fall* (Seattle, WA: University of Washington Press, 2020), 85–88.

[83] RHG RG/B 18, "Brief an Freunde von den Umweltblättern," July 10, 1989.

[84] Tim Grady, "A Shared Environment: German–German Relations along the Border, 1945–1972," *Journal of Contemporary History* 50, no. 3 (July 2015), 661. For more on the history of the Elbe, see Dirk Schubert, "Path Dependencies Managing the River Elbe and the Requirements of Hamburg's Open Tidal Seaport" in *Rivers Lost, Rivers Regained: Rethinking City-River Relations*, eds. Martin Knoll, Uwe Lübken, and Dieter Schott (Pittsburgh, PA: University of Pittsburgh Press, 2017), 157–158.

[85] Grady, "A Shared Environment," 667.

[86] The Black Triangle's pollution was both a matter of natural resource deposits and the region's relatively peripheral location in each of the three countries.

Polish Lower Silesia became a point of contention in the 1960s and 1970s.[87] Moreover, water pollution from Czechoslovakia had downstream effects on Poland and the GDR. Experts in the three countries clearly understood the transnational impact of pollution and viewed environmental protection as a project that "bound together socialist countries," physically and ideologically.[88]

The GDR's border with Poland also raised numerous natural resource concerns. For pragmatic, resource-related and idealistic reasons, Poland and the GDR signed a number of treaties and collaborated on various projects, including shared water and coastlines. The Oder and Neisse Rivers garnered attention because the border ran through them and both sides drew water for their own needs.[89] The two countries had cooperated on pollution in waterways since a Polish law on water quality had been set in 1961.[90] They signed another agreement about the Oder and Neisse in 1965, with both states then settling on specifics about what constituted navigable waters and who had access to them in 1969. The last of these agreements clarified that neither party could alter the course of the waterways so as to hinder the other. They had to "maintain the border waters in their appropriate conditions" by not permitting "physical, chemical, or bacterial contamination" of the Oder or Neisse via waters that flowed into those rivers.[91] While primarily focused on the economic impact of the pollution, the agreement also acknowledged the need for cooperation when it came to limited yet crucial natural resources.

All of this multifaceted environmental degradation and its impacts on the GDR and East Germans were compiled in the 1968 "prognosis report" that motivated the SED to act. The report's findings, which Werner Titel and his colleagues collected, exposed the many ways that pollution imperiled the GDR's interests at home – such as economic growth and social welfare – as well as its international reception. The public health consequences alone cost the economy, and by extension the state, valuable

---

[87] BArch DK 5/1831, Wambutt, "Information über den Stand und die Entwicklung des Umweltschutzes in der DDR," April 5, 1972, 10.

[88] Ibid., 18–19.

[89] BArch DK 5/5972, "Vereinbarung zwischen der Regierung der DDR und dem Bevollmächtigten der Regierung der VRP über die Zusammenarbeit auf dem Gebiet der Wasserwirtschaft an den Grenzgewässern zur Vorbeugung und Bekämpfung außergewöhnlicher Verunreinigungen der Grenzgewässer," 1989.

[90] BArch DK 5/6064, "Gesetz vom 31. Januar 1961 über den Schutz der Gewässer vor Verunreinigung," Quelle: poln. Gesetzestext.

[91] BArch DK 5/5972, "Vereinbarung zwischen der Regierung der Deutschen Demokratischen Republik und der Regierung der Republik Polen über die Schiffahrt auf den Grenzgewässern und über die Ausnutzung und Instandhaltung der Grenzgewässer," 1969.

resources. Smoke, particulate matter, and gases caused illnesses of the respiratory tract, eyes and skin, which compromised workers' health.[92] Moreover, polluted water endangered both domestic consumption and industrial production in addition to swimming, recreation, and nature conservation, all of which the SED purported to support for East Germans' overall wellbeing.[93] When citizens of a workers' state could barely breathe much less drink clean water or recreate outdoors, the SED realized it was more difficult for the people to be productive and build socialism. The report concluded that the social benefits of investing in regulation were decidedly higher than the numbers alone indicated; environmental protection constituted a component of the social contract between the state and its worker-citizens.

Titel and his colleagues further laid out the international implications of the GDR's pollution, noting above all Moscow's support for increased regulation. In the 1960s, Soviet leader Leonid Brezhnev also realized the need to use natural resources more prudently, claiming "all that is our very own communist mission." Other Soviet bloc states had also begun to implement new conservation laws, such as one in Bulgaria that reflected "not only traditional nature protection" but a broader understanding of the interconnectedness of ecological systems. In the nonsocialist world, Titel and the other authors worried that countries such as Sweden were already taking the lead in environmental protection and leaving the GDR behind.[94] The GDR's economic and environmental situation had cascading effects on society, political decisions, and diplomacy, forcing the SED to reconsider its priorities by the late 1960s.

Institutionalization

In recognizing environmental devastation, the SED reapplied socialism's mission of improving workers' lives to the protection of nature. As in other arenas, the SED sought to employ science and technological innovation to use resources ever more efficiently for industrial production so that nature could be left as a space for the workers to recreate. The party and state formalized this approach to environmental protection in a range of laws, state institutions, and mass social organizations. These measures addressed

---

[92] BArch DC 20-I/3/715, "Prognose: Industrielle Abprodukte und planmäßige Gestaltung einer sozialistischen Landeskultur in der DDR," 1968.

[93] Ibid.

[94] BArch DC 20-I/3/715, "Prognose: Industrielle Abprodukte und planmäßige Gestaltung einer sozialistischen Landeskultur in der DDR," 1968, 7.

the harm to nature in the GDR while leveraging the actions for external audiences.[95] Intended or not, the SED's support for protection ultimately cultivated popular investment in nature in the years following 1968 and set an expectation that East Germans deserved a clean environment.

A few months before the prognosis report was officially completed, the SED had already included the workers' right (and responsibility) to protect nature in the new constitution. The new law also reinforced more conventional forms of conservation and the preservation of plants and animals.[96] This inclusion served multiple purposes. It aimed to ameliorate existing conditions within the GDR by inspiring East German citizens to take better care of their natural surroundings as a task for the "entire society."[97] This tactic naturally obfuscated the fact that state-determined industrial production contributed significantly more to pollution than individual actions. Yet, from an optics standpoint, the constitutional right was also a calculation targeted at the capitalist west, which faced growing environmental protests at the same time. By inscribing protection in its constitution, the East German state sought favor at home and to discredit capitalism abroad.

The SED intended to signal the conviction that it could provide for its citizens and expand the place of nature in the GDR. The constitution used familiar language but also spoke more broadly of Landeskultur, which incorporated a sense of developing or cultivating the land along with engendering a national identity through nature. The constitution stated the need to keep the air and water clean *and* for the protection of plant and animal life and the beauty of the Heimat.[98] With these statements, the SED leadership blended older ideas about preserving the natural landscape with considerations about preventing water and air pollution. Yet the terms "environment" or "environmental protection" did not appear in the constitution. They first appeared in official documents a year or two later. This "conservation plus" mentality accounted for the challenges that

---

[95] Newer works that focus on the GDR have begun to integrate domestic and international implications but tend to focus either on one side or the other, such as Moranda, *The People's Own Landscape*, 116–126, or Dix and Gudermann's "Naturschutz in der DDR." Others have focused on the international side, such as Kai Hünemörder, "Environmental Crisis and Soft Politics: Détente and the Global Environment, 1968–1975," in *Environmental Histories of the Cold War*, eds. J.R. McNeill and Corinna R. Unger (New York: Cambridge University Press, 2010), 257–276, and Chaney and Gudermann, "The East's Contribution to International Conservation Part 1."

[96] Artikel 15, Absatz 2, Verfassung der Deutschen Demokratischen Republik, 1968.

[97] BArch DK 5/4454, "Entwurf: Prognostische Grundlagen über die Entwicklung von Hauptrichtungen des Umweltschutzes," 1973.

[98] Artikel 15, Absatz 2, Verfassung der Deutschen Demokratischen Republik, 1968.

the smokestack industrial economy generated but framed them in familiar and anthropocentric terms (i.e. "what can nature do for us," rather than seeing the environment as an integrated whole).[99]

The 1968 constitution marked a turning point in the dynamic between the economy and ecology, restricting the ways in which nature could be used.[100] This formulation stated that the GDR's "precious natural riches" must be protected and used efficiently, and it incorporated stronger language than the 1954 Conservation Law. The constitution stipulated, for instance, that land designated for agriculture or forestry could only be used for its intended purpose. The SED's embrace of nature acknowledged domestic concerns and signaled to East Germans that nature mattered to the leadership and ought to matter to them, too. At the same time, the constitution made a statement to the rest of the world. In the GDR's pursuit of recognition in a Cold War context, the SED hoped that being at the front of the environmental charge would curry favor beyond the borders of the GDR. This progressiveness was to speak to the benefits of socialism and stand in contrast to capitalist, imperialist countries in the west that refused to regulate industry.

Two years later, the Council of Ministers issued the Landeskultur Law to implement the constitutional promises, revealing a continuing evolution in official thinking. The law used hybrid language that both relied on traditional Heimat and resource conservation language as well as an evolving understanding of the term "environment" that treated humans and nature as part of a single, interconnected system. Still, in nearly all cases, either "natural" or "human" preceded the term, suggesting the law's authors failed to truly view humans and nature as truly interdependent. The law admitted that humans had an impact on the environment but still framed it as an object that could be shaped or constructed, a mentality reflecting the SED's worldview that anything and everything could be (re) built in a socialist society.[101] Natural riches were to be used prudently and economically, while at the same time industry and society were to work together to protect the socialist Heimat for current and future generations.[102] The SED sought to reconcile these many demands on nature through a scientific and technical revolution that would allow the

---

[99] Dix and Gudermann, "Naturschutz in der DDR," 572.
[100] Artikel 15, Absatz 1, Verfassung der Deutschen Demokratischen Republik, 1968.
[101] II. Gestaltung und Pflege der Landschaft sowie Schutz der heimatlichen Natur, § 10 Zielstellung Gesetz über die planmäßige Gestaltung der sozialistischen Landeskultur in der Deutschen Demokratischen Republik—Landeskulturgesetz—vom 14. Mai 1970.
[102] Ibid., Präambel.

economy to use resources ever more efficiently while leaving the rest as a place for workers.

The Landeskultur Law and its subordinate decrees demonstrated the SED's ongoing mediation between the needs of the economy and environmental protection. They included a combination of practical topics, such as noise pollution and sanitation, but also the conservation of plants and animals, and the "protection and care of the socialist national culture." The last of the four decrees specifically replaced the 1954 Conservation Law, because the old law ignored the "social demands on the complex development of the [natural] landscape." It placed conservation in a broader context, tying it to socialist Landeskultur while also arguing that protecting the environment was essential for both the citizens' wellbeing and the continued growth of the economy.[103] Nevertheless, the Landeskultur Law determined that the Council of Ministers had the responsibility to decide which interests should be given priority," permitting the leadership to place the economy over the environment.[104]

The challenge of navigating these two charges distinguished environmental protection under communism from western movements. Green movements under capitalism were explicitly protest movements, which called attention to industrial pollution, and to the governments that hesitated to regulate. The green movements did not need to legislate or consider the economic stance; they merely had to protest. The SED, however, walked a fine line between promising protections without criticizing its own industries and the pollution they generated. In trying to prove that socialism was more progressive and inclusive than the capitalist west, the SED became tangled in a web of being both polluter and protector. Environmental protection was more than a political talking point for the SED, but it faced an inherent contradiction that it struggled to reconcile.

Despite the SED's divided loyalties between economy and ecology, the SED persevered, approving a Ministry for Environmental Protection and Water Management (MUW) in late 1971. Dr. Werner Titel, the point person for the 1968 prognosis report, became its first minister. A relatively young man, born in 1931, Titel had recently received his doctorate in agricultural science from Humboldt University in 1965. In 1967, he became a member of the People's Chamber and one of many deputy chairs in the

---

[103] BArch DC 20/I/3/744, "Begründung des Gesetzes," Ministerrat Sitzung vom 1969.
[104] Artikel I, Absatz 3, Landeskulturgesetz, May 1970. Joachim Radkau, *The Age of Ecology: A Global History*, trans. Patrick Camiller (Malden, MA: Polity Press, 2014), 368.

Council of Ministers. In 1969, he became intimately involved in the writing of the Landeskultur Law. It followed logically that he assume leadership of the ministry in November 1971, even before it officially opened.[105] When Titel suddenly died of a heart attack at the age of forty on Christmas Day 1971, Hans Reichelt was tapped to lead the MUW when it was established in early 1972.[106] Reichelt remained in that position from the ministry's founding until January 1990, navigating economic and environmental interests.[107]

Reichelt guided the MUW's transition from using the concept of Landeskultur to a newer formulation of "socialist environmental protection" (*sozialistischer Umweltschutz*). He had served as the Minister for Agriculture and Forestry and then as a deputy minister for Agriculture, Forestry, and Foodstuffs Economy, before taking charge of the MUW for virtually the rest of the GDR's existence.[108] The transition to socialist environmental protection drew on Titel's balance between the material needs of the economy with the improvement of citizens' working and living conditions. It went further, however, to incorporate scientific and technological developments that would "strengthen and defend the power of socialism in contrast to the aggressive intention of imperialism."[109] Socialist progress and innovation would solve economic and environmental challenges, because it rationally applied a plan to the problems at hand. In the early 1970s, SED officials maintained that socialism and a planned economy could provide both environmental protection and economic

---

[105] Huff, *Natur und Industrie im Sozialismus*, 174.

[106] "Werner Titel," *Wer war wer in der DDR?*, http://bundesstiftung-aufarbeitung.de/wer-war-wer-in-der-ddr-%2363%3B-1424.html?ID=3547, accessed February 12, 2014. "Dr. Werner Titel Verstorben," *Neues Deutschland*, December 27, 1971, 1. BArch DK 5/5155, "Mitteilung," April 14, 1976.

[107] BArch DC 20/I-3/932, "Reichelt, Hans. Kurzbiographie," January 26, 1972. Reichelt had less than ideal socialist credentials but overcame them to rise within the ranks of the SED. Born in 1925 to an unwed mother, Reichelt finished school in 1943 and was then drafted into the *Wehrmacht*. He served in various infantry units and eventually rose to the rank of lieutenant before being caught by the Red Army. Between 1945 and 1949, Reichelt was a Soviet prisoner of war, during which time he attended an antifascist school. Upon his release, Reichelt traveled to the recently founded GDR and became politically active in the SED-backed agrarian party, the Democratic Farmers' Party of Germany (*Demokratische Bauernpartei Detuschlands*). As opposed to university-trained ecologists, the DBD and the agrarian interests it represented tended to be more pragmatic than idealistic. Huff suggests that the SED was not fully satisfied with Reichelt replacing Titel but had no better alternatives. Huff, *Natur und Industrie im Sozialismus*, 178.

[108] "Hans Reichelt," *Wer war wer in der DDR?*, www.bundesstiftung-aufarbeitung.de/wer-war-wer-in-der-ddr-%2363%3b-1424.html?ID=2790, accessed January 31, 2018.

[109] BArch DC 20/19102, "Die Entwicklung der sozialistischen Landeskultur—Ausdruck der kontinuierlichen Politik der SED zur Gestaltung der entwickelten sozialistischen Gesellschaft," January 20, 1971.

growth through regulation and the efficient use of resources, a goal the party struggled to meet in subsequent years.

Along with changes in state structures, the SED increased mass social activities that recruited East Germans to engage with the environment and reinforced its importance. In March 1969, before his death, Titel argued for closer coordination between state leadership and the social powers of the Cultural League to underscore the environment's place in socialism.[110] The Cultural League promptly charged the NHF's Central Commission with organizing campaigns on the district and local levels in order to disseminate information about the constitutional article and to educate East Germans. Projects such as "Nature Conservation Week" and regional "Landscape Days" wove together the familiar notions of Heimat and nature while introducing Landeskultur and socialist environmental protection to participants.[111] Typical of the SED's totalizing project, the party sought to realize a utopian and ideological ideal by using mass campaigns and tightly controlled social organizations to educate its citizens.

As the GDR wrestled with the consequences of smokestack industrialization, the SED sought to balance economic and environmental needs for domestic and international audiences. By 1968, the party was moving to support more environmental action on numerous fronts from the legal to the social at home, in the Soviet bloc, and the nonsocialist world. This decision built on existing conservationist traditions while addressing the obvious pollution occurring through socialist idealism. The SED's faith in science and technology to produce a better future created expectations among East Germans in the coming decades. The party and the state proudly proclaimed a socialist environmentalism would prevail, caring for both workers and nature against a Cold War backdrop.

A Global Environmental Moment

As the SED committed itself to environmental protection, objections to pollution resonated around the world in a larger moment of reckoning. 1968 marked both an endogenous East German and a global turning point for environmentalism as conferences and publications raised awareness about the devastating effects of industrialization and consumption across political systems. Most notably for the GDR, environmental – or green – issues gained traction in its Cold War rival, the FRG. The GDR therefore

[110] BArch-SAPMO DY 27/5649, "Sozialistische Heimatkunde – Zu den Hauptaufgaben," 1971.
[111] Ibid.

intentionally adopted what it considered to be progressive stances in contrast to the FRG and as a reaction to its precarious international standing. At the same time, the GDR also relied on Soviet bloc relations for diplomatic support and deliberately fostered those ties. Poland was particularly important for the GDR because the two states shared both economic systems and joint environmental concerns, such as in the Baltic Sea. A growing recognition of the pollution and its repercussions motivated the GDR – along with the states on either side of it – to seize a global, environmental moment in the late 1960s and early 1970s. Together, these influences explicitly and implicitly shaped East German understandings of the environment, alternately blending and clashing with socialist environmental protection.

Environmental degradation came under scrutiny around the world at the same time – in the 1960s – as in the GDR. With more freedoms in liberal democracies, however, exposés and conferences disseminated information more easily and resonated with worried citizens. Rachel Carson's 1962 *Silent Spring* sparked outcry in the United States and is generally credited with initiating the modern environmental movement.[112] Rather than listing a slew of pollutants and problems, Carson focused on just one, the effects of the pesticide DDT on the food chain that offered one tangible case with a concrete solution.[113] *Silent Spring* illuminated the interconnectedness of the environment, linking problems that had been treated as relatively discrete phenomena before. In the FRG, water and air pollution had already begun to be regulated in the 1950s and early 1960s but gained resonance in the late 1960s and into the 1970s.[114] Protests against other pollutants in the air and water, and especially questions about the repercussions of nuclear testing, reached a broader public, slowly compelling governments in western Europe and North America to reconsider their policies and institute regulation.[115]

In 1968, numerous conferences and published works underscored burgeoning international awareness about pollutants, population growth, and consumption. The United Nations' "Man and the Biosphere" conference in 1968 became the first occasion to discuss intergovernmental

---

[112] Uekötter, *The Greenest Nation?*, 78–79. Joachim Radkau, *Nature and Power: A Global History of the Environment* (New York: Cambridge University Press, 2008), 268.

[113] Radkau, *Nature and Power*, 269.

[114] Jens Ivo Engels, *Naturpolitik in der Bundesrepublik: Ideenwelt und politische Verhaltensstile in Naturschutz und Umweltbewegung, 1950–1980* (Paderborn: Ferdinand Schöningh, 2006), 32–33.

[115] Radkau, *Nature and Power*, 273–275. Radkau and Uekötter complicate this narrative somewhat, demonstrating that certain issues, such as clean air legislation in the FRG, found more resonance in the 1950s than around 1970.

coordination on the impact of humans on the environment.[116] That same year, *Only One Earth* and Paul Ehrlich's *The Population Bomb* illuminated the global impact of seemingly small-scale matters. The Club of Rome also first convened in 1968 as an informal collection of thirty individuals form ten countries to discuss "the present and future predicament of man." A group of experts with different backgrounds – scientists, educators, economists, humanists, industrialists, and civil servants – met to discuss the interdependent character of the "global system in which we all live," publishing the famous *Limits to Growth* report in 1972.[117] In it, the authors questioned contemporary rates of consumption and the use of the earth's finite resources.[118] These works and others like them argued that growing populations, waste and consumption damaged the natural environment. They became a rallying cry for more proactive and coordinated stances.

The student and extra-parliamentary protests of the late 1960s changed the face of both the United States and western Europe. Among other points of contention, such as the U.S. involvement in Vietnam and institutional hierarchy in universities, the environment along with women's rights and peace (and others) spawned a number of interrelated "New Social Movements" (NSMs) in the late 1960s and early 1970s. These movements tended to start at the grassroots level and be nonhierarchical, which intentionally stood in opposition to what students viewed as a rigid and old-fashioned society, reflecting a value change on a number of social issues.[119] The grassroots and informal character of the NSMs, and their corresponding citizens' initiatives, were very effective in targeting local polluters. Activists protested both against the businesses that produced the pollution and the governments that hesitated to regulate them.[120] In pushing for more protection, the green movement reshaped and broadened the scope of politics in the FRG, representing roughly half of the three to four thousand citizens' initiatives by the mid-1970s.[121]

The environment also found its way into mainstream media, reflecting broad resonance in West German society and offering the SED the means

---

[116] Michel Batisse, "MAB at age 25," *UNESCO Courier* 46, no. 10 (October 1993).

[117] Donella H. Meadows et al., "Forward," in *The Limits to Growth: A Report for the Club of Rome's Project on the Predicament of Mankind* (New York: Universe Books, 1972), 9.

[118] The term we now associate with this is "sustainability," but that term did not come into common usage until after the 1986 Brundtland Report.

[119] Roland Roth and Dieter Rucht, eds. *Neue soziale Bewegungen in der Bundesrepublik Detuschland* (Frankfurt: Campus Verlag, 1987), 20.

[120] Radkau, *The Age of Ecology*, 94–96.

[121] Engels, *Naturpolitik in der Bundesrepublik*, 20–21, 326.

to (hypocritically) criticize the west. By 1970, a major weekly news magazine in the FRG, *Der Spiegel*, led with articles such as "Poisoned Environment," which showcased the impact of pollution on wide swaths of the population. The article began with quotations from Dow Chemical, based primarily in the United States, and then pivoted to challenges in the FRG, including Bonn's intransigence. Despite promises for an action plan in 1970, the interior ministry instead had a "compendium of could, should, and ought to considerations."[122] It further incorporated warnings in *Only One Earth* and *The Limits to Growth*, namely that technological progress and consumption had been fetishized, and called for immediate action.[123] This combination of government inertia and fear about the future prompted a reconsideration of human interactions with the natural environment in the FRG in the 1970s, spurring protest that the East German leadership sought to exploit.[124]

In this period, environmentalism in the FRG shifted away from earlier conservation and toward an "ecologization" of the movement.[125] Activists and experts transitioned to treating nature – and human interaction with it – more holistically, recognizing the interconnectedness of biological life and habitat, natural or built.[126] The term "environment" originated in the United States and was translated as *Umwelt* in German. Using environment rather than nature reflected the evolution in thinking and was widely used in the West German context. It resonated deeply with individuals who viewed a range of problems, such as nuclear testing and industrial pollution, as part of a larger, complex system, not simply a matter of caring for the landscape. As students protested against the materialism and waste of affluent postwar society, they questioned human interaction with the natural world, the squandering of resources, and the resulting pollution. For them, the broader concept of "environment" became eminently useful.[127] Building on an internal evolution as well as external influences, the SED slowly adopted "environment" in the early 1970s, as the party grew to see nature and resources in a more inclusive and interconnected context.

---

[122] "Morgen kam gestern," *Der Spiegel*, October 5, 1970, 77.   [123] Ibid., 85.

[124] In the 1970s, much of the green movement would focus on the anti-nuclear question. For an evolution of anti-nuclear and environmental activism in the FRG, see Stephen Milder, *Greening Democracy: The Anti-Nuclear Movement and Political Environmentalism in West Germany and Beyond, 1968–1983* (New York: Cambridge University Press, 2017). Dolores Augustine, *Taking on Technocracy: Nuclear Power in Germany, 1945 to the Present* (New York: Berghahn Books, 2018).

[125] Engels, *Naturpolitik in der Bundesrepublik*, 294.   [126] Ibid, 295–296.

[127] Sandra Chaney, *Nature of the Miracle Years: Conservation in West Germany, 1945–1975* (New York: Berghahn Books, 2008), 176–177.

West German officials, such as those from the Federal Ministry of the Interior, began to promote the term around 1970 as it expanded regulation.[128] Like their East German counterparts, they viewed environmental protection as a state-planning project that could be managed through policy, improved technologies, and professional expertise.[129] Despite different ideological foundations, East and West German officials presented surprisingly similar ideas. Both argued that science and technology, along with planning, would alleviate the degradation both states faced. Typically, western democracies are considered the birthplace of the modern environmental movement, but that interpretation overlooks similar changes in other parts of the world.[130] The parallels between early official reactions to pollution and potential solutions in the FRG and the GDR overlapped more than has been previously acknowledged.

One major difference between the East and West German responses to environmental pollution stemmed from structural differences in the political systems. The green movement in the west opposed the government's stance on pollution and the corporations producing it. The government slowly reconsidered its position and adopted regulations to curb emissions and runoff as it worried about the economic impact it would have on the country. Structurally, the protesters, the government, and the corporations acted independently, each with different decision-making priorities and desired outcomes. In the totalizing system of the East German dictatorship, which lacked an autonomous civil society or market-based economy, the SED shouldered all three roles.[131] It called for environmental protection even as it caused the pollution and chose the economy over other considerations.[132] This contradictory situation eventually proved to be ineffective and led to the rise of an environmental movement outside – or at the very least, on the edges – of the dictatorship in the 1980s.

Despite the uneasy relationship between conservation and dictatorship, the SED pushed for international engagement – as ever – with the Cold

---

[128] Engels, *Naturpolitik in der Bundesrepublik*, 275–276.

[129] Chaney, *Nature of the Miracle Years*, 177.

[130] Hubertus Knabe, "Neue Soziale Bewegungen im Sozialismus. Zur Genesis alternativer politischer Orientierungen in der DDR," *Kölner Zeitschrift für Soziologie und Sozialpsychologie* 40, no. 3 (September 1988), 552. Roland Roth and Dieter Rucht, eds., *Die sozialen Bewegungen in Deutschland seit 1945: Ein Handbuch* (Frankfurt: Campus, 2008).

[131] Jarausch, "Beyond Uniformity," 6. Jürgen Kocka, *Civil Society and Dictatorship in Modern Germany* (Hanover, NH: University Press of New England, 2010), 21.

[132] David Blackbourn, *The Conquest of Nature: Water, Landscape, and the Making of Modern Germany* (New York: W. W. Norton & Company, 2006), 311–335, or Uekötter, *The Greenest Nation?*, 131–138.

War and the GDR's lack of diplomatic status in mind. The GDR lobbied hard and was finally approved for admission to the International Union for Conservation of Nature (IUCN) in 1965, and two years later became one of the founding members of the Eastern Europe Committee.[133] Though the GDR's involvement was primarily limited to that committee, it still gave the state a foothold on the world conservation stage. Mass social organizations as well as experts contributed to these networks, which were important for strengthening international ties and shaping attitudes toward nature.[134] As a member of the NHF's Central Commission stated in 1971, "Our socialist Landeskultur is an explicitly political mission, a part of the world-wide struggle between socialism and imperialism." Citizens' environmental activities were imbued with a sense of a greater, socialist purpose.

In 1972, the UN Conference on the Human Environment in Stockholm gathered representatives from both sides of the Iron Curtain who agreed on the importance of solving a global crisis of growth and consumption.[135] Building on the IUCN's 1968 Man and the Biosphere conference, the meeting hosted 113 countries and 400 intergovernmental and nongovernmental organizations.[136] In the leadup, western countries expected criticism from the Soviet bloc, but the SED refrained, stating the "problems of environmental protection are, according to their nature, universal."[137] Consistent with the GDR's efforts for diplomatic recognition, the East German leadership – with Titel as the point person until his death – worked tirelessly to join the conference, first proposing the GDR participate in 1970.[138] In a 1971 television interview, Titel emphasized the GDR's enthusiasm for the conference and its readiness to take part in work of environmental protection on an international level. He went so far as to claim lasting security in Europe rested on important joint projects such as protection and that the GDR's inclusion in the Stockholm conference was a precondition for all else.[139]

---

[133] Dix and Gudermann, "Naturschutz in der DDR," 579.
[134] BArch-SAPMO DY 27/9616, "Zuarbeit zur Rechenschaftsberichten in Vorbereitung des XI. Bundeskongresses des Kulturbundes der DDR," December 3, 1986. Chaney and Gudermann, "The East's Contribution to International Conservation Part 1," 121.
[135] Hünemörder, "Environmental Crisis and Soft Politics," 262.
[136] Chaney, *Nature of the Miracle Years*, 193.
[137] BArch DC 20-I/3/948, "Vertrauliche Ministerratssache: Beschluß über eine Erklärung der Regierung der Deutschen Demokratischen Republik zur Stockholmer Umweltkonferenz vom 13. März 1972."
[138] Hünemörder, "Environmental Crisis and Soft Politics," 264.
[139] BArch DC 20/19093, "Fernsehinterview mit dem Stellvertreter des Vorsitzenden des Ministerrates der DDR, Dr. Werner Titel," October 27, 1971.

Despite Titel's grand arguments, the West German Hallstein Doctrine made the GDR's situation precarious. Since the FRG did not recognize the GDR or any country that did, it was ultimately excluded from Stockholm, much to the East German leadership's frustration and chagrin. In a display of solidarity, other communist countries boycotted the conference, too, leaving primarily western countries in attendance.[140] Many of the countries that did participate considered Stockholm a success, and it remained the largest such conference until Rio de Janeiro in 1992, overlooking how many were ignored or excluded.[141] The absence of the Soviet bloc and sympathetic countries from Stockholm reinforced a narrative of western environmental commitment and communist neglect. That enduring interpretation ignored both the Soviet bloc's interest in the conference and the FRG's role in creating a situation that made it impossible for the GDR to attend, and by extension, fellow socialist states.

Within the communist bloc, the Soviet Union also admitted how problematic pollution was for the environment and people in the late 1960s and early 1970s.[142] Since Moscow insisted on a degree of uniformity in how the constitutive states operated, communist parties embraced a materialist, production-oriented worldview that shaped their rule.[143] As Brezhnev began to take the impact of pollution seriously, though, satellite states felt pressure to confront the devastation that their industries caused.[144] Soviet bloc countries similarly adopted regulation and bolstered mass social conservation associations, though the political situation in each country and its relationship to nature varied the reactions.[145] Bloc states initiated and participated in conferences on cross-border environmental issues, such as pollution in the Baltic Sea, even though they did not attend Stockholm. Bound both physically by shared pollution and Soviet structures, Poland instituted more regulation in the 1960s and cooperated with East German diplomats and scientists on environmental problems to create a common set of knowledge and solutions.[146] This program reflected

[140] Uekötter, *The Greenest Nation?*, 83.   [141] Radkau, *Nature and Power*, 288.

[142] OSA, "Steps Towards Pollution Control in the USSR," Radio Free Europe, April 6, 1972.

[143] Eagle Glassheim, "Ethnic Cleansing, Communism, and Environmental Devastation in Czechoslovakia's Borderlands, 1945–1989," *The Journal of Modern History* 78, no. 1 (March 2006), 68.

[144] Mark Kramer, "Stalin, Soviet Policy, and the Establishment of a Communist Bloc in Eastern Europe, 1941–1949," in *Imposing, Maintaining, and Tearing Open the Iron Curtain: The Cold War and East-Central Europe, 1945–1989*, eds. Mark Kramer and Vit Smetana (New York: Lexington Books, 2014), 26–28.

[145] Barbara Jancar-Webster, "Introduction," in *Environmental Action in Eastern Europe*, ed. Jancar-Webster, 1–8.

[146] BStU MfS ZKG/14310, Schreiber, "Umweltschutz in sozialistischen Ländern," 1.

a broader reckoning in Soviet-style communism regarding its relationship to the environment.

As part of these bloc-wide endeavors, Poland expanded its mass social efforts to raise environmental awareness. In the 1960s, the Nature Conservation League (LOP) recruited beyond expert circles to bring in youth organizations and schools. Membership grew dramatically.[147] In 1968, the PZPR further prioritized the LOP by elevating it to the status of "Association of Higher Interest." Though primarily an honorary promotion, the decision signaled the PZPR's recognition of environmental engagement.[148] The increased emphasis on popular action and attention to the LOP reflected the Soviet impulse to address resource management, the environment, and public health, into which the GDR also became invested.[149] In this moment of heightened environmental awareness in the late 1960s, the LOP and the NHF forged deeper friendships according to Soviet wishes, such as jointly declaring their responsibility for the development and protection of the environment through state and society.[150]

This sort of collaboration fed into international efforts to clean up the Baltic Sea. In the 1960s, the GDR and Poland participated in discussions about ameliorating pollution with the United Nations' Economic Commission for Europe, sending delegates to Geneva, Switzerland and Visby, Sweden. The Soviet Union's Minister for Melioration and Water Management, Comrade Borodavchenko, affirmed the importance of the topic with an East German delegation in Moscow in 1969. The USSR planned to publish about the "problem of keeping the Baltic Sea clean," and Borodavchenko wanted the GDR to take up the cause in Geneva the next year. East German and Polish delegations were to actively take part in talks in Visby, coordinating their messages in discussions with capitalist countries in order to maintain a coherent stance.[151] The East German

---

[147] Olaczek, "Konserwatorska Ochrona Przyrody w Polsce," 88–89. The organization had originally been founded in 1927 during Poland's short-lived interwar democracy and was reestablished under communist control in 1946 as part of the Party's mass social organizations and boasted branches in Warsaw, Lublin, and Gdynia.

[148] D19680227, "Rozporządzenie Rady Ministrów z dnia 20 sierpnia 1968 r. W sprawie uznania 'Ligi Ochrony Przyrody' za stowarzyszenie wyższej użyteczności," http://isap.sejm.gov.pl/isap.nsf/download.xsp/WDU19680330227/O/D19680227.pdf, accessed November 5, 2020.

[149] "Historia Ligi Ochrony Przyrody," www.lop.org.pl/O_nas, accessed May 3, 2021.

[150] BArch-SAPMO DY 27/5649, quoted in "Sozialistische Heimatkunde – Zu den Hauptaufgaben," 1971.

[151] BArch DK 5/27, "Bericht über die Teilnahme einer Delegation der DDR an der in Visby (Schweden) durchgeführten Konferenz über Maßnahmen zur Verhütung der Verschmutzung der Ostsee," September 10, 1969.

delegation, though, received instructions to advocate for a treaty to regulate pollution, because only states could properly manage these situations. Yet the delegates were forbidden from making any "binding statements about stipulations of financial provision that pertained to combatting oil pollution in the Baltic Sea."[152] The GDR and Poland supported a treaty to improve conditions, along with the Soviet Union, touting environmental protection but simultaneously limited any concrete commitments.

The Polish and East German approach illustrates the ongoing tension between economy and environment under communism. Experts aspired to be at the vanguard of international environmental protection while expanding industrial production and providing for their citizens at home. These goals pushed the SED and the PZPR to pursue a production-oriented plan, which conflicted with conservationist goals to preserve an untouched nature. The advancement of the economy, especially in highly industrial regions like Silesia, came at the expense of Poles' health and wellbeing. Despite various initiatives, nature conservation and environmental protection did not resonate as strongly in Poland as they did in the GDR, generally remaining within a cohort of scientists and experts. Moreover, the PZPR's response to pollution lacked the GDR's carefully cultivated connections between nature, national identity, and legitimacy. The Polish communists' tenuous hold on the population and a struggling economy added to their difficulties and created a somewhat different model for environmental protection and official activism than in the GDR.

Conclusion

By 1968, the GDR and countries around the world were forced to reevaluate their relationships with nature, industry, and consumption. The impact of postwar rebuilding and increased production on the environment resulted in a myriad of pollution problems that led to this moment of reckoning. Grounded in traditions of preservation and popular engagement with nature, along with a pragmatic need to manage resources, the SED responded by first embracing conservation and then institutionalizing a specifically socialist environmental protection. The East German leadership viewed these actions as a means of meeting the country's economic needs while advancing its social and diplomatic ambitions.

[152] BArch DK 5/27, "Direktive für die Teilnahme einer im Auftrage der Regierung der DDR entsandten Expertendelegation an einer internationalen Verhandlung zwischen den Ostseeanliegerstaaten zur Vorbereitung des Abschlusses eines Abkommens zum Schutz der Ostsee vor Verunreinigung," undated.

With a faith in science and technology to utilize natural resources more efficiently, and accordingly, raise productivity, the GDR aimed to improve material living standards alongside preserving a pristine nature. The SED determined that taking on environmental causes could be advantageous in winning over the East German population and demonstrate its progressiveness to the world. The GDR's aim was to gain legitimacy through having East Germans participate in the dictatorship, and in doing so, win the international recognition the SED so desired.[153]

The SED's changing position aligned with a global transformation as governments on both sides of the Iron Curtain came to terms with the toll that pollution took on people and nature. In the west, this anxiety invaded the public consciousness, generating a grassroots movement that pushed democratically elected officials to fix the problems. Additionally, the intellectual freedom of the west spurred an atmosphere of collaboration and mutual concern, which inspired such groups as the Club of Rome and, later, the 1972 Environmental Conference in Stockholm. In the east, however, protection was essentially dictated – and ignored – by the party and the state. In the GDR, the SED sought to make its economy more efficient as well as to paternalistically provide for its workers in a workers' state. The SED investigated the effects of pollution on the people and fostered a broader concept of environmentalism that extended beyond preservation and landscape management projects. Poland and the PZPR similarly reassessed their relationship to nature and joined partnerships with the GDR to address shared problems.

The GDR's treatment of the environment was uniquely situated at the confluence of German traditions of conservation and Soviet style communism. Even as East German officials and experts emphasized the material value of natural resources and focused on conservation, they also incorporated new understandings of the environment in the late 1960s. With the right to a clean environment secured in the constitution and a newly founded ministry, officials touted the GDR's progressiveness time and again over the next twenty years. More than anything, the SED showcased socialism's alleged successes while criticizing governments in the west for being slow to institute regulation. The SED believed that it had much to gain domestically and internationally from environmental protection and institutionalizing in law and through mass social organizations.

---

[153] Fulbrook, *The People's State*, 12.

CHAPTER 2

"Socialist Environmentalism": Between Ideal and Practice, 1971–1982

The 1970s began as a decade of promise for environmental protection in the GDR. With the legal framework in place, the SED and state bodies went about institutionalizing it on a cultural level and implementing regulations. They viewed the environment as an element of Honecker's "Unity of Economic and Social Policy," announced at the VIII Party Congress in 1971, which simultaneously pledged to raise production and living standards.[1] In the shadow of the Prague Spring unrest in neighboring Czechoslovakia, Cultural League officials worried that "the struggle for the People's thoughts and emotions had become a flashpoint" and that the environment presented the newest front in that battle.[2] Therefore, officials set about creating a socialist environmentalism distinct from related trends in the west through championing popular, party-sponsored activities and putting new regulations into practice. They expanded existing programs, invented traditions, and established new organizations. Officials also engaged with Eingaben, or petitions, from citizens to demonstrate the state's responsiveness to pollution problems.[3] The party and state united rhetoric with action and regulation to showcase its socialist environmental ideal.

These decisions came in a moment of confidence for the GDR as the state strengthened its position in central Europe as a hinge between east and west. The GDR normalized relations with the FRG, gained

---

[1] Bundesarchiv (BArch) DK 5/4454, "Entwurf: Prognostische Grundlagen über die Entiwcklung von Hauptrichtungen des Umweltschutzes," November 1973.

[2] BArch-Stiftungarchiv der Parteien und Massenorganisationen der DDR (SAPMO) DY 27/5649, "Zur Perspektive der Tätigkeit des Deutschen Kulturbundes auf dem Gebiet der sozialistischen Heimatkunde," February 20, 1969.

[3] Paul Betts, *Within Walls: Private Life in the German Democratic Republic* (New York: Oxford University Press, 2010); Mary Fulbrook, *The People's State: East German Society from Hitler to Honecker* (New Haven, CT: Yale University Press, 2005); see Christian Möller, *Umwelt und Herrschaft in der DDR: Politik, Protest und die Grenzen der Partizipation in der Diktatur* (Göttingen: Vanderhoeck & Ruprecht, 2020); Felix Mühlberg, *Bürger, Bitten und Behörden: Geschichte der Eingabe in der DDR* (Berlin: Karl Dietz Verlag, 2004).

international recognition, and joined the United Nations in 1973.[4] Contact between the two Germanys improved at a moment when environmental activism took off in West Germany. The rise of a green movement, and later the Green Party, both intrigued and disconcerted the SED leadership. Information between the GDR and FRG grew, and the two states influenced each other in an asymmetrical fashion with information and resources disproportionately flowing from west to east.[5] Exposés raised awareness about pollution in both East and West Germany. Further, West German opportunities for organizing and protest in a democracy inspired East Germans to wonder about alternatives, such as some form of a green party, in the GDR.[6]

At the same time, the GDR reached out to other countries in the Soviet bloc, including Poland and Czechoslovakia, with which it shared a border. In 1972, the three countries signed an agreement establishing the "borders of friendship" that eased travel restrictions between the countries and fostered educational and scientific cooperation.[7] The three states deepened relations through a variety of institutional and technological exchanges, especially regarding shared pollution. For the GDR and Poland, pollution in the Oder River, which formed the border, and in the Baltic Sea were of grave concern. The Baltic endeavors extended beyond bilateral agreements, solidifying the GDR's new international status through talks with Sweden and Finland as well as the Soviet Union. The GDR looked to strengthen diplomatic and environmental relations with socialist and non-socialist countries, underscoring is unique position as a link between east and west.

Yet the environmental promise of the 1970s did not last long in the GDR. Economic stagnation, political inertia, and renewed international tensions crippled the potential of socialist environmentalism. By most real measures, pollution was getting worse. Air and water quality were poor, and in many cases worsened, as the SED remained committed to a materialist, production-oriented system with aging infrastructure. The

---

[4] Carole Fink, *Cold War: An International History* (Boulder, CO: Westview Press, 2004).

[5] Frank Bösch, ed., *History Shared and Divided: East and West Germany since the 1970s*, trans. Jennifer Walcoff Neuheiser (New York: Berghahn Books, 2018); Tobias Hochscherf, Christoph Laucht, and Andrew Plowman, eds., *Divided but not Disconnected: German Experiences in the Cold War* (New York: Berghahn Press, 2005); Christoph Kleßmann, ed., *The Divided Past: Rewriting Post-War German History* (New York: Berghahn, 2001); Simon Mikkonen and Pia Koivunen, eds., *Beyond the Divide: Entangled Histories of Cold War Europe* (New York: Berghahn Books, 2015).

[6] BArch-SAPMO.DY 27/6112, "Information über Mitarbeit von Christen in der GNU in der Stadtorganisation Leipzig des KBs der DDR," September 26, 1983.

[7] Mark Keck-Szajbel, "A Cultural Shift in the 1970s: 'Texas' Jeans, Taboos, and Transnational Tourism," *East European Politics and Societies and Cultures* 29, no. 1 (February 2015), 217.

GDR redoubled its commitment to lignite when oil imports from the Soviet Union dropped in a period when western Europe turned to high-tech industries and outsourced other production to Asia.[8] While East German relations with western countries cooled at the end of the decade, other socialist countries became unreliable in the SED's eyes, too. Poland proved to be a particular source of consternation with economic underper-formance and constant strikes. 1982 formally marked a retreat that was already in progress when the SED moved to classify all environmental data, keeping it from domestic and international audiences.

This chapter argues that the SED succeeded in creating a more environ-mentally minded population and, at least initially, tried to address con-cerns within existing structures. The SED used mass social campaigns to unite East Germans around the issue of environmentalism and practiced protection through policy and negotiating petitions. The GDR simultan-eously reached out to other socialist countries to create coalitions around its brand of environmentalism in contrast to the one taking off in western Europe. This positioning intentionally placed the GDR in the middle of a regional and global phenomenon that spanned the Iron Curtain in the 1970s. Despite minor improvements and growing transnational networks, however, the discrepancy between rhetoric and lived reality produced an untenable situation for the SED. The GDR increasingly relied on the Ministry for State Security (Stasi) to make decisions and police the popu-lation, and ultimately opted to classify all data in 1982 when conditions did not – and would not – improve. In a paradox of success, the SED promoted an environmental expectation that it could not fulfill and placed the party and state in a tenuous position moving forward.

Social Policies: Official Environmental Engagement

After legally and institutionally enshrining environmental protection between 1968 and 1971, the SED turned to practicing it. At the VIII Party Congress in 1971, newly installed East German leader Erich Honecker proclaimed the SED's commitment to the development of Landeskultur and environmental protection. They now held the status of "principal mission" for the party on the premise that "the connection between the means of production and the GDR and the lived environment is a task for all of society central to the improvement of working and living

---

[8] Konrad H. Jarausch, *Out of Ashes: A New History of Europe in the Twentieth Century* (Princeton, NJ: Princeton University Press, 2015), 620–622.

conditions for workers." Protection mattered to the East Germans' health, capacity to work, and overall wellbeing.[9] Communist officials worried about keeping citizens satisfied in the wake of demands for reform in Czechoslovakia's Prague Spring, which the Warsaw Pact had put down with tanks in August 1968. In the GDR, the leadership viewed environmental protection and recreation in nature as a means of pacifying the population.[10] The SED believed that fostering East Germans' connectedness with a socialist Heimat would ensure loyalty.[11] Party leaders in the GDR and elsewhere looked to mass social organizations to introduce an approach to the environment that was ideological as well as practical.

The SED drew on socialist ideology and contemporary geopolitical debates along with projects to encourage broad engagement. As with many of the SED's undertakings, the Cultural League drummed up interest for the environment on a mass social level but limited activity to sanctioned venues. Officials formulated a narrative in which the environment had always been integral to socialism, drawing on the familiar pillars of socialist thought. Most notably, they turned to Friedrich Engels, who co-wrote the *Communist Manifesto* with Karl Marx, and quoted him frequently. Environmental Minister Reichelt turned to Engels' statement that "We should not flatter ourselves too much for our every human victory over nature. For every such victory, [nature] takes revenge upon us" to instill the importance of environmental protection in the population and, more importantly, to socialism.[12] In doing so, Reichelt attempted to demonstrate the environment's longstanding place in socialist and in the SED's thinking, inventing a tradition that was not necessarily well-founded.

The SED spent the first half of the 1970s signaling the importance of socialist environmental ideals – and the central role of technology – to various groups in the GDR. In 1972, Reichelt spoke to the Chamber of Technology, a voluntary society of engineers and scientists, charging members to protect nature through innovation. He contended, "Natural resources are the passive part of the means of production, and technology the active part that generates the intensity to transfigure nature." Nature,

---

[9] BArch DK 5/4454, "Entwurf: Prognostische Grundlagen über die Entiwcklung von Hauptrichtungen des Umweltschutzes," November 1973.

[10] BArch-SAPMO DY 27/5649, "Zur Perspektive der Tätigkeit des Deutschen Kulturbundes auf dem Gebiet der sozialistischen Heimatkunde," February 20, 1969.

[11] BArch-SAPMO DY 27/5649, "Überlegungen und Hinweise zur Perspektive der inhaltlichen Tätigkeit des DKBs auf dem Gebiet der sozialistischen Heimatkunde und zu einigen damit eng gebundenen Strukturfragen," undated.

[12] Quoted in RHG Th 02/01, "Friedrich Engels zur Umweltproblematik," undated.

like workers, could be used to build socialism, or exploited for *some* people's benefit (under capitalism, for example).[13] In socialism, technology could be employed to use nature's resources more efficiently without exploiting either the worker or nature. Extending the concept of exploitation beyond workers to incorporate the physical environment, Reichelt overlooked the inherent tension between material production that raised standards of living and resource conservation. Moreover, blaming capitalism as bequeathing pollution to the GDR explained away the current situation.[14]

Officials also invoked the environment to politicize geopolitical Cold War struggles. Reichelt and others claimed that monopoly capitalism in the United States and elsewhere sacrificed the fertile earth and protective forests for their own profit. Reichelt tied the Soviet Union's "camp of peace" rhetoric to environmental protection, proclaiming that capitalist countries were warmongering profiteers. This fact, he claimed, was manifest in the United States' bombing of South Vietnam, where the United States military took out resources, burned forests, and used dangerous insecticides and herbicides to destroy harvests. Reichelt argued that the United States was deeply and systematically destroying the environment in Vietnam to gain a military advantage.[15] Socialist environmentalism, then, was the opposite, a peaceful and equitable use of nature for the people. Critiquing the United States' unpopular war in Vietnam offered the SED a moral high ground on multiple fronts.

As an organization aimed at the technical and cultural elite, the Cultural League broadened the potential scope of socialist environmentalism and infused it into a range of disciplines. At an interdisciplinary colloquium in 1974, biologists, medical experts, architects, and others were asked to make the connections between ecology, health, and living conditions to the East German public. One participant elaborated on distinctions between capitalism and socialism, arguing that the goal of capitalism was profit, while in socialism, production was to satisfy workers' needs. He continued, "We produce not only chairs, houses, glasses frames but also recuperation, wellness, and such things that has value use. Avoiding environmental degradation is an additional [type of] production."[16] In reorienting the

---

[13] BArch DK 5/2428, "Referat von Dr. Hans Reichelt: Beitrag der Kammer der Technik bei der Gestaltung der sozialistischen Landeskultur und zum Umweltschutz," September 21, 1972.

[14] Umweltbibliothek Großhennersdorf (UBG) 80–113, Klaus Kluge in *Mensch und Umwelt: Aus dem Protokoll eines Kolloquiums des Kulturbundes der DDR* (Berlin: Kulturbund der DDR, 1975), 51.

[15] Ibid.   [16] UBG 80–113, Wilhelm Bartels in *Mensch und Umwelt*, 50–51.

definition of production, the participants consciously engaged in Cold War rhetoric while avoiding the "real existing pollution" in the GDR.[17]

The SED also deployed prominent academics to educate East Germans about the importance of socialist environmentalism through published works. Horst Paucke and Adolf Bauer from the Academy of Sciences specialized in strengthening the ideological case. Their 1979 book, *Environmental Problems: Humanity's Challenge*, reinterpreted Karl Marx to demonstrate environmentalism's centrality to socialism. Politically, though, they tied it to the Cold War and socialist, scientific progress. True human progress, they contended, could only be made through "the mastery of scientific-technological revolution, the development of new energy sources, advancement in space, more extensive use of the ocean, and consideration for the needs of the biosphere."[18] Following this logic, enhanced efficiency united the aims of improving living and working conditions and enacting environmental policies. Political, social, and academic leaders united behind scientific and technological innovation to move the GDR towards communism.

With the foundation laid, the Cultural League and the National Front fostered projects and campaigns that promoted participation from wide swaths of the population.[19] The Cultural League first established Landeskultur Conferences in 1966, and they became a mainstay of the vision in the 1970s. The Landeskultur Conferences celebrated nationally or regionally "meaningful and extensive protected areas" to inspire affinity toward and care of the GDR's nature, drawing on established notions of Heimat and nature conservation. Participants attended preserves and conservation sites where the SED had invested resources and declared them to be culturally significant.[20] The Landeskultur Conferences involved ensuring these spaces fulfilled the recreational needs of the urban population, and most especially industrial workers. As such, the events forbade building in some areas in addition to the maintenance of

---

[17] Conference leader Professor Werner Hartke dismissed the ideas of cost–benefit analysis and the expense of environmental protection, suggesting only that "We all want to live better." Ibid, 51–52.

[18] Horst Paucke and Adolf Bauer, *Umweltprobleme: Herausforderung der Menschheit* (Dietz Verlag: Berlin, 1979), 10.

[19] In part because there was no unified society for nature or the environment until 1980, these campaigns were jointly organized by two mass social organizations, the Cultural League and the National Front.

[20] Hermann Behrens, "Umweltprobleme eines Agrarbezirks im Spiegel von 'Landschaftstagen' – Beispiel Bezirk Neubrandenburg," in *Umweltschutz in der DDR: Analysen und Zeitzeugenberichte, Band 1: Rahmenbedingungen*, eds. Hermann Behrens and Jens Hoffmann (Munich: Oekom, 2008), 261.

some lakes and forests.[21] Practically, the Landeskultur Conferences' festivities combined working out of doors, planning future events, and rounding up party state, factory, and volunteer representatives to address the importance of the given region or natural monument.

The first Landeskultur Conference in Neubrandenburg showcased the Müritz Lake Park, which organizers hoped to turn into a national park according to UNESCO guidelines. Müritz already housed the education center for the Institute for Regional Research and Nature Protection, which made it an ideal site to confer national park status.[22] In addition to scientific and practical speeches and presentations, organizers led excursions into the protected area. Leaders also discussed and decided on plans for the maintenance and care of a given landscape.[23] As the engineer and scholar Hermann Behrens later commented, though, "next to nothing was done to solve problems like unsanctioned construction or water pollution from industrial agriculture."[24] The Müritz Lake Landeskultur Conference put East German nature on display, but it did not result in large scale investment. Officials eventually tabled discussions about creating a national park anywhere in the GDR. They deemed the designation an invention of the United States, a capitalist enemy, and therefore unfit for socialism.[25] More likely, the SED was concerned about not meeting international standards while economic planners hesitated to relinquish control over land and resource usage.[26]

Nevertheless, the Landeskultur Conferences expanded in scope and scale in the 1970s, demonstrating both the SED's commitment and the population's willingness to participate. Another one honoring the Thuringian Forest required collaboration across the three southern administrative districts (*Bezirk*) of Erfurt, Suhl, and Gera. Between 1968 and 1983, the districts carried out seven Landeskultur Conferences. Central officials in Berlin regarded them as successful, claiming that they had acquired the

[21] "'Wildes' Bauen ohne Chance," *Neue Zeit*, November 20, 1966, 6.
[22] Scott Moranda, *The People's Own Landscape: Nature, Tourism, and Dictatorship in East Germany* (Ann Arbor, MI: University of Michigan Press, 2014), 160–161. Hermann Behrens, "Das Institut für Landesforschung und Naturschutz (ILN) und die Biologischen Stationen," in *Umweltschutz in der DDR: Analysen und Zeitzeugenberichte, Band 3: Beruflicher, ehrenamtlicher und freiwilliger Umweltschutz*, eds. Hermann Behrens and Jens Hoffmann (Munich: Oekom, 2008), 71–72.
[23] BArch-SAPMO DY 27/9616, Joachim Berger, "Kulturbund der Deutschen Demokratischen Republik, Zentralvorstand der Deutschen Demokratischen Republik: Ziele, Methoden, Ergebnisse," April 12, 1983.
[24] Behrens, "Umweltprobleme eines Agrarbezirks im Spiegel von 'Landschaftstagen,'" 277.
[25] Sandra Chaney and Rita Gudermann, "The East's Contribution to International Conservation Part 1," *Environmental Policy and Law* 40, no. 2–3 (April 2010), 121.
[26] Moranda, *The People's Own Landscape*, 113.

status of a tradition in the region.[27] As in Neubrandenburg, experts and representatives from local clubs and factories discussed how to make the forest a more enjoyable place for recreation and research. Their activities involved planning for the maintenance of the Thuringian Forest over the next several years, leading excursions to learn about local flora and fauna, and maintaining hiking trails and markers.[28] By the 1980s, the district administration in Gera supported similar but smaller Landeskultur Conferences for the Upper Saale (River) and the *Holzland*, or woodland areas.[29] These events aimed at nurturing East Germans' sense of loyalty to nature and nation. The SED improved East Germans' understanding of the environment and the ecological implications of pollution, which would later undermine its legitimacy when the East German leadership could not deliver.[30]

The Cultural League instituted a related and at times overlapping program in 1971, a "Week of Socialist Landeskultur," to exhibit the SED's accomplishments. Such programs provided publicity and public goodwill without necessarily investing the large sums of money that systematic regulation would have required. Officials used the Week of Socialist Landeskultur and other projects to convince East Germans that the SED was mobilizing all of the social forces for the important cause of socialist environmentalism. The Cultural League juxtaposed geographically specific activities such as the Landeskultur Conferences with multilateral, international endeavors to deepen cooperation on environmental protection.[31] Werner Titel and the Cultural League publicized all of these dimensions, especially the Landeskultur Law, to support the GDR's unsuccessful bid for participation in the United Nations' 1972 Conference on Environmental Protection in Stockholm.[32] Though this approach failed to gain the GDR the diplomatic recognition – and

[27] BArch-SAPMO DY 27/9616, Joachim Berger, "Kulturbund der Deutschen Demokratischen Republik, Zentralvorstand der Deutschen Demokratischen Republik: Ziele, Methoden, Ergebnisse," April 12, 1983.

[28] BArch-SAPMO DY 27/6177, Kurt Harke, "Betr: Auftrag vom 8. Mai 79 zur Ermittlung der agra-Ausstellung in Markleeberg." BArch-SAPMO DY 27/5649, "Vorschlag: Gründung der Gesellschaft für Heimat und Umwelt im Kulturbund der DDR," August 21, 1974.

[29] BArch-SAPMO DY 27/6112, "Arbeitsvereinbarung: Zwischen dem Rat des Bezirkes Gera und der Bezirksleitung Gera des Kulturbundes der DDR zur weiteren Zusammenarbeit auf dem Gebiet der sozialistischen Landeskultur, des Umweltschutzes und des Erholungswesens," November 26, 1981.

[30] Jan Palmowski, *Inventing a Socialist Nation: Heimat and the Politics of Everyday Life in the GDR, 1945–1990* (New York: Cambridge University Press, 2009), 166–167.

[31] BArch DK 5/2428, "Referat von Dr. Hans Reichelt," September 21, 1972, Beitrag der Kammer der Technik bei der Gestaltung der sozialstischen Landeskultur und zum Umweltschutz.

[32] "Landeskultur geht alle an," *Neue Zeit*, August 21, 1971, 1–2.

participation in the conference – that Titel sought, the SED continued to pursue international collaboration and domestic achievements.

The same year, the Cultural League bridged longstanding traditions and evolving priorities by integrating an environmental dimension into the Baltic Sea Week events. Started in 1958 to ensure that the Baltic Sea remained "a sea of peace," the SED initially concentrated on securing the GDR's position in the region and legitimizing the state. These efforts began during a period when the FRG pursued its policy of non-recognition, placing the GDR in a precarious situation in which it did not enjoy diplomatic relations with many countries, especially outside of the Soviet bloc. The Baltic Sea represented a unique and important opportunity for the GDR to interact with socialist and non-socialist countries as economic and environmental regulations were necessary for any country that touched its shores. East German officials specifically viewed Baltic pollution as an issue for which they could leverage a sovereign role for the GDR and erode the power of the West German Hallstein Doctrine that forced states to choose which Germany they recognized.[33]

The East German leadership intentionally built up the Baltic Sea Week for an international and regional audience in an effort to exert influence in central Europe. Over time, it grew to incorporate a variety of political, cultural, and athletic events in addition to lectures, symposia and a sailing regatta.[34] In 1971, Poland's Nature Conservation League (LOP) and seventy representatives from the Soviet Nature Conservation Society joined diplomatic delegations from Scandinavian countries at the Baltic Sea Week celebrations in Rostock, East Germany.[35] In total, over twenty thousand international visitors, primarily from Soviet bloc and Baltic states, attended the opening ceremony.[36] With the theme "Man and Nature and Socialism: The Landeskultur Law and the Cultural League," the Baltic Sea Week showcased the SED's comprehensive new law and the progress it represented.

To emphasize intra-bloc cooperation, the GDR, Poland, and the Soviet Union cosponsored a 900-square-meter exhibition on socialist Landeskultur. The content specifically addressed the vital questions about environmental protection and how to join the Cultural League's many related projects. The Soviet and Polish components of the exhibition

---

[33] DC 20 19039, "Auskunftsbericht: Probleme der Verschmutzung der Ostsee," February 2, 1969.
[34] BArch DZ 4/206, "Ostseewoche, 1960."
[35] "DDR – wichtiger Friedensfaktor: Gespräch mit Nina Popowa," *Neues Deutschland*, July 2, 1971, 6.
[36] "Die Ostseewoche wird heute in Rostock eröffnet." *Neues Deutschland*, July 11, 1971, 1.

highlighted their respective organizations' methods and forms of Landeskultur activities. All three parts (the Soviet, Polish and East German) subsequently became a traveling exhibition that was intended to be shown in all districts and counties of the GDR by the end of the following year.[37] These endeavors fostered the domestic and bloc-wide transmission of knowledge about the environment, in this case the Baltic Sea, and its place in socialism.

The collaboration of multiple countries imbued the events with significance across the Soviet bloc and beyond. After the 1971 Baltic Sea Week, collaboration between the GDR, Poland, and the Soviet Union turned into a multilateral negotiation with Sweden, Finland, Denmark, and the FRG. Over the next five years, the countries worked together to limit pollution from industry, agriculture, and increasing ship traffic and agreed to reverse their effects on the sea. In part, the GDR took interest in the talks because the Baltic was crucial to transporting goods and the economy more generally. It was also a popular vacation destination for East German workers as well as citizens of other socialist countries.[38] In 1976, they signed an international agreement on the protection of the Baltic Sea in Helsinki.[39] After the GDR's exclusion from the 1972 Stockholm conference, the SED's ability to mobilize thousands of East Germans for the Baltic Sea Weeks helped to offset the international embarrassment and to make Helsinki possible.

In contrast to the expansive Baltic Sea Week or Week of Socialist Landeskultur, the Take Part! campaigns fostered small-scale beautification efforts that East Germans could easily join. After the 1971 VIII Party Congress, the National Front declared six priorities for Take Part! efforts that included repairing and building housing, tending to green spaces in residential areas, cleaning up industrial waste, and collecting and recycling materials.[40] Like the Landeskultur Conferences, and typical of the East German system, Take Part! brought together local industries, party and

---

[37] BArch-SAPMO DY 27/5649, "Sozialistische Heimatkunde: Zu den Hauptaufgaben," undated.

[38] Politisches Archiv des Auswärtigen Amtes (PA AA) M 2 B 1659 77, "Begründung (Konvention über den Schutz der Meeresumwelt des Ostseegebietes)," March 22, 1974.

[39] BArch DK 5/529, "Bericht über die ZA zwischen der DDR und der VRP auf dem Gebiet des Umweltschutzes auf der Grundlage des 'Protokolls über die Verhandlungen zwischen dem Stellvertreter des Vorsitzenden des Ministerrates der Deutschen Demokratischen Republik und Minister für Umweltschutz und Wasserwirtschaft, Dr. Hans Reichelt, und dem Stellvertreter des Vorsitzenden des Ministerrates der Volksrepublik Polen, Zdzislaw Tomal, zur weiteren Entwicklung der Zusammenarbeit auf dem Gebiet der Landeskultur und des Umweltschutzes,' vom 29. Juni 1972."

[40] Palmowski, *Inventing a Socialist Nation*, 157.

state officials, as well as ordinary East Germans to demonstrate support for cleanup projects from across society. Familiar thanks to older, ingrained notions of popular conservation and Heimat maintenance, Take Part! induced towns and neighborhoods to plant trees, install park benches, or paint buildings, again with little cost to the party or the state.

A 1976 report from Berlin praised improvements in targeted neighborhoods and presented the GDR as being at the forefront of environmental engagement. Take Part! initiatives recruited heavily, and the number of people agreeing to care for green spaces in the city rose from 2,157 to 2,385 between 1971 and 1974. The SED daily newspaper *Neues Deutschland* claimed that in 1974 alone the volunteer work cost saved an estimated 526,000 Marks. The media touted the campaign's achievements the same way it would a production target, emphasizing the scale of the project in terms of number of participants or trees planted or area of land protected.[41] In private, the Cultural League report acknowledged the limits on improving air and water quality. It concluded that given the high demand for energy sources with lower levels of sulfur, better air and water quality simply would not be attainable in the foreseeable future.[42] Even as mass social organizations called for engagement, experts recognized the constraints. Moreover, participants often joined these endeavors not out of patriotism, but because they would have done them anyway, which hinted at the limits of mass social organizations' ability to garner popular enthusiasm.[43]

The multiplicity of mass social efforts illuminates rhetorically and practically how the SED conceived of its relationship to the environment in the 1970s. These campaigns encouraged East Germans to "voluntarily" improve their neighborhoods with few resources, but the National Front and Cultural League also spun them as great acts of socialist progress. Landeskultur events and Take Part! campaigns were not intended to solve the country's degradation alone but comprised one component of socialist environmentalism. Within this social dimension, the SED aimed to raise awareness about its progressiveness, knit a bond between the population and the East German landscape, and promote its policies. It also encouraged East Germans to consider their surroundings – in the SED's intended

---

[41] Uwe Stemmler, "Schöneres Gesicht für 1300 Lichtenberger Höfe," *Neues Deutschland,* January 11/12, 1986.

[42] BArch DK 5/5155, "Schwerpunktprobleme: Auf dem Gebiet des Umweltschutzes in der Hauptstadt Berlin," 1976.

[43] Palmowski, *Inventing a Socialist Nation,* 166–168.

manner or not – providing a foundation for environmental observations and producing a corpus of knowledge about natural conditions.

Yet the Cultural League did not have a unified organization for environmental activities, such as the LOP in Poland, and so worked to establish one in the 1970s. As early as 1969 officials envisioned an association that consolidated various activities in the Cultural League and the National Front into what finally became the Society for Nature and the Environment (*Gesellschaft für Natur und Umwelt*, GNU) in 1980.[44] Despite a promising start under Werner Titel in the late 1960s, his death, as well as structural challenges typical to the GDR – lack of clear objectives or incentives and bureaucratic inertia – stalled the project. In the following years, the committee responsible for setting up the new organization renamed it the "Society for Heimat and the Environment," to move from conservation and Landeskultur and toward the newly popularized term, environment. Still, the Cultural League's political goals did not always align with the interests of the volunteers, nor did Cultural League employees always devote much attention to founding the society. These problems, along with the sufficient functioning of already existing groups, reduced the urgency to form a more comprehensive organization.

On March 28, 1980, the Cultural League finally created the GNU, not only the result of long-term internal pressure but also as response to the newly established Green Party in the FRG. Professor of Forest Management Harald Thomasius headed the new organization in order to lend it scientific credibility and expertise at home and abroad. He attended in international events, presented at conferences, and spoke with westerners visiting the GDR. Thomasius was well-versed both in socialist conceptions about the relationship between humans and nature and on more technical topics relating to forestry and the environment.[45] The GNU popularized socialist environmentalism across the GDR with every district creating its own chapter, and later every county (*Kreis*) too.[46] Under Thomasius, the GNU unified 40,000 members of the Cultural League who had been involved in related work and mobilized 1,600 working groups on such diverse topics as dendrology, city ecology, and nature and environment. By 1989, the GNU had expanded from 40,000 to

---

[44] BArch-SAPMO DY 27/5649, "Sozialistische Heimatkunde: zu den Hauptaufgaben (Zu a) der Konzeption)," 1969.

[45] BStU MfS/HA XVIII/12511, "Information, 29.5.86."

[46] BArch-SAPMO DY 27/6113, Dr. Manfred Fiedler, "Gedanken und Feststellungen zur Einschätzung der Entwicklung der Arbeit der GNU im KB im Berichtszeitraum der Abrechnung des Aktionsprogramms zum XI. Parteitag der SED," February 3, 1986.

nearly 60,000 members.[47] Although interest and activity level varied, the GNU represented one of its most popular subordinate organizations, comprising nearly one quarter of its 230,000 members in 1990.[48] The GNU attracted engaged individuals and provided a party-approved channel for participation.

The GNU's founding principles illustrate the evolution of domestic and international debates as well as the GDR's dimming environmental prospects during its eleven-year gestation. Still more technocratic in orientation than western environmentalism, the GNU broadened the definition of the word beyond the more limited concepts of nature, Heimat, and Landeskultur. Although these ideas remained imbedded in the text, they had evolved and taken on slightly different objectives, such as "increasing the beauty and *diversity* of the landscape" and "the *comprehensive* protection and improvement of the environment."[49] This vocabulary contrasted with the earlier emphasis on nature as a resource for the construction of socialism or for engendering a sense of national identity in the population. The SED was also keenly aware of the West German Green Party's electoral successes and founded the GNU in part to stave off interest in an independent environmental association.[50] Bringing the GNU into existence in 1980 was a calculated effort to keep up with domestic and international changes, and importantly, to confine environmental activism within official spaces.

The opening celebrations set a discouraging tone for the association's future, underscoring the tensions between the economy and social well-being under communism. One invited speaker, a young woman, had been involved in local nature organizations for some time. She argued that all the children and youth of her heavily industrial region around Halle and Leipzig were very concerned with pollution. She complained that after swimming outside, she and her friends had to go home and bathe again to get clean. When driving through the mining region, they felt they had landed on the moon given the dejected crater landscape. Furthermore, the filthy air from coal and chemical plants made it difficult to clean at home.

---

[47] Ehrhart Neubert, *Geschichte der Opposition in der DDR, 1949–1989* (Berlin: Ch. Links Verlag, 1997), 453.

[48] Hermann Behrens et al., *Wurzeln der Umweltbewegung: Die "Gesellschaft für Natur und Umwelt" (GNU) im Kulturbund der DDR* (Marburg: BdWi Verlag, 1993), 14. Naturally, some East Germans belonged to more than one Cultural League organization, but the number of people involved in the GNU remains impressive.

[49] BArch DK 5/1830, "Leitsätze der Gesellschaft für Natur und Umwelt im Kulturbund der DDR," January 1980. The italics are my own.

[50] Behrens et al., *Wurzeln der Umweltbewegung*, 52–53.

Appealing to the mostly older male party leaders by deploying a decidedly domestic discourse, the speaker explained, "We girls get just as vexed as our mothers when the freshly cleaned windows get dirty again after a light rain, or that we have to sweep out the windowsills after a gust of wind."[51] Although she blamed youth and naiveté for her statements, her comments highlighted the daily impact of pollution in the mining regions. From its creation, the GNU occupied a precarious position between promoting environmentalism and inviting critique.

The GNU's administration and activities varied by district and even county, but overall, the association drew enthusiasm from specialists in the 1980s. In Cottbus and elsewhere, the old NHF "interest groups" for specialists retained their earlier popularity and even grew in size.[52] In Halle, GNU members participated in Take Part! campaigns that included erecting signs for hiking trails, building fishponds, counting waterfowl populations, and preparing plans for local landscapes and parks, among other activities.[53] Farther south in Gera, officials proudly noted that roughly eighty percent of the GNU's leading members had not previously been a part of the Cultural League, having "won new forces" for the environment. Despite many positive reports about the GNU at the district level, officials also acknowledged that some counties had little leadership or no organization. In some cases, they failed to submit reports regarding their work.[54] Though the GNU certainly struggled at times, the proliferation of new chapters and swelling membership indicated popular interest in the environment.

The GDR was not alone in its pursuits; communist parties across the Soviet bloc expanded organizations and encouraged collaboration, such as Poland's role in the Baltic Sea Weeks. In the 1970s, the PZPR grew and reoriented the LOP as its official mass social conservation organization, rather than creating a new organization specifically targeted at environmentalism. The LOP worked with the East German Cultural League throughout the 1970s and then with the GNU after 1980 to organize partnerships. In 1974, the year after the two countries signed an environmental protection treaty, the Cultural League and the LOP agreed a series

---

[51] BArch-SAPMO DY 27/6112, "Stenografisches Protokoll: Gründung der Gesellschaft für Natur und Umwelt im Kulturbund der DDR am 28. März 1980."
[52] BArch-SAPMO DY 27/5649, "Bericht zur Entwicklung der GNU in den Kreisen," November 3, 1982.
[53] BArch-SAPMO DY 27/5649, "Stand der Entwicklung der GNU in Bezirk Halle," October 26, 1982.
[54] BArch-SAPMO DY 27/5649, "Einschätzung des Entwicklungsstandes der GNU im Bezirk Potsdam," October 27, 1982.

of cooperative undertakings. A Polish delegation would attend the fourth regional Landscape Conference in Thuringia, an exchange of experiences would be set up for East Germans to visit Poland, journalists from both countries would discuss environmental protection, and youth organizations would carry out exchanges.[55] These types of endeavors continued into the 1980s with correspondence between GNU and LOP members as well as trips, furthering environmental ties between the countries.[56]

As part of energizing environmental efforts in the 1970s, the LOP took over and reimagined the already existing conservation periodical *Przyroda Polska*, or *Polish Nature*, in 1975. The journal reported on the decisions of the mass social organizations relating to the environment, and even used the same language to describe the cultivation of nature and its importance to the country's socio-economic progress.[57] The LOP aimed to establish regional branches in all forty-nine voivodships, including in urban and rural communities, schools, universities and institutions. Whereas the East German Cultural League took ten years to found a new mass social organization, the PZPR redefined the existing one and pushed connections with schools to reach out to children and adolescents. Articles such as "Appeals from the youth" and "Young people gladly join the League" along with reports from schools and awards for "young nature friends" reinforced the appeal to the next generation and encouraged greater activity.[58] Through *Polish Nature*, the LOP reported on competitions and campaigns, widening its circles. By 1989, the LOP claimed a robust 1.7 million members.[59]

Participation in official conservation in both countries relied heavily on experts trained by the state and presumably loyal to communism. Scientists from the National Academy of Sciences wrote articles for official periodicals, gave speeches at major functions, and represented socialist environmentalism abroad. These efforts could be seen in the Baltic Sea Week and other projects, especially those dealing with tourism on the Baltic coast or shared rivers, such as the Oder. The GDR's Stasi, however, suspected

---

[55] BArch DK 5/529, "Arbeitsplan über die ZA 1974 und die Hauptrichtungen der ZA für 1975 zur Durchführung des Umweltschutz Abkommens DDR/VRP," January 11, 1974.

[56] BArch-SAPMO DY 27/10694, Correspondence between Adam Bazylczyk and Joachim Berger, 1986.

[57] Marian Gawroński, "Nowa organizacja Ligi Ochrony Przyrody," *Przyroda Polska*, April 1976, 1. The word "*Gestaltung*" in German is very closely related both in meaning and phonetically to the Polish word "*Kształtowanie*."

[58] "Apel młodzieży," *Przyroda Polska* (June 6, 1978), 3. Stanisław Orłowski, "Młodzież chętnie wstępuje do Ligi," *Przyroda Polska*, May 5, 1977, 4. "Nagrody dla młodych przyjaciół przyrody z Ponańskiego," Ibid., 5.

[59] Barbara Hicks, *Environmental Politics in Poland: A Social Movement between Regime and Opposition* (New York: Columbia University Press, 1996), 50–51.

Polish scientists of disloyalty as early as the beginning of the 1970s, worrying that they had extensive contacts to relatives and individuals they had met within the context of international conferences in the capitalist west.[60] The PZPR's generally more open attitude about criticism and degradation behind the Iron Curtain endlessly frustrated East German authorities despite their continued cooperation.

Socialist countries expanded popular participation in socialist environmental projects with limited means, a necessity given that these endeavors coincided with economic stagnation. Burdened with foreign debt and low-quality products that no one wanted undermined claims about a culture of efficient use of natural resources and environmental awareness. Socialist dictatorships had devoted time and resources to legislation and organization but by the end of the 1980s could not produce the solutions they had pledged. Laws could not be fulfilled through the social organizations or their activities, even though the GDR continued to make commitments domestically and internationally. The Cultural League championed awareness at the SED's behest at precisely the same moment that state ministries acknowledged they could not stop the degradation.

Political Transformation? Regulation and Its Limits

While mass social programs rallied East Germans to action, the MUW took up international cooperation and domestic regulation. The GDR signed an environmental treaty with Poland and expanded the number of academic and technological exchanges in 1973, a year after Poland, Czechoslovakia, and the GDR formalized the "borders of friendship." The Landeskultur Law and its mandates also went into effect in the 1970s and aimed to improve the natural environment, but the continual prioritization of the economy stymied these endeavors. Rather than systematically address degradation and make meaningful changes, East German leaders handed the Stasi more authority, signaling a willingness to use covert measures and repression to maintain the status quo.[61] Department XVIII of the Ministry for State Security ensured the functioning of the economy, and under its auspices, the Stasi became increasingly

---

[60] BStU MfS JHS MF VVS 681/76, "Die politisch-operative Aufgabenstellung bei der vorbeugenden Absicherung der zentralen staatlichen Leitung des Umweltschutzes unter besonderer Berücksichtigung seiner zunehmenden Bedeutung in den internationalen Beziehungen," 1977.

[61] Tobias Huff, *Natur und Industrie im Sozialismus: Eine Umweltgeschichte der DDR* (Göttingen: Vandenhoeck & Ruprecht, 2015), 180–183. Jens Gieseke, *The History of the Stasi: East Germany's Secret Police, 1945–1990* (New York: Berghahn Books, 2014), 8.

involved in handling environmental problems, most especially covering them up. Shifting responsibility to the secret police reinforced the SED's decision to only address pollution within the existing system. The East German leadership chose continuity and short-term gains over fulfilling its own environmental promises.

East German and Polish officials coordinated on a range of environmental topics, strengthening ties through the 1973 treaty. A year before, representatives built on a 1965 agreement regarding joint waterways, citing an accord among members of the Soviet Council on Mutual Economic Assistance (Comecon) on the protection of nature. They proposed strengthening collaboration on water issues, deepening the exchange of information for planning purposes, and working to build instruments for environmental protection, and they reiterated a mutual commitment to cleaning up the Baltic Sea.[62] When the two governments signed the treaty, they articulated common goals that spurred a decade of investment, specifying shared tasks, such as deepening scientific and technological cooperation, and developing the production of instruments. The GDR and Poland regarded the training and preparing of a cadre of experts on environmental protection and communal water management as important joint projects, indicating a mutual recognition of environmental interdependence in central Europe.[63] Throughout the 1970s and into the 1980s, delegations from the two countries remained in conversation, despite officials' limited authority to implement the improvements they discussed.

Research institutes, such as the Institute for Environmental Protection at the "Stanisław Staszic" Mining and Steel Works Academy in Kraków, became central to these efforts. Founded in 1972, it sought to improve conditions in Poland and take part in Soviet bloc conversations on how to re-cultivate old mines, enhance technologies to remove water from mines, and research air quality in industrial centers. The fledgling center forged relationships with counterparts in the Soviet Union and Czechoslovakia but especially with the GDR. In an interview for the East German

[62] BArch DK 5/529, "Protokoll über die Verhandlungen zwischen dem Stellvertreter des Vorsitzenden des Ministerrates der Deutschen Demokratischen Republik und Minister für Umweltschutz und Wasserwirtschaft, Dr. Hans Reichelt, und dem Stellvertreter des Vorsitzenden des Ministerrates der Volksrepublik Polen, Zdzisław Tomal, zur weiteren Entwicklung der Zusammenarbeit auf dem Gebiet der Landeskultur und des Umweltschutzes," June 29, 1972.

[63] BArch DK 5/529, "Information des Stellv des Minister für Örtliche Wirtschaft und Umweltschutz der VRP, Dr. Ludwik Ochocki, über die Einschätzung der Erfüllung und der Ergebnisse des Abkommens zwischen der DDR und der VRP über die Zusammenarbeit auf dem Gebiet der Landeskultur und des Umweltschutzes im Zeitraum vom 4.7.73–8.1.1974," July 4, 1973.

newspaper *Neue Zeit,* Polish lecturer and engineer Janusz Dziewanski told a reporter that researchers regularly analyzed publications from the GDR and the Soviet Union in order to collect new and relevant information. He emphasized, "These days, nature protection cannot be solved by one country alone."[64] Such initiatives and connections aided and reinforced the importance of the environment as well as a shared sense of purpose among experts.

Educational exchanges deepened the ties and technological information between the two states, particularly on the matters of water management and air quality. The 1972 Treaty of Friendship permitted travel between the two countries without a passport or visa, facilitating interactions between East Germans and Poles.[65] In the 1970s, East Germans and Poles traversed the Oder–Neisse Line millions of times on educational and youth exchanges, as well as for tourism and consumerism.[66] Visits back and forth meant sharing information and technology about the Baltic Sea, and other topics such as water treatment and air quality. An East German visit to the Marine Institute in Gdańsk in 1976 brought together scientists whose research explored biological and technical aspects of coastal protection. An East German report concluded that both countries faced the same technical problems and "foresaw essentially the same solutions." For better or worse, the GDR and Poland faced similar problems and conjured up similar solutions.[67] The structure of the Soviet bloc facilitated these bonds between the GDR and Poland, but the joint pollution incentivized pursuing common projects.

Within the GDR, after Honecker united economic and social policy at the VIII Party Congress, the MUW enacted environmental protection to improve conditions for citizens.[68] In 1973, a temporary MUW working group formulated the ministry's priorities through the year 1990. They targeted heavy pollution of the air, water, and ground in industrial regions as well as noise from factories and traffic as urgent issues. Intending to

[64] "Junges Institut schützt Umwelt: Interview mit Dozent Dr.-Ing. Janusz Dziewanski, Bergbau- und Hüttenakademie Krakow," *Neue Zeit,* June 17, 1973.

[65] BArch DK 5/516, "Anlage 5 zum Protokoll der XVII. Tagung des WA DDR/VRP – Bericht," undated.

[66] Keck-Szajbel, "A Cultural Shift in the 1970s," 213. Dariusz Stola, "Opening a Non-Exit State: The Passport Policy of Communist Poland, 1949–1980," *East European Politics and Societies and Cultures* 29, no. 1 (February 2015), 112.

[67] BArch DK 5/516, "Bericht über die Studienaufenthalt vom 25.5. bis 29.5.1976 im Instytut Morski, VR Polen."

[68] BArch DK 5/4454, "Entwurf: Prognostische Grundlagen über die Entwicklung von Hauptrichtungen des Umweltschutzes," November 1973.

handle "new kinds of environmental problems qualitatively," the working group emphasized the re-incorporation of waste, byproducts, and recycled goods to accommodate rising production quotas.[69] They offered suggestions for scientific and technological developments – a hallmark of the East German technocratic mentality – to protect the environment through more efficient use of resources.[70] The MUW officials would spend 9.1 billion Marks between 1971 and 1982 trying to remedy these issues.[71]

In that period, though, the MUW made limited headway with regulation. The ministry fell short of planned improvements, and even half measures required extensive negotiating with other state entities. One of the regulators' assignments was to approve construction and industrial projects. In the 1970s in Halle, for example, municipal administrators signed off on plans to build infrastructure that would ameliorate conditions in different parts of the city and expand industry.[72] Fast-growing parts of the city desperately needed water and electricity, and so bureaucrats from different departments went several rounds over where to lay district heating pipes for chemical plants in outlying Leuna, Buna, and Ammendorf. The city planning commission argued for a less invasive and more environmentally conscious option that avoided removing thousands of cubic meters of earth and a large stand of trees.[73] Economic and planning advisers made some accommodations to environmental concerns but undertook the intended project anyway. In the end, practicality helped determine the solution. Engineers compromised on where to lay the pipes, so that natural and built impediments least affected the construction. The city department of environmental protection mediated between the different industries' interests, earning some concessions from economic interests but making many, too.

Partial successes, like the one in Halle, challenged the MUW's sense of purpose and called into question officials' belief that the state could

---

[69] Ibid.

[70] This fits with a broader Soviet approach to technology as the solution to modernization and progress. Tobias Rupprecht, "Socialist High Modernity and Global Stagnation: A Shared History of Brazil and the Soviet Union during the Cold War," *Journal of Global History* 6, no. 3 (November 2011), 509.

[71] BArch DK 5/5111, "Ergebnisse und Probleme im Umweltschutz der DDR," undated. While Honecker shifted away from the rhetoric of experts and technocrats that Ulbricht had embraced, they nevertheless continued to operate in ministries and industries. See Huff, *Natur und Industrie im Sozialismus*, 187–188.

[72] The newly constructed Halle-Neustadt was so large that it was administered as its own city, independent of Halle.

[73] Stadtarchiv Halle Stadtplako 147, Correspondence, undated. The original for "district heating" is "Fernwärme" or "Fernheizleitung."

provide for its citizens. In the 1970s, factories were fitted with filters to decrease particle emissions.[74] By 1975, an energy plant in Halle had installed an electrostatic precipitator to reduce pollution from its generators, while three others had been converted to the much cleaner natural gas.[75] Halle witnessed reductions in dust emissions after officials implemented these measures, dropping from 20,280 to 17,083 tons per annum between 1975 and 1987. Yet even as particle levels decreased, sulfur dioxide emissions increased. Moreover, plants rarely replaced or repaired filters, like electrostatic precipitators that collected dust particles, when they broke. By the late 1970s, the SED had also reversed its transition to natural gas when the energy crises hit the GDR and forced a renewed dependence on lignite, further burdening coal plants charged with minimizing their pollution.[76]

In the Chemical Triangle, Halle's poor air quality combined with heavily polluted water from industry and coalmining to lead to disastrous environmental and public health conditions. Residents continued to inhale coal dust, smoke, lead from gasoline, and carbon monoxide and a host of other particles.[77] One local claimed, "Surely Halle is one of the dustiest, hottest, and driest cities in our country with high levels of pollution and decidedly little greenspace."[78] By one count, forty-five percent of Halle's flora had died out since the turn of the century.[79] Rates of chronic bronchitis were two and a half times higher in Halle than in the more rural Neubrandenburg.[80] Added to that, heavily contaminated water made life in Halle incredibly difficult. Drinking water contained heavy metals, and local lakes and rivers were not safe to swim in.[81] In

---

[74] Although the power plant put a filter on one of its generators' smokestacks to reduce particle emissions, it had not succeeded in introducing processes that reduced sulfur dioxide levels.

[75] The electrostatic precipitator uses the inherent partial charge in dust particles to draw them toward a charged metal plate, essentially catching them rather than releasing them into the atmosphere. Conversation with Dr. Andrew Ault, Department of Chemistry, University of Michigan, July 28, 2014.

[76] Stadtarchiv Halle A. 40 Nummer. 19, Band 1, "Konzeption zur Entwicklung der Umweltbedingungen in der Stadt Halle bis 1990," 1987 and Nummer 41, Band 5, "Zuarbeiten der Abteilung Umweltschutz und Wasserwirtschaft, 1973/74."

[77] BArch DK 5/3399, "Entwurf: Einschätzung zum Stand und zur Entwicklung auf dem Gebiet der sozialistischen Landeskultur in der DDR bis 1975," 1970.

[78] BArch DO 4/802, "Bäume und Sträucher in der Stadt: Wie wir schützen und pflegen," 1987.

[79] RHG Th 02/11, "Die Natur begegnet uns unübersehbar als vom Menschen verschmutzte, bedrohte und zerstörte Umwelt," undated.

[80] Archiv Bürgerbewegung Leipzig (ABL), Kirchliches Forschungsheim Wittenberg, "Die Erde ist zu Retten," 1985, 1.

[81] BArch DK 5/1982, "Bericht über Probleme des Geheimnisschutzes bei Informationen zum Umweltschutz," October 25, 1982.

short, conditions in Halle contradicted the SED's promise for a better future through technological innovation and left residents dissatisfied.

The GDR's bureaucratic character and its planned economy led to innumerable inefficiencies because responsibilities were divided between different organizations. Given that no single ministry or body had full jurisdiction, each partially responsible party tried to administer its portion or push its own agenda but lacked a comprehensive picture. Because the MUW nominally controlled regulation, out of necessity it had to work with the ministries that generated the pollution, such as the Ministry for Coal and Energy, the Ministry for Chemical Industry, the Ministry for Agriculture, Forestry and Food Production, and the Ministry for Construction.[82] Advancements in technology were supposed to improve conditions, but experts in the MUW unsurprisingly complained of insufficient coordination between individual problems and scientific-technical tasks.[83] The need for a united effort was abundantly obvious, and yet structurally difficult if not downright impossible.

Domestically and internationally, the SED's highest priority was the economy, and as such, factories could obtain exemptions to bypass the limits set by the state. High-level officials, such as Secretary of the Economy Günter Mittag, encouraged granting permits to circumvent the laws in order to keep production from being slowed.[84] The Landeskultur Law specified that "as far as incursions into the landscape and its recuperative properties are concerned, those that are unavoidable must receive special permission from the responsible local council."[85] Because the Council of Ministers made decisions about the environment based on the best interests of the entire society, it was possible to ignore limits, if other interests mattered more.[86] Officials installed environmental

[82] Jens Hoffmann und Hermann Behrens, "Organisation des Umweltschutzes," in *Umweltschutz in der DDR, Band 1*, eds. Behrens and Hoffmann, 42–45.

[83] BArch DK 5/3399, "Entwurf: Einschätzung zum Stand und zur Entwicklung auf dem Gebiet der sozialistischen Landeskultur in der DDR bis 1975."

[84] Günter Mittag was an SED party member and economic adviser. In 1976, he became the Secretary for the Economy for the Central Committee of the SED and was instrumental in shaping East German economic policy. "Hintergrund: Umweltpolitik in der DDR," September 22, 2011, Bundesministerium für Umweltschutz, Naturschutz, Bau und Reaktorsicherheit, www.umwelt-im-unterricht.de/hintergrund/umweltpolitik-in-der-ddr/, accessed August 17, 2014.

[85] BArch DC 20/I/3/744, "Entwurf: Durchführungsverordnung zum Gesetz über die planmäßige Gestaltung der sozialistischen Landeskultur in der DDR: Erschließung, Pflege und Entwicklung der Landschaft für die Erholung," 1969.

[86] "Gesetz über die planmäßige Gestaltung der sozialistischen Landeskultur in der Deutschen Demokratischen Republik—Landeskulturgesetz—vom 14. Mai 1970," Gesetzblatt der Deutschen Demokratischen Republik, Teil I Nr. 12, Berlin, den 28. Mai 1970.

controls only when they did not hinder economic performance and thereby the materialist mentality at the core of SED's self-conception.

The tension between economy and ecology manifested itself more clearly as the Stasi and its purview expanded in the 1970s. In general, the SED increasingly relied on the Stasi in the 1970s and 1980s to keep a watchful eye on the East German population after the Prague Spring and to suppress potential opposition.[87] Between 1968 and 1982, the Stasi's budget grew considerably, and the number of full time employees as well as unofficial collaborators swelled, creating an "apparatus of domination."[88] By the end of the GDR, there was roughly one Stasi employee per 180 East German citizens, an astonishing ratio of agents compared to the overall population. Nor did this number reflect the growing number of unofficial informants that the Stasi used in the 1970s and 1980s. In contrast, in Poland the ratio was one security official per 1,574 Polish citizens. Not even during Solidarność and Martial Law (1980–1983) did Poland come close approaching the GDR's reliance on a state security apparatus to mind the population.[89] In terms of money and personnel, the SED devoted significant resources to surveillance and security and held enormous sway within the party and state.

In that period between 1968 and 1982, the Stasi's reach extended into the economic realm, which the SED viewed as essential to maintaining legitimacy. Given the close relationship between production and pollution, the Stasi also became more involved in the environment. The Ministry of State Security's Department XVIII handled the functioning of the economy and accordingly assumed responsibility for various aspects of environment protection, such as handling spills, especially if they had international implications.[90] By the 1980s, the Stasi also kept tabs on environmentally related petitions (Eingaben) submitted to the MUW and other institutions.[91] East Germans submitted roughly four to five thousand petitions per year between 1977 and 1989.[92] Thus, the Stasi had a vested interest in both the domestic and international implications of environmental protection as well as its failures. The sensitivity of environmental issues revealed the party's willingness to use covert measures, surveillance, and repression to ensure economic performance and the SED's position of authority.

---

[87] Betts, *Within Walls*, 38–39.   [88] Gieseke, *The History of the Stasi*, 49, 8.

[89] Gary Bruce, *The Firm: The Inside Story of the Stasi* (New York: Oxford University Press, 2010), 10–11.

[90] BStU MfS HA XVIII 25108, "Arbeitsergebnisse 1973."

[91] BStU MfS HA XVIII 19276, "Erste Bestandaufnahme zu den bedeutendsten Umweltproblemen in der DDR," April 1981, 10.

[92] Martin Stief, *"Stellt die Bürger ruhig": Staatssicherheit und Umweltzerstörung im Chemierevier Halle-Bitterfeld* (Göttingen: Vanderhoeck & Ruprecht, 2019), 230–235.

The Stasi's jurisdiction over environmental problems underscored the emphasis on hiding pollution and relying on quick fixes instead of implementing meaningful protection. In 1977, for instance, an MUW worker informed the Stasi that between five and six hundred kilograms of a deadly pesticide called Wofatex had been spilled into the Mulde River. Senior inspection officials determined that the pesticide consisting of chlorobenzene and methyl-parathion did not present "a danger to local inhabitants or industry . . . yet the concentration of the [pesticide] would potentially be high enough to kill fish" when the Mulde flowed into the larger Elbe River.[93] Although the inspector could not confirm other repercussions from the spill, the Stasi prioritized the maintenance of appearances. Namely, the Stasi worried dead fish would float downstream and cross the border into the FRG. If that happened, it would tip off West German officials who had already registered numerous complaints about the Elbe's pollution and its impact on the FRG and especially Hamburg.[94] This time, the MUW and the Stasi succeeded in chemically neutralizing the pollutant before it flowed westward, but in the process, they downplayed damage to both the ecosystem and local, East German population.[95]

The Stasi's waxing influence relegated the MUW to a subordinate role with limited responsibilities, even as its officials observed rising pollution levels. One major task that remained in the MUW's purview related to water management. The ministry was to ensure the supply of water for industry and develop ways to reuse the byproducts and waste that various industries dumped into the water. In internal reports, the MUW acknowledged its inability to implement comprehensive strategies to improve water quality and reduce usage as well as the inefficacy of its environmental protection measures. Officials predicted a 137 percent increase in water usage would overwhelm sanitation plants between 1976 and 1980, so that two thirds of the waterways would fall into the categories of "heavily" or "very heavily" polluted.[96] Though these dire warnings perhaps constituted an appeal for better water sanitation, the ministry was forced to work

[93] BStU MfS HA XVIII 18216, "Information über Vergiftung durch Pflanzenschutzmittel," November 30, 1977.

[94] Tim Grady, "A Shared Environment: German–German Relations along the Border, 1945–1972," *Journal of Contemporary History* 50, no. 3 (July 2015), 660–679.

[95] For more on shared water problems between East and West Germany, see Astrid M. Eckert, *West Germany and the Iron Curtain: Environment, Economy, and Culture in the Borderland* (New York: Oxford University Press, 2019) and Grady, "A Shared Environment."

[96] BArch DK 5/3399, "Einschätzung zum Stand und zur Entwicklung auf dem Gebiet der sozialistischen Landeskultur in der DDR bis 1975," undated.

within the strictures of the SED's decision to subordinate the environment to the needs of the all-important economy. By the early 1980s, officials in the related ministries were often disheartened by their inability to solve the devastation, leading them to concentrate on crisis management and denial.

East Germans had the right to submit Eingaben, or petitions, to the state as recourse for problems they faced, and they did so consistently in response to pollution.[97] Enshrined in the constitution since 1949, petitions allowed East Germans to directly appeal to state bodies for help. While the SED did not allow open criticism, it did permit citizens to communicate frustration on any number of topics through them, annually submitting nearly a million of them over the course of the GDR's existence.[98] This tally, especially those directed to Honecker and the highest echelons of the state, mounted through the 1980s.[99] These petitions became a means of gauging East Germans' resentments as well as official responses to them, representing means of negotiating conflicts between citizens and administration.[100] As such, petitions provide insight into how East Germans presented their cases to the MUW and how the ministry operated. From its inception in 1971, the MUW was inundated by East Germans with petitions about living, work- ing, health, and general environmental conditions.[101] Petitions to the minis- try (and its district and county branches) overwhelmed officials in their often earnest attempts to address the wide range of individual or local problems.

In the ministry's first years, bureaucrats enthusiastically replied to citi- zens' frustrations, confident in their ability to solve them. East Germans wrote petitions about noise from auto repair shops and factories to general pollution from coalmining to wastewater from factories to bees poisoned from local industry.[102] One series of petitions complained about noise from the VEB Elektrokeramik "Otto Winzer" in Berlin in 1974 and 1975. After many rounds between the MUW, the VEB's director and the petitioners, the factory added a series of equipment to lower noise from production and, for a time, actually introduced a filter system in the outdoor facilities, so that the mill's filter system would not need to be used after 4:30 PM, the official closing time. The factory director later checked back with the petitioners and found that after the measures had been implemented, they could confirm a noticeable reduction in noise pollution.[103] A willingness to explore options and confront citizens'

---

[97] Fulbrook, *The People's State*, 280. [98] Mühlberg, *Bürger, Bitten und Behörden*, 7.
[99] Fulbrook, *The People's State*, 277. [100] Mühlberg, *Bürger, Bitten und Behörden*, 9.
[101] Fulbrook, *The People's State*, 280. [102] BArch DK 5/4509, Eingaben 1974/1975.
[103] BArch DK 5/4509, "Protokoll über die Kontrollberatung zum erreichten Stand der Verminderung des vom VEB EKB verursachten Lärms am 29.10.1975 im Klub der Werktätigen 'Julius Fučik.'"

grievances marked the MUW's early years and demonstrated an optimism in finding manageable solutions that balanced the economy's and the citizens' needs.

Yet many problems required complex solutions that the MUW could not provide, leading to half-measures and rising dissatisfaction among East Germans. In the village of Dorndorf, north of Jena in Thuringia, one mother criticized the pollution from the local chemical plant that affected her, her mother, and her three children. She illustrated how bad the air was by explaining that "if there is a northeasterly wind, it is impossible to remain outside in the garden. Even opening the windows is impossible, because it results in a thorough and demanding cleaning of the living area." Having suffered from tuberculosis for years, she was not at full strength and the extra work from cleaning up the pollution was an enormous burden. Moreover, in her yard, most of the trees were half dead, if not completely so, and flowers rarely bloomed. Even the Trabi in the garage was constantly covered in a thick, white dust and beginning to rust. In 1973, the family had received 1,000 Marks in cash as compensation, but it did not alter the situation. After again pleading for some kind of improvement, the petitioner concluded her letter by pleading "We only wish to live in a manner worthier of humans."[104] Such rhetoric embarrassed officials in a workers' state, but the MUW did not have the authority to hold polluters accountable or introduce new technologies.

Removing residents from dangerous situations became a standard tactic, which demonstrated responsiveness if not systemic solutions. Over in the district seat of Gera, the local officials debated how to resolve the Dorndorf petitioner's complaint, for surely the pollution affected other families, too. An engineer from the MUW tasked with responding to the petitioner, Comrade Guido Thoms, cited the Landeskultur Law's statute on clean air and demanded that something be done, while the director of the factory explained in detail all of the measures he had already taken. After the district health inspectors visited the home, the inspector and the factory director agreed that the family was in fact negatively affected. In the end, local officials provided the family with three options: to sell their house to the chemical plant and apply to the town council for another house in Dorndorf-Steudnitz, to have a new house built with the possible financial support of the chemical plant, or to move into a newly built apartment.[105]

---

[104] Barch DK 5/4509, "Betreff: Umweltverschmutzung," 1974/1975.
[105] BArch DK 5/4509, "Niederschrift über die Grundsatzaussprache beim Rat der Gemeinde Dorndorf-Steudnitz am 11.6.74 zur Klärung der Eingabe —————, vom 19.4.1974 an den Staatsrat der DDR über Umweltverschmutzung."

The officials' offer may have brought the family some relief, but it did not eliminate the larger problem: the factory's emissions.

In other cases, semi-solutions were relatively easy and inexpensive, but they often changed the character of the problem rather than addressing the root cause. In 1975, a temporary working group on the development of environmental protection argued that building taller smokestacks or chimneys on factories and homes could improve air quality and protect the local population. The theory was that taller smokestacks would diffuse the pollution over a greater area, reducing its effect on a single location. While the working group admitted it did not permanently resolve the air pollution, it pursued the idea anyway.[106] Near Magdeburg, petitioners from a small village lamented the smoke from recently built houses and requested some form of abatement. Local authorities then required the homeowners with flat roofs to raise their chimneys by three meters, though who was responsible for doing the work remained unclear. More commonly used in industry, and with taller smokestacks, district officials hoped higher chimneys would ameliorate air pollution by spreading it over a larger area and decreasing its density. Upon following up a few years later, the MUW learned that only one of the houses had added the chimney extension and the measure brought no noticeable improvement.[107]

Over time, as MUW officials could not fix the pollution, they became more adversarial toward petitioners, disputing their methods and grievances. In the early 1970s, officials had not balked when individuals from a community submitted petitions collectively, such as from communal housing associated with various industries complaining about pollution.[108] Yet by the 1980s, their procedure served as a reason for not passing on the petition to the appropriate ministry or for infinitely stalling its resolution. As one Stasi official pointed out when visiting the author of a petition in 1983, "a special permit is required to collect signatures for a petition," and therefore, no one would answer it. The Stasi officer further demanded the author turn over the list with all ninety signatures.[109] Collective petitions represented a public threat to the regime's stability, rather than being just

---

[106] BArch DK 5/4454, "Entwurf: Prognostische Grundlagen über die Entwicklung von Hauptrichtungen des Umweltschutzes," November 1973.

[107] Landeshauptarchiv Magdeburg M 1/9951, Eingaben, Umweltschutz 1976.

[108] See for example, BArch DK 5/4509, "Eingabe der Hausgemeinschaften der AWG 'Joliet Curie' in Liebertwolkwitz," April 22, 1974, or "Eingabe der Hausgemeinschaft 9101 Niederlichtenau, Hauptstr. 67; BVE – Nr. 138/74," August 5, 1974. See also Betts, *Within Walls*, 188–191. For more on collective petitions, see Möller, *Umwelt und Herrschaft in der* DDR, 29–32.

[109] BStU MfS/BV Bln AKG 3674, "Unrechtmäßige Unterschriftensammlung . . ." February 1983.

private grievances, and they had to be suppressed. In the early 1980s, officials noticed a slight rise in the number of petitions, though they strongly suspected that the scope of the pollution had expanded.[110] By the end of the decade, both petitions and frustration had greatly increased.

Bureaucrats navigated multiple administrative planes, at times putting them at odds with one another and highlighting polycratic elements within the dictatorship.[111] Inadequate funds and structural intransigence created formidable barriers for officials who tried to alleviate the multitude of ecological disasters facing East German society. Moreover, these highly polluting, state-owned factories operated on the assumption that they could pay for an exemption, which was significantly less expensive than implementing regulations. An entire system of bypassing regulation and half-implementing solutions undercut earlier environmental impetuses. As officials recognized the scale of the degradation and the insurmountable challenges it presented, their perspective changed on what petitions could tell them. Officials transitioned from viewing petitions as something to solve to a tool for identifying potential troublemakers and systemic short-comings. In reading the multitude of petitions, the MUW and the Stasi, along with the Council of Ministers, realized the situation could be used to make the GDR and the SED look incompetent.

Structural Challenges, Domestic and International Implications

By the early 1980s, the GDR was quickly retreating from its progressive environmental agenda in order to devote more resources to the economy and, by extension, its international status. After gaining admission to the United Nations in 1973 and committing to various agreements, such as the Helsinki Accords in 1975, the East German leadership sought to prove the GDR's legitimacy in new ways. Leaders decided not to transform but rather to hide weaknesses, economically and otherwise. Where Poland defaulted on western loans in 1981, the GDR took on more debt, primarily from the FRG because other bodies became warier of communist states' ability to pay.[112] The environment was intimately wrapped up in both economic performance and international status as pollution crossed bor-ders and undermined the SED's claims. This modus operandi became

[110] BArch DK 5/1982, "Bericht über Probleme des Geheimnisschutzes bei Informationen zum Umweltschutz," October 25, 1982.

[111] Ibid., 167–219.

[112] André Steiner, *The Plans that Failed: An Economic History of the GDR* (New York: Berghahn Books, 2010), 172.

apparent as environmental issues gained popularity in the FRG. The SED's focus, then, shifted to restricting access to environmental data to hide failings. On November 16, 1982, the SED took decisive action and classi-fied all data, concealing the figures if not the physical devastation. The SED attempted to starve East Germans as well as outside sources of information that could discredit the GDR, but doing so ultimately had the same effect.

When Honecker assumed power in 1971, he directed the SED to turn its attention to consumption and matters relating to quality of life. Given that three years earlier, the Prague Spring had proven there would be no "socialism with a human face," the best course of action for the ruling communist parties of eastern Europe was to placate the population with more consumer goods.[113] The SED's VIII Party Congress in 1971 reflected this consumer-oriented mentality, establishing the "unity of economic and social policy." Honecker declared that the party would target "the People's material and cultural standard of living on the basis of a fast developmental pace of socialist production, of higher efficiency, of scientific technological progress and the growth of productivity of labor."[114] Yet the GDR made little headway with the technology it so highly touted, while it simultan-eously devoted more resources to much desired consumer goods and social welfare programs. As a result, Honecker opted to improve material condi-tions first and hoped better economic performance would follow.[115]

The SED financed this expansion of consumer goods by borrowing money from the west, which became possible thanks to the easing of diplomatic tensions in the 1970s. West German Chancellor Willy Brandt's policies "toward the east," or *Ostpolitik*, and more generally Détente between the superpowers improved relations between the FRG and GDR. This new status provided the SED with opportunities to obtain hard money.[116] In the short term, such loans propped up the economy as Günter Mittag and other advisers devised a strategy to enhance efficiency through greater horizontal *and* vertical integration in conglomerates, or *Kombinate*. This large-scale form of industry consolidated all levels of production for a particular good or set of related goods into a single

---

[113] Paulina Bren, *The Greengrocer and His TV: The Culture of Communism after the 1968 Prague Spring* (Ithaca, NY: Cornell University Press, 2010), 197.

[114] *Protokoll der Verhandlungen des VIII. Parteitages der SED, 15. bis 19. Juni 1971*, Vol. II, Berlin (East) 1971, 296.

[115] Steiner, *The Plans that Failed*, 143.

[116] Charles S. Maier, *Dissolution: The Crisis of Communism and the End of East Germany* (Princeton, NJ: Princeton University Press, 1997), 94.

location, bringing together all raw materials to be processed as well as all manufacturing stages at one location. Kombinate became the hallmark of the East German economy, but the integration did not boost productivity and led to ever greater indebtedness. The Soviet Union's mounting economic and political difficulties, especially with the end of Détente in the late 1970s, resulted in less support for bloc states.[117] The GDR turned ever more to western countries for bailouts – primarily the FRG, with which the GDR had a unique relationship – while attempting to overcome domestic weaknesses by staying the course.

Despite remaining primarily dependent on solid fuel (lignite) throughout the GDR's existence, the oil crises contributed to the SED's deepening economic woes. Initial responses from chief economic planners such as Mittag expressed a certain amount of *Schadenfreude* over the west's struggles to adapt, and the GDR's petroleum-based products sold very well on the international market.[118] But, as the crisis deepened, the Soviet Union began to demand higher prices from its fellow bloc members as well as to sell more oil to the west for hard currency. This decision essentially cut out the bloc states like the GDR that also sought to profit from high oil prices in the west. In 1980, the Soviet Union reduced its oil deliveries to the GDR by two million tons, chopping the total amount from twenty to eighteen million. This ten percent reduction in crude oil threw the GDR's economy into disarray, as planners had already set production targets based on higher levels. Moreover, the GDR had to use a greater percentage of its oil domestically, leaving less available to produce petroleum-based goods and refined oil for the west, a crucial source of hard currency.

The combination of higher prices and less oil made it impossible for the GDR to shift away from lignite, a major source of the GDR's environmental woes.[119] Mittag authorized revived lignite mining in the late 1970s, and tacitly acknowledged the GDR's dependence on the low-quality coal for the foreseeable future.[120] In 1981, he specifically stated that the GDR must turn to lignite to replace imports of hard coal and crude oil, emphasizing that *"this amounts to a fundamental and permanent orientation of*

---

[117] Steiner, *The Plans that Failed*, 142.
[118] Raymond Stokes, "From Schadenfreude to Going-Out-of-Business Sale: East Germany and the Oil Crises of the 1970s," in *The East German Economy, 1945–2010: Falling Behind or Catching Up?*, eds. Hartmut Berghoff and Uta Andrea Balbier (New York: Cambridge University Press, 2013), 131.
[119] Ibid., 138–39.
[120] While the GDR did have four nuclear energy plants by the end of its existence, they were never the predominant energy source.

economic strategy."[121] Accordingly, between 1980 and 1987, lignite mining increased by 20 percent with disastrous results. Sulfur emissions rose by 30 percent over that time period, while the cost of mining crude coal rose from 7.70 Marks to 13.20 Marks between 1980 and 1988 as engineers had to access less accessible and lower quality seams.[122] This decision highlighted the SED's mentality that the economy – in its existing structure – must take priority over all else.

The oil crises forced western economies to undergo a structural transformation, which changed the character of the competition between communism and capitalism. The FRG, like much of western Europe, deindustrialized and shifted away from a production-oriented economy, in which the east and west had competed since the late 1940s. With the race to rebuild Europe – and its emphasis on heavy industry – essentially completed, the west transitioned to service, science, and technology industries.[123] Although the GDR technologically and economically surpassed the rest of the Soviet bloc, it trailed further and further behind advancements in western countries. This widening gap hurt both the SED's pride and its economy. The west did not need or want the GDR's technology-related exports. In 1977, the SED leadership decided to specialize in microelectronics, but where the GDR had been relatively close behind western science in 1970, it now trailed too far behind to catch up and make its electronics appealing on the world market.[124]

The rise of a green movement that focused on ecology and global interconnectedness reconfigured West German politics and provided a model of environmental change for East Germans. As the west underwent a structural transformation through deindustrialization and the rise of service and high-tech industries that struggled in the light of the oil crises, politics also shifted to new questions that Stephen Milder has argued broadened democratic input.[125] The green movement in the FRG influenced both East German officials and average citizens' perspective on degradation at home, both that a state could effectively regulate pollution and in methods of meaningful protest. Moreover, the West German government pressed the GDR for more regulation at a moment when its financial dependence on the FRG grew. Diversifying beyond older

---

[121] Quoted in Stokes, "From Schadenfreude to Going-Out-of-Business Sale," emphasis in the original. BArch-SAPMO DY 30/6474.
[122] Steiner, *The Plans that Failed*, 173.   [123] Jarausch, *Out of Ashes*, 620–622.   [124] Ibid., 153.
[125] Stephen Milder, *Greening Democracy: The Anti-Nuclear Movement and Political Environmentalism in West Germany and Beyond, 1968–1983* (New York: Cambridge University Press, 2017).

conservation efforts, the West German green movement gained widespread support across societal strata.[126]

In particular, locally organized petitions, or "citizens' initiatives," became a hallmark of West German environmental activism.[127] They protested any number of construction projects and sources of pollution, such as a new runway at the Frankfurt airport.[128] By the mid-1970s, estimates suggest that 60,000 to 120,000 citizens participated in 3,000 to 4,000 initiatives, leading to the creation of umbrella organizations to connect local and regional groups.[129] The largest of these associations, the Federal Alliance of Citizens' Initiatives, Environmental Protection (*Bundesverband Bürgerinitiativ Umweltschutz*, BBU), was founded in 1972. Within three years, over a hundred initiatives had joined. After the occupation of Wyhl, a proposed nuclear power plant in southwestern Germany, between 1973 and 1976, citizens' initiatives joined the BBU in even larger numbers as it embraced anti-nuclear protest as a key aspect of environmentalism. Citizens' initiatives' concrete and local character presented new modes of activism.

The green movement also built on older regional conservation organizations that developed more environmentally oriented stances in the 1970s.[130] With members from already existing organizations, the German Federation for the Environment and Nature Conservation (*Bund für Umwelt- und Naturschutz Deutschland*, BUND), was founded in 1975. It advocated for the reconceptualization of conservation in the FRG. With a younger generation that came out of the 1968 protests, the BUND took on a more confrontational form of protest than older conservation organizations and incorporated new topics, such as alternatives to industrial agriculture, protection of environmental data, and energy policy. Unlike the BBU, it allowed individuals rather than already existing citizens' initiatives to become members, though the two organizations overlapped and learned from one another. The more grassroots a BUND chapter was,

---

[126] Frank Uekötter, *The Greenest Nation? A New History of German Environmentalism* (Cambridge, MA: MIT Press, 2014), 92–98.

[127] Dieter Rucht, "Einleitung" in *Die sozialen Bewegungen in Deutschland seit 1945: Ein Handbuch* (Frankfurt am Main: Campus Verlag, 2008), 16–18.

[128] Milder, *Greening Democracy*, 1–2. Uekötter, *The Greenest Nation?*, 92. Sandra Chaney, *Nature of the Miracle Years: Conservation in West Germany, 1945–1975* (New York: Berghahn Books, 2008), 199–200.

[129] Chaney, *Nature of the Miracle Years*, 194–195.

[130] Jens Ivo Engels, *Naturpolitik in der Bundesrepublik: Ideenwelt und politische Verhaltensstile in Naturschutz und Umweltbewegung, 1950–1980* (Paderborn: Ferdinand Schöningh, 2006), 307. Chaney, *Nature of the Miracle Years*, 199.

the more citizens' initiatives shaped its mode of operation.[131] Together, the BBU and BUND represented a younger generation of more politically charged activists who radically transformed modes of thinking about and engaging with nature. To the SED, these developments offered both opportunities to critique the FRG as well as a source of concern should East Germans attempt to adopt similar tactics.

Growing environmental awareness in the FRG further came from experts that could hurt the GDR's reputation if the SED did not manage the situation carefully.[132] The SED had already established its GNU as a partial response to environmental concerns in the GDR and pushed to confine such sentiment into controlled spaces. Yet West German pieces, such as Ilka Nohara-Schnabel's 1976 article on policy in the GDR from the Federal Agency for Civic Education, undermined party and state efforts. Nohara-Schnabel contradicted official lines about the complementary nature of economic growth and environmental protection, specifically highlighting how the globally changing economy had "largely crippled" ecological investment.[133] Nohara-Schnabel further illuminated how the East German leadership conceived of and exploited natural resources, despite rhetoric to the contrary.[134] Such articles reached only a relatively limited audience but laid the groundwork for awareness as environmental politics gained greater acceptance in the FRG and provided East Germans with the knowledge to counter the SED.

With a contested relationship to the west, the East German leadership looked to Soviet bloc states for support, but there, too, the SED questioned the strength of socialist friendship. For the PZPR, combatting economic and social instability became virtually all-encompassing. Scarcity of goods and cutbacks in welfare expenditures led to strikes and general discontent.[135] Following student and intelligentsia protests in 1968, normalization in Poland reached an uneasy equilibrium. Though the unrest did not lead to attempted large-scale reforms like in Czechoslovakia, and the leader of the PZPR, Władysław Gomułka, retained power, dissatisfaction with the regime remained high.[136] By 1970, Polish society protested

---

[131] Engels, *Naturpolitik in der Bundesrepublik*, 316.
[132] BArch DO 4/801, Gräfe, "Die Haltung der Kirchen in der DDR zu Fragen des Umweltschutzes," October 1982.
[133] Ilka Nohara-Schnabel, "Zur Entwicklung der Umweltpolitik in der DDR," *Deutschland Archiv* 9 (1976), 809.
[134] Ibid., 819.
[135] Robert Zuzowski, *Political Dissent and Opposition in Poland: The Workers' Defense Committee "KOR"* (Westport, CT: Praeger, 1992), 44–50.
[136] Ibid., 38–39.

again over austerity measures. Workers led strikes that the state put down, in some cases brutally, but Gomułka's leadership did not survive this second series of protests, so he stepped down and Edward Gierek replaced him.[137]

Gierek precariously led Poland for the next decade, but economic struggles weakened the leadership and its claims to offer a desirable – and socialist – quality of life for workers.[138] As in the GDR, Poland turned to the west to solve its woes, taking out large loans to ensure some kind of stability. Between 1971 and 1975, Gierek generated a semblance of acceptance from the Polish population, using western money to raise living standards.[139] By the early 1980s, western lenders pushed to see returns from the preceding decade's investments, and the eastern European economies were "drawn into an inter-bloc network of commodity and capital flows."[140] As the Soviet Union proved unable or unwilling to prop up the eastern European economies, they became ever more closely tied to the capitalist economies. Despite economic dependence on the west, this relationship was uneasy. Most notably, tensions heightened when Poland declared it could not pay back loans and the communist bloc faced a de facto credit boycott.[141] These pressing economic concerns created a near constant state of crisis in Poland but represented much more far-reaching problems with Soviet style planned economies and the stability of the region. The GDR was increasingly estranged from its neighbors to both the west and the east.

In the context of economic downturn and bloc-wide uncertainty, in 1982, the East German Council of Ministers restricted access to environmental data as a matter of state security. The Council of Ministers expressed apprehension about the gathering, publication, and interpretation of relevant data, fearing that enemies both in and outside of the GDR used them to destabilize the socialist project. Socialist environmentalism had aimed to advance the SED's agenda and compete with green movements in the west but became a point of contention between the regime and the population. Ironically, the SED's success in promoting consciousness among East Germans ended up generating a new sense distrust.[142] Barely two years after creating the GNU to rally East Germans around

[137] Steiner, *The Plans that Failed*, 141.
[138] Zuzowski, *Political Dissent and Opposition in Poland*, 59.
[139] Jan Kubik, *The Power of Symbols against the Symbols of Power: The Rise of Solidarity and the Fall of State Socialism in Poland* (University Park, PA: Pennsylvania State University Press, 1994), 33.
[140] Maier, *Dissolution*, 104.   [141] Steiner, *The Plans that Failed*, 142.   [142] Ibid.

socialist environmentalism, the SED decided not to confront the pollution but tacitly admitted defeat and hid the data.

In 1981, the MUW reported internally on the extent of the degradation that it now sought to keep secret. The re-commitment to lignite resulted in higher levels of sulfur dioxide emissions across the GDR, but especially in the coalmining region of Lusatia. Moreover, filters in multiple power plants had worn out, resulting in increased particulate matter in the air, and former open-pit mines had not been "re-cultivated" as promised in the Five-Year Plan.[143] Industrial agriculture, especially pesticides and fertilizers, and slurry (a mixture of animal waste and other substances) polluted the water in rural areas, while cities combatted run-off and noise pollution from factories.[144] Deficiencies in East German environmental policies and mass social efforts exposed omnipresent degradation that the SED wished to conceal. The situation was not improving but growing more dire.

These thorough policies and the experts behind them had been intended to awe capitalist countries with progressiveness, but inadvertently revealed the GDR's weaknesses. An October report leading up to the resolution cited fears that the FRG and other capitalist countries had "systematically misused [environmental] publications from the GDR for political and economic purposes" and tried to internationally discredit real-existing socialism. The GDR participated in international activities, such as the second basket of the 1975 Helsinki Accords and the United Nations Environment Program (UNEP), but providing real data proved precarious.[145] The report resolved to only submit data from monitoring stations that were "unproblematic," or presented the GDR in the best light. East German scientists, too, swore not to reveal compromising information when abroad, despite accusations at international conferences about sulfur dioxide emissions in the air and water quality in rivers that ran from east to west.[146]

The Stasi also worried that East German experts that were not considered reliable enough for international travel attended conferences in the Soviet bloc and thereby came into contact with westerners anyway. Because travel within the Soviet bloc did not require the same credentials

---

[143] DK 5/1337, "Bericht über die Ergebnisse der Entwicklung des Umweltschutzes in der DDR, 1976–1980," 1981.

[144] Ibid.

[145] The GDR's international status changed dramatically in the 1970s, following the 1972 Basic Treaty when the GDR and the FRG recognized each other. Both countries were subsequently admitted to the United Nations.

[146] BArch DK 5/1982, "Bericht über Probleme des Geheimnisschutzes bei Informationen zum Umweltschutz," October 25, 1982.

as travel to the west, less politically reliable East German experts might be subverting the SED's efforts to conceal the extent of the pollution in the GDR.[147] Westerners, and especially West Germans, often attended events in Poland, Czechoslovakia, and Hungary, and might seek out such individuals. In the early 1980s, Poland was a suspicious socialist partner with the emergence of the independent trade union, Solidarność. The PZPR permitted much more open criticism than the SED, which worried the East German leadership. The SED perceived itself to be trapped between the capitalist west and an unreliable "friend" to the east, while simultaneously linking the two through its actions.

The Council of Ministers distrusted experts in ecology, biology, and water management at home and abroad, despite their centrality to economic and environmental planning. The October report stated alarm about veterinary and medical presentations at the university in Leipzig that openly discussed finding cadmium and other heavy metals in animal feed as well as human food. One expert cited in the report was Dr. Dobberkau, a member of the SED and the director of the GDR's leading center for the medical aspects of environmental protection. He questioned the reliability of young scientists who might not respect the "secrecy of environmental information."[148] Being suspicious of younger East Germans, who had come of age and gone to university in the years since 1968, illustrated the disparity between the party's ideals and stagnated reality. An ever more obvious generational divide posed a greater challenge for the SED elite than pollution; it questioned the party's ability to lead the GDR into the next decade.

This threat came not only from experts and scientists but also from writers and intellectuals such as Monika Maron. In 1981, her debut novel *Flight of Ashes* depicted the severe pollution in Bitterfeld, the bleakness of the gray landscape, and the despair of nothing staying clean. Maron based the novel off of her personal experience traveling around the country as a journalist in the late 1970s.[149] Ironically, a salesgirl in the novel notes that "white shirts sell best here" while the narrator wonders about the children on the playground, "you have to think how many of them must have bronchitis. You wonder about every tree that hasn't died."[150] Banned from

---

[147] BStU MfS JHS MF VVS 681/76, "Die politisch-operative Aufgabenstellung bei der vorbeugenden Absicherung der zentralen staatlichen Leitung des Umweltschutzes . . .," 1977.

[148] BArch DK 5/1982, "Bericht über Probleme des Geheimnisschutzes bei Informationen zum Umweltschutz," October 25, 1982.

[149] Thomas W. Goldstein, *Writing in Red: The East German Writers Union and the Role of Literary Intellectuals* (Rochester, NY: Camden House, 2017), 153–154.

[150] Monika Maron, *Flight of Ashes*, trans. David Newton Marinelli (New York: Readers International, 1986), 8.

publishing *Flight of Ashes* in the GDR, Maron signed with a West German publisher, familiarizing West German audiences with the devastation, and undermining the East German leadership's fear of international exposure.

The perceived danger from within East German society also drove the decision to restrict access to all environmental data. The SED believed that information about conditions would lead to – and already had led to – potential unrest. Though officials blamed western "provocateurs," such as the West Berlin-based Radio in the American Sector (RIAS), the SED feared its citizens were being turned against the party and fomenting a "movement." The report, though, was self-critical, too, admitting that its class enemies were justified in their concerns about pollution, because objectively they could not be resolved. The authors did not anticipate a solution to the GDR's degradation in the foreseeable future.[151] The Council of Ministers' decision became the lone viable means of restricting environmental knowledge. While it limited experts' ability to interact with the broader public, the decision also had the potential to fuel frustration over undisclosed pollution. The secrecy surrounding the data transformed the environment from a localized issue into a system destabilizing problem. The ban on data wove together pollution problems and information politics, which worked together to discredit the SED.

Conclusion

The 1970s began as a decade of promise for environmentalism in the GDR through the expansion of legal and mass social policies as well as international cooperation. Underpinned through theoretical and ideological writings, the Cultural League developed numerous programs, and eventually the GNU, to generate mass interest in a socialist environmentalism. The SED and its Cultural League did so by drawing on older traditions of nature and Heimat as well as the need to manage natural resources efficiently and on broader conceptions of the environment. An often-touted faith in progress and scientific innovation to build a better future played a role in the Cultural League's call to action. In Poland, too, new – if atomized – legislation and the reconceptualization of the LOP reflected similar advancements across eastern Europe as well as deepening interactions between Soviet bloc countries. Measures such as cleaning up parks,

---

[151] BArch DK 5/1982, "Bericht über Probleme des Geheimnisschutzes bei Informationen zum Umweltschutz," October 25, 1982.

planting trees, and sharing technology were welcome beacons for change in the early 1970s.

Ironically, just as the SED bolstered its environmental activities at the associational level, it began to fully grasp the challenges of implementation. Economically, introducing regulations would be expensive and time consuming, something which planners and the SED leadership sought to avoid at all costs. Rather than investing in long-term solutions for improving conditions, industries applied for exemptions on the grounds that any reduction in production or profits would hurt the national economy. As a scientist from Potsdam matter-of-factly reported, despite critical evaluations, key industries "functioned under exemptions."[152] Where industries sought to coordinate with regulators, both ended up applying haphazard measures with little real effect. At times officials and workers only installed filters in some (but not all) smokestacks of a factory or did not replace them when they broke. Factories dumped poisonous waste products without permits or following the law.[153] In this context, the GDR faced a world economy that was shifting from heavy to high-tech industry, received less support from the Soviet Union, and grew more indebted to capitalist countries.

The self-inflicted paradox of strict environmental regulation and reliance on dirty industries created a legitimacy gap. Although protection purported to serve the workers, and therefore the state, knowledge about the environment – and the effects of pollution – that the state and party had helped produce now became a liability. SED and Cultural League officials became ever more concerned that "environmental pessimists, enemies of technology and nihilistic opinions about the future" threatened the well-being of socialist environmentalism, and finally the GDR as a whole.[154] Rather than invest heavily in improvements, Honecker, Mittag, and the rest of the leadership denied the problem. On November 16, 1982, the Council of Ministers, in cooperation with the MUW, classified all data as a matter of state security in order to defend the GDR against the west. The SED tacitly admitted it could not or would not solve the GDR's pollution when it restricted access to the data and instead took the less expensive route of denial. It was a defeat for the ideal of a socialist environmentalism.

[152] BStU MfS/BV Pdm Abt. XVIII 1324, "Informationsvorlage Umweltschutz im Bezirk Potsdam," undated.
[153] BStU MfS/HA XX 13945, "Einige Probleme bei der Einleitung des Natur- und Umweltschutzes durch die Landwirtschaft im Bezirk Rostock," July 30, 1987.
[154] BArch-SAPMO DY 27/6112, "Stenograpfisches Protokoll: Gründungsversammlung der Gesellschaft für Natur und Umwelt," March 28, 1980.

CHAPTER 3

Church, Faith, and Nature: An Alternative Environmentalism, 1972–1983

The SED's decision to hide environmental data in 1982 underscored communism's economic and environmental weaknesses in the GDR. Non-party or state actors challenged the existing (im)balance between economy and ecology and demanded change. Most especially the Protestant Church, as the largest and most influential counterweight to the SED, led the charge.[1] Though the conflict between Church and party dated to the Soviet occupation after the World War II, the tension shifted in tone and character in the 1970s. With deepening ties to international ecumenical organizations and growing concerns about the environment, the Protestant Church increasingly participated in transnational debates about consumption and pollution, which led its membership to critique the SED's materialist worldview. The Church's institutional support in turn furnished new opportunities to build environmental networks that built on SED policies but also advocated for alternative modes of thinking about human interaction with the natural world.

Despite the Protestant Church's contentious position in communism, it provided a space for East Germans to learn about the environment in the early 1970s. Given its relative autonomy in the dictatorship, the Church developed ways of endorsing environmentalism long before the better known oppositional activities of the late 1980s.[2] Leaders in the Church

[1] Non-party and state actors were fewer in number and had less independence in various dictatorships when compared to democracies, but they still represented an important set of actors distinct from ruling communist parties. For more on debates surrounding the public sphere under communism, see David Bathrick's *The Powers of Speech: The Politics of Culture in the GDR* (Lincoln, NE: University of Nebraska Press, 1995) and Jürgen Kocka's *Civil Society and Dictatorship in Modern Germany* (Hanover, NH: University Press of New England, 2010).
[2] Detlef Pollack, *Politischer Protest: Politisch alternative Gruppen in der DDR* (Opladen: Leske + Budrich, 2000), 8. Pollack distinguishes between the larger citizens' movements of 1989 and "political-alternative" groups in the Church, arguing the latter were generally disconnected from society. Micheal Beleites, *Untergrund: Ein Konflikt mit der Stasi in der Uranprovinz* (Berlin: BasisDruck, 1991); Gareth Dale, *Popular Protest in East Germany, 1945–1989* (New York: Routledge, 2005); Carlo Jordan and Hans Michael Kloth, eds., *Arche Nova: Opposition in der*

responded to global concerns about the environment and consumption, working with the World Council of Churches (WCC) and its Church and Society Committee.[3] It also shifted the focus of the Ecclesiastical Research Center in Wittenberg to study the relationship between nature and Christianity. The Protestant Church further backed environmental protection by housing parish-based groups at the grassroots level. Environmental as well as peace, feminist, gay rights, human rights, and third world solidarity groups addressed interconnected concerns and evolved in conjunction with one another under the Church's roof. Environmentalism resonated among theologians, Christians, and activists, transcending traditional cleavages in East German society and participating in networks that spanned the Iron Curtain.

The environment attracted East Germans from a range of backgrounds with a variety of attitudes toward the state, many of whom joined both official and Church-based organizations. This "dual participation" became more feasible after the SED and the Church came to an understanding about the Church's place in socialism in 1978 that eased tensions.[4] Rather than the state actively discriminating against the Church, East Germans now experienced more leeway to participate in both Church and party-run organizations. The Church hosted activists with different perspectives on the environment and the SED, but those individuals also took part in party and state organizations. This dual participation suggests continuity and dialogue between official and Church-based environmentalism, entangling different outlooks on nature.[5] The overlap between these sets of individuals and ideas complicates and broadens interpretations of environmental engagement under communism by breaking down dichotomies between official and Church participation and expertise.

While environmental impulses were firmly grounded in the GDR, transformations abroad provided additional educational and political possibilities for East Germans. Independent actors in western democracies as

---

DDR, *"Das Grün-ökologische Netzwerk Arche,"* 1988–1990 (Berlin: BasisDruck, 1995); Hubertus Knabe, "Neue Soziale Bewegungen im Sozialismus. Zur Genesis alternativer politischer Orientierungen in der DDR," *Kölner Zeitschrift für Soziologie und Sozialpsychologie* 40, no. 3 (September 1988), 551–569; Wolfgang Rüddenklau, ed., *Störenfried: DDR-Opposition 1986–1989, mit Texten aus den "Umweltblättern"* (Berlin: BasisDruck, 1992).

[3] Evangelisches Zentralarchiv (EZA) 101/629, "Stellungnahme zum Bericht der Evangelischen Akademie Sachsen-Anhalt für die Kirchenleitung der Kirchenprovinz Sachsen ausgearbeitet von H. Schultz," January 23, 1973.

[4] Ehrhart Neubert, *Geschichte der Opposition in der DDR, 1949–1989* (Berlin: Ch. Links Verlag, 1997), 248–249.

[5] See, for example, works by former activists, who downplay the idea of dual participation. Jordan and Kloth, eds., *Arche Nova*; Rüddenklau, ed., *Störenfried*; Beleites, *Untergrund*.

well as Soviet-style dictatorships pushed against and changed the established order. Organizations such as the WCC gave the Church an international and ecumenical path to environmental engagement. In the FRG, citizens' initiatives and the green movement's transformation into a political party inspired further activism in the GDR. East Germans sought more opportunities for environmental action and collaboration with West Germans The Green Party's admission to the Bundestag in 1983 signaled a new era for partnership across the German–German border, while the Stasi worried about these West German influences.[6]

To the east, Solidarność's challenge to the PZPR in Poland exposed communism's fragility, undermining monopolies on information and discrediting dictatorship across the bloc. As a non-party or state actor, Solidarność's victory in 1980 guaranteed, at least briefly, the right for associations to organize outside of official channels. This flurry of activity included the first independent environmental organization behind the Iron Curtain.[7] Founded in September, the Polish Ecological Club primarily consisted of scientists and experts who advocated for reducing pollution and was not explicitly oppositional. Solidarność and the PKE domestically and internationally raised awareness about the devastation that smokestack industrialization wrought. East Germans used this example to advocate for more independent organization, looking eastward as well as westward for inspiration.[8] Unsurprisingly, the SED and other eastern European leaders became suspicious of Poland, viewing it as a point of weakness in the Soviet bloc.

This chapter argues that non-party or state actors formed alternative narratives to those presented by officials and, in doing so, disputed their claims. In the GDR, Church-based environmentalism evolved on the fringes of society and in a transnational context. Environmental engagement, its impetuses and forms, led to a critique with theological underpinnings as well as practical frustration about degradation. Church-based

---

[6] Bundesarchiv-Stiftungarchiv der Parteien und Massenorganisation der DDR (BArch-SAPMO) DY 27/6112, "Information über die Mitarbeit von Christen in der GNU in der Stadtorganisation Leipzig des Kulturbundes der DDR," September 26, 1983.

[7] RHG TH 12/03, "Polski Klub Ekologiczny (PKE) – wer wir sind …," undated.

[8] Ned Richardson-Little has similarly noted that East German human rights activists turned to Poland and Czechoslovakia for inspiration. Ned Richardson-Little, *The Human Rights Dictatorship: Socialism, Global Solidarity, and Revolution in East Germany* (New York: Cambridge University Press, 2020), 204. In general, references to Solidarność's influence on the GDR are relatively common only as a means of understanding 1989. They do not tend to explore inter-bloc dynamics. Timothy Garton Ash, *The Magic Lantern: The Revolution of '89 witnessed in Warsaw, Budapest, Berlin, and Prague* (New York: Vintage Books, 1993). Padraic Kenney, *A Carnival of Revolution: Central Europe, 1989* (Princeton, NJ: Princeton University Press, 2002).

activists fostered contacts with independent actors to the east and west, establishing networks across central Europe. In the FRG, the environmental movement became formalized in the Green Party, which underscored the SED's inability to adapt. In the Soviet bloc, Poland modeled a less repressive attitude toward society that opened opportunities for independent actors. These impulses encouraged East Germans to pursue means of improving the environment through the Church and at the fringes of state authority. The SED increasingly distrusted developments in neighboring countries and their impact at home, obsessing over state security. The GDR's position as hinge between east and west became a liability for domestic stability.

The Protestant Church and the East German State

The SED's relationship with religion – namely the Protestant and Catholic Churches – was contentious from the founding of the GDR. The party elite believed that churches were obsolete, and the SED sought to ensure their demise by limiting religion's influence.[9] Yet, given both the Protestant and Catholic Churches's cultural significance as well as their international stature, neither simply faded away. They remained the targets of SED policies for decades as it endeavored to control the official or socialist public sphere.[10] While relations between the SED and both the Protestant and Catholic Churches evolved over time, the Protestant Church turned into a refuge for those who did not fit into the mainstream or rejected SED rule.[11] As a non-party or state actor, it offered structural support and a non-socialist worldview that drew both state ire and Stasi attention for decades.

In the GDR, the vast majority of the population was Protestant, which afforded that Church a broader base and potentially more influence in East German society. Eighty to eighty-five percent identified as Protestant, and only about eleven percent as Catholic.[12] Catholic pockets existed, such as around Eichsfeld in Thuringia, but on the whole, the Catholic Church was

[9] Bernd Schaefer, The East German State and the Catholic Church, 1945–1989 (New York: Berghahn Books, 2010), 10.

[10] Esther Peperkamp and Małgorzata Rajtar, "Introduction," in Religion and the Secular in Eastern Germany, 1945 to the present, eds. Esther Peperkamp and Małgorzata Rajtar (Boston, MA: Brill, 2010), 7. Schaefer, The East German State and the Catholic Church, 1–2. Bathrick, The Powers of Speech; Kocka, Civil Society and Dictatorship in Modern Germany.

[11] Mary Fulbrook, Anatomy of a Dictatorship: Inside the GDR, 1949–1989 (New York: Oxford University Press, 1995), 201.

[12] Peperkamp and Rajtar, "Introduction," 5. Fulbrook, Anatomy of a Dictatorship, 88–89.

small and more inward-looking, viewing itself as a double minority in the GDR.[13] While both the Protestant and Catholic Churches cooperated with the State Secretariat for Church Questions after its creation in the 1950s, the Protestant Church tended to play a larger role in opposing the SED. It intentionally adopted social and political stances, especially in later years, that led to confrontations with the SED and made it the target of state surveillance.[14] While coopted through negotiation and infiltration in some ways, the Protestant Church remained a relatively autonomous actor that thwarted the SED's totalizing aims.

Since the founding of the GDR, the SED and the Protestant Church had been locked in conflict with one another. In the confusion of the immediate postwar years, the Protestant Church saw attendance swell in response to the suffering and uncertainty after defeat. It afforded parishioners a moral center and a familiar setting.[15] First Soviet occupiers and then communist East German leaders sought a pragmatic partnership with the Church, exempting it from various taxes and nationalization projects to avoid direct hostility. As the SED consolidated power in the early 1950s, though, the Church proved difficult to control. Given the long history of the Church and its established place in society, the SED struggled more to bring churches under political or social control than it had political parties and associational life.[16] Moreover, Christianity and Marxism–Leninism proffered all-encompassing and opposing worldviews. Given that these two approaches could not be reconciled, tensions between the Church and the SED rose.

East Germans had to choose between the prevailing sociopolitical system and the Church, or else face persecution from the state. The SED cracked down on churches and systematically discriminated against practicing Christians, reducing the odds of admission to university or making desirable jobs inaccessible.[17] The introduction of *Jugendweihe*, a secular ceremony to induct teenagers into socialism and to replace confirmation in the Church, became a serious point of contention in the 1950s. The Church opposed inducting youth into a worldview that meant to end the influence of religion, denying adolescents confirmation if they also went through Jugendweihe.[18] Eventually, the Church backed down on its stance on confirmation, because the number of confirmands declined as

---

[13] Peperkamp and Rajtar, "Introduction," 9.
[14] Schaefer, *The East German State and the Catholic Church*, 237.
[15] Fulbrook, *Anatomy of a Dictatorship*, 91–92. [16] Ibid., 91. [17] Ibid., 97.
[18] RHG RG/MV 01, "40 Jahre Kirche in der DDR—Konfrontation oder Kooperation," 3–4, Gruppe "Gewaltfrei Leben," undated.

East Germans opted for Jugendweihe. Many East Germans chose the SED's system rather than face discrimination. Attendance dropped and society became more secular, leaving the Church with less and less leverage. Between 1950 and 1964, those who identified as Protestant dropped from 80.5 percent of the population to 59.3 percent, while those who described themselves as unaffiliated increased from 7.6 percent to nearly one third.[19] Additionally, in 1960, Ulbricht halted official opposition to the Church, proclaiming that Christianity and the humanistic goals of socialism were not opposed to each other.[20] This accommodation weakened the Church's "either or" stance and eroded the Church's position in East German society.

The Church also faced internal divisions, especially a generational split regarding the role of the Church in a socialist state, that complicated the pursuit of a clear policy. The Church's ties to nationalism reached back to the nineteenth century and hindered its claims to moral authority.[21] Older Church leaders, in particular, had had dubious associations during the Third Reich and lacked integrity according to younger adherents. Some clergy thus wished to retreat from the earthly realm entirely and focus on the spiritual, which echoed the Catholic Church's tactic.[22] Nevertheless, a younger generation – one removed from the complicity of the Nazi period – chose to become more politicized. Leadership in the 1960s and 1970s believed the Church had a responsibility to engage with the socialist state and with political topics. This generation included many Christians who had been denied access to desirable jobs or university training based on their faith, and they challenged the SED in ways the older generation avoided. This cohort questioned the goals of socialism as well as the Church's stance on science and the environment.[23]

The SED persisted in monitoring Church activities even as the Church's influence waned over time. Since 1956, the Ministry for Church Affairs (renamed the State Secretariat for Church Questions in 1960) coordinated relations between the state and Church leaders.[24] On the one hand, it

---

[19] Fulbrook, *Anatomy of a Dictatorship*, 103.

[20] BP, O-4, Information No. 2/68, "Analyse der Vorbereitung und Durchführung des 450. Jahrestages der Reformation 1967," cited in Fulbrook, *Anatomy of a Dictatorship*, 104.

[21] Claudia Lepp, *Tabu der Einheit? Die Ost-West-Gemeinschaft der evangelischen Christen und die deutsche Teilung (1945–1969)* (Göttingen: Vandenhoeck & Ruprecht, 2005), 25–35.

[22] Benjamin Pearson, "Faith and Democracy: Political Transformations at the German Protestant *Kirchentag*, 1949–1969" (PhD Dissertation, University of North Carolina at Chapel Hill, 2007), 40.

[23] EZA 101/629, "Stellungnahme zum Bericht der Evangelischen Akademie Sachsen-Anhalt für die Kirchenleitung der Kirchenprovinz Sachsen ausgearbeitet von H. Schultz," January 23, 1973.

[24] Fulbrook, *Anatomy of a Dictatorship*, 98–99.

served as a means for the Church to express its concerns to officials; on the other hand, it kept the state informed on the mood in the Church. The Stasi additionally planted informants and unofficial collaborators, and placed compliant individuals in positions of authority to supplement its knowledge of Church affairs.[25] Although the level of scrutiny depended on the political climate, both the Church's cooperation with the SED and the Stasi's infamous infiltration strained the Church–state relationship until the GDR's collapse.

The Church's affiliation with its counterpart in the FRG also motivated the SED to closely observe it in a world of Cold War suspicion.[26] Politically speaking, associations with capitalist countries undermined the SED's project and potentially poisoned East Germans' opinion of their state. In practical terms, contacts in the west provided information and goods that were more difficult to attain in the east. The SED's attempts to limit communication and to divide the Church's shared structures fit into the larger East German narrative of being unable to compete and cutting itself off. Most obvious in the gradual closing of the German–German border, and the construction of the Berlin Wall in 1961, the SED chose to withdraw.[27] The SED actively sought to divide the Protestant Church in East and West Germany, and it eventually succeeded in 1969. The two sides officially separated, forming the *Bund der Evangelischen Kirchen in der DDR* (Alliance of Protestant Churches in the GDR, BEK).[28] Despite the split, western churches maintained financial aid for their East German counterparts, which helped to preserve bonds between adherents in east and west and undercut the SED.[29]

After the 1969 split, the Church turned to finding a place in East German society, resulting in a 1978 agreement between the BEK and the state. How closely the Church would collaborate with party or state officials remained debatable, but some level of cooperation emerged as the only option. Over the course of the 1970s, the BEK and state officials held a series of meetings, ultimately coming to an important understanding. On March 6, 1978, the Church declared itself to be "the Church in Socialism," citing common,

[25] Ibid., 88–89.

[26] For a detailed account of the relationship between the Protestant Churches in East and West Germany, see Lepp, *Tabu der Einheit?*

[27] Jens Gieseke, *The History of the Stasi : East Germany's Secret Police, 1945–1990* (New York: Berghahn Books, 2014), 53–54.

[28] From this point on, when referring to the "Church," I will be referring to the BEK, unless otherwise specified.

[29] Robert F. Goeckel, "The GDR Legacy and the German Protestant Church," *German Politics & Society*, 31 (Spring 1994), 97.

humanistic goals with the state.[30] Although it was independent of the party and state – the only large institution in the GDR to have that status – the Church had also admitted defeat. Christians abandoned hopes of fighting back communism and reuniting with the western Churches in an all-German union. The path forward required cooperation, or at least uneasy tolerance.

Ironically, in relinquishing its openly oppositional stance, the Church found a new measure of independence to act within the SED system. Because it accepted the SED's right to rule over the GDR, the Protestant Church could now question without posing a fundamental threat. As Bishop Werner Krusche stated, "the Church is trying to walk the narrow line between opposition and opportunism, the path of critical solidarity with shared responsibility."[31] East German officials reluctantly dialed down their distrust and, for a time, eased their targeting of Church activities and members. This leniency allowed for the creation of a space in which Christians and interested individuals could take up such causes as human rights, peace, and the environment. The Church delved into how to address problems with the premise that "we in a socialist society have different conditions than they do in capitalist countries."[32] Church leadership and members recognized that their situation varied from Christians in the west, but their lines of enquiry bridged the Iron Curtain.

West German *Ostpolitik* and Détente in the 1970s improved relations between the eastern and western blocs in Europe. The Basic Treaty between the two Germanys in 1972 further improved the GDR's international standing, and ultimately brought about recognition at the United Nations.[33] This trend toward recognition and cooperation between the GDR and FRG reached a highpoint at the Helsinki Accords in 1975. Signees at Helsinki agreed on matters relating to security, economic and scientific cooperation, and human rights.[34] On a smaller scale, agreements on travel between the two countries increased the movement of people and information.[35] These measures stabilized the GDR's existence, which in turn opened its borders – at least in a limited way – to neighbors on both sides of the Iron Curtain and reaffirmed the Church's existence in communist states.

---

[30] Fulbrook, *Anatomy of a Dictatorship*, 109.
[31] Cited in Neubert, *Geschichte der Opposition in der DDR*, 249.
[32] EZA 101/623, "Arbeitshilfe für Vorbereitungsgruppen zu dem Seminarthema: Was bedeutet Jesus auf unserer Suche nach einer Menschlichen Welt?" undated.
[33] Carole Fink, *Cold War: An International History* (Boulder, CO: Westview Press, 2004).
[34] Timothy Garton Ash, *In Europe's Name: Germany and the Divided Continent* (New York: Random House Publishing, 1993), 39, 42.
[35] Edith Sheffer, *Burned Bridge: How East and West Germans Made the Iron Curtain* (New York: Oxford University Press, 2011), 168–169.

German–German diplomacy became strained again toward the end of the decade with the beginning of the Second Cold War. In 1976, the Soviet Union began stationing SS-20 (intermediate range ballistic) missiles in eastern Europe.[36] This military buildup, along with the invasion of Afghanistan three years later, cooled relations between the US and Soviet camps. The GDR followed the Soviet Union's lead, introducing additional military service requirements and military education in schools. The SED also clamped down on protest, such as the famous singer and songwriter Wolf Biermann's performances, leading to calls of human rights violations.[37] The Church, with its relative freedom, expressed concern about the changing political and military situation, and used human rights language in the Helsinki Accords to justify its position.[38] In response to the Cold War flareup, the Church became more involved in the peace movement and protested mandatory military service.[39]

The Church's adoption of politically charged issues appealed to a broad cross-section of East German society, and especially to a younger generation, which revived religious activity. Leaders remained divided on many of the topics that resonated with its newest members, with many who had experienced the repression of the 1950s and 1960s hesitant to disturb the recent truce with the SED. Though high ranking Church officials disagreed with one another, often along generational lines, grassroots sympathy for peace and human rights grew.[40] East Germans returned to the Church and joined parish-level groups and services in numbers unparalleled since the 1950s.[41] The Church became a "safety valve" for East German society, offering a space to vent frustrations and discontent in a controlled setting.[42] These movements allowed for a release that was also constructive; they became the nexus of alternative social networks. In

---

[36] Oliver Bange, "SS-20 and Pershing II: Weapons Systems and the Dynamization of East–West Relations," in *The Nuclear Crisis: The Arms Race, Cold War Anxiety, and the German Peace Movement of the 1980s*, eds. Christoph Becker-Schaum, Philipp Gassert, Martin Klimke, Wilfried Mausbach, and Marianne Zepp (New York: Berghahn Books, 2016), 72–73.

[37] Mary Fulbrook, *The People's State: East German Society from Hitler to Honecker* (New Haven, CT: Yale University Press, 2005), 209.

[38] Ned Richardson-Little, "Dictatorship and Dissent: Human Rights in East Germany in the 1970s," in *The Breakthrough: Human Rights in the 1970s*, eds. Jan Eckel and Samuel Moyn (Philadelphia, PA: University of Pennsylvania Press, 2013), 60.

[39] In contrast to the environmental groups, the Stasi immediately understood the peace movement to be a threat to state security. Fulbrook, *Anatomy of a Dictatorship*, 207–209.

[40] Steven Pfaff, "The Politics of Peace in the GDR: The Independent Peace Movement, the Church, and the Origins of the East German Opposition," *Peace & Change* 26, no. 3 (July 2001), 284.

[41] RGH RG/B 19, "Gruppen in der Kirche—Orientierung für Konfliktfelder," undated.

[42] Michel de Certeau, *The Practice of Everyday Life*, trans. Steven Rendall (Berkeley, CA: University of California Press, 1984), xix.

different forms, they all critiqued not only SED policies but ultimately the system as a whole.

Peace and human rights activists, along with like-minded clergy such as Bishop Gottfried Forck, censured the state for failing to fulfill promises made at the Helsinki Accords. They used Christian language to underscore the importance of human rights and the state's violation of them by refusing to let East Germans leave the country or punishing them for applying to move to the west.[43] Church leaders contended in 1978, "In our time, human rights have become important. We must deeply lament that human worth and rights have become such a point of contention between east and west." They further argued that because God created man, a "man's freedom can only be achieved through accepting the Creator, to whom this power belongs."[44] In the years after the Helsinki Declaration, with its commitment to human rights, these accusations proved difficult for the SED to ignore.

The peace movement led East and West German activists to protest NATO's response to the Soviet Union's SS-20s by placing nuclear missiles in the FRG. Contending that "peace can only be maintained, agreed upon, and strengthened when people continually talk with one another anew," East and West Germans reached out to one another outside of official channels.[45] It was not necessarily a unified oppositional movement, but numerous independent and loosely associated initiatives arose. The so-called "Peace Seminars," the group "Swords to Plowshares," and innumerable other peace circles tied to individual parishes all contributed to the growth of the peace movement in the GDR.[46] In the early 1980s, such groups in the Protestant Church flourished on the edge of East German society, casting doubt on the SED's agenda and challenging the Soviet "camp of peace" narrative.[47]

State officials reacted to this movement by closely tracking Church-based groups through both the State Secretariat for Church Questions and the Stasi. Church leaders like Manfred Stolpe regularly met with state officials to alleviate the strain, leaving Stolpe and others open to accusations of informing on activists.[48] Still, Church leaders kept a handle on

---

[43] RHG Ki 02/01, "Wo stehen wir? Kirchenleitung Bericht 1984 – Teil II."

[44] RHG Ki 05, "Information des Evangelischen Konsistoriums Görlitz an die Gemeindekirchenräte und kirchlichen Werke der Görlitzer Kirchen zur Verhaftung und Verurteilung von Uwe Reimann (telef. Mitschnitt) vom 19.12.1978."

[45] Ibid.　　[46] Pfaff, "The Politics of Peace in the GDR," 90.

[47] RHGo Ki 21/01, "Ökumenische Versammlung: Informationsdienst, März 1988."

[48] BArch-SAPMO DO 4/801, "Persönlicher Referent," June 6, 1979. Goeckel, "The GDR Legacy and the German Protestant Church," 101.

developments, at times cracking down on the groups' activities and independence. When these tactics did not garner enough information, the Stasi
coopted participants, paying them for information, and planting agents.
The work of these agents and unofficial informants successfully divided
circles, sowing distrust and hindering their ability to expand or to have an
influence on the wider society. The peace movement's momentum further
declined in 1983 when they lost the battle to stop NATO from stationing
the missiles in the FRG. In contrast, the Church-based environmental
movement's focus on small-scale efforts often attracted less attention from
party or state apparatuses than peace or human rights activism. Well into
the 1980s, the Stasi explicitly differentiated between the "class neutral
environmental movement" and the "antagonistic-negative forces" of the
peace movement.[49] The perceived apolitical character of environmental
groups provided them cover and an opportunity to expand as the peace
movement received greater attention from state authorities.

The Church's conflicts with the SED were not unique to the GDR;
across the Soviet bloc religious institutions clashed with communist parties, disputing their monopoly on power. Most notably in Poland, where
Catholicism was intimately tied to national identity and independence, the
socially conservative Catholic Church became a space of opposition. In
contrast to the GDR, Poland was one of the most religiously homogenous
countries in Europe after World War II, and from the beginning, the
Catholic Church's anticommunist stance resisted the PZPR's government
as a foreign and atheist occupation.[50] The Catholic Church became the
primary voice of opposition in Poland as well as internationally, spreading
word of the PZPR's attacks on religion. In light of these tensions, the
Catholic Church retreated to the "religious sphere" for a time before 1970,
not unlike the Catholic Church in the GDR. Later, it became more
political once the Polish cardinal Karol Wojtyła was elected to the papacy
as John Paul II in 1978.[51] In light of the Helsinki Accords and shifting
attitudes toward religion in communist states, churches across the Soviet
bloc intensified their political engagement, voicing alternative worldviews
to the ruling parties in the 1970s.

---

[49] Bundesbeauftragten für die Stasi-Unterlagen (BStU) MfS JHS 20205 "Diplomarbeit: Die
Organisierung der politisch-operativen Arbeit zur Verhinderung des Mißbrauchs von
Umweltschutzproblemen für politische Untergrundtätigkeit," October 31, 1984, 8.

[50] Michael Fleming, "The Ethno-Religious Ambitions of the Roman Catholic Church and the
Ascendency of Communism in Postwar Poland (1945–1950)," *Nations and Nationalism* 16, no. 4
(October 2003), 638.

[51] Robert Zuzowski, *Political Dissent and Opposition in Poland: The Workers' Defense Committee "KOR"*
(Westport, CT: Praeger, 1992), 120–122.

Independent actors counterbalanced the ruling parties' authority in the Soviet bloc in the 1970s and 1980s. Churches, with their ingrained antagonism towards communism and international connections, subverted the status quo. In the GDR, too, the Protestant Church's position changed once it acknowledged the permanence of the East German state and agreed to work within the SED's parameters. Yet in conceding that it was the "Church in Socialism" in 1978, the Church received the freedom to take on contemporary concerns, such as peace and human rights. Within the Church, leaders debated how much to welcome these nascent groups – with some wholeheartedly embracing them and others remaining highly suspicious – but they did not shut them down. The SED disliked these trends, kept the groups and their contacts to the west under constant surveillance, and infiltrated them.

Environment, Faith, and the Protestant Church

Church-based environmentalism, organized beyond party and state authority, in the GDR traces back to the global moment of reckoning at the end of the 1960s and beginning of the 1970s.[52] Since the early 1970s, elements in the Church had joined discussions about consumption and materialism, often from an intellectual and theological perspective. Leadership encouraged this engagement through the Ecclesiastical Research Center (*Kirchliches Forschungsheim*, KFH), the Church and Society Committee, as well as in other ways. Moreover, these organizations fostered international associations, such as with the WCC, placing them in a global, ecumenical network. Despite state interference, the Church cultivated environmentalism, connecting East Germans with ideas and activists across borders. The Church built on and reacted to concepts that the SED and the state had established, as well as global trends, which broadened East Germans' understanding of the environment and called into question communist states' actions.

The Church began to systematically delve into such topics in the early 1970s when the Diocese of Saxony based in Magdeburg charged the KFH with studying the environment. Located in Wittenberg, the KFH's purpose since the 1920s was to grapple with the relationship between theology

---

[52] Tobias Huff, *Natur und Industrie im Sozialismus: Eine Umweltgeschichte der DDR* (Göttingen: Vandenhoeck & Ruprecht, 2015), 11. From a broader Eastern European perspective, Kenney's *A Carnival of Revolution*. Pollack, *Politischer Protest*, 7.

and science.[53] In 1973, the diocese directed the staff theologian and scientist, Hans Kleinschmidt and Charlotte Boost, respectively, to examine the place of the environment in Christianity, drawing on anxieties about consumption, growth, and the perils of modern life. This emphasis was reinforced when Dr. Hans-Peter Gensichen, a young minister from Pritzwalk, Brandenburg, became the director of the KFH in 1975. In the years thereafter, he and Boost formed working groups on the environment and religion, namely "Earth" in 1977 and "Agriculture and Environment" in 1980. That same year Boost retired, and Gerd Pfeiffer, a biologist and ecologist, replaced her, further demonstrating the KFH's deepening commitment to the environment.[54]

From its inception, Earth was a space for scientists, engineers, and theologians to share expertise and disseminate information to larger Church audiences through publications. For Gensichen and Boost, having a scientific knowledge base was crucial, so they focused on cultivating young professionals in those fields. Participation in Earth depended on both background and presence within the Church but elicited members from across the GDR. Invitations in 1977 intentionally drew on existing networks to invite known and recommended individuals. Gensichen clarified that the working group sought "university graduates your age or younger" and welcomed "various denominations and ideological backgrounds."[55] In part because it was selective, the semiannual retreats welcomed families, including childcare and group activities.[56] This form of recruitment worked; several of the members were involved for many years. Although Earth represented a small circle, its writings and ideas became staples of environmental discourse in the Church in the 1980s.

---

[53] BArch DO 4/800, Hans-Peter Gensichen, "Eine neue Phase des Umweltengagements in den Kirchen," *Die Zeichen der Zeit* 7/88, Heinz Blauer, ed., Berlin (Ost), Evangelische Verlagsanstalt. The KFH dates back to 1927 when it was established to explore the relationship between religion and the natural sciences. The focus of its first director, Otto Kleinschmidt, was on the theory of evolution and zoological biology. In the 1960s and 1970s, the center also began to consider the ethics of genetics. Given its focus, the KFH generally had one scientist (usually a biologist) and one theologian on staff.

[54] Hans-Peter Gensichen, "Die Beiträge des Wittenberger Forschungsheimes für die kritische Umweltbewegung in der DDR," in *Umweltschutz in der DDR: Analysen und Zeitzeugenberichte, Band 3: Beruflicher, ehrenamtlicher und freiwilliger Umweltschutz*, ed. Hermann Behrens and Jens Hoffmann (Munich: Oekom, 2007), 151–152.

[55] RHG KFH 01, Form Letter, Arbeitskreis "Erde," April 1977.

[56] Providing childcare for young parents was essential to garnering participation in weekend long events. For more on reproduction policies in the GDR, see Donna Harsch, *Revenge of the Domestic: Women, the Family, and Communism in the German Democratic Republic* (Princeton, NJ: Princeton University Press, 2007).

Exploring the connections between Christianity and environmentalism drove Earth's work in the early years. Participants discussed awareness, technology, and quality of life as they debated how to address the problems that industrialization and modern life caused. They concluded that contemporary discourse surrounding "man versus nature" suggested an ephemeral and contained crisis, but, in fact, this tension had existed "as long as man." The members further worried that humans altered and cultivated nature, and became increasingly removed from it, which led to a loss of respect for nature and overexploitation.[57] This perspective fit into the German "life reform" tradition, which the SED also utilized to gain interest in nature, and which dated back to the early twentieth century.[58]

In the face of a system that exploited nature, Earth's participants unsurprisingly argued that returning to faith and rejecting communism constituted the only viable solution. The members believed that a "loss of harmony and alienation were the price of civilization and economic progress, because man had not only forgotten the hidden wisdom of the great religions but actually repudiated them."[59] For them, religion remedied the environmental destruction that communism caused. Thus, they connected nature and religion in a way that challenged the SED's materialist worldview, exposed its failings, and offered a different model for understanding how the world should function. Earth was well aware of the criticisms of Christianity's impact on nature, such as those put forward by the well-known medieval historian Lynn T. White. White was one of numerous scholars who scrutinized the relationship between Christianity and nature in the 1960s and 1970s. In his 1967 article in *Science*, "The Historical Roots of our Ecological Crisis," White argued that Europeans had a particular and exploitative relationship with nature that was in part defined by their interpretation of Christianity.[60] Earth countered this interpretation with a Christian answer to the GDR's woes, a response that also competed with the SED's approach to environmentalism.

Earth consolidated its findings in a 1980 pamphlet, "The Earth is to be saved," which became immensely popular in Church circles over the next decade. Parish-based groups and others cited and reprinted this eighty-page

---

[57] RHG KFH 01, Diskussionspapier aus Arbeitsgruppe 2, October 21–23, 1977.

[58] John Alexander Williams, *Turning to Nature in Germany: Hiking, Nudism and Conservation, 1900–1940* (Stanford, CA: Stanford University Press, 2007), 11–13.

[59] RHG KFH 01, Diskussionspapier aus Arbeitsgruppe 2, October 21–23, 1977.

[60] Lynn White, Jr., "The Historical Roots of our Ecological Crisis," *Science* 155 (March 1967), 1203–1207.

booklet, cementing the relationship between religion and nature. Gensichen explained the intentionally ambiguous title, stating it was both optimistic (that the world could still be saved) and a moral imperative to do so.[61] He further quoted the Polish pope, John Paul II, who had been elected to the papacy in 1978 and was a vocal opponent of communism in eastern Europe. He declared the earth was not a limitless reservoir to exploit, but a part of the mystery of creation.[62] The booklet focused on specific global and domestic problems and strategies, namely the Club of Rome report, Marxism-Leninism's attitude toward the environment, technological solutions for environmental protection, and opportunities for cooperation with the Cultural League's GNU. The authors did not catalog forms of pollution but affirmed a commitment to cooperating with the party and state. They believed that their faith commanded them to not only think environmentally but also take action. This approach linked spiritual and cultural activities, social engagement, and an attitude of solidarity that intentionally distinguished Christian thinking from the SED's materialist conception of socialism.[63]

"The Earth is to be saved" resonated with a burgeoning number of individual Christians and small groups, spreading knowledge about the environment through Church networks.[64] Earth's members shared their expertise with others, listing large- and small-scale suggestions for improving environmental conditions. These tips ranged from turning off the light when leaving a room to reducing the use of pesticides in intensive agriculture. The authors argued for everyday actions, because "how can one reasonably demand more action on the part of the state if one doesn't take – on a small scale – these measures for oneself?"[65] This mindset in conjunction with the larger intended audience for this booklet called for personal responsibility and independent action, as charged by a higher, non-socialist authority. "The Earth is to be saved" circulated through Church and independent circles throughout the 1980s and was often cited as the work that made readers want to learn more.

Beyond the KFH, the Church and Society Committee became a source of institutional Church support for the environment with international ties. In the 1970s, it grew more active in the WCC's umbrella Church and Society Committee based in Geneva, Switzerland. The WCC and its various sub-organizations created larger, international fora for member

---

[61] Hans-Peter Gensichen, "Einleitung," in "Die Erde ist zu retten" (Wittenberg: Kirchliches Forschungsheim, 1980), 1.
[62] Ibid., 54.   [63] Ibid., 27.   [64] Ibid., 1.   [65] Ibid., 40–42.

churches.[66] Thuringia's provost and chair of the East German committee, Dr. Heino Falcke, became one of the most outspoken advocates for the environment. Having studied in Göttingen and Basel in the late 1940s, Falcke had extensive contacts in the FRG before voluntarily moving to the GDR in 1952. Later, after earning a doctorate in theology at the University of Rostock and serving as a parish priest, Falcke rose in the Church hierarchy to assume the position of provost in 1973.[67] His international work in the Church and Society Committee furthered his environmental pursuits within the GDR.

In 1978, Falcke prepared for the WCC's international conference on "Faith, Science, and the Future" (held a year later) by organizing a smaller but related meeting in the GDR. Some fifty interested individuals, which included the KFH's Gensichen, gathered to consider the "responsibility of our Church and our society" for environmental problems and the future of humankind.[68] In highlighting the tensions between ecology and economic growth in industrialized countries, they placed Christian theology and the GDR at the center of numerous relevant debates. Participants offered an alternative to the technocratic socialist environmentalism that the SED had advocated throughout the 1970s. In asserting Christian responsibility and developing their own sets of knowledge surrounding environmental conditions, Church-based activists disputed the efficacy of the SED's approach.

The KFH and Church and Society Committee's shared work also permeated other institutions within the Church, spreading the influence of Christian environmental thought. In 1980, Gensichen introduced a newsletter, *Briefe*, on human–nature conflicts for Christians, inspired by the WCC Congress. He continued to produce *Briefe* until the collapse of the GDR.[69] This publication and others encouraged additional theological and student organizations to investigate creative forms of cooperation with nature, and in Saxony, Church leaders formed a working group on "Environment and Church." Pressure for this shift overwhelmingly came from younger clergy and interested individuals, such as those

---

[66] EZA 101/603, "Protokoll über die Sitzung des Ausschusses KuG am 21.11.1970 in Berlin-Weißensee, 10–17.00 Uhr."

[67] Pfarrer Ricklef Münnich, "Dr. Dr. H.c. Heino Falcke zum 85. Geburtstag am 12. Mai 2014," *Gesellschaft für Zeitgeschichte*, May 12, 2014, www.gesellschaft-zeitgeschichte.de/geschichte/perso nen/heino-falcke/, accessed November 7, 2019.

[68] EZA 101/624, "Einführungsreferat zu der Konsultation, 'Unsere Verantwortung für Umwelt und Zukunft des Menschen', Buckow, 28 und 29 Januar 1978."

[69] Robert Havemann Gesellschaft (RHG), Hans-Peter Gensichen, *Briefe zur Orientierung im Konflikt Mensch-Natur*, Kirchliches Forschungsheim Wittenberg, 1. Brief – Januar 1980.

studying theology. Specifically, men banned from studying at university for political reasons turned to the Church to pursue an education.[70] These initiatives did not necessarily reflect wide-ranging societal interest but demonstrated that both local and international concerns informed the Protestant Church's direction in the 1970s and 1980s.

Organizational and intellectual centers for environmentalism remained active within the Church until the collapse of the GDR, expanding awareness and involvement. Some activists' respective positions within the Church and focus on theology frustrated more oppositional figures who condemned the SED system as a whole. For others, the Church provided a space for people to meet and the theological backbone that undergirded wider critiques of the system. While some involved in the KFH became actively involved in the opposition in the late 1980s, Gensichen embodied a moderate approach, cooperating with officials and often negotiating between more radical figures and the SED.[71] The KFH navigated condemning the SED's policies while not provoking a crackdown. To complicate matters, not all clergy and bishops were equally devoted to environmental protection. Church-based activism defied binaries of church versus opposition, or opposition versus state, or state versus church, revealing entanglements within East German society.

Pollution and the Parishes

While the Church became more committed to environmental protection as an institution, distress about pollution concurrently grew at the parish level in grassroots groups. These two strands of Church-based environmentalism informed and reinforced one another, producing a more varied and diverse approach. Gaining momentum in the late 1970s, environmental groups found common ground with the already established peace movement, especially over the nuclear issue.[72] At first, though, environmental groups devoted their efforts to small-scale matters with local activities, which led the Stasi to believe these circles were less subversive than the peace movement.[73] Their rise in the early 1980s was a response to a number

---

[70] Neubert, *Geschichte der Opposition in der DDR*, 268, 273.

[71] This position has led to criticism of the organization's efficacy, but the KFH served a fundamentally different purpose, and we must acknowledge the variety of responses to the SED state within the Church and the opposition.

[72] Pfaff, "The Politics of Peace in the GDR," 291.

[73] BStU MfS/JHS 2025, "Diplomarbeit: Die Organisierung der politisch-operativen Arbeit zur Verhinderung des Mißbrauchs von Umweltschutzproblemen für politische Untergrundtätigkeit," October 31, 1984, 8.

of key changes, namely the peace movement's loss of momentum in 1983, the Church's apparent approval of environmental activism, and the SED's restriction of data in 1982. Groups relied on the Church's structure and theology to confront the degradation, despite cooperation with authorities, which blurred distinctions between sets of actors. Church-based inter-actions with the party and state illustrate the interconnectedness of envir-onmental efforts. Networks of interested individuals overlapped with dual participation and the sharing of information. Engagement with the envir-onment transcended traditional social cleavages in the GDR and created a shared knowledge base for involved individuals.

Some of the first groups appeared in Berlin, the epicenter of the peace movement. The "Peace and Environmental Circle in the Parish Berlin-Lichtenberg," for example, united the messages of peace and environment through the New Testament command to "love thy neighbor as thyself." The Lichtenberg circle expressed solidarity with "the least amongst us" when forming a new human community in accordance with Jesus' teach-ings and fulfilled through a new covenant with God. By their definition, Jesus' message to love another encompassed ecological justice in a Cold War context. In their founding document, the members stated that "Given the increasing number of environmental problems and growing danger of atomic self-destruction, a critical assessment of our attitude towards oppression, militarism and our relationship with nature is absolutely vital."[74] In linking threats to peace and to nature, groups tied local issues to larger ones facing the GDR; they developed an alternative conception of environmentalism that stood in contrast to the SED's socialist interpretation.

Parish-based environmental groups also sprang up in heavily polluted areas across the GDR, not only in Berlin or other cities. The Christian Environmental Seminar Rötha (*Christliches Umweltseminar Rötha*, CUR), based in the coalmining area outside of Leipzig, began to take action in 1981. With a desire to improve local living conditions, the members started with a tree planting campaign in November of that year, in which seventy-five participants between the ages of one and eighty-five took part. Rötha suffered from poor air quality from the nearby beneficiation plants and briquette factories that prepared coal for widespread distribution. The CUR started in 1981 with a coffee klatch with a pastor, two Protestants, one Catholic, and an atheist. Under the leadership of Pastor Walter

---

[74] RGH RG/B 08, "Protokoll der Gründungssitzung des Friedens- und Umweltkreises in der Evangelischen Pfarr- und Glaubensgemeinde Lichtenberg: in der Glaubenskirche am 28. 6. 83."

Christian Steinbach, the group sought to draw attention to the region's pollution and mitigate it where possible by writing petitions, organizing tree planting campaigns, and shocking people with information. The aim was to inspire hope and enhance ecological education.[75] In the years to come, the members garnered local support in addition to the notice of Church leadership and groups from around the country.

In the early 1980s, the CUR devoted considerable effort to working with local authorities for a common goal. Citing noticeably more open and constructive relations with officials since the mid-1970s, the CUR's members took part in National Front and GNU activities, serving on the GNU's executive board for the county level. Their cooperation led to the organization of a local Landscape Day that unfortunately did not succeed in generating much interest in improving living conditions. These partnerships demonstrated the Church-based groups' willingness to work with party and state organizations as part of their call for individual action. The activists recognized the limits of their ability to effect change in a dictatorship without official cooperation, so they sought at least tacit permission from local authorities in order to meet publicly and to carry out activities, such as tree planting campaigns.

Other early groups similarly acknowledged the benefits of working through the GNU and other official channels to foster goodwill. In Magdeburg, Antje Wilde justified her group's commitment to the environment because the number of public events, interest among fellow humans, and GNU memberships were all increasing.[76] In 1982, the Eco-Seminar in Schwerin emphasized the importance of communication and cooperation between Church and the official channels as a means of achieving its real goal: better environmental protection. The seminar claimed that dual participation, or collaboration between the GNU and individual Christians, was possible and often even requested. The authors further suggested attending public lectures to seek out points of constructive collaboration, such as practical projects including cleaning up trash, greening neighborhoods, and nature walks.[77] Working with the party and state offered more opportunities to achieve small-scale goals without – at least intentionally – provoking local officials.

Cooperation only partly represented a gesture of goodwill from Christian groups; it was also a matter of necessity. Freedom of information

[75] RGH TH 02/03, "Eine Mark für Espenhain oder ein Protest bekommt Flügel," 1988.
[76] RHG Wi 06, Personal Notes of Antje Wilde, undated.
[77] RHG SWV 02/02, "Ergebnisse der Gruppe 2," February 19–21, 1982.

was not a given in the GDR, especially after the 1982 decision to restrict access to data. Working with the GNU and other official venues proved essential for Church-based groups. The Eco-Seminar in Schwerin nodded to this state of affairs. In listing ways to gather information, members suggested personal observation, the Church, and western media sources. The majority of the list, however, cited a variety of official sources, such as GNU pamphlets, lectures, the academic publisher Urania, and literature from the Academy of Sciences. Participants added that personal contacts and discussions with teachers, forest rangers, conservation agents from Urania, and other specialists could also be beneficial for gaining a better understanding of the topic.[78] These networks brought together official, expert, and Church-based sets of knowledge that provided more insight into actual environmental conditions than the pro forma responses found in the East German media.

Naturally, the groups also relied heavily on the Church to orient themselves on the issues and activities. Antje Wilde's group based at the cathedral in Magdeburg openly cited the KFH's literature, such as "The Earth is to be saved," as a major impetus for forming and an important basis for its work.[79] Based on information from the KFH and western news sources, Wilde and her co-founder, Johannes Drenger, held their first informational stand at the 1983 Church Congress taking place at the cathedral. They wrote out alternative recipes and environmental cartoons and literature. That the Magdeburg cathedral hosted for a group early on came as no surprise. After all, the KFH lay in the same diocese, and it had already been encouraged to move in an environmental direction a decade before. New and expanded networks took off in the early 1980s, and venues such as Church Congresses became vital nodes for exchanging ideas and information.

Early success must be understood in a relative sense, because distrust and wariness flourished once the Stasi became more skeptical of environmental groups after 1982. The Stasi scrutinized works such as "The Earth is to be saved" and the Church-based groups, seeking to disrupt their rising popularity and stir up discontent within the Church.[80] For example, the Stasi recruited Antje Wilde as a minor and coerced her to inform on her group. Wilde had lost her father at a young age and, in her teenage years, had a difficult relationship with her mother. The Stasi played on these

---

[78] Ibid.   [79] RHG Wi 06, "Präambel, Juni 1983."

[80] BStU BV Bln AKG 72, "Arbeitshinweise über die Entwicklung, Pläne, Absichten und Aktivitäten gegnerischer und feinderlich-negativer Kräfte zur Schaffung einer sogenannten Ökologie- und Umweltschutzbewegung in der DDR und deren operative Bekämpfung," October 22, 1985, 29–31.

Figure 3 Church Congress of the Protestant Church of Saxony in Leipzig. (Photo by Mehner/ullstein bild via Getty Images)

insecurities in recruiting her to be an unofficial informant with the pseudonym "Simone Pietsch" when she was sixteen years old. The Stasi directed her to remain active in the organization and to take on leadership positions. Although she later apologized, Wilde informed on her friends and colleagues for more than three years. She later explained that she felt like she had a "split personality: on the one hand participating in the eco-group and on the other uncritically doing as the Stasi asked."[81] Wilde's example underscores the Stasi's extreme measures to sow distrust and to limit environmentalism in the Church.

Although central Church bodies and parishes approached the environment from different perspectives, they relied on one another to cultivate a cohort of interested individuals. Combining theological considerations with grassroots responses to local problems, the movement appeared simultaneously abstract yet locally specific, initially making it seem less threatening to the SED. Importantly, these two impulses intertwined in the Protestant Church and provided a foundation on which to build broader interest from across different segments of East German society. They incorporated official information and rhetoric but rejected its interpretation and highlighted its failures. Despite competing interpretations, these overlapping stimuli worked together to create a larger body of knowledge that East Germans could access to learn about the environment.

Environment and the West: The WCC and the Green Party

Church-based environmentalists responded not only to the visible degradation at home but also to mounting alarm about growth and waste on the international stage. Western critiques of consumption, material production, and excess resonated with Christian theology and motivated religious leaders on both sides of the Iron Curtain to champion similar concerns. Ecumenical and church conferences opened avenues for East Germans to learn about transnational discussions, such as when clergy members attended WCC conferences on technology and science in Bucharest, Nairobi, Boston, and Vancouver between 1974 and 1983. Moreover, the waxing popularity of the green movement in the FRG and the founding of the Green Party became crucial influences on Church-based environmentalism in the GDR. They were also a fount of information across the Cold War divide. Western environmental thought, movements, and political

---

[81] *Die ZEIT TV-Magazin*, April 18, 1996, www.zeit.de/1996/17/tv17.19960419.xml/seite-3, accessed July 19, 2015.

parties became intellectual sources of inspiration and a practical means of support for East German environmentalists, intertwining global and local issues in central Europe.[82]

WCC meetings in 1974 and 1975, in Bucharest and Nairobi, respectively, exposed the GDR's Church leadership to evolving ideas about the environment beyond the Soviet bloc. As in the parish-based groups, nuclear capabilities and weaponry shaped debates about nature and peace. The Bucharest conference linked fears about technology's ability to damage humanity with its ability to destroy the physical environment. At the 1975 conference in Nairobi, the WCC fought to "live without the protection of weapons," referring to the deadly capacity of nuclear arms. Subsequently, a peace group in Rostock cited Nairobi in its decision to pursue "personal peace treaties" in the early 1980s, in which individuals from either side of the Iron Curtain swore not to fight one another if their countries went to war.[83] The treaty pledged to show the connections between the war and armament through their work in ecology, third world, and feminist groups.[84] The emphasis on peace in the early to mid-1970s served as a shared point of Christian apprehension in the west and in the GDR.

At the 1979 WCC conference on "Faith, Science, and the Future," the environment emerged as a central theme. For Falcke, western perspectives also proved crucial in expanding his perspective on the relationship between humans and the environment.[85] Visits to the west were a gateway to new modes of thinking. Obtaining travel permits to the west was less complicated for clergy and Church officials than for average East Germans, so opportunities to go abroad became all the more important to those who had them.[86] While out of the country, East Germans – at least the few who could get permission to travel abroad – learned about different approaches to difficulties they had faced for decades. The WCC's consideration of "the Christian understanding of nature, humanity, and God and its implications for our engagement in the realization of a just, participatory and viable society" stood in contrast to the SED's technocratic understanding of environmentalism.[87] Given the SED's propaganda and its efforts to strictly control information, Church contacts in the FRG and the west in general became vital conduits for ideas.

---

[82] Jens Gieseke and Andrea Bahr, *Die Staatssicherheit und die Grünen* (Berlin: Ch. Links Verlag, 2017) focuses on the Stasi's attempts to limit these types of interactions.
[83] Ibid., 55.   [84] RHG RG MV 01, "Elemente für einen persönlichen Friedensvertrag," undated.
[85] Neubert, *Geschichte der Opposition in der DDR*, 273.   [86] Fulbrook, *The People's State*, 88.
[87] EZA 101/1209, "Glaube, Wissenschaft und die Zukunft: Weltkonferenz 1979," January 1978.

The "Faith, Science, and the Future" conference influenced not only the six East German attendees but also those with whom they shared their experiences upon returning to the GDR. Falcke, already involved in environmental questions, sought to implement what he had learned in the west in the GDR, disseminating information across the Iron Curtain.[88] After his 1979 visit to the United States, Falcke convinced the Church to establish four subcommittees: "Agriculture and Environment," "Forest, Forestry, and Environment," "Lifestyle," and "Ethics of Science." Each of these four groups prepared extensive reports on the state of the environment in the GDR over the next decade, more than one of which was republished by Church presses. Given the GDR's ban on releasing environmental data, and with the Church wishing to avoid direct confrontation with the SED, these reports were only distributed for within the Church.[89] The pamphlets circulated in parishes and environmental groups across the GDR, helping to raise awareness about the situation that East Germans faced within the confines of the dictatorship.

The first report, "Agriculture and Environment," appeared in 1982, citing the WCC's conference as a reason for investigating the GDR's industrial agricultural practices.[90] Highlighting the interconnectedness of industry and agriculture and their impact on the air, water, and soil, the authors detailed the multiple ways in which food production was fraught. Monoculture farming and planting the same crop year after year, the report argued, reduced genetic variety, and led them to be susceptible to pests, diseases, and weeds. Acid rain destroyed plants and crops, it asserted, and made the soil more acidic, which then ran into streams and rivers. Fertilizers and pesticides further damaged the quality of the soil and water, rendering it unpotable. Finally, the report claimed that harvests were exposed to toxins in the air and soil such as lead, cadmium, and arsenic, contaminating the food and poisoning those who consumed it.[91]

A large fraction of the report was devoted to meat production. Increased use of antibiotics and hormones, poor conditions for livestock, and

[88] BArch DO 4/801, "Konzeption zum Informationsgespräch mit der Konferenz der ev. Kirchenleitungen in der DDR (KKL) zu Fragen: 'Wissenschaftlich-technischen Fortschritt und die Aufgaben auf dem Gebiet der Ökologie'," January 24, 1980.
[89] Siegfried Lokatis and Ingrid Sonntag, eds., *Heimliche Leser in der DDR: Kontrolle und Verbreitung unerlaubter Literatur* (Berlin: Ch. Links Verlag, 2007).
[90] Archiv Bürgerbewegung Leipzig (ABL) 4.21.14, "Agrarwirtschaft und Umwelt," 1984, 0–1.
[91] Ibid., 7–13.

ammonia-laced stench from excrement were but a few of the ecological issues that the authors raised.[92] Working in or living near animal, and especially pig, farms stank. And they damaged the forest. The "Forest, Forestry, and Environment" subcommittee confirmed these findings in its report, which was published in 1986. The authors of that pamphlet highlighted how a single facility could harm over a thousand hectares of forest, as in Schleiz in southern Thuringia.[93] Information about the disastrous effects of industrialized food production spread through Church networks, countering official narratives about the boundless progress of science. The "Agriculture and Environment" report was so widely read that the committee printed a revised edition in 1984, and it inspired similar projects on other topics.[94]

Within the Church hierarchy, Falcke used his WCC experiences to present on the relationship between economy and ecology to the leadership and make the case for more support. At a Conference of the Church Leadership in 1979, he pushed the main takeaways from *The Limits to Growth* to argue that "indeed, our state desires economic growth and rejects the thesis of zero growth." The book primarily responded to capitalism, but Falcke believed the message applied to socialism, too. He acknowledged the different capitalist and communist premises, insisting, "It is not a growth that gains momentum from capital . . . but should be a growth that serves to satisfy humans' material and cultural needs." Nevertheless, Falcke contended that humans' needs included a clean environment.[95] The prioritization of the economy in the GDR and the obsession with matching "western standards of consumption" had resulted in ecological compromises. Falcke's speech reinforced the similarities between planned and market economies – much to the SED's consternation – and used western approaches to expose communism's failings.

Falcke was not alone in his appropriation of western literature to dispute the efficacy of socialist environmentalism and intertwine western, religious, and socialist environmentalisms. Jürgen Morgenstern, pastor, theologian, and member of the KFH's working group Earth, also highlighted how the SED ignored its own pollution and treated warnings about growth

[92] Ibid., 33–39. For more on livestock, see Thomas Fleischman, *Communist Pigs: An Animal History of East Germany's Rise and Fall* (Seattle, WA: University of Washington Press, 2020).

[93] RHG TH 02, Kirche und Gesellschaft, "Wald-, Fortwirtschaft und Umwelt," 1985–1986.

[94] "Agrarwirtschaft und Umwelt," 0–1.

[95] BArch DO 4/801, "Konzeption zum Informationsgespräch mit der Konferenz der ev. Kirchenleitungen in der DDR (KKL) zu Fragen: 'Wissenschaftlich-technischer Fortschritt und die Aufgaben auf dem Gebiet der Ökologie',' January 24, 1980.

as "complete nonsense."[96] The official line went: because the ownership of the means of production was different under socialism, no ecological crisis existed like in capitalist countries, only "dangers" and "threats."[97] Morgenstern invoked W. Harich, a reformed communist East German author whose work could only be published outside the Soviet bloc. As with many dissidents, Harich's work found a ready audience in the FRG. His book, *Communism without Growth?* became the foundation of Morgenstern's assessment, relying on western conceptions of environmentalism and "zero-growth" to illuminate how the East German system rejected alternative opinions.

By the time of the WCC meeting in Vancouver in 1983, the East German Church was disseminating information about the GDR abroad to further international conversations about nature and faith. In 1978, the Erfurt Church Congress included an exhibit that a "large and active environmental group" organized.[98] Two years later, and just one year after the Boston conference, Church and state officials met to discuss points of contention, especially nuclear energy.[99] Church Congresses regularly covered the environment, and grassroots activities were on the rise. At the conference in Vancouver, Falcke confirmed this commitment, lecturing on "Survival Threats Encounter Theological Aspects." He argued that "life and the future of the world as we know it are vitally and radically threatened" and contended that the solution to these dangers was to live a Christian and ethical life.[100] Falcke's speech and attendance at the conference shared information about communist states in the west and used trends from western peace and environmental movements to bolster his interpretation.

WCC conferences offered a theological yet narrow perspective, but green movements in capitalist countries, especially the FRG, modeled wider engagement for East Germans. The success of the movement, its protests, and its ability to influence policy gave many East Germans a hope for change. More broadly, the greening of West German society and the information that its media reported were crucial to developing challenges to authorities as well as ideas about how activism operated. Western

---

[96] RHG KFH 01, Jürgen Morgenstern, "Die Verarbeitung des ökologischen Problems, speziell der Ergebnisse und Schlußfogerungen des Clubs of Rome, in unserer sozialistischen Fachliteratur," undated.

[97] Ibid.   [98] Neubert, *Geschichte der Opposition in der DDR*, 273.

[99] RHG Ki 18/02, Untitled copy of a BStU report, undated.

[100] BArch DO 4/802, Dr. Heino Falcke, "Die Bedrohungen des Überlebens Begegnen Theologische Aspekte," Sechste Versammlung der Ökumenischen Rat der Kirchen, July 24–August 10, 1983.

movements tended to be secular in orientation and accordingly exemplified a way to embrace environmentalism that did not require theologically rigorous debate. Some western churches did join these conversations, especially regarding nuclear energy, but the West German movement as a whole represented environmental activism that was neither state socialist nor religious.[101] While activism in the GDR was clearly conscribed to specific spaces, such as the GNU and the Church, the green movement in the FRG provided information, inspiration, and practical support for "independent" East German activism.

The West German citizens' initiatives and the BBU of the 1970s popularized patterns of protest that East Germans wished for and hoped to replicate.[102] Their concrete and local character, protesting sites of pollution, presented innovative modes of activism in the FRG but also had implications for East Germans who sought to reapply citizens' initiatives to their own political context. As East Germans' frustration with the handling – or non-handling – of petitions mounted in the 1980s, they began to demand "real" citizens' initiatives instead. The CUR returned to this concept later in the 1980s, calling for democratic citizens' initiatives and electoral mandates for reform. The group grew resentful of the official channels when they proved rigid and unresponsive.[103] West German citizens' initiatives, especially as part of the anti-nuclear movement, cultivated "counter experts" to authoritatively respond to official or industry narratives.[104] In a sense, East German activists in the Church followed this model to learn about environmental problems and circumvent state secrecy. The West German green movement set an example East Germans sought to implement at home while simultaneously aggravating the SED by using the "imperialist" language of the west.[105]

By the end of the 1970s, the green movement transformed and professionalized into the first new political party in the FRG since the World War II. The Green Party declared it was an "anti-party party" that rejected traditional politics and instead followed the principles of grassroots

---

[101] Michael Schüring, *"Bekennen gegen den Atomstaat": Die evangelischen Kirchen in der Bundesrepublik Deutschlnd und die Konflikte um die Atomenergie, 1970–1990* (Göttingen: Wallstein Verlag, 2015).

[102] Dieter Rucht, "Einleitung," in *Die sozialen Bewegungen in Deutschland seit 1945: Ein Handbuch*, eds. Roland Roth and Dieter Rucht (Frankfurt: Campus, 2008), 16–18.

[103] RGH TH 02/03, "Eine Mark für Espenhain oder ein Protest bekommt Flügel," 1988.

[104] Dolores Augustine, *Taking on Technocracy: Nuclear Power in Germany, 1945 to the Present* (New York: Berghahn Books, 2018), 74–87.

[105] BArch-SAPMO DY 27/6177, "Entwurf: Vorschlag für die Gründung einer Gesellschaft im Kulturbund der DDR," November 4, 1974.

organization, social justice, nonviolence, and ecological wisdom.[106] The Greens quickly made their way into local and state governments, and eventually into the Bundestag in 1983 with 5.6 percent of the vote.[107] The SED viewed the Greens' success as an opportunity to register disapproval of the FRG and to expose its weaknesses. This tactic presented unanticipated challenges, however, as the SED realized that the West German Greens' ideas also resonated in the GDR, especially among activists in the Protestant Church. Throughout the 1980s, then, Honecker and the SED oscillated in their stance on the Green Party, at times welcoming its ideas and politicians while shunning and spying on them at others.

The Green Party's electoral success drew significant attention both from the SED and the Church as East Germans established relationships in the other Germany. Direct contacts with West German Greens lent legitimacy to official visits between Greens and the SED while also giving East German environmentalists information and aid. Parliamentarian and ecologist, Dr. Wilhelm Knabe, became a prominent figure in the Greens' German–German endeavors. Born in 1923 in Saxony and attaining a university education in the GDR, Knabe became a linchpin between the Germanys on environmental topics. He had completed a doctorate in agriculture at Humboldt University in 1957 before fleeing with his family to the FRG in 1959.[108] Knabe worked at a number of ecological and forestry establishments, such as the Institute for World Forestry in Reinbek bei Hamburg and the Provincial Institute for Ecology in Essen. In the late 1970s, he became involved in politics, joining local and provincial green lists, despite being roughly a generation older than many of his fellow Greens. Over the course of the 1980s, as a spokesperson for the party and later a member of parliament, Knabe had both the scientific training and the political clout to tackle official and Church-based East German environmental concerns.[109]

On October 31, 1983, Knabe and a delegation of Greens traveled to the GDR and met with East German environmental minister Hans Reichelt. For six hours, they sparred over the role of nature in modern society.[110] Whereas Reichelt emphasized the pragmatic, narrow subjects such as the GDR's need to conserve its limited water supply – with which East

[106] Belinda Davis, "A Brief Cosmology of the West German Green Party," *German Politics & Society* 33, no. 4 (Winter 2015), 53.

[107] Frank Uekötter, *The Greenest Nation? A New History of German Environmentalism* (Cambridge, MA: MIT Press, 2014), 114.

[108] "Die Autorin und die Autoren," in *Umweltschutz in der DDR, Band 3*, 369.   [109] Ibid.

[110] Gieseke and Bahr, *Die Staatssicherheit und die Grünen*, 54–55.

German experts had some success – Knabe explained that the Greens viewed humans as being in a partnership with nature; it was not a resource to exploit.[111] Knabe noted being surprised at the GDR's efforts to reclaim used materials, because they contrasted with Reichelt's refusal to recognize other issues, such as acid rain. Knabe's report likened the GDR's warnings to not dramatize the situation to an official statement from West German industries. Reichelt's stance illuminated the GDR's commitment to the existing economic model and his refusal to condemn East German polluters. After the meeting, the Greens fumed over the East German press release, which did not describe their positions. The state censors also removed the Greens' call for more citizen participation, which the SED had interpreted as a provocation.[112] This contentious meeting set the tone for future ones between the Greens and East German policymakers.[113]

The day after meeting with Reichelt, Knabe and his delegation met with Church-based activists, a move that the SED did not appreciate.[114] Although the Greens were not as familiar with the theological foundations of Christian environmental engagement, they found numerous points of agreement, including the seriousness of the pollution levels and a distaste for modern consumerist society.[115] In the following years, Knabe spearheaded making contact with Church-based environmentalists, including Gensichen at the KFH, Falcke in Erfurt, the Working Group for Environmental Protection (*Arbeitsgruppe Umwelt*, AGU) in Leipzig, and others.[116] In cultivating these ties, Wilhelm Knabe worked closely with his son, Hubertus, who also became involved in environmental politics in the GDR. The elder Knabe's efforts deepened East and West German collaboration and contributed to a shared knowledge base, just not always through official or diplomatic channels.

The SED's relationship with the Greens fluctuated; it used the anti-party party to critique the FRG but was also suspicious of their support for alternative groups in the GDR.[117] The SED and various ministries enjoyed pointing out that the Green Party gained momentum as a "reaction to

---

[111] Raymond Dominick, "Capitalism, Communism, and Environmental Protection: Lessons from the German Experience," *Environmental History* 3, no. 3 (July 1998), 321. Archiv Grünes Gedächtnis (AGG) B II 1/1766, "Kontaktaufnahme zu Umweltfragen, von Wilhelm Knabe, Sprecher im Bundestagsfraktion der GRÜNEN," undated.

[112] Ibid.   [113] Gieseke and Bahr, *Die Staatssicherheit und die Grünen*, 56.

[114] AGG A 56, Correspondence between Wilhelm Knabe and Erich Honecker, October 10, 1984.

[115] AGG A 56, "Besuch von den Grünen," *Der Sonntag: Gemeindeblatt der Evangelisch-Lutheranisch Landeskirche Sachsens*, November 18, 1983.

[116] AGG A 56, "Vorschläge für Gespräche der 'GRÜNEN' mit und in der DDR," undated.

[117] Gieseke and Bahr, *Die Staatssicherheit und die Grünen*, 9–10.

environmentally despicable economic policies of large corporations, as well as problems with the disgraceful politics" in Bonn.[118] Yet the SED, Stasi, and other state officials worried about the Greens' influence in the Church. The State Secretariat for Church Questions noted that the Greens introduced East Germans active in the Church to "opinions that do not mesh with the concrete possibilities and conditions of a developed socialist society, either conceptually or in the specifics."[119] When a Green delegation visited an SED Club of Intelligence in Leipzig for a discussion, a number of students active in Protestant circles showed up, eagerly asking about the possibility of establishing a green party in the GDR.[120] As East Germans turned to ideas and methods learned from the Greens, the SED alternately praised and condemned the party, at times even barring members from entering the GDR.[121]

Poland and the Pull of Solidarność

Communist authorities faced pressure from non-party or state actors, such as churches, but the greatest threat to them yet came from Poland with the rise of Solidarność. By the summer of 1980, the PZPR conceded the trade union Solidarność's right to organize independently of party and state structures. This move unnerved other communist parties in the Soviet bloc, which feared similar questions about their monopoly on power. Even during periods of closer "friendship," the SED distrusted the PZPR, citing poor economic performance and workers' propensity to strike.[122] Environmentalism was not central to Solidarność, but it did provide the framework for the first independent environmental organization in eastern Europe, the Polish Ecological Club (*Polski Klub Ekologiczny*, PKE), to emerge.[123] The PKE's activism modeled how non-state actors could shape the narrative from the margins of socialism. Many of the PKE's members also represented a form of "dual participation," in which they held both

---

[118] BStU MfS BV Potsdam/AKG 1873, "Referat 'Ordnung, Sicherheit und Disziplin in der Volkswirtschaft – unsere gemeinsame Aufgabe und Verantwortung', 8.11.88."

[119] BArch DO 4/801, "Die Haltung der Kirchen in der DDR zu Fragen des Umweltschutzes," October 1982.

[120] BArch-SAPMO DY 27/6112, "Information über Mitarbeit von Christen in der GNU in der Stadtorganisation Leipzig des KBs der DDR," September 26, 1983.

[121] Gieseke and Bahr, *Die Staatssicherheit und die Grünen*, 10.

[122] Politisches Archiv des Auswärtigen Amtes (PA AA) M 39 693 09, "An das Politbüro des ZK der PVAP z.H. des I. Sekretärs des ZK, Genossen Eward Gierek," October 1978, 1–5.

[123] Polski Klub Ekologiczny – Historia PKE, www.pkeko.pl/historia.php, accessed May 5, 2021. Barbara Hicks, *Environmental Politics in Poland: A Social Movement between Regime and Opposition* (New York: Columbia University Press, 1996), 4, 9–11.

official positions as scientists and experts but also joined an independent advocacy group. Over the course of the 1980s, the PKE became a critical node for independent environmental movements across the Soviet bloc. Church-based groups in the GDR hoped for similar liberties, making the SED feel increasingly besieged and contributing to its 1982 decision. Situated in the heart of central Europe and along the Cold War fault line, the SED environmental initiatives were caught between an influential green movement to the west and a powerful anti-communist opposition in Poland that created space for independent activism.

Strikes and protests in Poland opened up spaces for independent organization that did not exist on the same scale in other satellite states. Even as the GDR strengthened its relationship with Poland through the 1972 Treaty of Friendship, unrest in Poland made East German authorities wary. Throughout the 1970s, frustration over working conditions, wages, and price increases increasingly united workers.[124] This groundwork paved the way for Solidarność, which emerged in the summer of 1980 when a price hike led to another series of strikes. They started in the shipyards in Gdańsk and spread across the country.[125] By the end of August, Gomułka relented on twenty-one different points, including the right to organize independently.[126] The largest independent organization was the trade union, Solidarność, which mushroomed to an unprecedented ten million members.[127] From the summer of 1980 until December 1981, when General Wojciech Jaruzelski declared Martial Law, Poles established a multitude of associations outside the purview of party or state.

Observing from across the Oder River, the GDR considered Solidarność to be an economic problem and a threat to the stability of the bloc, souring relations between the two countries. East German officials canceled official visits and invoked stringent restrictions for delegations when they did travel to Poland. In late 1980, after months of coordinating with Polish cartographers to map the shelf and shoreline of the Baltic Sea, at the last minute, East German representatives from the interior ministry were directed not to go. Given the situation in Poland, the entire excursion was to be set aside for the time being. The East German coordinator of the

---

[124] Jan Kubik, *The Power of Symbols against the Symbols of Power: The Rise of Solidarity and the Fall of State Socialism in Poland* (University Park, PA: Pennsylvania State University Press, 1994), 154–155.
[125] Ibid., 185–186.
[126] Brian Porter-Szüsc, *Poland in the Modern World: Beyond Martyrdom* (Malden, MA: Wiley-Blackwell, 2014), 301–302.
[127] Magdalena Kubow, "The Solidarity Movement in Poland: Its History and Meaning in Collective Memory," *The Polish Review* 58, no. 2 (2013), 12.

operation instead recommended seeking out the Soviet Union.[128] The trip to Poland was rescheduled a month and a half later, but the East German delegation received explicit instructions. The interior ministry official was to convey that the GDR supported Polish communists' efforts, as "the true patriots of People's Poland," to overcome the current situation and to strengthen socialism.[129] The delegation thus conducted its visit while also reprimanding Polish officials for not containing Solidarność.

In the Baltic Sea, where economic and environmental collaboration had been strong, Solidarność and non-state actors jeopardized tripartite Soviet–East German–Polish exploration for oil. Regarding the *Gemeinsame Organisation Petrobaltic* (GO Petrobaltic), Stasi reports expressed frustration over the Polish independent press's doubts about the endeavor. This tension heightened when articles accused the GO Petrobaltic of endangering the safety of workers and Poland's coast. The articles also claimed that the venture presented a danger to shipping on the Baltic and the neighboring countries' natural environment.[130] At sea, among trained engineers, environmental and working conditions called into question the Soviet bloc's shared economic interests and environmental objectives. The Stasi particularly worried about the presence of Solidarność members among the crew. As of May 1981, it determined that Solidarność had only had a "passive and conspiratorial character" at GO Petrobaltic but also believed the trade union undermined the entire project. East German managers expressed dismay that sixty of the Polish workers (those working on the platforms and ships were almost exclusively Polish) were members of Solidarność and that the drilling depended on them.[131] By October, 117 Polish workers declared themselves to be members, roughly a quarter of the Polish workforce. The situation led to problems in decision-making (would Solidarność be legally recognized on board?), but more broadly, in the context of the Soviet cuts in oil deliveries, GO Petrobaltic's smooth functioning had significant economic ramifications.[132] The interconnectedness of the Soviet bloc economies meant potential difficulties when another member faced unrest

[128] BArch DK 5/1018, "Telegram: 'konsultationsreise in die vrp zur tiefenkartierung in der juestenzone (sic)'," Lindner to Thoms, November 24, 1980.
[129] BArch DK 5/1018, "Teildirektive für die Teilnahme eines Delegierten des Ministeriums des Innern an einer Arbeitsberatung zum Thema 'Methodik der Kartierung des Schorre- und Schelfgebietes'," January 1981.
[130] BStU MfS/HA XVIII 19276, "Information zur Erdölfündigkeit auf dem Ostseeschelf der VRP," May 11, 1981.
[131] Ibid.
[132] PA AA M 39 2547 87, "Genossen Dr. Krolikowski: Aus einem Gespräch mit dem Leiter der Abteilung IB des Ministeriums für Geologie ergeben sich folgende Informationen," November 1981.

at home. Uncooperative Polish workers struck fear in the SED's relatively smooth functioning economy, which factored into East German pressure for Soviet intervention.[133]

Despite uneasy relations with other Soviet bloc states, Poland continued to permit the freedoms that Solidarność secured, including organizing outside of official channels. The PKE was founded as an "independent social movement without political or religious orientation" on September 23, 1980.[134] Accordingly, the PKE revolved around scientists and interested individuals who combined expertise with grassroots concern, forming a "dual participation" similar to East German activists in the Protestant Church who also joined the GNU.[135] Within months, the club counted 3,000 members nationally, 700 of whom lived in Kraków.[136] Members described their primary goal as "opening the eyes of their fellow humans to environmental destruction in Poland and the dangers to health and life that it brings." The PKE aimed to bring people together and create a society in which ecological development, a clean environment, and human rights were valued. Members therefore began a campaign to raise awareness through fliers, regular reports on pollution, and other publications. These pamphlets made their way into the hands of citizens as well as government ministries.[137]

The PKE swiftly published an open letter to the legislature, the Sejm, about pollution and its damaging effects on humans, the environment, and Poland's cultural heritage. Speaking as representatives of science, culture, trade unions, and conservationists, the founding members drew on the language of the 1975 Helsinki Accords to argue for the human right to live in an unpolluted environment.[138] Citing heavy industrialization, indifferent authorities, and disinformation as the causes of Poland's devastation, the PKE pushed the Sejm to make immediate changes. Their demands included complying with existing laws, giving informed policy its due, and taking immediate action to provide citizens with uncontaminated food and water. As in the GDR, access to information about the pollution and

---

[133] Hermann Wentker, *Außenpolitik in engen Grenzen: Die DDR im internationalen System, 1949–1989* (Munich: Oldenbourg, 2007), 437–448.

[134] RHG TH 12/03, "Polski Klub Ekologiczny (PKE) – wer wir sind . . . , " undated.

[135] Hicks, *Environmental Politics in Poland*, 105, 173.

[136] Sabine Rosenbladt, *Der Osten ist grün? Ökoreportagen aus der DDR, Sowjetunion, Tschechoslowakei, Polen, Ungarn* (Hamburg: Rasch und Röhring Verlag, 1988), 14–15. The numbers would reach as high at 6,000 by 1989. Hicks, *Environmental Politics in Poland*, 99.

[137] RHG TH 12/03, "Polski Klub Ekologiczny (PKE) – wer wir sind . . . ," undated.

[138] "List Otwarty do Sejmu Polskiej Rzeczpospolitej Ludowej," *Życie Literackie*, No. 42, October 19, 1980.

extent of the ecological damage was a serious point of contention. The PKE claimed to safeguard civil and national obligations regarding environmental protection, positioning itself as the expert and authentic voice on the subject.[139]

Before Martial Law was declared in December 1981, the PKE pressured officials on a number of issues, most famously the Skawina aluminum smelting plant near Kraków.[140] While Solidarność was essential to the rise of independent environmental activism in Poland, the PKE built on a foundation that already existed.[141] The Skawina works had long been a major source of pollution and frustration in the region, based in the Stalinist mode of heavy industry and technologically outdated from the beginning of its construction in the 1950s. Built for a capacity of 15,000 tons per annum, its output reached some 53,000 tons in 1980.[142] Moreover, Skawina's smelting led to fluorine levels in the soil that measured between five and thirty-five times the national average, and were dangerous to cattle grazing in the area.[143] With its closure, emissions sank roughly thirty percent.[144] Popular activism in Kraków helped coerce the PZPR to respond quickly, but the involvement of scientists and their frustration with official channels also contributed greatly to the campaign. Complaints about the pollution surfaced well before the PKE, but this period of liberalization enabled activists to successfully push for the plant's closure.[145]

While the environment was not at the center of Solidarność's platform, it did form part of a larger critique of communism in Poland, a trend that mirrored developments in the GDR.[146] The program for Solidarność's First National Congress in the fall of 1981 included environmental concerns. Proposals suggested regulating and modernizing enterprises, setting up inspections on the regional level, and having unions weigh in on

[139] Ibid.   [140] RHG TH 12/03, "Polski Klub Ekologiczny (PKE) – wer wir sind . . .," undated.

[141] Stanley J. Kabala, "The History of Environmental Protection in Poland and the Growth of Awareness and Activism," in Environmental Action in Eastern Europe: Responses to Crisis, ed. Barbara Jancar-Webster (Armonk, NY: M.E. Sharpe, 1993), 118.

[142] Open Society Archive (OSA), A. S., "More About Pollution," in Polish Situation Report, January 30, 1981, 2.

[143] Magnus Andersson, "National Environmental Policy in the 1980s," in Change and Continuity in Poland's Environmental Policy, ed. Magnus Andersson (Dordrecht: Springer, 1999), 64–67.

[144] Wolf Oschlies, Bald ist Polen doch verloren: Umweltzerstörung hinter Oder und Neisse (Cologne: Böhlau, 1987), 60.

[145] Hicks, Environmental Politics in Poland, 123–124.

[146] Well-known narratives of Solidarność, such as Kubik's The Power of Symbols against the Symbols of Power or Garton Ash's The Magic Lantern tend to overlook environmental activism.

government plans and bills.[147] The environment factored into workers' wellbeing, and accordingly, Solidarność had an interest in cultivating an environmental condemnation of the PZPR and the state. Unfortunately, these proposals were never implemented, and Solidarność's focus remained on other forms of political rights. Still, pollution and workers' safety fit into its larger censure of the system and generated awareness about environmental issues.

As the peace movement in the GDR expanded between 1980 and 1982, Solidarność's popularity unnerved the SED while it simultaneously provided fodder for oppositional voices. Police notoriously arrested Roland Jahn, a member of the peace movement who later fled to the FRG, for displaying a Solidarność flag and imprisoned him for twenty-two months.[148] Jahn's treatment sparked international uproar, especially from members of the West German Green Party who sympathized with the peace movement in the GDR. The connections between the peace movement and Solidarność were not lost on West German Greens. Wilhelm Knabe argued that the western peace movement's credibility would only be guaranteed, "if [we] protect democratic structures, solidarity with the grassroots movement Solidarity in Poland, and the peace movement in the GDR."[149] Solidarność posed a threat to the SED's domestic legitimacy as well as its image abroad.

On December 13, 1981, Solidarność's right to exist ended when General Jaruzelski declared Martial Law and reasserted communist authority. Though other Soviet bloc leaders remained suspicious of Poland, Jaruzelski eliminated the liberties of the preceding fifteen months, arrested roughly 5,000 of the union's leaders – killing as many as 100 – and implemented a curfew.[150] The state systematically broke down the movement's networks, weakening it significantly and forcing those not arrested to go underground. Still, the SED and other communist parties in the bloc distrusted Poland. Well into 1982 and 1983, relations between the GDR and Poland were slow to rekindle. A few years later setbacks in cultural and

---

[147] Hicks, *Environmental Politics in Poland*, 125.
[148] Sarina Pfauth, "Unverwüstlich für die Freiheit," *Süddeutsche Zeitung*, November 30, 2010, www .sueddeutsche.de/politik/roland-jahn-soll-auf-marianne-birthler-folgen-liebhaber-der-gerechtig keit-1.1017087, accessed December 17, 2014.
[149] RHG OWK 01, "Um Glaubwürdigkeit und Perspektive der Friedensbewegung: Beitrag zur BHA-Sitzung am 24.4.1982 in Bonn von Wilhelm Knabe, Mülheim an der Ruhr," Ost-West Kontakte. I use the English "Solidarity" here, because Knabe uses the German "Solidarität" rather than the Polish.
[150] Piotr Lipiński, "Ofiary stanu wojennego i lat następnych do 1989," *Gazeta Wyborcza*, December 12, 2006.

scientific collaboration had not yet fully recovered.[151] Poland continued to be an outcast among the Soviet bloc countries after the institution of Martial Law.

During that crackdown, Solidarność, the PKE, and other organizations struggled to maintain their networks, which were forced underground. Women took over running the oppositional newspapers, because officials considered women less likely to be subversive, and so they avoided the scrutiny assigned to well-known male leaders.[152] In their publications, articles focused on arrests and protest, while those banned from studying formed so-called Flying Universities.[153] Individuals who had been banned or expelled from universities found their way into these underground networks to discuss topics forbidden at official universities. The participants gathered and maintained politically damaging materials, including environmental information. When the repression lessened with the lifting of Martial Law in 1983, they functioned more publicly again, picking up where they left off in December 1981.

Solidarność, indirectly, and the PKE, directly, succeeded at connecting environmentally minded individuals and inspired groups in both Poland and the GDR. Independent of the party and state, the PKE's regional and national reach became a goal for East German activists. The PKE's focus on value change, raising consciousness, and education coincided with East German activists' goals.[154] More specifically, the "Flying Universities" during Martial Law became a stimulus for later organizations, such as the Environmental Libraries (*Umweltbibliotheken*), the first of which activists established in Berlin in 1986.[155] Environmental Libraries shared information and held events as well as seminars on forbidden subjects, such as pollution. These practical and philosophical exchanges reflected diversity within the communist bloc as well as contacts with the west in the early 1980s, revealing a larger central European network of environmental engagement.

---

[151] PA AA M 39 2531 87, "Stand der bilateralen Beziehungen DDR-VRP," August 6, 1982, 6. "Beziehungen DDR-VR Polen," February 1983, 1.

[152] For more information on women in Solidarność during Martial Law, see Shana Penn, *Solidarity's Secret: The Women Who Defeated Communism in Poland* (Ann Arbor, MI: University of Michigan Press, 2005), 100–147.

[153] "Flying Universities" date back to the nineteenth century as a way of keeping Polish intellectual traditions alive during Partition: "Fliegende Universitäten," Bundeszentrale für politische Bildung und Robert-Havemann-Gesellschaft e.V., www.jugendopposition.de/index.php?id=3180, accessed December 9, 2014.

[154] Hicks, *Environmental Politics in Poland*, 96.

[155] "Fliegende Universitäten," Bundeszentrale für politische Bildung und Robert-Havemann-Gesellschaft e.V., www.jugendopposition.de/index.php?id=3180, accessed December 17, 2014.

Conclusion

The social and political developments on either side of the GDR evoked a range of responses from East Germans. The SED attempted to coopt the green movement in the FRG as a critique of the imperialist west while condemning the rise of Solidarność to the east. Early on, the SED realized that the Green Party in the FRG might undermine its authority rather than weaken western democracy. On both sides of the Iron Curtain, non-state actors challenged the status quo, and the SED recognized the domestic implications of these forces and sought to limit their influence in the GDR. Events in neighboring countries quickly became liabilities for the SED's monopoly on power. The Cultural League's founding of the GNU in 1980 was a response to both the West German Green Party as well as the proliferation of Church-based environmental groups. Similarly, the GDR virtually cut off relations with Poland during Solidarność and only slowly rebuilt them in subsequent years. Most especially, the East German leadership sought to limit the impact of these stresses on the SED system by restricting access to data in 1982 and increasing Stasi surveillance.

This transformation, however, also signified new connections and opportunities to advocate for an alternative environmentalism. In the Church, these impulses stemmed from a range of domestic influences and larger changes in central Europe that exposed the SED's (im)balance between ecology and economy. The Church, grassroots concern, international anxiety, and inspiration within the Soviet bloc all resonated with secular and religious, expert and lay East Germans. Still, the motivations were not entirely disparate. Information and environmentalists passed back and forth between party, state, and Church. Whether it was the SED, the Stasi, the MUW, the GNU, the KFH, the Church and Society Committee, or parish-based groups, questions about environmental devastation and the regime that produced it arose. They did so as actors relied on networks that transcended traditional cleavages within the GDR and crossed political boundaries.

Church-based environmentalism revealed the shortcomings of the SED's socialist environmentalism, attracting a range of interested individuals that only grew in the 1980s. Falcke and Gensichen promulgated Christian, theological debates about human interaction with the natural world and connected them to western discussions. Parish-based groups formed in conjunction with the peace movement and in response to local conditions. These circles took off after the peace movement lost momentum in 1983. But Church-based environmentalism also resonated across wide swaths of East German society. In the context of the SED's "socialist environmentalism," the Church offered a different interpretation of human engagement with nature. It defied the SED's rational, progressivist outlook and grounded itself in religious rhetoric that undermined the totalizing claims of the socialist vision. Concerns about the environment in the GDR incorporated a range of critiques and increasingly tied East Germans – if not the leadership – to one another, to nature, and to networks beyond their borders.

CHAPTER 4

Intertwining Environmentalisms: Transboundary Pollution and Protest in Central Europe

Despite the SED's efforts to hide environmental degradation in the GDR and along its borders, activism only proliferated in central Europe after 1982. Border-crossing pollution betrayed the SED's failures to international audiences, pushing the GDR's neighbors to call for greater environmental protection. One of the SED's greatest sources of concern was West Germany. The rise in environmental awareness in the FRG bred public frustration about transboundary pollution, which motivated West German officials to negotiate with the GDR on behalf of West German citizens and the environment. In the 1980s, West German journalists and academics traveled behind the Iron Curtain, uncovering the extent of the devastation that West Germans had only glimpsed before. Much of this information made its way back to the GDR through illicit western radio and television, smuggled print media, and personal contacts. These asymmetrical German–German transfers underscore how pollution and information flowed across the Iron Curtain and challenged the SED's alleged "balance of economy and ecology."[1]

Nonetheless, the East German leadership endeavored to keep up appearances regarding its domestic and international environmental commitments. The party and state created new institutions and opportunities for approved engagement among East Germans, maintaining that environmental protection was "directly tied to realizing the economic strategy of the 1980s."[2] The SED intensified GNU projects, and the state established new bodies, trumpeting them in the press. Founded within the MUW in 1982, the Center for Environmental Development served as the "central

---

[1] BArch-SAPMO DY 27/6113, Dr. Manfred Fiedler, "Gedanken und Feststellungen zur Einschätzung der Entwicklung der Arbeit der GNU im KB im Berichtszeitraum der Abrechnung des Aktionsprogramms zum XI. Parteitag der SED," February 3, 1986.
[2] BArch DO 4/803, "Länderbericht: Deutsche Demokratische Republik," vorgelegt zur Multilateralen Konferenz über die Ursachen und Verhinderung von Wald- und Gewässerschäden durch Luftverschmutzung in Europa, München, June 24–27, 1984, 2.

scientific-technical institution" that implemented environmental policy within the SED's broader plan for the 1980s.[3] Three years later, the State Environmental Inspection brought together trained scientists and volunteers to monitor and improve conditions.[4] These new initiatives strained relations within party and state structures. Stasi investigations of these organizations precipitated distrust among experts, creating the malcontents the Stasi so worried were there.[5]

As the state's responses to environmental degradation rang hollow, the independent movement grew dramatically. The number of individual participants, groups, and activities expanded in the Church and across the GDR. From Schwerin and Rostock in the north to Lusatia and the Erzgebirge in the south, activists gathered to raise consciousness and take action, networking in the Church and through official means. To explore how independent activism spread, this chapter examines three regions – Berlin, Leipzig/Halle, and Lusatia – to highlight the geographic and thematic breadth of the environmental movement.[6] The SED dictatorship restricted engaged individuals' ability to convene publicly and conducted additional surveillance on them. Despite these obstacles, the mid-1980s represented a period of networking and expansion within Church-based circles, drawing on western movements as well as other protest under socialism.

Across the Soviet bloc, environmental activism was already gaining ground in the years before Mikhail Gorbachev came to power in the Soviet Union in 1985. After the end of Martial Law in Poland in 1983, the easing of restrictions permitted greater protests. Transboundary pollution in southwestern Poland yielded particular frustration, as much of the

---

[3] BArch DK 5/4595, Hans Reichelt, "Stellung, Aufgaben und Struktur des Zentrums für Umweltgestaltung," 1985.

[4] Uwe Zuppke, "Aus der Tätigkeit des Zentrums für Umweltgestaltung," in *Umweltschutz in der DDR: Analysen und Zeitzeugenberichte, Band 3: Beruflicher, ehrenamtlicher und freiwilliger Umweltschutz*, eds. Hermann Behrens and Jens Hoffmann (Munich: Oekom, 2008), 73.

[5] BStU MfS HA XX/13945, "Ehrenamtliche Inspekteure der Staatlichen Umweltinspektion," 1986.

[6] Numerous scholars and former activists have emphasized the importance of the Berlin-based groups, overlooking developments across the GDR. Carlo Jordan and Hans Michael Kloth's (eds.) *Arche Nova: Opposition in der DDR, "Das Grün-ökologische Netzwerk Arche,"* 1988–90 (Berlin: BasisDruck, 1995); Wolfgang Rüddenklau 's (ed.) *Störenfried: DDR-Opposition 1986–1989, mit Texten aus den "Umweltblättern"* (Berlin: BasisDruck, 1992). Scholars have furthered this interpretation. Gareth Dale, *Popular Protest in East Germany, 1945–1989* (New York: Routledge, 2005), 124–125; Mary Fulbrook, *Anatomy of a Dictatorship: Inside the GDR, 1949–1989* (New York: Oxford University Press, 1995), 232–234; Nathan Stoltzfus, "Public Space and the Dynamics of Environmental Action: Green Protest in the GDR," *Archiv für Sozialgeschichte* 43 (2003), 399; Dieter Rink, "Environmental Policy and the Environmental Movement in East Germany," *Capitalism, Nature, and Socialism* 13, no. 3 (September 2002), 79–81.

acid rain that destroyed the forest stemmed from East German industry.[7] Poland's relative freedom turned it into a hub for engagement across eastern Europe. Independent and official organizations publicly cooperated, which East German activists envied, but they also benefited from Poland's relative freedom. As in the GDR, environmental groups possessed an assortment of attitudes toward the state and drew from a cross section of society, including experts working for the state and oppositional activists. Starting in 1985, these individuals helped establish and operate Greenway, a network of independent eastern European environmental groups intent on sharing experiences within the bloc. This web of connections proliferated behind and across the Iron Curtain.

The GDR was a link between east and west, connecting it to neighboring states through shared environmental hazards, policies, and protest movements. Moving geographically from west to east, this chapter traces the entangled evolution of policies and protest within the GDR and between the GDR and its neighbors after 1982 and (mostly) prior to Chernobyl in 1986. The chapter first explores growing dismay in the FRG and redoubled attempts to work with the GDR. Next, the chapter looks at responses to pollution in official channels and Church-based circles. The chapter argues that outcries over the environmental situation were not limited to the dissident hotspot of Berlin but emerged across the country and from an array of individuals. Lastly, the chapter demonstrates that environmental protest reawakened in Poland as the PZPR loosened its control over independent organization, making it an obvious node for activism. Ultimately, denunciations of pollution from within and outside the bloc heightened a sense of crisis that transcended political divisions and revealed the ecological interconnectedness of central Europe.

The West German Factor

The "greening" of the FRG systematically shifted domestic and foreign decisions and priorities, leading to renewed efforts to curb German–German environmental degradation. Very real transboundary pollution, such as water quality in the Elbe River and sulfur dioxide emissions, motivated West German officials as well as independent organizations to meet with the East German state as well as develop ties to Church-based

---

[7] BArch DK 5/5829, "Information für den Vorsitzenden des Ministerrates, Willi Stoph, zum Abschluss des Abkommens DDR-VRP-CSSR über die Zusammenarbeit auf dem Gebiet des Umweltschutzes," 1987.

groups. Interactions across the border brought the other side into focus and opened new channels of communication. Through diplomatic meetings, journalists' visits and research, West German media, and more, East and West Germans learned about and from one another. Enhanced contact and mutual exposure produced a more common sense of purpose.[8] A wide range of West German state and non-state actors brought new attention to problems that crossed the German–German border, pressuring the recalcitrant SED to change its ways.

West Germans had contended with East German pollution for decades, a source of dissatisfaction that became more publicized in the 1980s. Contaminated water in border-crossing rivers was one of most common accusations that West German politicians and media leveled against the GDR. East German rivers typically flowed west into the FRG, disproportionately affecting the West German side.[9] Infamously, the Elbe River accumulated significant contamination from heavy metals and chemical spills in northern Bohemia (Czechoslovakia) and the GDR before crossing the Iron Curtain into Lower Saxony and Hamburg, and ultimately the North Sea. For decades, West Germans living in the vicinity of the Elbe had faced unclean waters, spills that killed biological life in the river, and all of the repercussions from that. Instances like the 1976 hydrochloric acid spill into the Jeetze River, a tributary of the Elbe's, were common. Border troops erected barriers to collect the resulting dead fish – the majority of the population in the river – so that West Germans would not realize the extent of the spill.[10] Yet two days later, East German officials determined that the water's acidity could not be sufficiently neutralized, and they finally admitted what had happened to West German counterparts.[11] A year later, the Stasi similarly debated informing the FRG of a pesticide spill in another Elbe tributary, the Mulde.[12]

By the 1980s, West German members of parliament and city officials also reached out to the GDR about the condition of the Elbe. In 1985, the Christian Democratic Union's Dietrich Austermann, a Bundestag

---

[8] Frank Uekötter, *The Greenest Nation? A New History of German Environmentalism* (Cambridge, MA: MIT Press, 2014), 116.

[9] Astrid M. Eckert, *West Germany and the Iron Curtain: Environment, Economy, and Culture in the Borderland* (New York: Oxford University Press, 2019), 126.

[10] BStU HA XVIII 19386, "Information über Fischsterben in der Jeetze, Kreis Salzwedel," September 11, 1976.

[11] BStU HA XVIII 19386, "Information: 1. Ergänzung über Fischsterben in der Jeetze, Kreis Salzwedel," September 13, 1976.

[12] BStU HA XVIII 18216, "Information über Vergiftung der Mulde durch Pflanzenschutzmittel," November 30, 1977.

member, directly contacted East German environmental minister Hans Reichelt to meet about the Elbe. More than once, East Berlin declined to respond to Austermann's overtures.[13] Similarly, a year later, Hamburg's environmental senator, Wolfgang Curilla, attempted to contact Reichelt about the Elbe. He approached Reichelt on behalf of the Working Group for Protection of the Elbe as part of a consortium of water management offices in the three affected states. Again, the GDR denied this request.[14] East German officials commonly refused meetings or declined to respond to West German initiatives, fearing that engagement might be an acknowledgment of the SED's weaknesses. The primary exception to that was if the East German leadership saw an opportunity to gain an advantage, such as through acquiring western technology or hard currency. The SED's approach made real improvements to the Elbe virtually impossible.

In November 1987, a joint protest of West German Greenpeace and East German environmentalists finally forced the SED's hand and brought the GDR to the negotiating table. The activists distributed fliers that revealed the high levels of pollution and their impact on "Dresden-Hamburg-North Sea."[15] They pushed for the GDR and Czechoslovakia to participate in a conference on ecological conditions in the North Sea. Shortly thereafter, in December, the SED agreed to trilateral talks with the FRG and Czechoslovakia to address the Elbe.[16] In the last year or two of the GDR's existence, Honecker and the SED tentatively agreed to work with, or to essentially receive aid from, the FRG to improve the water quality of the Elbe.[17] The West German province of Schleswig-Holstein independently offered help to lower mercury and cadmium levels.[18] These typical tactics from Honecker, Mittag, and the Stasi stymied pollution abatement across the German–German border, despite the GDR's tacit acknowledgment of the degradation.

[13] PA AA M 41 633 89, "Standpunkt zum Anliegen eines Bundestagsabgeordneten der BRD bezüglich eines Gespräches über die Reinhaltung der Elbe," May 20, 1985.

[14] PA AA M 41 812 88, Correspondence between the East German Permanent Diplomatic Mission in Bonn (Glienke) and the FRG Department of the East German Foreign Ministry (Seidel), April 15, 1986.

[15] BStU MfS HA XVIII 21998, "Stellungnahme zu den Flugblättern der Internationalen Umweltschutzorganisation, 'Greenpeace,' die von 5 Mitgliedern der Organisation am 14.11.1987 in Dresden verteilt wurden."

[16] AGG B II 1 567, "Kurzprokoll der 13. Sitzung des Ausschusses für Umwelt, Naturschutz und Reaktorsicherheit," December 9, 1987.

[17] Hermann Wentker, *Außenpolitik in engen Grenzen: Die DDR im internationalen System, 1949–1989* (Munich: Oldenbourg, 2007), 519–520.

[18] BStU MfS HA XVIII 24797, Correspondence between Hans Reichelt and Gunter Mittag, June 5, 1989.

West German politicians and activists similarly advocated for improved water quality in the Werra River, whose water was highly salinized from potash mining.[19] The Werra River flows primarily through Thuringia and across the border into Lower Saxony before emptying into the North Sea north of Bremen. A source of tension between the Germanys for decades, the environmental and German–German ministries in West Germany worked to improve transboundary pollution in the 1980s. Both sides mined for potash in this border region, but the industry's effects disproportionately affected West German waterways. Different from earlier efforts at cooperation, the SED was interested in working together to solve the problem, if only to acquire desirable West German currency and technology.[20] The West German government, along with the three affected provinces (Lower Saxony, Hessen, and Bremen) promised to provide 200 million Deutsch Marks to the process. With Green politician Joschka Fischer as the environmental minister in Hessen, it looked as if discussions would move forward with greater urgency.[21]

The process stalled, though, when Reichelt and other East German officials proved unwilling to make concrete obligations. In October 1987, the two countries had agreed for West German Greens to visit the East German mining operation, but on the day before the visit, Reichelt rescinded the offer, which the Greens considered a strong disservice to both German states. As the Green Party press release concluded, the last-minute cancellation must be understood as an affront, because the Werra, Weser, fish and plants, and above all local residents were in great need of improved conditions.[22] The cooperation moved shakily forward as West Germans provided the means for new equipment, and each side agreed to certain responsibilities.[23] Ultimately, in 1988, the FRG worked with the GDR to supply the technology for an electrostatic separation process and 200 million Marks to install the equipment.[24] These agreements, however, did not have much of an impact on the Werra's pollution, which remained a point of contention until the end of the GDR.

---

[19] Potash generally refers to a variety of potassium-based salts used for various industrial processes.

[20] Eckert, *West Germany and the Iron Curtain*, 254.

[21] "Positiver Ansatz: Ein Erdbeben wurde zum deutschdeutschen Politikum," *Der Spiegel*, March 11, 1985.

[22] RHG OWK/01, "Werra Entsalzung braucht Zusammenarbeit und Dialog – Doch DDR nimmt Zusage an Grüne zurück," Pressemitteilung Nr. 981/87, October 23, 1987.

[23] BStU MfS Rechtsstelle 210, "Beschluß des Politbüros des ZK der SED vom 12. April 1988: Information über den Stand, die Probleme und das weitere Vorgehen zur Gewährleistung der Bergbau- und öffentlichen Sicherheit und zur Rohstoffsicherung im Kalibetrieb 'Werra.'"

[24] Eckert, *West Germany and the Iron Curtain*, 256–257.

A second issue with transnational implications whipped the West German media into a frenzy in the 1980s, namely, Waldsterben (dying of the forest) from acid rain. The phenomenon damaged forests across Europe, but the sense of crisis surrounding it reached nigh panic levels in the FRG.[25] Images of yellow and brittle needles across swaths of German forests, especially in mountainous regions, mobilized a large number of West Germans to advocate for solutions. Fear of forests dying tapped into long-standing traditions of nature conservation and invigorated the Green Party, which organized a major protest against forest decline in 1981.[26] While that gathering focused primarily on West German polluters, most recognized that intensive and often outdated industries in socialist countries contributed significantly to acid rain.[27] The BBU and BUND wrote to Honecker, too, with the BBU sending a delegation to meet with him in 1984.[28] These negotiations mattered greatly, because a significant portion of the FRG's Waldsterben stemmed from sulfur dioxide emissions produced in the GDR and Czechoslovakia. Lignite mining and refining across the GDR became infamous both domestically and internationally.

Professor Martin Jänicke, a political scientist based in West Berlin, figured prominently in publicizing East German emissions and the impact of sulfur dioxide emissions on central Europe. Multipage spreads, such as his 1984 "Death by Smokestack: Air Pollution Reaches Catastrophic Levels in the GDR" in the popular newspaper *Frankfurter Rundschau*, highlighted the harmful effects of East German industry. He recounted a West German expert's recent visit to the Erzgebirge along the East German–Czechoslovak border, in which he witnessed "dead trees for kilometers, which simply cannot be used. Residents have to leave the region; there is no more basis for existence here." Jänicke further clarified that this crisis existed throughout the GDR, southern Poland, and northern Czechoslovakia.[29] In the 1980s, the pollution and public health crisis in northern Bohemia was so bad that residents received an annual subsidy,

---

[25] Birgit Metzger, *"Erst stirbt der Wald, dann Du!" Das Waldsterben als westdeutsches Politikum (1978–1968)* (Frankfurt am Main: Campus Verlag, 2015), 17. Franz-Josef Brüggemeier, "Waldsterben: The Construction and Deconstruction of an Environmental Problem," in *Nature in German History*, ed. Christof Mauch (New York: Berghahn Books, 2004), 119–131.

[26] Ibid., 119–120.

[27] Simo Laakkonen, Viktor Pal, and Richard Tucker, "The Cold War and Environmental History: Complementary Fields," *Cold War History* 16, no. 4 (Fall 2016), 380–381.

[28] AGG B II 1/1766, "Gesprächsnotiz von einem Treffen mit Gunnar Seitz vom geschäftsführenden Vorstand des BBU über die DDR-Reise der BBU-Delegation, der er angehörte (7.9.84)."

[29] Copy found in Petra Kelly Archiv (PKA) A Kelly 333, Martin Jänicke, "Der Tod aus dem Schornstein: In der DDR nimmt die Luftverschmutzung allmählich katastrophale Formen an," *Frankfurter Rundschau*, January 28, 1984. Jänicke was an environmental policy adviser for the

which locals cynically referred to as their "burial bonus."[30] In another newspaper article later that year, Jänicke returned to the topic of sulfur dioxide emissions, stating that the air pollution not only disastrously killed trees but resulted in higher instances of illness among residents of southern East Germany.[31] The implications for the FRG were obvious, furthering the Waldsterben panic and generating concern across political boundaries.

In response, the West German government enlisted experts to share desulfurization technology with their socialist neighbors for the "sake of the population" and the forests.[32] The GDR approved of these deals, because they typically brought in hard currency from the west – something the SED was desperate for by the mid-1980s – as well as new technology.[33] The Czechoslovak leadership also welcomed the increased contact with the FRG and West German willingness to share desulfurization processes for coal-burning power plants.[34] Despite a deepening environmental commitment, socialist countries, and the GDR in particular, continued to deny the extent of the pollution. As the BBU delegation discovered in 1984, the SED categorically denied the existence of Waldsterben and strictly forbade the term. One of the BBU delegates noted after the fact the phones in their hotel rooms had been disconnected so that they could not contact western media outlets during the visit.[35] Even two years later, Honecker explicitly stated in a West German interview that dying forests ("*sterbende Wälder*," not "Waldsterben") were something East Germans did not understand. Though the GDR faced some damage to trees along the Czechoslovak border, "our forests are healthy. Also, there is no 'acid rain' here either."[36] Thus, the GDR accepted West German aid while also attempting to obscure actual conditions.

Alternative List in West Berlin (a party that would later join with the Green Party) from 1981 to 1983 before receiving his chair at the Free University.

[30] Eagle Glassheim, "Building a Socialist Environment: Czechoslovak Environmental Policy from the 1960s to the 1980s," in *Nature and the Iron Curtain: Environmental Policy and Social Movements in Communist and Capitalist Countries, 1945–1990*, eds. Astrid Mignon Kirchhof and J.R. McNeill (Pittsburgh, PA: University of Pittsburgh Press, 2019), 149.

[31] Copy found in Petra Kelly Archiv (PKA) A Kelly 334, Martin Jänicke, "Die real existierende Luftverschmutzung in der DDR," *Tages Allgemeine Zeitung*, November 6, 1984.

[32] PA AA M 41 633 89, Correspondence between Oskar Fischer and Hans Reichelt, February 14, 1985.

[33] PA AA M 41 631, "Vorschläge zur weiteren Entwicklung der Beziehungen zwischen der DDR und der BRD bzw. Westberlin auf dem Gebiet des Umweltschutzes," April 4, 1984.

[34] PA AA M 41 633 89, Unofficial Translation (of a summary of West German–Czechoslovak negotiations), Prague, February 1, 1985.

[35] AGG B II 1 1766, "Gesprächsnotiz von einem Treffen mit Gunnar Seitz," September 7, 1984.

[36] "Das Interview Erich Honeckers für die BRD-Wochenzeitung," *Die Zeit*, published in *Neues Deutschland*, January 31, 1986, 3.

Despite the SED's restrictions, information about the East German situation circulated as West German visitors, journalists, and activists educated Germans on either side of the border. West German journalist Peter Wensierski, for example, authored numerous books on society and the environment in the GDR.[37] His radio interviews, especially for West Berlin's Radio in the American Sector (RIAS), became so damaging that the SED specifically cited him as a reason for classifying environmental data in 1982.[38] Hubertus Knabe, son of Green politician Wilhelm Knabe, researched related topics, focusing on the rise of independent groups in the Protestant Church from a sociological perspective. Through personal contacts, he informed West Germans while also enlightening East Germans about various developments. Over the course of the 1980s, H. Knabe gave numerous interviews on West German radio about the Church groups' ambitions for "ecology over economy" as opposed to the SED's rhetoric about balancing the two.[39] Personal contacts, travel abroad, and West German media all transmitted knowledge about East German degradation to a range of audiences.

For many West Germans, however, the GDR remained foreign, placing the onus on East Germans to explain the differences in activism under dictatorship versus a democracy. In a letter to a Greenpeace chapter in Hamburg in 1984, two Church-based environmentalists in Leipzig enlightened the West Germans as to the practical realities of life in a dictatorship. They explained that if Greenpeace sent a letter with the logo on it, the authorities would immediately open it; there was no right to privacy.[40] They further described the difficulties of raising awareness when it was illegal to publicly display bulletins or photos of sludgy rivers or dying forests; nor could they freely publish materials to inform citizens about the devastation.[41] These complications inhibited their ability to effect change or policy, inducing them to work within the system, such as participating in the GNU, rather than fight against it. The authors illustrated disparities

[37] In the 1970s and 1980s, Wensierski published numerous books on the GDR, including *Beton ist Beton: Zivilisationskritik aus der DDR* (Hattingen: Scandica-Verlag, 1981), *Null Bock auf DDR: Aussteigerjugend im anderen Deutschland* (Reinbek bei Hamburg: Rowohlt, 1984), and *Von oben nach unten wächst gar nichts: Umweltzerstörung und Protest in der DDR* (Frankfurt: Fischer Verlag, 1986).

[38] BArch DK 5/1982, "Bericht über Probleme des Geheimnisschutzes bei Informationen zum Umweltschutz," October 25, 1982.

[39] RHG HK 01, Hubertus Knabe, "'Erste Hilfe für die Umwelt': Ökologisches Engagement in den evangelischen Kirchen der DDR," *Bayerischer Rundfunk*, September 26, 1983.

[40] Archiv Bürgerbewegung Leipzig (ABL) 22.14, Letter to Wolfgang Lohbeck, Hamburg (Greenpeace member), December 18, 1984.

[41] Ibid.

in a social movement's opportunities under a dictatorship, even as they sought information and materials from the other side.

Within the West German Green Party, questions about the GDR's diplomatic status complicated environmental cooperation.[42] Leftist political positions made some Green politicians sympathetic to the SED project and accordingly hesitant to criticize the GDR. Party leaders like Lothar Probst and Jürgen Schnappertz pushed for a transformation from "Germany policy" to "German–German relations," in an attempt to acknowledge the reality of the Cold War divide. They viewed Green policies toward the GDR as a means of democratizing the dictatorship through foreign policy.[43] Some of those deeply involved in policy toward the GDR included Elisabeth Weber, Schnappertz, and Dirk Schneider, though Schneider was later revealed as a longtime unofficial collaborator for the Stasi.[44] Despite the Greens being the only West German political party to promise the GDR full diplomatic recognition, the East German situation did not comprise the core of the Greens' agenda.[45]

The position of the Greens' most outspoken leader, Petra Kelly, in relation to the GDR reflected some of the complications that the party faced in engaging with their socialist neighbor. Devoted to the peace movement in the early 1980s, Kelly became a point of contact between East German dissidents and the Greens. She championed the signing of "personal peace treaties," in which East and West Germans individually swore not to fight each other. In 1983, on a visit to the GDR, Kelly and a delegation of Greens tried to commit Honecker to signing a treaty.[46] He declined. Regardless, Kelly's efforts reflected the tone of the Greens' relationship to the GDR. Still, Kelly used her contacts established in this period and remained a supporter of peace and opposition circles in the GDR throughout the 1980s. Despite networking with feminist and peace groups and having personal friendships with many of their members, the West German Greens' engagement with the environment remained somewhat piecemeal.

---

[42] Roland Roth and Detlef Murphy, "From Competing Factions to the Rise of the Realos," in *The German Greens: Paradox between Movement and Party*, eds. Margit Mayer and John Ely (Philadelphia, PA: Temple University Press, 1998), 49–71.

[43] AGG B II 1/1766, "Entwurf eines Grundsatzpapiers: Ansätze und Perspektiven Grüner Politik in den deutsch-deutschen Beziehungen," 1983–1984.

[44] "Fürst von Kreuzberg: Agenten des DDR-Ministeriums für Staatssicherheit steuerten Grüne und westdeutsche Friedensfreunde," *Der Spiegel*, November 11, 1991, 80.

[45] Jens Gieseke and Andrea Bahr, *Die Staatssicherheit und die Grünen* (Berlin: Ch. Links Verlag, 2017), 71.

[46] PKA A 077, "Presse Berichte und Zeitungs-/Zeitschriftenartikel zu DDR und Besuch der Grünen 31.10/1.11.1983."

The Greens also lent practical support to activists, such as criticizing the SED when the Stasi harassed oppositional figures, rather than only engaging in high-level diplomacy. In April 1985, the Stasi imprisoned Udo Zeitz for "denigration" of the republic after condemning pollution in Biesenthal. Green Party parliamentary spokesperson Hannegret Hönes released an open appeal to Honecker. Declaring that Zeitz was only trying to "improv[e] the quality of life in his ecologically endangered hometown," Hönes expressed dismay that his actions could be interpreted negatively by the state.[47] She further argued that personal engagement with an important cause was exemplary, not punishable, and called for his release. When the major West German news weekly, *Der Spiegel*, picked up Zeitz's story in May, the SED came under international pressure.[48] Support for East German activists bolstered cross-border networks and posed new questions about accountability and legitimacy for the SED.

At the same time, the West German government pushed the GDR on environmental issues and their centrality to German–German relations through international avenues. At the landmark Economic Commission for Europe conference in Munich in 1984, thirty-four countries from across Europe – including the GDR, Czechoslovakia, and Poland, among others – convened to address the environment. Environmental and interior ministers committed themselves to working on the "causes and prevention of forest and water damage from air pollution in Europe."[49] On behalf of the GDR, Reichelt pledged to reduce sulfur dioxide levels by thirty percent by 1993 at the conference, a surprisingly concrete obligation to make on an international stage. His decision stemmed from a 1983 plan he had developed for desulfurization of coal.[50] In the short term, East German newspapers lauded the progressive step.[51] Officials viewed it as "responsible environmental policy" and as a logical extension of the 1975 Helsinki Accords.[52]

---

[47] RHG OWK 01, "Pressemitteilung Nr. 314/85," May 30, 1985.
[48] "Ständig Treibel: Grüner Protest ist in der DDR unerwünscht: Eine Umwelt-Initiative wurde zerschlagen, ihr Gründer kaltgestellt und festgenommen," *Der Spiegel* 1985, http://magazin .spiegel.de/EpubDelivery/spiegel/pdf/13514913, accessed June 20, 2018.
[49] AGG B II 3 1172, "Multilaterale Umweltkonferenz in München, vom 24. bis 27. Juni 1984," Presse- und Informationsamt der Bundesregierung, Nr. 79/S.697, June 30, 1984.
[50] Tobias Huff, *Natur und Industrie im Sozialismus: Eine Umweltgeschichte der DDR* (Göttingen: Vandenhoeck & Ruprecht, 2015), 265.
[51] AGG B II 3 1172, "Hauptziele der DDR-Umweltpolitik," veröffentlicht in *Der Morgen (LDPD)*, Ost-Berlin, no. 150, June 27, 1984.
[52] BArch DO 4/803, "Deutsche Demokratische Republik: Länderbericht, vorgelegt zur Multilateralen Konferenz über Ursache und Verhinderung von Wald- und Gewässerschäden durch Luftverschmutzung in Europa, München, 24.–27. Juni 1984."

Following through on emissions reduction in the long term, however, proved impossible. East German officials deflected responsibility, claiming that achieving the goal depended on other countries decisively implementing measures to lower sulfur dioxide levels. They blamed neighboring countries rather than acknowledge their own lack of filters and processes to reduce emissions.[53] To ward off any accusations, the GDR jealously guarded its environmental data and refused to ratify the subsequent Helsinki Protocol, which twenty-one countries signed in 1985.[54] The GDR continued to rely on low quality lignite, rendering the thirty percent pledge futile.[55] Western pressure and international agreements called into question the GDR's handling of the environmental situation in the 1980s, forcing the East German leadership to crack down on foreign and domestic critics of its policies. This repression only handed them additional fodder, however, and weakened the SED's overall credibility.

Domestic Efforts and their Limits

While the party and state faced real challenges from abroad, they nevertheless continued to profess their commitment to the environment at home. Both the SED and state structures further developed institutions and programs throughout the 1980s and widely touted them in the state-run media to boost the GDR's environmental image.[56] Most significantly, the MUW created a new Center for Environmental Development in 1982, and in collaboration with the Cultural League, a voluntary State Environmental Inspection in 1985. To complicate matters, the GDR's signing of the 1984 Munich Agreement strained already underfunded programs.[57] Experts tried to reconcile their training and official promises with the reality of environmental degradation, but with no real investment, many became frustrated with the system in which they worked.

---

[53] BArch DK 5/3386, "Information über das Protokoll zur Reduzierung des Schwefeldioxidausstoßes um 30 Prozent," undated.

[54] Eckert, West Germany and the Iron Curtain, 149.

[55] RHG Th 02/08, "Aus 'Umwelt,' 4/83, Dr. Cord Schwartau, 'Umweltschutz in der DDR. Zunehmende Luftverschmutzung durch Renaissance der Braunkohle?' Fassung des DIW Wochenberichte, 4/1983."

[56] Huff, Natur und Industrie im Sozialismus, 263–264.

[57] BArch DK 5/3386, "Korrektur der an die ECE übergebenen Daten und der im Statistischen Jahrbuch der DDR veröffentlichten Angaben zu Schwefeldioxid und Stickoxiden der DDR einschließlich der Strategie zu deren Minderung (Rauchgasentschwefelung)," November 21, 1989.

The same year the state restricted access to data, the MUW established a center dedicated to improving the environment as part of the GDR's technological avant-garde. With Hans Lütke as director, the new Center for Environmental Development (*Zentrum für Umweltgestaltung*, ZUG) employed 225 scientists, who worked at five locations across the GDR, and collected and analyzed data from different entities within the MUW.[58] The Center monitored pollution levels, evaluated potential dangers for the population and the economy, and alleviated them where possible.[59] ZUG scientists worked most closely with the Meteorological Service and the State Hygiene Inspection, which monitored air pollution and its impact on humans. After the Munich Agreement in 1984, they also set up state monitoring stations.[60] The ZUG further made policy recommendations to high level party and state officials about how to include the environment in the SED's economic planning.[61] Newspapers touted the ZUG's work, such as technology for low-waste and waste-free production, insisting its processes had international acclaim.[62]

Scientists in the institute perennially complained about insufficient funding, and the data they collected was incredibly damning, which belied the SED's optimistic rhetoric.[63] Secret reports collected between 1976 and 1988 detailed rising sulfur dioxide emissions in at least five of the GDR's districts (Berlin, Cottbus, Dresden, Karl-Marx-Stadt, and Leipzig). These areas represented the most densely populated parts of the GDR, indicating that a significant percentage of East Germans lived in highly polluted conditions and suffered from higher rates of respiratory infections.[64] Data gathered over the 1980s indicated that roughly ten percent of drinking water contained levels of nitrates and other pollutants that exceeded MUW regulations. According to the ZUG's own calculations, some 450,000 East Germans consumed water containing nitrates and another 1.7 million drank water that held various contaminants. Scientists further blamed industry and agriculture for improperly using fertilizers, pesticides, and other nitrogen compounds that poisoned the groundwater.[65] These reports illuminated the expertise at hand as well as the structural inertia

---

[58] Huff, *Natur und Industrie im Sozialismus*, 263.
[59] Zuppke, "Aus der Tätigkeit des Zentrums für Umweltgestaltung," 73.
[60] Huff, *Natur und Industrie im Sozialismus*, 264–267.
[61] BArch DK 5/4595, "Stellung, Aufgaben und Struktur des Zentrums für Umweltgestaltung," 1986.
[62] Prof. Dr.-Ing. Manfred Schubert, "Auf den Halden liegen noch zu viele Schätze," *Neues Deutschland*, June 16, 1984, 12.
[63] Zuppke, "Aus der Tätigkeit des Zentrums für Umweltgestaltung," 73.
[64] BArch DK 5/1347, "Analyse der Umweltbedingungen – DDR, 1976–1988," October 31, 1989, 18.
[65] Ibid., 19–20.

that impeded action. Much of the data they collected only officially came to light in the "Environmental Report of the GDR" that was published in 1990 as the GDR disintegrated.[66]

As a scientific center, the ZUG also took a principal role technological innovation to alleviate environmental problems. Drawing on language developed in the 1970s, the ZUG focused on "low waste production" processes in industry, the reapplication of "secondary raw materials," and the use of "more renewable natural resources, especially air, water, soil, and eco-systems."[67] Under Lütke, the ZUG presented its recommendations to the Council of Ministers' Advisory Committee for Environmental Protection, offering pointed commentary on the need to reduce energy consumption in absolute terms and to more efficiently use areas of production, prioritizing landfills and waste heaps.[68] They further highlighted the importance of developing economical and effective desulfurization processes for lignite, especially a limestone additive to absorb sulfur oxides.[69] Explanations of the improvements' benefits did not gain traction with planners, reinforcing the imbalance between economy and ecology.

Despite internal frustration in the ZUG, its experts were still expected to engage with Church-based groups on behalf of the state. These meetings became more hostile over the 1980s as official and independent interpretations of the environmental situation increasingly diverged. ZUG officials addressed petitions and deflected complaints, leading their offices in Berlin to become a site of negotiation and confrontation.[70] Activist Wolfgang Rüddenklau was among those invited to discuss a petition he had submitted in January 1984. Building on earlier petitions and meetings with the same ZUG bureaucrats, Rüddenklau and his cosigners articulated their problems with the coal industry and its many repercussions on the Cottbus and Leipzig areas. Lütke and his colleagues provided formulaic responses about impending new technology for desulfurization. Rüddenklau countered that they had stumbled upon various contradictions between what ZUG officials told them and what they personally observed. As such, they did not believe new technology was imminent.[71] With no substantive resolution, the petitioners requested another audience,

[66] *Umweltbericht der DDR: Information zur Analyse der Umweltbedingungen in der DDR und zu weiteren Maßnahmen* (West Berlin: Institut für Umweltschutz, 1990).
[67] BArch DK 500/22, "Ausgewählte Aufgaben des Planes Wissenschaft und Technik auf dem Gebiet des Umweltschutzes und der rationellen Wasserverwendung im Zeitraum 1986 bis 1990 und darüber hinaus," November 20, 1984.
[68] Ibid.   [69] BArch DK 5/5111, "Ergebnisse und Probleme im Umweltschutz der DDR," 1984.
[70] RHG B 08, Letter to Wolfgang Rüddenklau from Lütke, January 1984.
[71] RHG Th 02/06, "Eingabe: Betr.: die Waldschäden im Erzgebirge. Ihre l. Antwort auf unsere frühere Eingabe, gegeben am 2.12.83 in Ihrem Institut," January 27, 1984.

which was set for later that year, but both sides left that meeting unsatisfied, too. The status of the environment fractured East German society along a range of fault lines that the SED struggled to identify and address.

Within the ZUG, divisions deepened over the lack of response to the environmental devastation they documented. As officials defended state actions to Church-based activists, the Center's administration and the Stasi began to doubt the ZUG scientists' loyalty. As it turned out, they were somewhat justified in their concern. In December 1987, someone on the staff at the ZUG in the Environmental Planning department wrote a letter to the attorney general of East Berlin about the "illegal" operation of a heating and power plant in Berlin-Rummelsburg. The author was a trained lawyer and long-time party member, who cited recent news articles as well as the Landeskultur Law regarding the unlawful functioning of the plant (without proper desulfurization filters).[72] His behavior prompted an internal inquiry. The concluding report determined that the author had not betrayed classified information but suspected he and a coworker of undermining the "credibility of environmental policy in the GDR."[73]

The coworker formally withdrew from the SED in December 1987, the same month that the lawyer submitted his letter to the attorney general, compounding the perceived need for an investigation. The coworker explained his decision by insisting that he did not have time to fulfill his party responsibilities and obligations. In fact, he had been considering leaving the SED for two years. The report claimed that he had already been critical of the regime for a long time, tended to have one-sided opinions, and generally believed the work was mostly senseless.[74] More problematic for the ZUG was the fact that he openly doubted the MUW's ability to execute the policy and thought it all formalities and whitewashing. Moreover, his frequent visits to West Berlin made him politically unreliable and a threat to the ZUG's objectives.[75] The two malcontents, along with other likeminded colleagues, revealed the GDR's weaknesses. They exposed how hollow the SED's claim rang even from within. The tension between scientists and the repressive system in which they functioned underscores the SED's desperation as well as its unwillingness to implement the reforms that its own experts proposed.

---

[72] BArch DK 5/5624, "Hausmitteilung von Inspektion an Genossen Minister Dr. Reichelt," January 12, 1988.
[73] Ibid.   [74] Ibid.   [75] Ibid.

Their actions prompted an investigation of the entire Center, suggesting that the SED and ZUG leadership viewed morale as a serious concern. In cooperation with the Stasi, the inquiry examined the political loyalty and behaviors of selected personnel at the ZUG.[76] Looking at multiple sites – Berlin, Wittenberg, and Cottbus – the assessment regarded the workers as "focused on specific tasks requiring technical expertise but lacking a foundational knowledge of political-ideological" positions. Additionally, the Stasi determined that the majority of employees were prone to "rumors, conjecture, speculation, and unrealistic ideas, which were partially propagated in the ZUG itself." The report then analyzed the contributions of fourteen coworkers, including secretaries and language interpreters. The Stasi went so far as to scrutinize the department head, Dr. Egon Seidel, even though he was known for his strict party-line mentality and was therefore "demonized in Church circles."[77] The SED's preoccupation with political stability bred distrust of scientists, ignoring their expertise and undermining the state's claims to environmental protection.

The report notably expressed anxiety over specialists' international contacts, despite the fact that representing the GDR abroad was part of the ZUG's intended purpose. The colleague in charge of international relations was deemed to be "ready to compromise on ideology," strongly influenced by reforms (glasnost and perestroika) in the Soviet Union, and impressed by the successes of western environmentalism.[78] Another delinquent colleague took part in the United Nations Environment Program in 1986 and 1987. During that time, he became involved with a Mexican woman and only broke off contact with her when pressured to do so.[79] Apparently, his disillusionment reached a breaking point in April 1989, when he did precisely what security forces feared: he defected. After attending an international fair in the FRG in April 1989, he decided not to return.[80] The ZUG's scientists became the malcontents the Stasi had always feared them to be.

This tension between expertise and loyalty also played out in the State Environmental Inspection (*Staatliche Umweltinspektion*, SU), which the MUW established in 1985. Without a sufficient budget or commitment from political leadership, the SU was formed to take up the task of

---

[76] BArch DK 5/5624, "Einschätzung zur aktuellen politisch-ideologischen Lage und zu Verhaltensweisen ausgewählter Kader des ZUG," November 28, 1988.
[77] Ibid.   [78] Ibid.   [79] Ibid.
[80] BStU MfS HA XVIII 27513, "HINWEIS über die Nichtrückkehr eines Abteilungsleiters des MUW von einer Dienstreise in die BRD," April 1989.

collecting data without additional jobs. The inspection was professional-ized on the national level but relied on approved volunteers at the district level and below.[81] In recruiting voluntary inspectors, many of whom participated in the Cultural League's GNU, the ministry struggled to determine who was politically trustworthy enough to collect classified data. The SU's position at the intersection of party-run organizations, science, and popular frustration quickly transformed it into a space for contesting access to environmental knowledge.

From its founding, applicants to be SU volunteer inspectors did not match the MUW's vision, because engaged individuals came from a wide range of backgrounds. The SU imagined the data gatherers would be loyal scientists with a passion for nature who participated organizations such as the GNU and were highly trained. To tap inspectors, the MUW worked with district-level GNU chapters to select inspectors. They had to be at least eighteen years old and "of qualified personality and training," mean-ing that they were educated in a technical or scientific field and had knowledge of economics. Finally, the GNU recommended volunteers from its ranks in order to control who had access to the information.[82] Despite being dependent on volunteers, the data's classified status made the screening process rigorous and political. The district council could revoke an inspector's badge if he or she became a "liability to the proper measuring of data."[83] Finding inspectors who would not reveal damaging information to the general public, especially to West German media, was essential.

Despite structural obstacles, the SU's voluntary inspectors in East Berlin moved swiftly to improve conditions and hold polluters accountable. They found that nine plants exceeded emissions limits. The state then charged them 129,000 Marks in fines, of which 26,400 Marks went back into unspecified Landeskultur projects.[84] These fines were minimal and did nothing to deter various industries from further violations, but the SU's ambitiousness annoyed officials, who complained that it was above all members of the GNU acting as inspectors who pushed for the fines. After that, the Stasi increasingly scrutinized the SU's volunteers. It sought

---

[81] BArch-SAPMO DY 27/6113, "Entwurf: Anordnung: Über die Zulassung und Tätigkeit ehrenam-tlicher Inspekteure der Staatlichen Umweltinspektion bei den Räten der Bezirke vom_____," February 1987.
[82] Ibid. [83] Ibid.
[84] BStU MfS BV Berlin AKG 72, Budnick, "Information zum Stand des Aufbaus der Staatlichen Umweltinspektion, den Ergebnissen des Umweltschutzes 1986 und über die Zusammenarbeit mit der Gesellschaft für Natur und Umwelt," April 20, 1987, 2.

to ensure that information remained secret and that inspectors did not get overly ambitious in pursing environmental objectives. The MUW and the Stasi wanted data collectors, not individuals who would interpret and judge what they found.

Determining candidates' worthiness became fraught for the GNU, as dual participants who took part in both independent and official organizations applied to become inspectors.[85] In the case of Dr. Christian Hönemann, his technical knowledge and standing in the community were valued. Additionally, he was well versed in the complications surrounding open-pit mining, the combustion of lignite, and their health complications.[86] Hönemann, however, also worked with the Church-based *Christliches Umweltseminar Rötha* (CUR) , which publicly reprimanded the SED's inaction. The CUR organized the campaign, "A Mark for Espenhain," which collected donations for a nearby beneficiation plant that the state refused to update.[87] Hönemann was ultimately approved to become an inspector but not without much consideration on the part of the state. Much to the SU's consternation, finding competent and loyal inspectors was not as straightforward as its leadership had hoped.

The SU had to draw the line somewhere and rejected applicants they deemed too questionable. Stefan Plaszkorski, for example, was a member of Torgau's GNU as well as the town's Church-based group. He tried more than once to become an inspector for the SU and was denied each time. His initial application was rejected by the district level official in Leipzig, who claimed that "We must guarantee an optimal operation across the entire district and can only consider a limited portion of the applications."[88] But Plaszkorski doubted the inspector, because he continued to hear calls for volunteer inspectors on the radio and television. He reapplied six months later, asserting that he wished to participate in the GDR's "socialist democracy" and citing the continuing shortage of volunteers.[89] The SU's refused him again. Most likely, Plaszkorski's association with Church-based activity was the reason for his rejection; fear of "oppositional and hostile-negative" forces in Church-based groups outweighed the need for

[85] ABL 39.6.01, "Ehrenamtlicher Inspekteur der Staatlichen Umweltinspektion, 7.3.1988."

[86] ABL 39.6.16, "Informationsmaterial," and "Braunkohlenverarbeitung und Umweltschutz," 1988.

[87] RGH TH 02/03, "Eine Mark für Espenhain oder Ein Protest bekommt Flügel," 1988.

[88] ABL Stefan Plaszkorski 42.3.5, "Ausübung der Tätigkeit als ehrenamtlicher Inspekteur der Staatlichen Umweltinspektion," April 5, 1988.

[89] ABL Stefan Plaszkorski 42.3.5, "Betrifft: Ausübung der Tätigkeit als ehrenamtlicher Inspekteur der Staatlichen Umweltinspektion," October 9, 1988.

inspectors.[90] The state's restrictions on participation inadvertently divulged insecurities about the GDR's environmental record, and by extension its political stability.

The SU made concessions, though, in order to obtain the required number of inspectors. A Halle-based SU employee, Dr. Neuhofer, found his patience tested when university students pushed him on degradation. They condemned the general lack of information and called for better waste disposal and noise reduction. Neuhofer tried to highlight successes, such as a reduction in chlorine emissions in Bitterfeld between 1971 and 1987, but the students remained unimpressed with these meager improvements.[91] Neuhofer then pressed for more people to be involved in protecting the environment and tried to recruit new inspectors, suggesting that he was willing to work with dual participants as long as their work in all Church circles was "clean."[92] Unlike Plaszkorski's experience in Leipzig, the SU in Halle recognized the need to compromise but illuminated the arbitrary decision-making process that fueled resentment of official channels. The SED failed in its attempt to hold a monopoly on environmental engagement.

Broadening the Base

As Hönemann, Plaszkorski, and the Halle students all indicate, by the mid-1980s, Church-based environmental groups were prevalent across the GDR. They formed in response to local conditions but also networked with one another to share concerns and information. The more these Church-based circles expanded, the more they challenged the primacy of official narratives and countered with their own research, observation, and understanding of environmentalism.[93] Taking East Berlin, Leipzig, and Lusatia as cases of environmental degradation and Church-based protest, patterns of discontent emerge and connect seemingly disparate regions

---

[90] BStU MfS BV Berlin AKG 72, "Arbeitshinweise über die Entwicklung, Pläne, Absichten und Aktivitäten gegnerischer und feindlich-negativer Kräfte zur Schaffung einer sogenannten Ökologie- und Umweltschutzbewegung in der DDR und deren operative Bekämpfung," October 22, 1985.

[91] Stadtarchiv Halle A 3.18 Nr. 148, Memo "Staatliche Umweltschutzinspektion Halle," undated.

[92] Ibid.

[93] In a sense, their work was not unlike the "counter experts" in the FRG, who challenged government and scientific authorities' arguments for nuclear technology, among other issues. Dolores Augustine, *Taking on Technocracy: Nuclear Power in Germany, 1945 to the Present* (New York: Berghahn Press, 2018), 74–75. Jens Ivo Engels, *Naturpolitik in der Bundesrepublik: Ideenwelt und politische Verhaltensstile in Naturschutz und Umweltbewegung, 1950–1980* (Paderborn: Ferdinand Schöningh, 2006), 330–331.

across the GDR. This grassroots networking strengthened the movement domestically and internationally.

In East Berlin, urban ecology and provocative political action greatly shaped the character of environmental protest. Some in East Berlin already had a reputation for developing a political opposition, stemming primarily from the peace movement.[94] They considered themselves to be part of an opposition, and in light of their role in the fall of 1989, these circles have received significant public and scholarly attention.[95] Flouting the SED's authority, more than the KFH, for example, the Berlin-based groups created a different type of space for activists and widened opportunities for participation beyond those who identified as Christians. Many of the new recruits were less invested in the Church's theological engagement with nature and more interested in utilizing the relative freedom it provided for organizing. Berlin-based groups engaged with these multiple strains of activism and became a vital node in the environmental network, gathering and disseminating information to and from other regions.

Leveraging existing interest in the fading peace movement, the "Peace and Environmental Circle" incorporated ecological questions at its inaugural meeting in Berlin-Lichtenberg in 1983. The Circle argued that destruction of nature through militarism and oppression contradicted God's command to love your neighbor as yourself; they also pointed to the "growing danger of atomic self-destruction."[96] Even before the 1986 nuclear disaster at Chernobyl, the Berlin-Lichtenberg group held seminars to remember the victims of Hiroshima and Nagasaki and to interrogate the impact of nuclear technology on peace and the environment.[97] The activists tied the nuclear question and overconsumption in modern industrial society through the expansion of energy use needed to produce "unnecessary" material goods.[98] Unsurprisingly, the participants framed their involvement similarly to the KFH's Earth. They drew on theological and anti-consumption arguments to formulate a common critique and expose a broken system.

---

[94] Detlef Pollack, *Politischer Protest: Politisch alternative Gruppen in der DDR* (Opladen: Leske + Budrich, 2000), 123–125.

[95] Dale, *Popular Protest*; Jordan and Kloth, eds., *Arche Nova*; Pollack, *Politischer Protest*; Rüddenklau, ed., *Störenfried*; Stoltzfus, "Public Space and the Dynamics of Environmental Action."

[96] RHG RG/B 08, "Plattform des Friedens- und Umweltkreises," June 28, 1983.

[97] RHG RG/B 08, "Das Friedensseminar zum Gedenken an die Opfer des Atombombenabwurf auf Hiroshima und Nagasaki, 11. und 12. August," undated.

[98] RHG RG/B 08, "Plattform des Friedens- und Umweltkreises," June 28, 1983. These types of concerns can be understood as echoes of the "life reform" movements from the early twentieth century, which questioned the first wave of consumerism.

The Circle's members also advocated for a more environmentally aware lifestyle to combat East Berlin's constant pollution. Wolfgang Rüddenklau and Christian Halbrock authored numerous petitions on Berlin-specific topics, such as the development of urban ecology. They requested, for example, more bicycle paths and higher quality replacement parts, so they could be "mobile without cars." These petitions echoed both a campaign that Church-based activists began in 1981 and a bicycle demonstration that took place in East Berlin in July 1982.[99] Halbrock further spearheaded petitions about air quality near Lichtenberg's coal-powered energy plant, VEB Elektrokohle.[100] Using Berlin's unique status as a divided city, Halbrock inquired why West Berlin received "Smog-Alarms" but East Berlin did not. Officials sidestepped that question, only responding that concrete steps had been taken to lower the concentration of pollutants on the day in question.[101] The proximity of West German environmentalism gave protestors concrete alternatives to East German solutions and accordingly supported a more confrontational approach.[102]

A second Berlin collective, the Ecology Working Group, crucially linked environmentalists from across the GDR and expanded the movement's reach. It began as a suborganization within the larger Friedrichsfelde Peace Circle but conducted the important work of sharing hard to attain information and reducing the sense of isolation among independent environmentalists. In 1984, the group started hosting "Eco-Seminars," the first of which boasted between 200 and 250 people from Berlin and many other cities. Given the limitations of gathering in the SED dictatorship, this turnout reflected a distinct interest in the topic. The participants convened to discuss the theme "Life in the City," delving into how to live amid the filth and the stress of an urban setting.[103] Traffic, dying plants and flowers, worsening air quality, and the destruction of buildings and monuments

---

[99] RHG RG/B 08, "Eingabe an das Ministerium für Handel und Versorgung," October 30, 1985. RHG Ki 03/02, "Gerechtigkeit, Frieden und die Bewahrung der Schöpfung." "Aktionen der DDR-Umwelt-Bewegung," Photo: Robert Havemann Gesellschaft/Johannes Bittner, www .jugendopposition.de/themen/145389/ddr-umweltbewegung?video=145150, accessed February 21, 2019.

[100] BArch DK 5/5155, "Schwerpunktprobleme auf dem Gebiet des Umweltschutzes in der Hauptstadt Berlin," 1976.

[101] RHG RG/B 08, "Eingabe vom 11.1.1985" and response on February 22, 1985.

[102] RHG Ki 18/02, "Die Karteibroschüre der kirchlichen Umweltgruppen in der DDR: Stand vom November 1988."

[103] The Stasi report on the event suggested only about 180 people attended, though it noted that sixty (or roughly one third) came from outside of Berlin. BStU MfS/BV Bln AKG 3275, "Information, Nr. 28/84. Über den Ablauf des sogenannten 'Ökologie-Seminars' vom 28. Bis 30. 9. 1984 in der Kirchengemeinde Berlin-Friedrichsfelde-Ost," October 5, 1984.

from air quality were among the conveners' top complaints. The attendees claimed that the cityscape's hectic and stressful lifestyle combined with monotony and lack of communication contributed to a sense of alienation that had implications on their health and quality of life.[104] The seminars embraced a broad definition of ecology, viewing humans, nature, and the built environment as interconnected, such that a shared sense of responsibility was essential to improvement.[105] Thus, the participants consciously linked local and structural problems in the GDR and beyond.

A year later, the second seminar was so popular that the conveners had to limit attendance to one or two representatives per Church-based group.[106] By requesting delegates, the seminar balanced its important role as a node of communication between groups in various regions with the restrictions on assembly that the movement faced. With the Stasi watching the seminar and Church leaders somewhat uneasy, the activists descended on the East Berlin parish. Using knowledge from both official and unofficial channels, the participants developed their own narratives and then disseminated that information back to their colleagues at home. Over time, the seminars became more openly critical of the state and took on a more oppositional character. The Stasi deemed them to be politically dangerous and, in 1986, demanded Bishop Forck get these events under control.[107] Until the end of the GDR, these seminars crucially connected the independent movement and infuriated the Stasi.

In the Leipzig-Halle area, activism adopted a different approach, generally taking a more conciliatory stance toward party and state officials and emphasizing religious motivations. The groups, especially the Working Group for Environmental Protection (AGU) in Leipzig and the already mentioned Christian Environmental Seminar Rötha (CUR), collaborated closely with local bureaucrats and the Church. This attitude stood in contrast to the Berliners who antagonized the SED and sometimes the more conservative Church leadership. Housed in Leipzig's Youth Pastoral

---

[104] RHG RG/B 02/05, "Bericht über das Ökologie-Seminar 'Leben in der Stadt.'" This report also reflects the expanding number of newly built communities in places like Hellersdorf, Hohenschönhausen, and Marzahn that efficiently housed tens of thousands of people. See Eli Rubin, "Amnesiopolis: From Mietskaserne to Wohnungsbauserie 70 in East Berlin's Northeast," *Central European History*, 47, no. 2 (June 2014), 334–374.

[105] RHG RG/B 02/05, "Bericht über das Ökologie-Seminar 'Leben in der Stadt.'"

[106] BstU BV Bln AKG, "Information, Nr. 28/84, Über den Ablauf des sogenannten 'Ökologie-Seminars' vom 28. bis 30.9.1984 in der Kirchengemeinde Berlin-Friedrichsfelde-Ost," October 5, 1984. RHG SWV 02/1, "Liebe Umweltfreunde," 1984.

[107] BStU BV Bln AKG 375, "Die Durchführung des '3. Berliner Ökologieseminars' vom 28. bis 30. November 1986 in der Evangelischen Kirchgemeinde Zion in Berlin-Mitte," December 4, 1986.

Office, the AGU in particular gravitated toward more theologically minded and less directly oppositional pursuits. Environmental knowledge produced and shared by groups around Leipzig and Halle developed in response to the region's greatest sources of pollution, namely open-pit coalmining and refining. Over time, the groups in Leipzig and Halle developed greater relationships with the Berliners – in part thanks to the Eco-Seminars – as the movement gained momentum.

The AGU was founded in 1981 in close collaboration with the KFH and with the goal of working within existing political structures. It eschewed more radical positions in favor of (hopefully) achievable solutions.[108] One of the AGU's organizers, Ralf Elsässer, described a "real hunger for information" and a desire "to live completely differently," rejecting the consumer-oriented lifestyle that the SED championed.[109] Like other groups, the AGU hosted small events, such as tree planting campaigns and informational evenings, and its members joined the GNU.[110] They also searched for new methods to improve the degradation around them, because they believed that "demands for an intact environment will only lead to meaningful reforms if it becomes a domestic security issue."[111] Given the SED's restrictions on data and censorship of the press, the AGU tried to raise environmental consciousness through the Church, in conversation with the party and state, and by broadening its base.

The AGU also pushed the Church to not confine the environment to specific circles but rather to engage with a variety religious and non-religious impulses for activism. In a 1984 letter to the Protestant Church's synod, the AGU expressed gratitude that the synod would pass a formal resolution to support environmental protection, as it did on September 25, 1984. The AGU, along with a number of others, had convened at the KFH over a year before to prepare materials for the synod's review. The AGU laid out seven practical and theological "hopes and wishes" that it felt illustrated the intersection of Christianity and environmentalism. The members requested the synod's support for their cause in a similar way to the Church's support of the "Peace Decade" movement,

---

[108] "Christliches Umweltseminar Rötha," www.runde-ecke-leipzig.de/sammlung/Zusatz.php?w=w00174, accessed February 21, 2015.

[109] ABL, Ralf Elsässer "Bildung von Umweltbewußtsein in den Kirchengemeinden – Gedanken zum methodischen Herangehen," in *Grünheft: 22 Beiträge zur ökologischen Situation*, ed. Hans-Peter Gensichen (Wittenberg: Kirchliches Forschungsheim, 1990), 48–49.

[110] ABL 22.14, Letter to Wolfgang Lohbeck, Hamburg (Greenpeace member), December 18, 1984.

[111] Ibid.

but the synod declined.[112] In the end, the synod's resolution reflected many of the AGU's sentiments but in more general and diplomatic terms. When it came to setting Church policy, the synod embraced environmentalism abstractly but often pushed the groups to the margins. Nevertheless, the self-described "young Christians" of the AGU continued to advocate for the environment at the grassroots level as well as to strengthen institutional Church support.[113]

In Rötha, the CUR concentrated less on theology and more on the physical and psychological toll the mining industry had on residents. Under the guidance of Pastor Steinbach, the group's first annual environmental church service took place in 1983 in the nearby village of Mölbis, in the long shadow of the Espenhain beneficiation plant, which refined coal to burn relatively more cleanly by removing minerals and extraneous matter. The plant's processes, however, seriously degraded the local air and water quality.[114] The motto for that year's event, "Our Future has already begun in Mölbis," referred to the "filth, stench, alcoholism, and deep and debilitating resignation" that characterized life in – and the future of – that village. With an emphasis on sharing information during an exhibition before the service, the organizers even invited representatives from the county council, including from the interior department.[115] Their message was that "We are living off of an antiquated fuel, at the expense of the future."[116] Until the collapse of the GDR, the CUR continued to describe life near Espenhain as an "industrial apocalypse" with air that was impossible to breathe, pollution that dirtied and corroded everything it touched, and insufficient medical care to treat headaches, chronic respiratory infections, and asthma.[117] The aftereffects of open-pit mining left scarred landscapes with pits that were turned into dumps for waste and coal ash.[118]

---

[112] Ibid. The "Peace Decade," or *Friedensdekade*, was an integral part of the peace movement in the GDR in the early 1980s and was connected to the larger European peace movement, especially in West Germany. Initially, it had been seen as a single event or series of events but became an integral part of the peace movement. For more on the "Peace Decade," see Anke Silomon, *"Schwerter zu Pflugscharen" und die DDR: Die Friedensarbeit der evangelischen Kirchen in der DDR im Rahmen der Friedensdekaden 1980 bis 1982* (Göttingen: Vandenhoeck & Ruprecht, 1999).

[113] BArch DO 4/802, Letter from AGU to Herr Krause of the Bundessynod, September 1984.

[114] Bruce G. Miller, *Coal Energy Systems* (New York: Elsevier Academic Press, 2005), 295.

[115] Walter Christian Steinbach, *Eine Mark für Espenhain: Vom Christlichen Umweltseminar Rötha* (Leipzig: Evangelische Verlagsanstalt, 2018), 60–80.

[116] RGH TH 02/03, "Eine Mark für Espenhain oder Ein Protest bekommt Flügel," 1988.

[117] Umweltbibliothek Großhennersdorf (UBG), Corina Kluttig and Grit Jüttler, "Die Opposition in der DDR am Beispiel der Umweltbibliothek und dem Grün-ökologischen Netzwerk Arche," undated.

[118] RGH TH 02/03, "Eine Mark für Espenhain oder Ein Protest bekommt Flügel," 1988.

The CUR's environmental service became a tradition that was hosted annually to raise awareness and disseminate information in the region. The events critiqued the existing social order as well as spreading word about their plight. Attendees wondered if socialism in the GDR and other socialist countries would be able to "meet the global question of human survival." They argued that ultimately the SED must either restructure itself or that economic pressures would force transformation.[119] The SED's inability to end its dependence on a low-grade coal that poisoned its own people exemplified failures within the larger system. By 1984, the service had garnered the attention of West German journalists, whom authorities closely monitored.[120] The group's activities cast doubt on the SED's competence to champion local or international environmental causes.[121]

To raise awareness about their region's plight, CUR members attended a Church conference in Dresden. After hearing how many children suffered from respiratory illnesses, a number of women spontaneously invited children from Mölbis to spend their school vacations in the mountainous Erzgebirge.[122] For the next several years, Dresden's Ecological Working Group hosted school-aged children, so they could enjoy fresh air and a respite from the pollution at home.[123] The organizers argued that the pollution in Mölbis endangered the children because it could be detrimental to their development, a somewhat ironic argument given that the Erzgebirge suffered severely from Waldsterben.[124] In the first year of the program, thirty children from the Leipzig area visited the Erzgebirge, and by 1985 organizers had arranged for one hundred exchanges.[125] Over the course of the 1980s, parents and younger children joined the older ones, which lifted some of the burden on hosts, while Church publications such as the KFH's *Briefe* drummed up financial support.[126] Sending children to the mountains became so popular that between January and August 1989, the organizers received 118 applications for 207 children.[127] The CUR's

---

[119] Ibid.
[120] BArch DO 4/805, "Information über den Verlauf des Umweltgottesdiensts am 17.06.1984 in Mölbis."
[121] RGH TH 02/03, "Eine Mark für Espenhain oder Ein Protest bekommt Flügel," 1988.
[122] Steinbach, *Eine Mark für Espenhain*.
[123] This is somewhat ironic given the high levels of pollution from acid rain in the Erzgebirge.
[124] RHG AB 07, "Saubere Luft für Ferienkinder: Aktion der ökologischen Arbeitskreises der Dresdner Kirchenbezirke."
[125] Ibid.   [126] Ibid.
[127] ABL, Karin Flachowsky, "Die Aktion 'Saubere Luft für Ferienkinder,'" in *Grünheft*, ed. Gensichen, 70–71.

partnership with Dresden provided grassroots support for those who lived in devastated areas and the networking of groups within the GDR.

In a third region, Lusatia, environmental activism took on yet another set of dynamics that involved the local Slavic minority. Like the Leipzig area, Lusatia was – and still is – know for coalmining and refining. Located in the southeastern quadrant of the GDR, Lusatia stretched from Cottbus – the largest city in the area and a district capital – in the north down to the corner where the GDR, Czechoslovakia, and Poland met, a tri-border region known as the Black Triangle. Lusatia strained under the burden of extensive open-pit mining and coal refining without many other industries. Roughly two-thirds of the GDR's coalmining took place in Lusatia, leaving residents to suffer from high levels of pollution.[128] Lusatia's activism, however, remained relatively isolated and on the edges of the larger networks until the late 1980s when plans to mine a coal seam under the town of Zittau became controversial. With the presence of a Slavic minority, the Sorbs, who had long been marginalized, the absence of a major metropolitan center, and close ties to the mining industry, environmental devastation only slowly coalesced into social protest in Lusatia.

Lusatia had a long history of lignite mining, but after the oil crises of the 1970s when the Soviet Union cut energy exports to the GDR, the SED redoubled lignite extraction in the region.[129] While smaller in terms of population, the district of Cottbus's coal production rivaled the most industrialized parts of the country. Multiple reports from the MUW acknowledged that Cottbus, along with Leipzig, Halle, and Berlin, was among the most polluted districts in the country. A 1979 report concluded that "Berlin, and the highly industrialized districts of Halle, Leipzig, Cottbus, Dresden, and Karl-Marx-Stadt [now Chemnitz] made up thirty two percent of the GDR's area, but fifty-four percent of the population, and two thirds of the industrial production."[130] Officials hesitated to admit it, but by 1981, over twenty percent of Cottbus's territory (some 666 square miles) was either already devoted to mining or held in reserve for that purpose.[131] Economic planners foresaw that rising to forty-five percent within sixty years. In the county of Weißwasser, that number was projected

---

[128] UBG 4.29, Letter from Lusatian environmental groups to the Görlitzer Provincial Synod of the Protestant Church, October 2, 1988.

[129] BArch DK 5/5219, "Bericht über Entwicklung des Umweltschutzes," 1978–1979. Raymond Stokes, "From Schadenfreude to Going-Out-of-Business Sale: East Germany and the Oil Crises of the 1970s," in *The East German Economy, 1945–2010: Falling Behind or Catching Up?*, eds. Hartmut Berghoff and Uta Andrea Balbier (New York: Cambridge University Press, 2013), 138–139.

[130] BArch DK 5/5219, "Bericht über Entwicklung des Umweltschutzes," 1978–1979.

[131] RHG Ki 18/01, "Fakten und Zahlen zur DDR-Braunkohlenpolitik," undated.

to reach sixty percent.[132] The MUW intended to install new electro-filters to improve the air quality and convert abandoned open-pit mines into lakes for swimming, thereby improving quality of life.[133] Few of those projects ever came to fruition, leaving Lusatia marked with massive pits and covered in coal dust.

To accommodate the expansion of operations, the state forced Lusatians to evacuate their villages to use the land for coalmining. Between 1945 and 1989, some 13,000 residents had to leave the area, with most of the "resettlements" occurring after 1974.[134] The most affected areas tended to be in Lower Lusatia, where the coal seams were easier to access, but by the 1980s, officials planned further expansions. The drive to fuel the economy led engineers and politicians to look for ever more seams that inevitably were increasingly difficult to access. One particularly rich but controversial seam – the so-called *Neissepfeiler* – ran directly under the town of Zittau in Upper Lusatia, stretching from the large open-pit mine in Bogatynia, Poland, into the GDR and a small section of Czechoslovakia. By the mid-1980s, engineers aimed to level the entire town and remove its roughly 40,000 residents in order to access the seam.[135] Open-pit mining, the relocation – or potential relocation – of residents, and numerous power plants led to serious pollution and uncertainty.

Gradually, Church-based initiatives to protest local conditions began thanks to the work of a few medical doctors as well as youth and peace groups in Görlitz, Zittau, and Hoyerswerda. Often, they prioritized reaching out to both Church officials and state authorities for some kind of improvement, and the Stasi quickly took notice.[136] The groups often highlighted the evacuation and destruction of villages as detrimental to both Sorbian culture as well as nature. The Dubringer Moor, which was a nature conservation area and old morainic landscape, a drift landscape

---

[132] UBG 4.29, Letter from Lusatian environmental groups to the Görlitzer Provincial Synod of the Protestant Church, 2.10.1988.

[133] BArch DK 5/5219, "Bericht über Entwicklung des Umweltschutzes," 1978–1979.

[134] Cora Granata, "The Cold War Politics of Cultural Minorities: Jews and Sorbs in the German Democratic Republic, 1976–1989," *German History* 27, no. 1 (January 2009), 75.

[135] Dieter Liebig, "Begleitbuch zur Ausstellung: Anspruch und Wirklichkeit: Die Energie- und Umweltpolitik in der DDR am Beispiel des Energieträgers Braunkohle" (Großhennersdorf: Umweltbibliothek Großhennersdorf, e.V., 2009), 98. Protests against these plans became a major rallying point in the fall of 1989 as the SED-system was collapsing.

[136] UBG, unfiled, Roland Brauckmann, "Die Umweltschutzgruppen in Görlitz: Auslöser der friedlichen Wende in der niederschlesischen Lausitz," undated.

created by the older ice ages, was endangered by the expansion of open-pit mining.[137] Complaints, such as Ralf Engel's petition to district officials, emphasized the terrible living conditions. Engel noted that in Zittau it was impossible to open windows because floors and curtains instantly became covered in dust and dirt. Like the young woman who complained at the GNU's inaugural ceremonies, Engel noted it was impossible to wash or hang clothing out of doors, because soot and grime left the clothes dirtier than before. Beyond the everyday stench and dreck, the forest was dying from acid rain.[138]

When environmental concerns coalesced into a movement, Lusatia's unique history and demographics shaped its character, merging local identity and pollution concerns. The Sorbian minority, which totals about 60,000 individuals today, had been viewed as a privileged minority since the GDR's early years, but it still remained on the edges. Many Sorbs had lost interest in their minority identity and moved away from the region.[139] For those who stayed, the 1980s saw a reinvestment in Sorbian culture and traditions. They began to intertwine their minority status with environmental problems, blaming the SED for not protecting the community's needs and destroying the landscape with open-pit mines.[140] Prominent Sorbian author Jurij Koch highlighted these difficulties at the Tenth Writers' Congress in 1987.[141] He warned, "With every bit of warmth we take from the earth, in order to thoughtlessly waste it, it becomes colder around us." Koch then called for alternative solutions, such as solar energy, in order to reduce the burden that fossil fuels put on the population.[142] While he did not refer to Lusatia by name, his graphic descriptions of "gigantic machines" digging into the earth clearly invoked familiar images of the GDR's open-pit mining operations.

Removed from major urban centers with an organized opposition, Lusatia was largely rural and geographically isolated. Notably, large parts of Lusatia fell into the area known as the "valley of the clueless" (*Tal der*

---

[137] UBG 4.29, Letter from Lusatian environmental groups to the Görlitzer Provincial Synod of the Protestant Church, 2.10.1988.

[138] Ralf Engel, "Eingabe – Umweltverschmutzung durch Schornstein vom TKZ Werk 6!," February 6, 1988.

[139] Granata, "The Cold War Politics of Cultural Minorities," 74.

[140] Ibid., 75. John Andrew Reaves, "The Development of an Ecologically Critical Sorbian Literature as a Consequence of the German Democratic Republic's Dependence on Soft Coal as an Energy Source" (PhD Dissertation, University of Wisconsin at Madison, 1996).

[141] Thomas W. Goldstein, *Writing in Red: The East German Writers Union and the Role of Literary Intellectuals* (Rochester, NY: Camden House, 2017), 186.

[142] RHG TH 02/01, cited in "Lassen sich Umweltprobleme in der DDR noch abwenden?" 1988.

Ahnungslosen), which did not receive western radio or television signals. Lusatia lacked any universities, which often brought together the younger generation who had been involved in the peace movement, expressed discontent with the political situation, and advocated for policy if not system change. Before 1986 or 1987, individuals had to travel to Dresden or Leipzig to attend events.[143] Despite these structural obstacles, Lusatia became folded into a larger, more vocal Church-based movement that pushed back against the SED's claims to environmental protection. The Black Triangle's transboundary pollution underscored the structural problems that Soviet-style communism posed even though it remained a rural area far from the seats of power. Drawing on local challenges, and increasingly international influences, these groups gained momentum.

Socialist Pollution, Reform, and Networking

Transformations elsewhere in the Soviet bloc informed growing environmental activism in the GDR, inspiring East Germans and leading them to connect with eastern European activists. In particular, independent groups sprang up in Poland after the end of Martial Law, with the more industrialized southern half of the country becoming a hub for activism. In the southwest, East German and Czechoslovak pollution deteriorated air and water quality, generating frustration over transboundary acid rain. Farther east, renewed activism in and around Kraków responded to degradation in Upper Silesia. Once the new Soviet leader Mikhail Gorbachev introduced reforms, *glasnost* (openness) and *perestroika* (restructuring) in 1985, the PZPR quickly embraced them.[144] Poland's relative freedom fueled discussions about economic underperformance, corruption, pollution, human rights, and above all, alternatives to communist control. In this atmosphere, activism became more public and contact with other countries broadened environmental and political horizons as knowledge and networks transcended borders through media, correspondence, and visits. These deepening societal and environmental connections isolated the anti-reform East German leadership, making it wary of socialist and non-socialist neighbors alike.

The GDR contributed to a border-crossing, regional environmental disaster through shared waters and weather in the Black Triangle. In this

---

[143] UBG 16-3, "Leben in Gottes Schöpfung: Woche der Verantwortung für Gottes Schöpfung vom 2.–9. Juni 1985 – eine Handreichung."

[144] Padraic Kenney, *A Carnival of Revolution: Central Europe, 1989* (Princeton, NJ: Princeton University Press, 2002), 19.

Figure 4 Altenberg, GDR. July 11, 1987. Waldsterben in the Erzgebirge along the
East German–Czechoslovakian border

area where the GDR, Czechoslovakia, and Poland's borders met, all three
faced interrelated difficulties, but Poland received a net import of air
pollution from the other two countries. By the 1980s, reports estimated
that nearly half of Poland's air pollution came from the GDR and
Czechoslovakia.[145] In 1988, the GDR exported around 1,158 kilotons of
sulfur dioxide to Poland, meaning that about twenty-two percent of its
total sulfur dioxide emissions crossed the Oder–Neisse Line from west to
east.[146] This flow of pollution, along with Poland's domestic industry,

---

[145] Open Society Archive (OSA), Jacek Rostowski, "Environmental Deterioration in Poland," RAD
Background Report/169, September 5, 1984.
[146] BArch DK 5/1347, "Analyse der Umweltbedingungen – DDR, 1976–1988," 11–14.

killed roughly 10,000 hectares of Polish forest in the "Westsudeten" region along the East German and Czechoslovak borders and damaged another 5,000 hectares between 1981 and 1987. East German officials worried that "Wide circles in Poland, especially among the intelligentsia and students, demanded concrete action in response to the real danger of losing the forest entirely."[147] As awareness of the devastation spread, the connections between these countries – and with western Europe – also became more apparent.

While socialist states prioritized their own economies and industrial output, they were not above objecting to other countries' inaction. The tri-border region underscored the ecological interconnectedness of central Europe. Rivers and air crossed from northern Bohemia into the GDR, leading to Waldsterben in the Erzgebirge and pollution in the Elbe River. Yet the GDR polluted Czechoslovakia's air and forest in almost equal amounts by the mid-1980s.[148] Poland, too, complained about water quality from Czechoslovakia and lack of transparency. In 1986, for example, heating oil from Ostrava spilled into the Lucina River, a tributary of the Ostravice that eventually flows into the Oder River. This accident as well as others allowed contaminants to cross unchecked into Polish and East German waters, exasperating the downstream recipients.[149] Czechoslovakia only slowly admitted to such incidents, and even then, hesitated to provide hard numbers.[150] In response, the PZPR began publishing pollution levels from the other two countries, which a Solidarność paper in Wrocław noted was an attempt to deflect from Polish failures.[151] Miscommunication, distrust, and health problems frustrated the governments, but they did not succeed in addressing the mess or its knock-on effects, which further disenchanted citizens.

The end of Martial Law in Poland in 1983 marked the resurgence of independent activism, making the environment not only a diplomatic but also a sociopolitical issue again. The PKE reemerged and became stronger than it had been in 1980–1981. In part it succeeded in doing so because, as leader of the organization Zygmunt Fura stated, the PKE was not explicitly

---

[147] BArch DK 5/5829, "Information für den Vorsitzenden des Ministerrates, Willi Stoph, zum Abschluss des Abkommens DDR-VRP-CSSR über die Zusammenarbeit auf dem Gebiet des Umweltschutzes," 1987.

[148] BArch DK 5/1991, "Direktive für das Auftreten auf dem dreiseitigen Treffen der Stellv der Vors des MR der DDR, CSSR und VRP zu Fragen des Umweltschutzes und der Wawi im Februar 1988 in der VRP," undated.

[149] Ibid.   [150] OSA, Czechoslovakia – Situation Report, December 1986.

[151] K. Sanducci, "Bójcie się Czarnego Luda," *Prawda: Pismo Myśli Niezależnej*, no. 29–31 (1986), 51.

oppositional and not as directly targeted as Solidarność.[152] In the mid-1980s, the PKE fostered a form of dual participation, perhaps more successfully than the Church-based movement in the GDR. Fura viewed the PKE as a collection of doctors, scientists, journalists, and members of workers' councils who all viewed the environment as part of Poland's larger social and economic challenges but cooperated with officials. Although this stance generated tension between them and some Solidarność leaders who called PKE members "regime-loyal," Fura and the PKE simply viewed their position in communist Poland as different from the trade union.[153] The PKE prioritized bringing together "researchers and organizers of activities in the fields of environmental protection and education" and further incorporated economic and political aims.[154] It did not oppose the PZPR but aimed to improve environmental conditions and consciousness.

In 1985, the PKE held its first national meeting since Martial Law had been instituted in 1981. The organizers held the convention on June 5, "World Environmental Day," to intentionally situate the PKE in global trends. It brought together scholars from a spectrum of backgrounds – humanists to scientists to engineers to architects to psychologists – to address ecological development, foundations, elements, and methods. Despite diverse approaches, the participants intentionally depicted their seemingly local issues as part of a crisis that counted as "one of the most serious diseases of the modern world."[155] They came together to formulate a more unified response to pollution in Poland and around the world. The PKE succeeded in establishing an independent space in which specialists shared ideas and solutions that their training informed, and yet remained still outside of party and state venues.

Whereas the PKE generally recruited from established scholars and specialists, independent groups appealed to a younger generation and were more openly oppositional. The most prominent example, *Wolność i Pokój* (Freedom and Peace, WiP), established in 1985 in Kraków and Warsaw, later developed a presence in Wrocław and other cities. WiP rejected any collaboration with officials, and while its members did not necessarily have direct ties to Solidarność, they were strongly in support of

---

[152] Sabine Rosenbladt, *Der Osten ist grün? Ökoreportagen aus der DDR, Sowjetunion, Tschechoslowakei, Polen, Ungarn* (Hamburg: Rasch und Röhring Verlag, 1988), 15.

[153] Ibid., 14–15.

[154] Stanisław Juchnowicz, "Słowo Wstępne," in *Ekorozwój Szansą Przetrwania Cywilizacji: Materiały z Konferencji PKE, 4–5 Czerwiec 1985* (Kraków: Wydawnictwo Akademii Górniczo-Hutniczej, 1986), 9.

[155] Ibid., 9.

it. As in the GDR and FRG, linking peace and environment concerns aligned these Polish activists with a broader, transnational movement.[156] Drawing on Polish Pope John Paul II's message of peace and arguing that "There is no peace in a Poland controlled by communists," the self-proclaimed independent movement rejected any cooperation with the authorities.[157] WiP declared that it was antimilitary and ecological, acting on behalf of the environment but focused on peace, too.[158] WiP never sought to negotiate with the party or state, representing a generational shift from older workers and professionals toward new goals and agendas.

As in 1980–1981, Solidarność emerged as the leading voice of dissent in the mid-1980s, and also like earlier, the trade union did not prioritize the environment in its platform. Nevertheless, Solidarność published articles about pollution for foreign audiences, recognizing that the environment played well abroad, especially in the FRG. The union's German-language *Information Bulletin* incorporated relevant stories, such as the founding of WiP, in one issue.[159] In another, the bulletin highlighted collaboration between Solidarność in Dąbrowa (Silesia) and a BUND chapter in Rhineland-Westphalia (FRG). The two organizations agreed to exchange information and experiences; test soil, water, and air quality; and print the results in Solidarność publications and other related venues.[160] That same publication included a multipage report of environmental conditions in the Upper Silesian city of Opole, which had been part of Germany with a mixed Polish and German population until 1945.[161] After cataloging the degradation, the authors sought amelioration efforts for the Oder River similar to ones that "brought life back to the Rhine and the Thames."[162] Solidarność incorporated the environment to appeal to western sensibilities and win international support.

Environmental groups and awareness were thus already gaining popularity when Gorbachev introduced reforms in 1985 and 1986. Under the

[156] Kenney, *A Carnival of Revolution*, 59–60.

[157] Biblioteka Ossolineum, WiP 1985–1987, "Deklaracja założycielska Ruchu Wolność i Pokój," April 14, 1985.

[158] Biblioteka Ossolineum WiP 1985–1987, "Wsplnoty 'WiP' (sic)," 1985.

[159] AGG B II 3/1101, "Freiheit und Frieden – Wolność i Pokój," *Informationsbulletin – Solidarność*, no. 37 (March 1986), 3–6.

[160] AGG B II 3/1101, "Kommunique – Ökologie," *Informationsbulletin – Solidarność*, no. 53–54 (August 1987), 35.

[161] Brendan Karch, "Instrumental nationalism in Upper Silesia," in *National Indifference and the History of Nationalism in Modern Europe*, eds. Maarten van Ginderachter and Jon Fox (New York: Routledge, 2019), 196.

[162] AGG B II 3/1101, "Kommunique – Ökologie," *Informationsbulletin – Solidarność*, no. 53–54 (August 1987), 41.

motto of perestroika, glasnost, and democratization, Gorbachev first eased restrictions in the Soviet Union, especially economic restructuring. Quickly, the spirit of reform spread across the Soviet bloc as people hoped for change and mentalities shifted under the surface. Communist leaders responded differently to Gorbachev's programs, creating unequal opportunities for producing and strengthening environmental knowledge in eastern Europe. In Poland, the reforms continued a trajectory the PZPR had already set, because officials had tolerated freer speech since the end of Martial Law two years earlier. Gorbachev had the most influence in the Soviet Union itself, while on the other end of the spectrum, the GDR and Czechoslovakia outright rejected reform.[163] These changes coincided with a crisis of confidence on the part of the ruling communist parties in eastern Europe. Officialdom lost faith in its own system and its willingness to repress alternative thinkers was waning.[164]

Though Poles already enjoyed relatively more freedoms than other communist countries, they expanded further after 1985.[165] WiP wrote openly provocative publications, such as *A-Capella*, in which the members embraced the slogan of "Live and Let Live." They undermined the state by establishing an "anarchists' library," where people could inform themselves on the topic. Unsurprisingly, the library did not have much at its disposal, and organizers asked for donations of books and materials so they could gather and disseminate environmental and other forms of restricted knowledge.[166] WiP's more radical response revealed limits on the state's willingness to suppress oppositional activities and material. The PZPR did relatively little suppress them, but the East German Stasi kept tabs on WiP, honing in on contacts with "hostile and negative forces" in the GDR.[167] The East German officials conducted surveillance on Polish activists, both because they believed the Polish ministry of security was too weak and because they feared Polish influence at home.

With Gorbachev's reforms, travel across the Iron Curtain became easier, bringing groups into closer contact with the west, and a transnational network emerged. In 1985, a few activists from Poland and Hungary attended a Friends of the Earth (FOE) conference on acid rain in

---

[163] Brian Porter-Szücs, *Poland in the Modern World: Beyond Martyrdom* (Malden, MA: Wiley-Blackwell, 2014), 314.

[164] Stephen Kotkin, *Uncivil Society: 1989 and the Implosion of the Communist Establishment* (Chapel Hill, NC: University of North Carolina Press, 2009), xiv–xv.

[165] Porter-Szücs, *Poland in the Modern World*, 313.   [166] PKA A Kelly 461, *A-Capella*, undated.

[167] BStU MfS ZAIG 13842, "Geplante Aktivitäten der antisozialistischen Organisation Wolnosc i Pokoj (Freiheit u. Frieden)," 1987.

Eerbeek in the Netherlands. While there, the eastern Europeans found it to be an "excellent opportunity, not only for meeting other participants, but for also starting contacts between both countries."[168] At this conference, and with the aid of FOE and a handful of other western organizations, the Polish and Hungarian representatives developed the idea of networking in eastern Europe. Along with a few interested individuals from Czechoslovakia, activists took advantage of the eased travel regulations to meet in Hungary later in the year to found Greenway, an English-language collaboration between independent groups in the Soviet bloc. This network did not seek to become a single organization but tried to help activists recognize challenges and opportunities shared across Soviet satellite states.[169] By permitting at least some criticism at home and more travel abroad, new impulses from east and west transformed the possibilities for environmental action.

Conclusion

The GDR's position as a link between east and west in central Europe became ever clearer in the 1980s as awareness of environmental degradation and transboundary pollution grew. Activists and concerned individuals read, watched, and traveled across the Iron Curtain to protest multiple issues, perhaps most notoriously sulfur dioxide emissions and Waldsterben. Activists in Poland and the GDR pursued different avenues to pressure their communist parties, and they did so with help from western European governments and non-state actors. Together, they learned about and drew attention to eastern European environmental devastation, with western European actors providing technology and other forms of aid to states and independent groups alike. Moreover, the 1984 Munich Agreement to reduce sulfur dioxide emissions permitted East Germans as well as neighbors to point to concrete communist failures against the backdrop of the Waldsterben panic in the FRG.

Given rising environmental consciousness in the GDR, the SED increasingly fielded criticism from domestic actors, even as it tried to curb access to damaging information. Security organs distrusted scientists, Church-based activists, and international observers, viewing them as potential threats to East German stability. Activists independent of the state (whether explicitly tied to the Church or not) became bolder in their

---

[168] AGG B II 3/1101, "Greenway: The Youth Environmental Network in Eastern Europe," 1985.
[169] Ibid.

demands for substantial, measurable improvements. The SED's paranoia about environmental groups was justified as calls for change in the GDR grew louder and created a tenuous situation for Honecker's regime. As other eastern European countries embraced glasnost and perestroika after 1985, travel and flow of information increased across borders. With Honecker's rejection of Gorbachev's reforms, however, the GDR became more isolated. The East German leadership viewed its neighbors as unreliable and dangerous, but knowledge and frustration among environmental activists grew anyway.

CHAPTER 5

Coming Out From Behind the Cloud:
Environmentalism after Chernobyl

Disaster struck at the Chernobyl nuclear power plant in Ukraine on April 26, 1986. Shortly after midnight, a routine test of emergency shutdown procedures in reactor number four set off an explosion that ignited an uncontrollable fire. In the five hours before it could be contained, the fire released twenty thousand roentgens of radiation per hour, roughly two hundred times the standard lethal dose over the same amount of time. Levels near the reactor core reached thirty thousand roentgens, enough to kill a person in a mere forty-eight seconds.[1] A Swedish measuring station publicly announced the radiation emanating from Chernobyl, triggering an international outcry. In the FRG, the media reported images of gas-masked people with subtitles like "Fear! Flight from Kiev, Fear of Exposure across Europe" and "Death Cloud already over Denmark: Are we next?".[2] In the Soviet bloc, satellite states wavered in their transparency, hesitating for days before finally releasing statements. News from and contacts in western Europe, however, undermined that decision, feeding fears and frustration behind the Iron Curtain.[3] East Germans voraciously consumed West German reports on the fallout, which led to demands for more and better information.[4]

In the GDR, and the Soviet bloc more generally, Chernobyl symbolized communism's environmental shortcomings as well as its problematic information politics. Protests over the nuclear disaster built on existing

---

[1] Kate Brown, "Blinkered Science: Why We Know So Little about Chernobyl's Health Effects," *Culture, Theory, and Critique* 58, no. 4 (September 2017), 414. Adam Higginbotham, "Chernobyl 20 Years On," *The Guardian*, March 26, 2006, www.theguardian.com/world/2006/mar/26/nuclear.russia, accessed July 6, 2015.

[2] See *Der Spiegel* cover page from May 12, 1986, and *Bild* cover page from April 29, 1986, for examples of such titles.

[3] Padraic Kenney, *A Carnival of Revolution: Central Europe, 1989* (Princeton, NJ: Princeton University Press, 2002), 71.

[4] "Dokumentation: Eingabe von DDR-Umweltgruppen zur Kernenergie nach Tschernobyl," *Umweltblätter* 3, 1986.

tensions regarding pollution and access to environmental data.[5] In response, newly founded groups sought out a deeper knowledge of nuclear dangers, existing groups grew in number of participants, and communication between groups deepened. The relative absence of antinuclear sentiment before 1986 stemmed both from a sense that nuclear energy was cleaner than coal – the source of so many Soviet bloc problems – and a culture of secrecy surrounding nuclear spills.[6] In the wake of Chernobyl, however, antinuclear protest erupted across central Europe as the dangers of Soviet-designed power plants became terrifyingly real. Environmental protest was intrinsically tied to the Soviet bloc's mounting political and economic crises.[7] Glasnost created a more open atmosphere in which eastern Europeans, including East Germans, demanded not only policy reform but changes to the system as a whole.

As activists in the Soviet bloc looked westward after Chernobyl, they further developed a sense of solidarity and common purpose across political divides. Signs reading "Chernobyl affects everyone," "Chernobyl is everywhere," and "better active today than radioactive tomorrow" appeared in multiple languages in the weeks and months after the disaster, tying together concerned individuals across Europe.[8] This alliance led to activists pursuing multiple, interrelated environmental issues by exchanging information and visiting one another on an unprecedented scale. Co-organized and western sponsored conferences in Poland and other Soviet bloc countries defied the impermeability of the Iron Curtain, weaving a network of eastern and western activists. In an era of easing censorship and swelling communication, these factors shaped the environmental

[5] The literature has considered Chernobyl to be one of the many delegitimizing challenges that late communism faced in the second half of the 1980s, but responses to Chernobyl often seem surprising, or to come out of nowhere. Works on eastern Europe teleologically look to the end of communism, primarily through political and economic considerations, without linking it to environmental considerations. Stephen Kotkin, *Uncivil Society: 1989 and the Implosion of the Communist Establishment* (Chapel Hill, NC: University of North Carolina Press, 2009); Kenney, *A Carnival of Revolution*; Detlef Pollack, *Politischer Protest: Politisch alternative Gruppen in der DDR* (Opladen: Leske + Budrich, 2000).

[6] Dolores Augustine, *Taking on Technocracy: Nuclear Power in Germany, 1945 to the Present* (New York: Berghahn Press, 2018), 214. Open Society Archive (OSA), Vladimir Kusin, "Chernobyl: The Greening of Eastern Europe?" 3, May 27, 1986.

[7] Valerie Bunce, *Subversive Institutions: The Design and the Destruction of Socialism and the State* (New York: Cambridge University Press, 1999); Ilko-Sascha Kowalczuk, *Endspiel: Die Revolution von 1989 in der DDR* (Munich: C.H. Beck Verlag, 2009); Charles S. Maier, *Dissolution: The Crisis of Communism and the End of East Germany* (Princeton, NJ: Princeton University Press, 1997); Michael Richter, *Die friedliche Revolution: Aufbruch zur Demokratie in Sachsen 1989/90* (Göttingen: Vandenhoeck & Ruprecht, 2009).

[8] Ossolineum Biblioteka, WiP, "Lepiej dzisiaj być aktywnym, niż jutro radioaktywnym!" undated, and "Czernobyl jest Wszędzie," 1989. RHG, *Umweltblätter*, September 1986, 1.

movements across central Europe. While eastern Europeans gained access to information and financial support, western Europeans learned more about pollution and the limits of protest in the east. This process of two-way learning entangled histories of eastern and western Europe, revealing commonalties as well as differences.

This chapter traces protest after Chernobyl, which increasingly became public and political in the GDR and eastern Europe. Bolstered by western support, this movement expanded swiftly in communism's final years. This chapter first examines how Chernobyl became a rallying point for environmental action. The movement's growth, however, generated friction between old-timers and new participants that limited its influence in the GDR. The chapter then turns to Poland to explore broader eastern European responses to Chernobyl, delving into how it fueled discussion of a range of environmental problems. Poland's openness solidified the country's position as facilitator of environmental exchange across borders within the region. Finally, the chapter illuminates West German interactions with eastern European pollution and protest in the late 1980s, focusing on moments of cooperation and distrust. This chapter argues that Chernobyl reshaped environmental movements, anti-communist rhetoric, and connections in central Europe. Critiques of the pollution and restricted access to data undermined a system that was already on shaky ground.

Expanding the Movement: The GDR after Chernobyl

Chernobyl – and the SED's bungled response to it – motivated East Germans to join existing environmental groups and to establish new ones across the GDR. The SED's initial silence fed East Germans' demand for transparency and contributed to a heightened sense of betrayal by the government. East Germans who were not otherwise active members of the Church now became involved in protest, reinforcing the idea that the movement was overflowing the Church's confines. This growth marked a transition from earlier "Church-based" to "independent" activism. By 1988, the KHF estimated that fifty-eight environmental groups with an average of ten to thirty individuals existed in the GDR, though specific events could mobilize larger crowds.[9] This burgeoning movement

---

[9] RHG Ki 18/02, "Die Karteibroschüre der kirchlichen Umweltgruppen in der DDR: Stand vom November 1988." Merrill Jones estimated 100 groups of twenty to thirty members in the 1993 *German Studies Review*, "Origins of the East German Environmental Movement," as did activist Henry Schramm in 1988. RHG ÜG 03, "Erwiderung zur Veröffentlichung des arche Artikels in den

united local environmental concerns with larger existential questions about the SED's ability to protect its citizens. Yet these developments also posed new challenges for an environmental movement struggling within the strictures of the dictatorship.

The Environmental Library (*Umweltbibliothek*) in East Berlin, which was founded in direct response to Chernobyl, reflected the expansion and diversity of the movement.[10] A core group of the Environmental Library's members had been active in Berlin-Lichtenberg's Peace and Environmental Circle since 1983 but moved to a new parish, the Zion Church in Berlin-Mitte, in September 1986. Modeled on Polish "flying universities" during Martial Law, the Environmental Library was both a physical library and group of activists. Its purpose was to offer information and materials to anyone interested in learning more about ecology.[11] According to one of the founders, Wolfgang Rüddenklau, the Environmental Library had about fifty members when it opened.[12] Over the next three years, participation grew, and the library functioned as a node in networks across the GDR. It served as an important point of contact for isolated groups and a model for others. By 1988, other similarly named "Environmental Libraries" sprang up in a number of municipalities, such as Leipzig, Erfurt, Zittau, and even the village of Großhennersdorf in Upper Lusatia. Each location provided much-needed information about local as well as global environmental problems, underscoring demands for data and changes in policy after 1986.

At the heart of the Environmental Library's efforts were the GDR-wide Eco-Seminars, which the Berlin-Friedrichsfelde group had initiated in 1984. Now hosted at the Zion Church, environmentalists came together each year to discuss a pressing topic. Reflective of concerns about Chernobyl and the Soviet bloc's continuing dependence on coal, the seminar focused on the dangers of nuclear energy, the problems of using

---

Umweltblättern 6/88," Arche, Grün-ökologisches Netzwerk in den Ev. Kirchen der DDR, Archiv der Opposition, Robert Havemann Gesellschaft, Berlin. Schramm himself was later revealed to have been an unofficial collaborator for the Stasi. Christian Halbrock, "Die unabhängigen Umweltgruppen in der DDR: Forschungsstand und Überblick," *Bundeszentrale für politische Bildung*, December 15, 2011, www.bpb.de/geschichte/zeitgeschichte/deutschlandarchiv/61423/umw eltgruppen?p=all, accessed July 22, 2015.

[10] "Fliegende Universitäten," Bundeszentrale für politische Bildung und Robert-Havemann-Gesellschaft e.V., www.jugendopposition.de/index.php?id=3180, accessed December 17, 2014.

[11] The members of the Environmental Library had previously been associated with a different congregation in Lichtenberg, Berlin, and had a different name but moved to the Zion Church in September 1986.

[12] Wolfgang Rüddenklau, ed., *Störenfried: DDR-Opposition 1986–1989, mit Texten aus den "Umweltblättern"* (Berlin: BasisDruck, 1992), 69.

fossil fuels, and the possibility of alternative energy sources.[13] The flier announcing the weekend's gathering requested that individuals and groups bring "materials, exhibits, petitions, and presentations," so that everyone could share what they knew. The roughly 120 attendees (104 of whom the Stasi could identify) divided their time between smaller discussions and larger presentations. A number of the talks clearly drew on West German sources, including the "anti-nuclear movement in West Germany" and "western media's perspective on the GDR's nuclear energy problem."[14] The Eco-Seminars brought people together from various parts of the country to discuss environmental subjects and to spread information difficult to obtain from the west.

The Environmental Library also importantly published what would become the highest circulated East German samizdat – underground and self-published – newsletter, the *Umweltblätter*. It provided a means of communication between independent groups, especially for those who could not travel to Berlin for seminars and similar events. It sought to reach non-Church audiences and provide an alternative to party-run newspapers, such as *Neues Deutschland*. Initially, the *Umweltblätter* spread news about Chernobyl, but it also disseminated information regarding peace and environmental movements in the GDR as well as other dissident movements in other eastern European countries. When the newsletter began in the fall of 1986, the Environmental Library printed between 150 and 200 copies. In 1987, Wilhelm Knabe smuggled a better printing press into the GDR, so the Environmental Library could expand its circulation of the *Umweltblätter*.[15] By 1989, circulation had mushroomed to over 2,000, which given that the newsletter was illegal, demonstrated a willingness to flout authorities and demand for its content.[16]

Thanks to the *Umweltblätter*, western news, and other venues, fears of nuclear disaster from civilian sources such as power stations skyrocketed after Chernobyl. The GDR already had three functioning nuclear power

[13] RHG SWV 02/01, "Drittes Berliner Ökologieseminar."

[14] BStU MfS BV Bln AG XXII 275, "Erste Erkenntnisse zum sogenannten 3. 'Berliner Ökologieseminar' vom 28.11.1986 bis zum 30.11.1986 in der Evangelischen Kirchgemeinde Zion."

[15] "Schmuggel für die Umweltbibliothek," Bundesbeauftrager für Stasiunterlagen der ehemaligen DDR, https://fallofthewall25.com/mauergeschichten/schmuggel-fuer-die-umwelt-bibliothek, accessed October 19, 2018.

[16] German History in Documents and Images, Robert-Havemann Gesellschaft, http://germanhistor ydocs.ghi-dc.org/sub_image.cfm?image_id=2836, accessed February 6, 2015. Given the illicit nature of the publication, we can assume significantly higher readership. Individuals would read the newsletter before passing it on to likeminded acquaintances. One letter to the editors explained how the author had come across the *Umweltblätter* at an Ecumenical Assembly and asked if it was possible to obtain a subscription. RHG RG B 19/08, Letter to the editor, May 12, 1989.

plants, but a fourth was under construction near Stendal, outside of Magdeburg, which drew significant attention after the April 26 disaster. Two local doctors, a married couple named Erika and Ludwig Drees, sparked opposition to the plant, which was supposed to become the largest nuclear installation in the GDR.[17] Active in Christian peace and environmental circles, the doctors linked fears about Chernobyl to the local situation, and thence to larger health and environmental questions. As medical doctors, their criticisms gained credibility that might otherwise have been lacking, which pushed the GDR to reexamine its nuclear power policy. Although the GDR continued with the project, the plant remained incomplete as the regime collapsed in 1989 and was scrapped during reunification in 1990.

Just weeks after the disaster at Chernobyl, the Dreeses spearheaded a two-pronged protest, attempting to gain support within the Church and to directly petition the state through Eingaben. In the first letter, addressed to the bishop of Saxony in Magdeburg, Christoph Demke, Erika Drees asked for the Church to take up the topic of the responsible use of nuclear energy with the government of the GDR. Signed by twenty-five local Christians, she explained that in light of the Chernobyl catastrophe and radioactivity's known dangers to life on earth, they believed the continued construction of the nuclear power plant near Stendal was a grave violation of their duty to be stewards of creation. She concluded the Church could no longer be silent, because "Christians and the Church have a prophetic duty here."[18] Her vivid language about the dangers of radiation to human health and nature pushed the Church to speak out against Chernobyl and Stendal.

Residents of Magdeburg and antinuclear activists also addressed petitions to the SED demanding that construction cease. Drawing on the nuclear spills at Three Mile Island in the United States and Chernobyl, one petition argued that the consequences of an accident would be unimaginable and evacuation impossible in an area as densely populated as Stendal.[19] Another petition sent to Honecker outlined the dangers of a nuclear disaster for Stendal but also emphasized the importance of energy to economic growth and consumption. They contended that the larger

[17] RHG Th 02/05 Eingabe von Dr. med. Ludwig Drees, Dr. med. Erika Drees an den Staatsrat der DDR, October 20, 1986.

[18] RHG Th 02/05a, Eingabe von Erika Drees an die Kirchenleitung der Kirchenprovinz Sachsen, May 21, 1986.

[19] RHG RG/SA 01, Eingabe vom Friedenskreis der ev. Martinsgemeinde an den Rat des Bezirkes Magdeburg, February 4, 1987.

solution, then, was to "transform people's consciousness to have a more responsible relationship between energy and affluence."[20] In both petitions, calls for more information about what had happened at Chernobyl went hand-in-hand with concerns about specific plans for emergency evacuation plans for Stendal. More broadly, appeals to end the use of nuclear power in the GDR illuminated the SED's untenable energy situation – caught between coal and nuclear – and its economic ossification.

As such, Stendal became a symbol of both nuclear danger and the shortcomings of Soviet-style communism. In 1988, activists gathered there to remember Chernobyl and to call attention to environmental degradation. Members of the AGU in Leipzig attended the protest and then submitted petitions to the Church, the Parliament of the GDR, and the Council of Ministers. The petitioners believed that the risks of nuclear energy were simply too great and stated that the most developed countries were already exploring how to end their reliance on it. As an alternative, they advocated for renewable energy sources, contending that phasing out nuclear power in the GDR was possible. Based on this line of reasoning, they concluded that they must "demand the immediate suspension of construction at Stendal."[21] Although officials at virtually every level of bureaucracy held meetings with activists and Church leaders – going so far as to give Bishop Demke a tour of the construction site – work on Stendal continued.[22] Despite these many protests and petitions, the SED remained unresponsive, revealing the intransigence of the system by the late 1980s.

The expansion of an increasingly oppositional movement, however, caused discord between older and newer participants as well as difficulty in defining goals. The Environmental Library's purpose and functioning, for example, generated conflict between organizers. For some, the Environmental Library was explicitly about opposing the state and carrying out self-described anarchist goals.[23] Ever more comprehensive issues of *Umweltblätter* indicated that the Environmental Library dedicated itself to

---

[20] RHG Th 02/05a, Eingabe von Ludwig und Erika Drees an Erich Honecker, October 20, 1986.
[21] BArch DO 4/805, Eingabe an die Volkskammer der DDR, den Ministerrat der DDR und die Landessynode des Bundes der Evangelischen Kirchen der DDR von der Arbeitsgruppe Umweltschutz Leipzig, June 11, 1988.
[22] BArch DO 4/801, "Auszug aus dem Gästebuch des VEB KKW Stendal über den Besuch des Bischof zu Magdeburg," 21 March 1988. Bishop Demke signed the guestbook, writing "I hope this difficult task finds a solution . . . that respects humans, their peaceful development, and the preservation of nature."
[23] Halbrock, "Die unabhängigen Umweltgruppen in der DDR."

a number of anti-SED causes, not just the environment. By 1987 and 1988, the newsletter had broadened to glasnost and perestroika in the Soviet Union, skinheads, and the march organized in protest of the assassination of Swedish politician Olof Palme, among other topics.[24] For some, then, the environment was more a weapon to be wielded against the SED's corruption and intransigence rather than a cause for its own sake. This divide heightened frustrations within the group.

Stasi interference further strained trust and curbed productivity within environmental circles. While the Environmental Library's inner circle remained more or less free of infiltration, a good number of its associates, such as Falk Zimmermann, were later revealed as unofficial informants.[25] Stasi reports illuminate the intensity of the surveillance, which officers carefully documented. They noted the attendance at environmental events, materials available in the library, the samizdat publications the Environmental Library and other groups produced, and the types of conferences and gatherings that activists held.[26] One report on the third Eco-Seminar in 1986 explained the importance of unofficial informants to the Stasi's work, stating "It is only through the use of unofficial informants that an objective analysis of the discussion and a differentiation between organizers can be reached." It went on to assert that one unofficial inform-ant had failed in his goal to assume a more prominent position because "all of his suggestions relating to this task had been rejected."[27] The constant surveillance and manipulation by unofficial informants added tension and an atmosphere of distrust.

The threat of Stasi interference became a reality on the night of November 24–25, 1987, when the Stasi raided the Environmental Library's rooms in the basement of the Zion Church. Officers arrested seven members and confiscated the illegal printing press.[28] Authorities released the arrested within a few days after domestic and international outcry produced a public relations nightmare for the GDR. The politically moderate KFH in Wittenberg spoke out against the arrests, while green

---

[24] ABL, *Umweltblätter*, Issues from February and July 1987, for example.   [25] 81, 90–91.
[26] BStU MfS BV Bln AKG 371, Hähnel, "Information über die Tätigkeit der sogenannten 'Umweltbibliothek' des 'Öko- und Friedenskreises' der Evangelischen Kirchengemeinde Zion in Berlin-Mitte," November 23, 1986.
[27] BStU MfS BV Bln AG XXII 275, "Erste Erkenntnisse zum sogenannten 3. 'Berliner Ökologieseminar' vom 28.11.1986 bis zum 30.11.1986 in der Evangelischen Kirchgemeinde Zion."
[28] The arrested were Till Böttcher, Bert Schlegel, Andreas Kalk, Bodo Wolff, Wolfgang Rüddenklau, Uta Ihlow, and Tim Eisenlohr. See "MfS-Aktion gegen die Umwelt-Bibliothek," hrsg. v. Bundeszentrale für politische Bildung und Robert-Havemann-Gesellschaft e.V., letzte Änderung September 2008, www.jugendopposition.de/index.php?id=203, accessed May 19, 2015.

parties and activists across western Europe demanded they be released.[29] New contacts abroad brought awareness of the events to a larger audience. The Dutch-based newsletter that the PKE had published in for some time, *Airplan*, wrote about the crackdown. Authors emphasized that the raid overshadowed the important work to be done at the Eco-Seminar scheduled for November 28 and 29.[30] Though the Stasi raid raised the Environmental Library's international profile, the mood within it darkened.

Further strife in the Environmental Library emerged over the group's main objectives, leading to a split in 1988. Relations soured after a failed proposal to build a network instead of a single umbrella organization in 1987. A former member later recalled that by the beginning of 1988 there were no longer substantive discussions. Conversations devolved into ruthless accusations, peppered with personal animosities and prejudices.[31] Therefore, in January 1988, just a year and a half after the library opened, a group led by Carlo Jordan broke off and established the *Grün-Ökologisches Netzwerk Arche in der Evangelischen Kirche Arche* (Green-Ecological Network, Ark, in the Protestant Church, Arche).[32] It took nearly two years for the groups to work together again, but they continued to share limited resources.[33] According to Jordan, in June 1988, Rüddenklau stormed into the Zion Church's office and tried to take off with an Arche computer. Custodian and fellow activist, Matthias Voigt, attempted to discuss the matter, but Rüddenklau threw a punch at Voigt. Voigt then locked himself in the office and waited for Rüddenklau to calm down or leave. When Voigt emerged, Rüddenklau was still there and allegedly assaulted him again, yelling, "If you didn't work here, you'd get one in the nose every day," stating that "That's how we did it in prison." During the scuffle, Voigt fell to the ground and sustained some minor injuries.[34] Personal animosities and suspicion pervaded environmental groups, not least in the more politicized Berlin scene.

[29] AGG OWK 01, "Abschrift der Tonbandprotokolle Der DDR-Veranstaltung in der Fraktion, DIE GRÜNEN IM BUNDESTAG, Am 12. April 1988."
[30] AGG B II 3 1101, "Arrests Shadow Seminar," *Airplan: Air Pollution Action Network* (December 1987), 12.
[31] Neumann, "Was war, war wenig und viel," 81.
[32] Christian Halbrock, "Störfaktor Jugend: Die Anfänge der unabhängigen Umweltbewegung in der DDR," in *Arche Nova: Opposition in der DDR, "Das Grün-ökologische Netzwerk Arche," 1988–90*, eds. Carlo Jordan and Hans Michael Kloth (Berlin: BasisDruck, 1995), 32. Other key founding members of Arche included Ulrich Neumann, Matthias Voigt, and Mario Hamel.
[33] For a competing narrative of the conflict between the Environmental Library and Arche, see Wolfgang Rüddenklau's (ed.) *Störenfried*, 178–180.
[34] RHG ÜG 03, "Information an den GKR – Zion," July 4, 1988, Carlo Jordan and Matthias Voigt. Rüddenklau had been arrested for his activities in oppositional environmental circles as well as for

Interpersonal conflicts aside, Arche's objective was distinct from the Environmental Library's, intentionally constructing a network, not an organization, to improve collaboration. Its samizdat publication, *Arche Info*, laid out the network's goal as "coordinating activities of single-minded environmental groups in the Protestant Church." Arche rejected a centralized structure and supported local or grassroots ecological activities, specifically concerning air quality, acid rain, clean water, waste disposal, lignite, urban ecology and human ecology.[35] Arche argued that misinformation and accusations hindered greater connection between groups, which could at best be described as "regionally bounded."[36] The other elements of the Environmental Library, such as those with anarchist tendencies, took a back seat in Arche, so that the focus remained on ecological issues and disseminating relevant information.

Arche linked groups in Halle, Leipzig, and even the Lusatian village of Großhennersdorf, relying on Church administration to distribute materials. The dioceses of Berlin-Brandenburg, Mecklenburg, Saxony-Anhalt, Dresden, and Thuringia all became part of Arche's network.[37] Before, activism had depended primarily on regional or local groups with a few contacts in Berlin and Leipzig, but Arche now helped to better connect the actors within the movement, improving communication and placing pressure on the progressively paralyzed SED. With events at Environmental Libraries, especially East Berlin's, and Arche's distributing of materials, East Germans more publicly engaged with the environment. The swelling independent environmental activism in the late 1980s exposed the SED's failures to enact its objectives, leaving the state with no choice but repression and Stasi meddling.

The growth of the CUR's "A Mark for Espenhain" campaign demonstrates the rise in environmental awareness by the late 1980s. On June 12, 1988, approximately 800 East Germans attended a widely publicized pilgrimage through the devastated coalmining region. The podium discussion with both Church and local authorities revolved around the antiquated machinery and techniques used at Espenhain, which led to "unbearable living conditions for residents."[38] It was the CUR's sixth annual environmental service, but unlike earlier ones, reports of the day's

anti-sodomy laws. BStU MfS BV Bln AKG 371, Hähnel, "Information über die Tätigkeit der sogenannten 'Umweltbibliothek,'" November 23, 1986.

[35] ABL, "Arche: Das Grüne Netzwerk i. Der Ev. Kirche – (vorläufige) Gründungserklärung," *Arche Info* I/88.

[36] ABL, "Warum Arche? Warum ein Netzwerk in der ev. Kirche?," *Arche Info* I/88.

[37] ABL, "Kontaktadressen," *Arche Info* I/88.   [38] ABL, 42.4.4, "Eine Mark für Espenhain," 1988.

happenings appeared in Church and samizdat publications that reached across the GDR, including *Briefe*, *Arche Info*, and the *Umweltblätter*. The CUR further published multiple pamphlets about the campaign. The authors asked for a single mark from individuals to renovate the nearby plant, claiming that reducing emissions by fifty percent could lower the death rate by 4.5 percent, raise life expectancy, and cut heart and circulatory diseases by ten to fifteen percent.

This truly GDR-wide campaign garnered an unprecedented level of interconnectedness among independent activists. The symbolic contribution was not a collection or donation but an "act of solidarity" to generate the funds that state officials could not or would not spend to improve living standards.[39] Rather than being a local effort to clean up a park or plant trees, "A Mark for Espenhain" asked East Germans to bypass the state's inertia. That the Church had to raise funds to improve the coal refining process when the centrally planned economy could not provide new filters for the plant had to gall local and central officials. This effrontery did not come from Berlin or Leipzig, though groups there publicized the campaign, but from one of the most devastated regions of the GDR. Activists from Dresden to Erfurt to Leipzig and Berlin donated, critiquing the human and environmental repercussions of the pollution.[40]

The inaugural "Ecumenical Air Seminar" held in Erfurt later that year also collected money for Espenhain, invoking the SED's commitment to the 1984 Munich Agreement. Participants demanded that the GDR reduce sulfur dioxide levels by thirty percent of 1980 levels by 1993, as it had promised internationally.[41] The working group "Air Pollution and Illnesses of the Respiratory Tract" prepared fliers that gave guidelines on how to pressure the SED. It recommended East Germans write petitions to local authorities and to district level ones, too, asking about progress toward the new standards. The authors also encouraged petitioners to demand the release of data, especially sulfur dioxide levels and "what measures were being taken in light of increasing incidences of asthma and chronic bronchitis."[42] Finally, beyond confronting local and district officials, the working group asked people to forward their correspondence with officials to Johannes Staemmler in Erfurt. By consolidating material, the group gained a better impression of their own movement's strength as

---

[39] RHG Th 02/03, "Erläuterung zum Aufruf," October 1988. For the percentages specified in the pamphlet, they cited K. Horn, "Vorwort," *Wissenschaftl. Zeitschrift*, Jg. 19, H. 5 (1970), 448.
[40] RHG Th 02/03, "Aktion: Eine Mark für Espenhain," undated.
[41] RHG Th 02/03, "Aktion 30%," October 1988.
[42] RHG Th 02/03, "Beteiligt Euch an der Aktion 30%."

well as the ability to challenge the state's messaging on pollution and public health.

In Lusatia, too, Chernobyl proved to be a turning point and was often cited as a reason for residents connecting and sharing concerns. The Ecology Circle in Hoyerswerda specifically stated the group sought to learn more about the effects of the nuclear disaster from East and West German sources. This decision could be somewhat surprising given that nuclear power was often viewed as a clean alternative to the ubiquitous devastation from coalmining and refining in the area.[43] In Großhennersdorf and Zittau, groups actually built on existing anxiety about open-pit mining and acid rain, and then framed them in terms of broader questions about energy sources. The degradation inspired them to found two Environmental Libraries, one in the village of Großhennersdorf and another in the nearby town of Zittau. In Großhennersdorf, workers from a local home for the disabled, Andreas Schönfelder and Thomas Pilz, founded the library. Schönfelder had established contact with the Environmental Library in Berlin in 1987 and distributed the *Umweltblätter* and another samizdat publication, *Grenzfall*, in Lusatia.[44] Travel and hand-to-hand dissemination of information facilitated ties between Lusatia and the larger movement.

In conjunction with a group in Zittau, Schönfelder and Pilz began publishing about pollution in their *Lausitz Botin* (*Lusatian Messenger*) to coordinate efforts "in a bigger context."[45] Starting in 1988, the *Lausitz Botin* appeared sporadically but focused especially on-air quality and the impact of acid rain on the forest. The first issue proclaimed, "WE, THE CITIZENS OF ZITTAU, ARE AFFECTED!" They went on to detail the effects of the "environmental catastrophe of Waldsterben" in the Zittauer Gebirge and the Black Triangle more broadly. They asserted, "We cannot find the beauty anymore. Many of us are sick in our souls to see our Heimat destroyed this way." They also made the case for environmental protection because living in a recreation area, which Pilz as the editor noted, meant that people from all over the GDR came to Upper Lusatia for health reasons. The devastation belied its status as a respite for vacationers.[46]

---

[43] Umweltbibliothek Großhennersdorf (UBG), unfiled, "Ökologiekreis Hoyerswerda," undated.

[44] Arnaud Liszka and Thomas Pilz, eds., *Lausitz Botin: Das Jahr 1989 in der sächsischen Provinz im Spiegel einer Zittauer Oppositionszeitschrift* (Bautzen: Lusatia Verlag, 1999), 13.

[45] UBG, Roland Brauckmann, "Entwurf: Entstehungsgeschichte der unabhängigen Hefte 'Lausitzbotin,' Zittau," September 15, 1997.

[46] Original document reprinted in Liszka and Pilz, eds., *Lausitz Botin*, 50–51.

The high levels of air pollution, acid rain, and Waldsterben led to continuing demands to make data regarding local conditions public. One of the leaders of the Zittau Church-based group was Andreas Prescher, a technologist at VEB Deutsche Piano-Union Leipzig in Olbersdorf. He repeatedly petitioned for the release of data on his own while also frequently speaking to different parishes about "Living for a livable Earth."[47] Despite attracting Stasi attention for his activism, Prescher received commendation from his state employer for changing the technical parameters of the centrifugal separator in order to reduce environmental pollution.[48] He also worked with officials to allow Christian and GNU environmentalists to clean up the surrounding forest. He appealed to state officials by insisting that all individual activists, groups, friends of nature, and the "ecologically affected" needed the opportunity to take responsibility.[49] Thus, Prescher attempted to improve the environment through work, Church, and official avenues, cutting across different sections of East German society to raise awareness and hopefully improve local conditions.

In October 1988, activists convened the first "Meeting of the Lusatian Environmental Groups," reflecting the spread of regional and trans-national networks. Convening in Görlitz, groups from Hoyerswerda, Weißwasser, and Forst also attended. These gatherings, of course, garnered attention from the Stasi. Meetings were reported to district level authorities, especially when it became clear that Schönfelder of Großhennersdorf could obtain Greenpeace newspapers and that someone else had connections with a peace group in Czechoslovakia.[50] One of the major players in this group, Dieter Goernert, was also known to have attended the founding meeting of Arche in Berlin. Goernert and Schönfelder's friends in Arche provided them with Greenpeace and Greenway materials, which worried local Stasi officials, and brought Lusatians into conversation with organizations active on both sides of the Iron Curtain.[51] Arche's approach to connecting groups was working. Even in the "valley of the clueless," western Greenpeace and eastern European Greenway materials were accessible and undermined the state's credibility.

---

[47] UBG, Andreas Prescher 27-8, "Herzliche Einladung zum Geprächsabend," undated.
[48] UBG, Andreas Prescher 27-6, "Urkunde," August 23, 1988.
[49] UBG, Andreas Prescher 27-8, "Liebe Mitglieder des Kirchenvorstandes," February 1, 1989.
[50] MfS KD Görlitz Abteilung XX 403-2 Nr. 13, "Information zum Ökologie- und Umweltschutzkreis in Görlitz am 15.12.88," found in UBG Personalbestand Andreas Schönfelder 35-7.
[51] MfS KD Görlitz Abteilung XX XIV 1431/81, AOP "Pfleger" 215/92 Bd. V, "Informationen zu Vernetzungsbestrebungen feindlich-negativer Kräfte innerhalb des Grün-Ökologisches Bundes/ Arche," June 17, 1988, found at UBG Personalbestand Andreas Schönfelder 35-7.

As the independent movement in the GDR attracted a larger following, the participants became more diverse, posing unforeseen challenges. Although the Church remained committed to the environment and formed a new Ecumenical Council in 1988 to reflect that, a growing number of activists wanted little or nothing to do with religion. Ironically, the Christian rhetoric on which the movement had initially based its critique of socialism was also self-limiting, which put off many of those who joined after Chernobyl to push the state on its inaction and secrecy. Moreover, longer standing members distrusted newcomers, fearing that they might be Stasi infiltrators. The Church continued to support a theological investigation of the environment and religion, as the KFH had since the 1970s, but it hesitated to support more radical objections. The movement's expansion in the GDR's final years produced tensions between the Church's strictures and activists who pushed against them.

In 1988, the new Ecumenical Council brought together virtually all of the churches in the GDR to discuss "Justice, Peace and the Preservation of Creation."[52] This plenum was a huge success, drawing over a thousand attendees for the opening service and 6,500 for the ecumenical peace service on Saturday evening.[53] The registered participants largely accepted the structure of East German society, explaining that as Christians they should also be ready to work together with all "societal forces" to reduce the destruction of nature.[54] Six months later, a second Ecumenical Council further criticized the SED, arguing that "shortsighted successes in offering consumer goods and statistically successful reports do not suffice as definitions of societal effectiveness."[55] As the movement evolved, one strand of it remained closely tied to theological justifications, focusing on questions about responsibility to God's creation, but they were becoming a minority as more East Germans joined the independent environmental movement.

The moralizing tone of the Christian ethic did not appeal to many of the new participants, dividing them in terms of method and message. The Ecumenical Council critiqued consumption as a means of making life

---

[52] Two more were held within the next year and a half, one in Magdeburg in October 1988 and a third in Dresden again in April 1989.

[53] This council included not only members of the mainstream Lutheran and Catholic Churches but also the Moravian Church, Methodists, the Old Catholic Church, Mennonites, the Russian Orthodox Church, Seventh Day Adventists, the Friends, and others. See RHG Ki 21/01, "Ökumenische Versammlung: Informationsdienst, März 1988."

[54] RHG Ki 21/2, "Ökumenische Vollversammlung, Arbeitsgruppe 11: Ökologie und Ökonomie," February 12–15, 1988.

[55] RHG Ki 21/2, "Ökumenische Vollversammlung, Arbeitsgruppe 11: Ökologie und Ökonomie," October 8–11, 1988.

more comfortable and to ward off boredom while squandering energy and resources for future generations. This mentality stood in direct conflict with many East Germans' desire for more consumer goods.[56] Noting that products were made "as cheaply as possible … [and] poisoned the air, water and earth" did not endear the more religious elements of independent environmentalism to a wider audience.[57] While targeting the SED system's inefficiencies and shortcomings, such rhetoric inadvertently criticized the population. Many could see that pollution was a serious problem, and may have wanted to address it, but did not want to be preached at to change their own lives while they protested the SED's policies.

From the perspective of the Church, too, the increasing number of groups posed a series of complications. Leaders in the churches, especially the Protestant Church, faced a difficult balancing act between permitting groups to use their space and placating officials. Naturally, some such as the pastor of the Zion Church in Berlin, Hans Simon, supported oppositional groups like the Environmental Library. Others, such as Hans-Peter Gensichen of the KFH in Wittenberg and Heino Falcke, remained dedicated to environmental causes and avoided the explicitly oppositional. Gensichen and Falcke were both deeply involved in the organization of the Ecumenical Councils. But others were hesitant to unreservedly back the groups' activities. Prominent Church leader Manfred Stolpe was known for telling more radical activists to keep it down.[58] As part of being the Church in Socialism, the Protestant Church was obligated to maintain some amount of control over the people it housed as well as to remain in contact with the authorities. Environmental issues had drawn together individuals from a range of backgrounds, but without changes to the communist system, the movement had grown about as much as it could.

"Żarnobyl" as a Turning Point: Protest in Poland

While East German environmental activism reached an impasse in the mid to late 1980s, other eastern European activists took full advantage of new

---

[56] Katherine Pence and Paul Betts, "Introduction" in *Socialist Modern: East German Everyday Culture and Politics*, eds. Katherine Pence and Paul Betts (Ann Arbor, MI: University of Michigan Press, 2008), 6–8.

[57] RHG TH 02/01, "Und ich will bei Euch wohnen," Die Evangelische Umweltgruppe Adlershof, 1987.

[58] Conversation with Lothar Rochau cited in Nathan Stoltzfus, "Public Space and the Dynamics of Environmental Action: Green Protest in the GDR," *Archiv für Sozialgeschichte* 43 (2003), 394.

freedoms under Gorbachev. Again, Chernobyl became a rallying cry for change, raising questions not only about nuclear technology but also pollution and energy sources more broadly. In Poland, protests against nuclear power had not been strong before, but in 1986 they gained momentum, uniting people from across the political spectrum and tapping into broader environmental discontent. Opposition to communist control continued to swell as opportunities for change were more tolerated than in the GDR. Greenway, the network of environmental groups in eastern European countries stretching from Yugoslavia to Estonia, linked pro-testors on an unprecedented level, with the PKE in Kraków taking a leading role in that organization. Poland became an important node in the movement, building bridges within the Soviet bloc and across the Iron Curtain. Transnational collaboration and solidarity grew among activists after Chernobyl, despite difficulties such as limited funds and mobility, repressive state security apparatuses, and cultural and linguistic barriers that impeded environmentalists' efforts.[59]

Initial outrage over the disaster led to numerous rallies in Wrocław, Kraków, and Warsaw, and linked Polish dissatisfaction with parallel reac-tions across the bloc. As in the GDR, the Polish press did not officially make the spill at Chernobyl known for several days – until after May Day celebrations – but the first vague reports were released late on April 28.[60] Of course, those paying attention to western media had already begun to hear about it and to raise the alarm. Though the PZPR expressed complete satisfaction with the way it handled Chernobyl, observers charged that the selective release of information was aimed at public acquiescence rather than safety.[61] Given Poles' access to news from non-communist sources, this response was not sufficient. In the week after Chernobyl, at least two new groups were formed: the Independent Ecological Commission in Lublin and the Working Group for Protection of the Environment in Wrocław. The Independent Ecological Commission declared in its founding statement that "this glaring example of the manipulation of information and the subordin-ation of the population's biological health to the regime's feeble aims forces us to energetic action."[62] As in the GDR, Chernobyl merged nuclear fears with information politics about the environment.

---

[59] Andrew Tompkins points to important limits on grassroots transnationalisms in his article, "Grassroots Transnationalism(s): Franco-German Opposition to Nuclear Energy in the 1970s," *Contemporary European History* 25, no. 1 (February 2016), 117–142.
[60] OSA, Radio Free Europe. 1986, *Research* 11:27 (June 27). Polish Situation Report 10/86, 13.
[61] Ibid., 17.   [62] Ibid., 17.

Poles also worried about potential nuclear disaster at home. In early May 1986, the oppositional Freedom and Peace (WiP) staged demonstrations in response to Chernobyl and the construction of Poland's first nuclear power plant at Żarnowiec. Fears over Chernobyl ("Czernobyl" in Polish) united with the potential for disaster at Żarnowiec, near Gdańsk, as protestors railed against "Żarnobyl." In Wrocław, several members of WiP publicly protested against what they called a "blockade of information" about the course and consequences of the catastrophe as well as the Soviet Union's rejection of western aid. The activists warned "Żarnowiec is next" and that contamination was spreading.[63] In the end, several hundred people stopped to observe the protest, and the police detained five WiP members involved. These demonstrations were then publicized in independent newsletters across the country, indicating that Chernobyl and Żarnowiec were not isolated concerns.

In Kraków, protests against Chernobyl built on already planned environmental initiatives, such as one on Children's Day (June 1) in Kraków. For the demonstration in Kraków, WiP became more active in orchestrating the events after Chernobyl came to light. Women carried dead flowers as they left the Marian church in the center of Kraków to symbolize the death of nature. As they entered the market square, WiP posters greeted them and the group began to sing songs that had been part of Solidarność in 1980–1981.[64] A Radio Free Europe situation report estimated that roughly 2,000 Krakowians participated in the Children's Day protests. In the wake of Chernobyl, WiP began to engage more actively with the environmental aspects of its platform and more explicitly protest against pollution on many levels. Chernobyl sparked a wave of antinuclear protest that was unprecedented for the country.

Despite popular frustration, construction on Żarnowiec, which was based on the same model as Chernobyl, continued. Located thirty-five miles northwest of Gdańsk, Żarnowiec raised questions about the future of nuclear energy in Poland, especially for a nuclear power plant that relied on the same technology and safety systems. Although Radio Free Europe concluded, "Public opposition to Żarnowiec will probably be of little consequence, simply because construction is unlikely to make much headway soon," nuclear energy remained contentious for environmental and

---

[63] OSA, Katarzyna Uroń et al., eds., "Czernobyl," *Wydaje: Komitet Oporu Społecznego*, Numer 84 dodatek, May 4, 1986, http://storage.osaarchivum.org/low/56/27/5627a0f7-89c6-4d5a-b400-c3abf9405bfe_l.pdf, accessed October 13, 2017.

[64] Kenney, *A Carnival of Revolution*, 71–73.

opposition groups.[65] In the weeks after Chernobyl, 3,000 Poles from the northern city of Białystok signed a petition to the Sejm demanding a stop to the construction of Żarnowiec. In nearby Gdańsk, the local WiP chapter wrote to fellow activists in the GDR as well as western Europe for support in stopping the construction.[66] Frustration over the danger posed by Chernobyl fed into larger discontent with the PZPR over its secrecy and lack of responsiveness.

Two years later, a WiP chapter in Wrocław was still writing to the PZPR's Presidium demanding a move away from nuclear energy, though general outrage over Chernobyl had quieted. The letter highlighted the economic costs associated with the construction and operation of nuclear power plants. The petitioners also warned of the social and environmental hazards they posed, especially the storage of nuclear waste that power stations generated.[67] They were, of course, also concerned with the dangers of nuclear weapons, but that seemed further removed in the months and years after Chernobyl. The letter concluded with a demand to end the construction of nuclear power plants in Poland. WiP's transition to fully incorporating more ecological issues – not just peace – became exemplified in petitions like this one and spoke to the broadening environmental base in eastern Europe.

Storing nuclear waste also became a flashpoint in Poland, as WiP spearheaded protests against a proposed disposal site near the small town of Międzyrzecz in western Poland. In 1987, WiP members and residents of the town at large opposed using a local World War II bunker for storage. They were troubled by the local geology and climate, fearing that humidity would erode the bunker and contaminate the groundwater.[68] The protests included a week-long hunger strike followed by a march through the town. Police permitted the 5,000 demonstrators to walk through the town, though numerous residents were fined over the course of the protests.[69] Relative to the size of the population, the mobilization in Międzyrzecz was unmatched anywhere in Poland between 1981 and 1989.[70] In light of

---

[65] OSA, 1986, *Research* 11:27 (June 27). Polish Situation Report 10/86, 18.

[66] RHG TH 12/03, "Freedom and Peace Gdańsk," undated.

[67] Ossolineum Biblioteka, Różne, Wolność i Pokój, Oddział Życia Społecznego, Letter to the Presidium on "Nuclear energy," March 15, 1988.

[68] Archiv Grünes Gedächtnis (AGG) B II 3 1101, "Do we need Żarnowiec?" *Greenway: An East European Environmental Newsletter*, 1987/3.

[69] Bogdan Turek, "Poles Stage Anti-Nuclear Protest," United Press International (Warsaw), October 4, 1987, www.upi.com/Archives/1987/10/04/Poles-stage-anti-nuclear-protest/3653560318400, accessed February 22, 2019.

[70] Kenney, *A Carnival of Revolution*, 75.

Chernobyl, the threat of nuclear energy loomed large. In 1987, Polish activists writing in Greenway's self-titled, pan-eastern European newsletter, *Greenway*, contended that "the invested expenses are not yet too big" and that there was still time to stop the construction.[71] Solidarność also joined the debate, printing calendars for 1988 that read "Atomic Trash Dump in Międzyrzecz – No!"[72] Resentment over eroding environmental conditions now intertwined with an immediate fear of nuclear power and the need to store waste if Poland continued its nuclear pursuits.

News regarding Żarnowiec, Międzyrzecz, and a second nuclear reactor planned near Klempicz made their way into German-speaking countries, where antinuclear movements were already strong. Given that Międzyrzecz and Klempicz were in parts of Poland that had gone back and forth between Polish and German control numerous times over the previous centuries, these regions were relatively more familiar to German readers.[73] Solidarność's German language publication made an "ecological appeal" to especially West Germans to protest against the three sites. Emphasizing that "in a system in which there is not democratic control" economic considerations had the power to destroy the natural environment.[74] East German samizdat publications, most notably *Umweltblätter*, also raised concerns about Polish nuclear power projects, such as Klempicz, which lay not far from Poznań (also in western Poland). The proposed plant would draw water from the Noteć River, disturbing the local water table and potentially contaminating the surrounding forest.[75] Gorbachev's reforms and outrage from Chernobyl riled up a sense of crisis in central European over existing and planned nuclear power plants – and the associated facilities – in the Soviet bloc for activists on either side of the Iron Curtain.

Chernobyl also provided an opportunity for activists to bring other environmental issues to the public's attention both at home and abroad. Another Kraków-based group, the *Naukowe Koło Chemików* (Chemists' Scientific Club, NKCh), became more prolific in the mid-1980s, coordinating with the PKE on numerous projects. In 1987, the NKCh began measuring water quality in the Vistula River in Kraków. It also operated

---

[71] AGG B II 3 1101, "Do we need Żarnowiec?" *Greenway: An East European Environmental Newsletter*, 1987/3.

[72] OSA, "Śmietnik Atomowy w Międzyrzeczu – Nie!" 1988, http://storage.osaarchivum.org/low/85/do/85dobba1-299f-47de-b226-d7c7ddfddc73_l_001.jpg, accessed February 22, 2019.

[73] Brian Joseph McCook, *The Borders of Integration: Polish Migrants in Germany and the United States, 1870–1924* (Athens, OH: Ohio University Press, 2011), 8–13.

[74] AGG B I 3 1101, "Ökologischer Appell," *Information Bulletin*, June 12, 1986.

[75] RHG, "Atomkraftwerk im Wald," *Umweltblätter*, April 1988, 18–19.

a second-hand bookstore, arranged for summer and winter scientific and ecological camps, and helped take part in investigations of contamination.[76] The NKCh published its findings abroad, such as in the Dutch-based newsletter, *Airplan*. Highlighting Poland's pollution to an international audience, the NKCh reported that roughly seventy percent – or nearly two-and-a-half-million people – lived "in conditions which are harmful to health." About one million inhabitants were continually exposed to carcinogens, while Upper Silesia had forty-seven percent more respiratory illnesses than other parts of Poland.[77] Through *Airplan* and similar publications, western audiences, such as the West German Greens, learned about degradation behind the Iron Curtain and then offered support.

The PZPR's leniency proved to be a boon for organizing environmental groups across Europe, allowing them a voice at home and representation in international associations. In addition to tolerating the PKE's existence on the margins, the PZPR permitted the PKE to become a full member of Friends of the Earth (FOE). To formalize this new affiliation, a PKE representative from Warsaw, Andrzej Kassenberg, attended an executive committee meeting in Geneva. A professor at Warsaw's Central School of Planning and Statistics as well as a former vice-president of PKE, Kassenberg straddled official and independent associations.[78] While at the meeting, he aimed to make western Europeans more aware of conditions in Poland and eastern Europe more generally. He contended, "The environment – and air pollution – do not care about boundaries, and environmental protection isn't defined by politics or profit factors." Kassenberg further pointed out – self-critically – that Poland was a large contributor of air pollution in Europe in addition to being in a "difficult economic situation."[79] Kassenberg worked to both show the ecological and environmental ties between east and west, which would strengthen contacts and mutual concern across the Iron Curtain.

At the same time, Poland became an integral site of transnational networking and cooperation. Still under Zygmunt Fura's leadership, the

---

[76] AGG B II 3 1101, "Chemists in Krakow," *Airplan: Air Pollution Action Network* (December 1987), 12.

[77] AGG B II 3 1101, "Upper Silesia: From the Information Leaflet of Naukowe Kolo Chemikówe," *Airplan* (December 1987), 12.

[78] Barbara Hicks, *Environmental Politics in Poland: A Social Movement between Regime and Opposition* (New York: Columbia University Press, 1996), 87.

[79] AGG B II 3 1101, "Perspective from the East," *Airplan* (December 1987), 10. While weather patterns in Europe typically move from west to east, Kassenberg means overall pollution levels. Moreover, the major Polish rivers empty into the Baltic Sea, adding to water pollution that affected non-communist countries. Also, radiation from Chernobyl did affect western Europe.

PKE hosted numerous international conferences, which brought together activists from the Soviet Union, communist bloc, and western Europe. The debates and resolutions were then published in *Greenway* as well as in samizdat publications in other eastern European countries. In the summers of 1987 and 1988, for example, the PKE hosted multiday events for participants from all over eastern Europe, including Poles, Czechoslovaks, Hungarians, East Germans, and Soviets. They concluded that the environmental situation in socialist countries was bad and it seemed to be getting worse, despite government programs and policies. The authors argued that activists should play a larger role in pushing for solutions to ecological problems.[80] This banding-together of Soviet bloc countries, with Poland as a central node, created a sense of purpose and unity among eastern European activists.

The PZPR's relative tolerance, however, was the source of much consternation for the East German authorities. The Stasi sought to limit East Germans' access to Polish gatherings and contacts, fearing that such exposure would weaken socialism in the GDR. Coordination between the GDR and Poland, albeit sometimes reluctantly on the Polish side, restricted East German activists' ability to travel. For known oppositional and environmental figures in the GDR, travel to Poland – much less beyond the bloc – remained uncertain. After having entered Poland with the intended destination of Katowice, one known activist was reported to have surfaced at the port of Gdańsk in an attempt to take the ferry to Finland for an international conference there.[81] The activist's visa only permitted travel to Poland, Czechoslovakia, and the Soviet Union, and on those grounds, Polish border authorities denied him passage to Finland. Polish police went so far as to confiscate a "note of protest" that the activist had planned to pass on to his Finnish companion, should he be detained. Ever thorough, the Stasi then requested that the note be handed over to them for safekeeping.[82]

---

[80] AGG B II 3 1101, Greenway Meeting, September 17–20, 1987.

[81] BStU MfS Abt X 257, Correspondence between Ministry for State Security, Regional Department Berlin, and the Polish Foreign Ministry, June–August 1989.

[82] BStU MfS Abt X 257, Correspondence between the Bezirksverwaltung für Staatssicherheit Berlin, Abteilung XX and the Ministerium für Staatssicherheit, 14, 1989. In his book, *Przyjaźń, której nie było*, Tytus Jaskułowski explores the cooperation (or lack thereof) between the Stasi and the Polish Interior Ministry. He argues that they rarely worked together and that it was often counterproductive when they did, typically trying to use their partner ministries for their own purposes. While this does seem to generally hold true for environmental activists, in Jordan's case, they did cooperate. Tytus Jaskułowski, *Przyjaźń, której nie było: Ministerstwo Bezpieczeństwa Państwowego NRD wobec MSW, 1974–1990* (Warsaw: Wydawnictwa Uniwersytetu Warszawskiego, 2014).

In other cases, East Germans were not permitted to visit other socialist countries; the Stasi cited Poland, Czechoslovakia, and Hungary as the three most problematic. The Stasi complained that for years "nonsocialist representatives" had used meetings in other Soviet bloc states to meet with GDR-people, particularly East Germans forbidden from leaving the bloc for political reasons.[83] East German officials even maintained the practice of banning East Germans from traveling within the Soviet bloc up to the GDR's final months. Moreover, the Stasi denied representatives from Ukraine, Estonia, Lithuania, Russia, and Latvia entrance into the GDR for a Greenway meeting in Berlin in the summer of 1989. Fearing that "'Greens' from different capitalist countries wanted to participate," the Stasi declared that the conference was not officially registered or permitted, and therefore forbade environmentalists from the Soviet Union from entering.[84] Even as communication increased between Soviet bloc countries, the continued vigilance of security apparatuses hindered the expansion of a movement and limited the coordination of independent public spheres.

When East Germans did manage to travel to Poland, they gained an appreciation for independent groups' more constructive relationship with the authorities. Just as the Stasi feared, East Germans praised the level of support the PKE received from local officials. Not only did the PKE's Fura have a good working relationship with the head environmental inspector of Kraków, Bronisław Kaminski, but Kaminski led visitors on a tour of the infamous local polluter, the Lenin Steelworks at Nowa Huta. Moreover, the government funded scientific projects, including measuring and publishing data, and went so far as to encourage international collaboration.[85] This more tolerant atmosphere signaled to East Germans that glasnost was taking hold in other countries and spurred calls for change in the GDR.

After such international gatherings, participants returned to their home countries to disseminate the results and their impressions from these meetings for those who could not attend. Reports on visits to Poland in 1987 and 1988 were written for multiple samizdat and Church publications in the GDR, such as *Umweltblätter* and *Briefe*, the newsletter published in

[83] BStU MfS JHS MF VVS 681 76, Fachschulabschlußarbeit, "Die politisch-operative Aufgabenstellung bei der vorbeugenden Absicherung der zentralen staatlichen Leitung des Umweltschutzes unter besondere Berücksichtigung seiner zunehmenden Bedeutung in den internationalen Beziehungen," January 4, 1977.
[84] BStU MfS HA XX 17175, "Information über ein geplantes 'Greenway-Arbeitstreffen' vom 28.9. bis 1.10.1989 in der Kirchgemeinde Berlin-Friedrichsfelde."
[85] Ibid.

Wittenberg at the KFH.[86] A report from East German activists on the European Youth Forest Action conference in July 1988 discussed the relative acceptance of independent groups in various countries, helping to contextualize the East German efforts. As the author explained, "In Hungary, Poland, Estonia, and Ukraine, autonomous environmental groups can exist and register as independent organizations ... [But] the situation is substantially more problematic in the GDR, Czechoslovakia, and Romania, where these groups are only partially tolerated."[87] In-person contacts and written distribution of knowledge supported further networking that undermined the SED's attempts to maintain a monopoly on power and information.

These transnational connections, however, sometimes experienced setbacks, as language barriers, misunderstandings, and cultural mispercep-tions tarnished encounters.[88] An article in *Umweltblätter* praised a 1988 meeting in Kraków as a high point in European environmental activists' work and a building block in overcoming barriers, but at least one East German disagreed and wrote in detail about his disillusionment with the visit.[89] After the conference finished, some of the male activists decided to go to a local disco. Despite the reasonable cost of drinks, the East Germans were unimpressed with the shabby club and loose women. The author complained that after dancing with two Polish women, they "excused themselves saying that sex [*Beischlaf*] would cost 150 DM, and if we were interested, we could follow them." East German activists further alleged the disc jockey demanded 1,000 zloty to keep the music playing.[90] The disgruntled author clearly found the experience distasteful, revealing real and perceived differences that at times dampened transnational interactions.

Opposition to the PZPR continued to strengthen in Poland after 1986, making it a crucial site for environmental activism and collaboration. Concerns about Chernobyl and Polish nuclear projects brought environ-mentalism to the fore and engaged a larger central European community

---

[86] RGH HJT 14, Jörg Naumann, "3. Greenway-Treffen in Krakow," *Briefe*, April 1988, 3–6. Archiv Bürgerbewegung Leipzig (ABL), "Europäische Waldaktion – Sommertreffen der EYFA in Krakow," *Arche Nova II*, October 1988, 19–21.

[87] RHG Th 02/06, "Europäische Waldaktion – Sommertreffen der E.Y.F.A. in Krakow."

[88] Tompkins, "Grassroots Transnationalism(s)," 128.

[89] ABL, "Europäische Waldaktion – Sommertreffen der EYFA in Krakow," *Umweltblätter*, September 27, 1988.

[90] RHG TH 02/01, "Youth Forest Action in Cracow (Poland) 10.–14.7.1988." 100 Złoty was about 1.40 DM at the time, as referenced in Sabine Rosenbladt, *Der Osten ist grün? Ökoreportagen aus der DDR, Sowjetunion, Tschechoslowakei, Polen, Ungarn* (Hamburg: Rasch und Röhring Verlag, 1988), 13.

about the physical and intellectual interconnectedness of the region. Increasingly, Poland served as a hub for environmentalists from behind and across the Iron Curtain to interact with one another, even if these exchanges occasionally led to misunderstandings and frustration. More than ever before, environmental activists were able to not only think transnationally but to act and be transnational through travel and in-person meetings. Moreover, by 1988, the PZPR was in negotiations with Solidarność about reforming and democratizing Poland, indicating it was the weakest link in the Soviet bloc and foreshadowing further challenges to communism in Europe. Deepening contacts between eastern and western Europe – through Poland – added to a mutual sense of environmental responsibility.

Building a Shared Responsibility: Entangled Environments

Overarching fear of nuclear disaster as well as concrete and well-established pollution forged new bonds between officials and activists in central Europe after 1986. Western Europeans, and especially West Germans, took a more concrete interest in environmental pollution and protests that they shared with Germans on the other side of the border. Journalists traveled to eastern Europe to report on conditions, while East German activists smuggled documentaries to the west and collaborated with western green groups, such as Greenpeace and Robin Wood.[91] These interactions forged a common body of knowledge on multiple levels that brought together Europeans from both sides of the Iron Curtain, and especially the two Germanys. Despite political as well as cultural differences that led to misunderstandings, the transnational networks continued to grow after Chernobyl. The entangled German–German environment and shared environmental concern laid a foundation for cooperation on multiple levels.

As early as April 30, 1986 – four days after Chernobyl – the West German province of Lower Saxony reached out to Reichelt to push for greater transparency. Minister Wilfried Hasselmann claimed that the accident at Chernobyl, "of which we learned with great regret and deep concern," was actually an opportunity to improve the exchange of information.[92]

---

[91] Astrid M. Eckert, "Geteilt aber nicht unverbunden: Grenzgewässer als deutsch-deutsches Umweltproblem," *Vierteljahrshefte für Zeitgeschichte* 62, no. 1 (January 2014), 69–99. Astrid Mignon Kirchhof, "'For a Decent Quality of Life': Environmental Groups in East and West Berlin," *Journal of Urban History* 41, no. 4 (April 2015), 625–646.

[92] PA AA M 41 812 88, Correspondence between Wilfried Hasselmann and Hans Reichelt, April 30, 1986.

Hasselmann was especially invested in sharing radiation levels, needling the GDR by stating that Lower Saxony already had such agreements with Switzerland, the Netherlands, and France. Oskar Fischer, Minister of Foreign Affairs, dismissed Hasselmann's letter as a tactic primarily aimed at the upcoming election campaign. Fischer recommended that Reichelt reply that the GDR did not meet with states of the Federal Republic. Reichelt's and Fischer's responses reaffirmed that the GDR did not see Chernobyl as a turning point in its relationship with the FRG – or its states – but rather became further entrenched in its distrust of West German initiatives.

With burgeoning interest in eastern Europe after Chernobyl, West German journalists, authors, and activists familiarized West Germans with developments in the Soviet bloc. These non-state actors worked to present a broader picture of pollution under communist rule. Wolf Oschlies' 1987 book explained Poland's environmental and political situation to readers. Though much of the research had been conducted before Chernobyl and there were only a handful of references to nuclear energy, increased interest in all things eastern European drew readers.[93] Oschlies introduced West Germans to the existence of "an open, honest and self-critical ecology debate" in eastern Europe.[94] Moreover, Poland's relative openness after 1985 shone through when Oschlies stated that the causes, character, and scope of the environmental degradation were unreservedly disclosed, implicitly contrasting that context with the more repressive GDR. Oschlies used this transparency to blame the planned economy for the exploitation of natural resources and devastating pollution. For example, he pointed out such absurdity as placing intensive industry and national parks side by side and exacerbating Waldsterben.[95] Works such as Oschlies' helped translate Poland's – and more broadly eastern Europe's – circumstances into comprehensible terms for western European audiences.

Other exposés more explicitly compared environmental pollution and movements in eastern Europe, painting a picture of devastation with regional variation for western audiences. Sabine Rosenbladt, a journalist with ties to the West German Greens, traveled through Soviet bloc countries to research her book on the environment behind the Iron

---

[93] Wolf Oschlies, *Bald ist Polen doch Verloren: Umweltzerstörung hinter Oder und Neisse* (Cologne: Böhlau, 1987). The title, *Poland Is Indeed Nearly Lost*, referenced the Polish national anthem, which begins, "Poland is not yet lost, so long as we still live." Wolf Oschlies was born in Königsberg (now Kaliningrad) in 1941 and lived in the GDR until he fled to the west in 1959. He later became a professor of political science at the University of Gießen with a focus on eastern Europe and the Balkans.

[94] Ibid., 7. [95] Ibid., 19.

Curtain. She cited a professor from the Polish Academy of Sciences who admitted that the Silesian region around Katowice was "probably one of the most polluted regions on the earth."[96] In Czechoslovakia, however, Rosenbladt's tale highlighted the denial of pollution and accused officials of disregarding critical reports. Northern Bohemia was a "horror scenario" and a "ticking time bomb" of ecological disaster thanks to heavy reliance on sulfur heavy lignite.[97] The pollution in the Black Triangle had already made headlines in the FRG when images of needle-less pine trees raised awareness about acid rain earlier in the 1980s, but she now reinforced a sense of impending doom in her work.[98] While some countries were more upfront about their pollution, the recurring message in Rosenbladt's work was the hopelessness of the environment under communism.

Yet while teaching western readers about eastern Europe, West German journalists displayed ongoing ignorance about what it meant to live in a dictatorship.[99] They tended to credit the developments in western European states with bringing about this transformation in eastern Europe, which was certainly true, while at times overlooking domestic impulses and the narrow opportunities to protest in Soviet-style communism. Journalist Robert Jungk noted in his introduction to Rosenbladt's book, that "'Eastern' partners, letters, and underground texts" explained the importance of western green movements as models of protest.[100] In a *Der Spiegel* article, Rosenbladt similarly criticized the lack of an "independent, critical green lobby" in Czechoslovakia, and complained that the learning process was not making sufficient headway.[101] While exposing West German readers to serious issues in the Soviet bloc, journalists and activists took credit for their influence in eastern Europe while simultaneously criticizing the subjects of their works for not improving conditions quickly enough.

Despite such misperceptions, GDR activists continued to request western works to counteract the information deficit at home.[102] East German reliance on West German publications reflected asymmetrical entanglements between the Germanys; East Germans depended on West Germans to better understand their own situation. The works provided outsider perspectives into the GDR as well as other eastern Europe states, thus also

---

[96] Rosenbladt, *Der Osten ist grün?*, 19.   [97] Ibid., 56.
[98] "Aktionen der DDR-Umwelt-Bewegung," Jugendopposition in der DDR, www.jugendopposition.de /themen/145389/ddr-umweltbewegung, accessed November 11, 2018.
[99] Rosenbladt, *Der Osten ist grün?*   [100] Ibid., 7.
[101] AGG B II 3 1101, Sabine Rosenbladt, "Der Lernprozeß ist langsam – zu langsam" *Der Spiegel*, 1987/ 7, 100–102.
[102] RHG OWK 07, "Bücherliste für uns," undated.

bolstering awareness among eastern Europeans. To gain access to western sources, East German activists had to work with western contacts to illegally bring the materials into the GDR. Wilhelm Knabe and other West German Green Party politicians frequently used their diplomatic status to bring books with them, and of course, the *Umweltblätter*'s upgraded printing press in 1987.[103] These networks and the accounts that visitors from the west brought with them strengthened environmental knowledge, especially about Chernobyl, across the Iron Curtain while also generating an aura of impending crisis in eastern Europe.

While West Germans read newspaper accounts and exposés about eastern Europe, pollution in the GDR that had a direct impact on the FRG was their most pressing concern. East and West Germans began to more frequently undertake joint demonstrations. This partnership stemmed from either projects that raised the profile of environmental disasters in the GDR or ones that affected both countries, such as the scandalous levels of pollution in the Chemical Triangle and the FRG paying the GDR to dispose of its waste. Through protests, and radio and television broadcasts, cooperation between activists from both Germanys hinted that a larger change might be afoot. Nevertheless, these projects remained the exception not the rule, standing out more for their rarity than their regularity. The activists operated in different systems, creating cultural and political if not linguistic obstacles that succeeded in limiting the transnational collaboration.

On September 27, 1988, two West German television stations, ARD and ZDF, broadcast a thirty-minute documentary entitled, *Bitteres aus Bitterfeld*. While airing shorter segments on the GDR was relatively common, the documentary captured public interest, allowing West Germans to see the extent of the pollution, and bringing home the reality of the problem.[104] East German activists Ulrich Neumann, Rainer Hällfritzsch, and Margit Miosga from Arche wrote, filmed, and smuggled the footage into the west. From there, the West German journalist Peter Wensierski orchestrated producing and airing the segment. The film depicted the many forms of pollution in and around Bitterfeld, which lay in the heart of the Chemical Triangle in the Halle district. The matter of Bitterfeld's water quality resonated with West German audiences, because the highly

---

[103] "Schmuggel für die Umweltbibliothek," Bundesbeauftrager für Stasiunterlagen der ehemaligen DDR, https://fallofthewall25.com/mauergeschichten/schmuggel-fuer-die-umwelt-bibliothek, accessed October 19, 2018.

[104] AGG POL 509-3, "Teil II. Die Grünen aus dem Blickwinkel der Bürgerbewegungen der DDR," undated.

poisonous wastewater was dumped into the Mulde River, a tributary of the border-crossing Elbe.[105]

Voiceovers shocked viewers with tales of unregulated dumping of byproducts into abandoned open-pit mines as images of the gray and corpse-like landscape appeared on screen. Photo processing chemicals, pesticides, fertilizers, and other harmful chemicals were unceremoniously unloaded into mines without any regard for proper disposal. When the ground froze in the winter, runoff from factories flooded the gardens of a nearby housing complex.[106] Polluted water and tainted soil made it virtually impossible to drink, swim in, or otherwise use local bodies of water. The documentary was so successful that the Environmental Library screened it at the Eco-Seminar in October of that year, helping to resolve

Figure 5 Greenpeace demonstration of environmental degradation near Bitterfeld-Wolfen. "We're turning the Earth into the moon. *Yours, the Chemical Industry*"

---

[105] BArch DO 4/1022, Correspondence between Hans Reichelt and Willi Stoph, October 6, 1988. "Müll: Grube ohne Grenze," *Der Spiegel*, July 18, 1983, 48–49.

[106] For a ten-minute clip of the video with commentary by Peter Wensierski, see www.youtube.com /watch?v=ULaE503n3Bc, accessed May 24, 2015.

the bitter feud between Arche and the Environmental Library.[107] Moreover, East Germans not explicitly tied to environmental circles illicitly watched the film on West German television, confirming what they already suspected.

Beyond Bitterfeld, waste disposal became a major flashpoint for shared protest in the late 1980s. Complaints about unsanctioned and unregulated "wild trash dumps" came from across the GDR. In a 1988 list of Church-based environmental groups that the KFH produced, eleven of fifty-eight groups identified waste disposal as an area of focus.[108] While the GDR mismanaged its own waste, the economically struggling regime also accepted West German trash in exchange for hard currency. Activists from both Germanys worried that the GDR had become West Germany's "waste colony." These accusations transformed the East German dumps at Schöneiche, Schönberg, and Vorketzin into symbols of geopolitical inequality.[109] Activists protested that accepting money for waste did not provide much of an incentive to properly dispose of it. Moreover, the trash sent to Schöneiche was largely the "waste of prosperity."[110] They also argued that there was a double standard, because West Berlin was not responsible for what happened to the trash in the GDR, and that Schöneiche's management did not follow the same standards as would have been required in the FRG. This discrepancy in regulation was particularly prevalent at Schöneiche and its partner dump in nearby Vorketzin, because they handled hazardous as well as regular waste.[111] West Germans also feared that this pollution in the GDR would return to them. Lübeck policymakers' expressed unease at the idea that their city's drinking water and groundwater would be poisoned beyond use if the FRG did not immediately end waste transports east.[112] Entangled environments and politics brought the two Germanys together, in this case through export and subsequent pollution via shared waterways.

To protest the opening of a new incinerator at Schöneiche, Robin Wood and the Environmental Library held a joint demonstration in the GDR on November 1, 1988. Given that it was a workday, the protest was to only consist of a "small circle of reliable people."[113] Robin Wood activists

[107] Matthias Voigt, "Zangengeburt unterm Kirchendach," *Die Tageszeitung*, May 4, 1990.
[108] RHG Ki 18/02, "Karteibroschüre der kirchlichen Umweltgruppen in der DDR: Stand vom November 1988."
[109] RHG Th 02/09, "Greenpeace Dossier – Müllkolonie Ostdeutschland: Müllexport," 1990.
[110] RHG ÜG 03, "Alternativen zum Müll," undated.
[111] RHG Th 02/09, "Infos zur Sonermüllverbrennung (sic) (SVA) und Deponie (MD) Schöneiche," undated.
[112] "Müll: Grube ohne Grenze," *Der Spiegel*, July 18, 1983, 29.
[113] RHG RG/B 19/09, "Robin Wood und Umwelt-Bibliothek gegen Giftmüllexport."

attempted to block West Berlin trash trucks from crossing the border into the GDR near Lichtenrade and then join East Berliners demonstrating at the landfill in Schöneiche. Unfortunately, there was some organizational confusion, and the Stasi was tipped off ahead of time thanks to a West Berlin press conference. As a result, the protest was broken up before anyone could reach the site. As one participant later wrote in the *Umweltblätter*, "By 11:30, there wasn't an unguarded bush" in Schöneiche county anymore, and police rounded up the demonstrators.[114] Though the November demonstration fell through and did not garner much attention, waste disposal galvanized East and West German activists and forged unprecedented cooperation on a grassroots level.

Activists protested not only the Schöneiche "waste for western currency" exchange but other similar arrangements, too. Various western European countries as well as the West German provinces of Schleswig-Holstein and Hessen were also guilty of selling their waste to the GDR. The hazardous waste site in Schönberg (not to be confused with Schöneiche) not far from the northern East German town of Wismar received trash from all over western Europe. Greenpeace protesters in the FRG and the Netherlands claimed that Schönberg had accepted roughly seven million tons of poisonous substances so far. From the FRG, Italy, France, Belgium, the Netherlands, Austria, and Switzerland, nearly 1.3 million tons of waste were brought there annually. For these countries, shipping waste to the GDR was significantly cheaper than following environmental regulations for disposal at home.[115] Thus, while purporting to have become greener themselves, western European countries exported their waste and turned a blind eye to East German practices.

The East German residents of Wismar actually petitioned West German politicians in the hope of gaining environmental concessions that the SED had refused to make. In a letter to the West German minister president, a Wismar group begged him to use his influence to end West German waste exports. They added, "Our country has enough problems with its own waste. The GDR cannot become Europe's trash dump!"[116] Western activists' conscience about the larger balance of ecology in Europe accordingly melded with East Germans' apprehension about local conditions and deepened collaboration on the interconnected subject of buying and selling

[114] Ibid.

[115] RHG Th 02/09, "Greenpeace Presse-Information, 31.11.89" and "Resolution," undated.

[116] RHG Th 02/09, Letter to the West German Minister President from the Wismar Ökumenisches Zentrum für Umweltarbeit, March 2, 1989.

trash. In the more transparent world of late 1988 and early 1989, the citizens of Wismar turned to western politicians for help, apparently a more viable option than their own government. Environmental networks built up over the course of the 1980s offered new opportunities, effectively writing off the East German state when it could not or would not respond. Still, these German–German partnerships faced challenges. Structural inertia, political expediency, and miscommunication became apparent in new ways as communism collapsed a year later.

Conclusion

The environmental and political landscape of the Soviet bloc changed dramatically after Gorbachev's rise to power in 1985 and in the wake of Chernobyl a year later. Increased freedoms under glasnost permitted greater expressions of dissatisfaction, as immediate calls for accurate updates about the disaster transformed into larger questions about the system as a whole. Travel within the Soviet bloc and across the Iron Curtain allowed more people to share more information in an expanding geographic space. The borders between east and west grew more porous, and knowledge about conditions bolstered social and political critiques. Western Europeans visiting eastern Europe relayed data and tactics that were previously difficult to obtain, and groups shared concern for air, water, and human health in central Europe, regardless of political boundaries. Chernobyl sparked not only antinuclear sentiment but a broader awareness of a range of environmental issues and politicized them on an unprecedented level. Poland's more relaxed attitude and mounting opposition foretold that larger changes might be coming in the Soviet bloc.

Despite enhanced contact, transnational endeavors faced challenges before and after 1986. Western European states, especially the FRG, struggled to obtain firm commitments from Soviet bloc states on pollution reduction. The FRG typically found greatest success in these negotiations if it promised technology and/or cash, essentially paying the GDR (or Czechoslovakia) for cleanup and providing the tools to do so. Western visitors also did not always understand the underlying differences in opportunities for organization and protest, leading to miscommunication and, occasionally, high-handed attitudes toward activists in the Soviet bloc. Even among eastern Europeans, cultural and linguistic barriers – in addition to security surveillance – generated friction in expectations about interactions and protest. Border-crossing environmental cooperation absolutely increased through the flow of people and ideas, media, common awareness of problems, a sense of mutual purpose, and state-level negotiations. Activism and new policy initiatives also encountered setbacks that complicated those gains.

In the GDR, abstract fears about nuclear disaster merged with concrete pollution problems to construct a larger ecological framework after Chernobyl. Small but growing networks of environmental activists in – or on the fringes of – the Protestant Church exerted pressure on party and state officials as new members joined, groups emerged, and samizdat publications spread after Chernobyl. Yet this expansion was not enough to comprehensively address the serious, systemic degradation they faced. Moreover, constant police and Stasi interference effectively sowed discord among activists, creating a toxic attitude of distrust and fear. Without larger, structural changes, the environmental movement in the GDR was reaching a saturation point. The political system refused to – or was incapable of – altering its priorities to improve environmental conditions. Continued repression and censorship would keep the SED uneasily in power until systemic changes undermined its power and the GDR unraveled.

CHAPTER 6

Growing Together? The Environment in the Collapse of Communism

The East German state continued to suppress environmental and oppositional movements after 1986, blindly crafting antiquated Five- and Ten-Year Plans. Under the surface, however, cracks in the system weakened the SED and its monopoly on power. Gorbachev's glasnost and perestroika, which some eastern European states quickly embraced, left Honecker isolated. In September 1988, Poland's PZPR agreed to Round Table Talks with Solidarność, heralding the end of communist monopolies on power in the Soviet bloc and opening up opportunities to discuss the regimes' environmental failures.[1] The following year, calls for democracy and capitalism, the right to unrestricted travel, and western consumer goods brought down communism in the GDR. The revolutions of 1989–1990 restructured central Europe in terms of environmental protection and cleanup as well as economic and political systems. The environment was not distinct from these often-dominant narratives of communist collapse but intricately woven into them and into questions about the future.[2]

Environmental concerns shaped the disintegration of communism, and increasing political freedoms provided an unprecedented opportunity for

---

[1] Padraic Kenney, *A Carnival of Revolution: Central Europe, 1989* (Princeton, NJ: Princeton University Press, 2002), 192.

[2] Jerzy Borejsza and Klaus Ziemer's edited volume *Totalitarian and Authoritarian Regimes in Europe: Legacies and Lessons from the Twentieth Century* (New York: Berghahn Books, 2006) and Grzegorz Ekiert and Stephen E. Hanson's *Capitalism and Democracy in Central and Eastern Europe: Assessing the Legacy of Communist Rule* (New York: Cambridge University Press, 2003) focus almost exclusively on political institutions and the market economy. Other historians emphasize the undoing of the communist systems, devoting special attention to oppositional leaders and protests, later turning to the failures within the communist structures. See Timothy Garton Ash, *The Magic Lantern: The Revolution of '89 Witnessed in Warsaw, Budapest, Berlin, and Prague* (New York: Vintage Books, 1993); Kenney, *A Carnival of Revolution*; Stephen Kotkin, *Uncivil Society: 1989 and the Implosion of the Communist Establishment* (Chapel Hill, NC: University of North Carolina Press, 2009); Ilko-Sascha Kowalczuk, *Endspiel: Die Revolution von 1989 in der DDR* (Munich: C.H. Beck Verlag, 2009).

new policy and activism. Poland became the model for other countries as oppositional and communist parties met to hand over power and to transition to more capitalist and democratic systems. Activists from eastern and western Europe watched anxiously as Poland led the way and pioneered new avenues for cleanup and participation, though Solidarność warned of "hyper-democracy" and prioritized the economy. In the GDR, frustration over pollution and public health helped fuel protests that brought down the SED, which then fed into calls for unification with the FRG.[3] During that period of transition, East German environmental officials found new freedom to implement reforms they had long desired, taking unprecedented measures to push for additional conservation and the creation of national parks.[4] As the system crumbled, new possibilities for environmental protection and politics arose.

With the imminent demise of communism in the GDR, debates over how to improve the environment and who would be responsible for the cleanup became central questions to moving forward. The human and economic costs of pollution and implementation of effective regulation were all enormous burdens that came into the spotlight in 1989–1990, which West German experts and bureaucrats increasingly shouldered. The environment was not especially controversial during unification, because East and West Germans agreed on the urgency of ameliorating the GDR's degradation.[5] Rather than salvaging useful East German ideas or informed individuals, during unification in the spring and summer of 1990, West German officials disregarded East German perspectives. They maintained that earlier failures had no place in a unified "greenest nation," also overlooking the variety of environmental impulses in the GDR before 1990.[6] Cleanup efforts were largely funded by the FRG and often excluded East German activists and experts, establishing a top down process from the outside. Moreover, the influx of West German money created

---

[3] Some of the works on environmental policy and protest in the GDR tend to shy away from the transformations in 1989 and 1990. See Hermann Behrens and Jens Hoffmann, eds., *Umweltschutz in der DDR: Analysen und Zeitzeugen, Band 1–3* (Munich: Oekom, 2008); Tobias Huff, *Natur und Industrie im Sozialismus: Eine Umweltgeschichte der DDR* (Göttingen: Vandenhoeck & Ruprecht, 2015); Christian Möller, *Umwelt und Herrschaft in der DDR: Politik, Protest und die Grenzen der Partizipation in der Diktatur* (Göttingen: Vanderhoeck & Ruprecht, 2020); Martin Stief, *"Stellt die Bürger ruhig": Staatssicherheit und Umweltzerstörung im Chemierevier Halle-Bitterfeld* (Göttingen: Vanderhoeck & Ruprecht, 2019).

[4] Astrid M. Eckert, *West Germany and the Iron Curtain: Environment, Economy, and Culture in the Borderland* (New York: Oxford University Press, 2019), 192–193.

[5] Konrad H. Jarausch, *The Rush to German Unity* (New York: Oxford University Press, 1994), 171–173.

[6] Frank Uekötter, *The Greenest Nation? A New History of German Environmentalism* (Cambridge, MA: MIT Press, 2014).

a divergence between the GDR and the other Soviet bloc states that lacked comparable support.

This chapter argues that the environment was crucial to the reconfiguration of central European politics, economies, and relationships in the collapse of communism. Pollution challenged Cold War political divisions, yet questions surrounding policy and cleanup generated continuities and change across the rupture of 1989–1990. The chapter first examines the place of the environment and environmental politics in Poland as a precursor to developments in other Soviet bloc states, laying out opportunities and pitfalls. Next, the chapter turns to the GDR, illuminating the environment as a source of protest against communism in the fall and winter of 1989. Then, the chapter examines how pollution abatement and environmental protection became central tenets of unification for both East and West Germans, concluding with the Environmental Framework Law as a prerequisite for the Unification Treaty. Capitalism and democracy introduced powerful new actors that exerted influence and undercut the existing structures of environmental movements in former communist states. The attempt to balance economic and ecological concerns did not cease as communism disintegrated, but new environmental regulation came from the top down and ignored activists and experts who had labored under communism. The shifts that came with the end of Soviet power in eastern Europe resolved much of the pollution, especially in the GDR, which benefited from the FRG's affluence. Yet improved environmental protection came at the expense of the activists and networks built up in the 1980s.

Leading the Way? Polish Democratization and the Environment

The PZPR's embrace of Gorbachev's glasnost and perestroika resulted in a more open atmosphere in Poland that permitted environmental activists to gather publicly. Moreover, Poland, the GDR, and Czechoslovakia continued to pursue joint efforts to clean up the Black Triangle border region. However, these were little different from earlier toothless initiatives. Still, momentum for political and economic changes in Poland inspired reform in other eastern European countries, too.[7] As historian Jan Behrends has noted, the end of German division – and Soviet control of the bloc – began in Poland.[8] As communism fell apart, environmental

---

[7] AGG A Kelly 3860, Carlo Jordan, "Greenway 1989–90, The Foundation of the East European Green Parties," *Green Light on Europe*, 2.

[8] Jan Claas Behrends, "Das Ende der Teilung Deutschlands begann in Polen," *Vorwärts*, June 4, 2020, www.vorwaerts.de/artikel/ende-teilung-deutschlands-begann-polen?fbclid=IwAR0FKuY4LUWZe1 b-dfN7jmvXBCzGbre74opN1iCYUUH_xYg2ZZy0UtS35Sg, accessed June 8, 2020.

connections and activist networks across the Iron Curtain continued to
shape central Europe amid changing political and economic regimes. The
Cold War blocs disappeared and new actors emerged, such that democratization and privatization presented activists and environmental protection
with unforeseen obstacles.

Even as the PZPR relinquished power, the environment remained
a serious issue, weaving together ecology, economy, and politics in
a moment of transition. A trilateral commission between the GDR,
Poland, and Czechoslovakia began meeting in the late 1980s to discuss
transboundary pollution. Poland pushed for the GDR and Czechoslovakia
to reduce sulfur dioxide emissions to abate acid rain and Waldsterben.
Polish officials drew on the thirty percent promise laid out in the 1984
Munich Agreement, because Polish forests in border regions disproportionately suffered from pollution generated in the other two countries.[9] Yet
when the East German and Czechoslovak delegates said such
a commitment was not possible, Polish officials relented. Ultimately, all
three states affirmed their support for Munich without any binding obligations. In this three-way dynamic, the GDR and Poland partnered up to
exert pressure on Czechoslovakia regarding water quality, especially in the
Lusatian Neisse River. The transboundary pollution that had plagued the
three states for the entire postwar period endured until the very end of the
regimes' existence.

A trilateral agreement was finally signed on July 1, 1989, though cracks
were already emerging in the communist system, especially in Poland. The
three states ultimately reinforced scientific and technological cooperation
with an emphasis on communication, monitoring, and developing better
methods of production.[10] They also pledged to help one another abate
certain dangers, such as from spills, but did not provide concrete explanations of how this collaboration would work. Nevertheless, the agreement
did not fundamentally improve environmental conditions or accountability and instead relied on stale language and promises from the 1970s. In
essence, it promised aid in an emergency but not for longstanding or
ongoing pollution. While setting up structures to strengthen communication, it did not fully address Poland's position as the primary recipient. By

---

[9] BArch DK 5/5841, "Bericht über die zweite Beratung der gemeinsamen Arbeitsgruppe DDR-VRP-
CSSR zur Vorbereitung eines dreiseitigen Abkommens über die Zusammenarbeit auf dem Gebiet
des Umweltschutzes, 28.11.–2.12.1988."

[10] BArch DK 5/2265, "Abkommen zwischen der Regierung der Deutschen Demokratischen Republik,
der Regierung der Volksrepublik Polen und die Regierung der Tschechoslawkischen Sozialistischen
Republik über die Zusammenarbeit auf dem Gebiet des Umweltschutzes," July 1, 1989.

the time of the signing, Poland had held elections in which the PZPR had allowed other parties to win seats in the legislature, ending its monopoly on power. The changing situation in Poland created new opportunities for participation in a more democratic process, much to the SED's dismay.[11]

Almost a year earlier, in September 1988, the PZPR and Solidarność negotiated Round Table Talks to discuss Poland's future and pave the way for a multi-party system. The PKE angled to have an active role in the talks alongside Solidarność, the main voice of the opposition. The PKE had announced the establishment of the Polish Ecological Party the same month for that express purpose and sent the West German Greens notice of its actions to gain greater visibility and credibility. The Polish Ecological Party, however, had a mere thirteen members at its founding.[12] Therefore, in December, the PKE organized a larger assembly for the official meeting to establish the Polish Green Party that drew on the club's membership, shifting it from an expert-based movement to a political party. West German Green Elisabeth Weber attended and reported on the events. She observed that between seventy and a hundred delegates represented roughly 400 members from twenty-four locales.[13] Under Fura's leadership, the Green Party sought to demonstrate that environmental degradation was central to Poland's problems. With an eye toward future elections, the party worked to use ecological themes to "expand the bounds of political activity."[14] The Green Party wished to offer an alternative to the Solidarność–PZPR dichotomy.

The emerging bipolar constellation between the PZPR and Solidarność did dominate the political sphere, though, exacerbating tensions within the Green Party. Solidarność organizers in Warsaw, such as Jacek Kuroń, asserted they had never even heard of the party, though in general, they believed that "Pluralism is good. All efforts to this end are worth pursuing."[15] Because the PKE had situated itself as neither party line nor explicitly oppositional in the communist system, formulating a coherent position now proved difficult. Some PKE members decided not to join the party, contending they were "interested in ecology not politics."[16] Others identified more strongly with Solidarność than the Green Party. Potential

---

[11] Politisches Archiv des Auswärtigen Amtes (PA AA) M 39 693 09, "Zum Verhältnnis PVAP – polnische Außenpolitik," December 28, 1989.

[12] AGG B II 3 1110, "Declaration," September 1988.

[13] AGG B II 1 5732, Elisabeth Weber, "Bericht über eine kurze Polen-Reise im Dezember 1988 anläßlich der Gründung einer Grünen Partei in Polen," 6.

[14] Ibid., 6.   [15] Ibid., 7.   [16] Ibid.

leaders who had been engaged in the movement detached themselves from the debate, leaving the party without their direction or charisma. As the Green Party attempted to gain a foothold, the dominance of the PZPR and Solidarność as well as petty conflicts within the Green Party limited its influence and appeal to the population.[17]

To gain attention and strengthen contacts across the Iron Curtain, the Green Party members did something that had been difficult earlier: they reached out to partner parties in western Europe. West German Greens Elisabeth Weber and Thomas Kuhl, Ali Gronner from the Austrian Green Party, and Sara Parkin of the European Greens all attended the constitutive meeting in December 1988, entangling environmental politics between eastern and western Europe.[18] The Polish Greens further shared their activities via letters and press releases, often translated into German or English for an international audience. Despite losing the vote to be the party's spokesperson, Fura deemed himself in charge of information and international outreach, mailing letters to the West German Greens to announce the party's existence and agenda. He explained that the party had 2,000 members and was "playing an important role in the democratization process."[19] Fura and others recognized that western European financial support could buoy the fledgling party while poor economic performance dominated the media. The swiftly evolving political constellation and international context offered a chance for increased connections with other green parties.

Still, the Green Party's bid to speak at the environmental "sub-table" of the Round Table Talks in early 1989 was sidelined in favor of the larger and more popular Solidarność. The PZPR and Solidarność both provided experts for the meetings, focusing on air and water pollution, but the topic did not garner much public attention. At the Round Table, Solidarność used primarily PKE experts to outflank the PZPR, as these scientists raised pressing ecological matters.[20] The PKE was acceptable,

---

[17] Barbara Jancar-Webster notes that across eastern Europe, greens fared better when they joined with a leading coalition rather than remaining independent. Barbara Jancar-Webster, "The Eastern European Environmental Movement and the Transformation of East European Society," in *Environmental Action in Eastern Europe: Responses to Crisis*, ed. Barbara Jancar-Webster (Armonk, NY: M.E. Sharpe, 1993), 195.

[18] AGG B II 1 5732, Elisabeth Weber, "Bericht über eine kurze Polen-Reise im Dezember 1988 anläßlich der Gründung einer Grünen Partei in Polen," 7–8.

[19] Umweltbibliothek Großhennersdorf (UBG) 80–114, "Die Polnische Partei von Grünen," undated.

[20] Barbara Hicks, *Environmental Politics in Poland: A Social Movement between Regime and Opposition* (New York: Columbia University Press, 1996), 94. The PKE represented about forty percent of all environmental experts at the Round Table, according to Hicks.

because it had been part of the "constructive opposition," in contrast to the strictly oppositional WiP, for example. The PKE's presence also rested on its members' technical knowledge and established relationships with officials. Exactly as the Green Party had feared, the ecology sub-table received little media attention, with the PZPR and Solidarność finding common ground on essentially every topic except nuclear energy.[21] A potential opportunity to raise the profile of environmental pollution and cleanup had fizzled out, dashing the hopes of activists in Poland and for other activists across the Soviet bloc.

The Green Party took part in the subsequent semi-independent election but did not win a single available seat, leaving observers to wonder about the fate of environmental politics.[22] Non-PZPR parties were permitted to run candidates for thirty-five percent of the seats in the lower house of parliament, the Sejm, and all the seats in the upper house, the Senate. For many, defeating the PZPR was of the utmost importance, so voters placed their confidence in Solidarność, which won all the contested seats in the Sejm and all but one in the Senate.[23] In part, Solidarność undercut the Green Party by tapping environmental experts to run on Solidarność lists, calling the Green Party's relevance into question.[24] West German journalist Klaus Bachmann complained that members of the Green Party argued over topics such as hunting, pesticides, and abortion that were non-issues in the FRG. Similar to Weber a year and a half earlier, he concluded that the Polish Greens did not have the requisite consciousness to be truly green, reflecting divisions that became more apparent with the end of Cold War solidarity.[25] From the West German perspective, the Polish Greens were distinctly lacking in greenness, while at the same time, Solidarność considered them an "embarrassing consequence of hyper-democracy."[26] The environmental movement in Poland, and eastern Europe more generally, faced numerous domestic as well as international obstacles as communism collapsed.

---

[21] Kenney, *A Carnival of Revolution*, 251. Hicks, *Environmental Politics in Poland*, 149.

[22] Glenn E. Curtis, ed., *Poland: A Country Study* (Washington, DC: Library of Congress, Federal Research Division, 1992), 175.

[23] Kenney, *A Carnival of Revolution*, 259. Kotkin, *Uncivil Society*, 129.

[24] AGG B II 1 5732, Weber, "Bericht über eine kurze Polen-Reise im Dezember 1988 anläßlich der Gründung einer Grünen Partei in Polen," 7. Radosław Gawlik from Wrocław is an example of an ecologist who sided with Solidarność over the PKE or Polish Green Party.

[25] Klaus Bachmann, "Polens Grüne sind sich nicht grün," *Die Tageszeitung*, July 18, 1989, found in Materiały ogólne, Oddział Życia Społecznego, Biblioteka Ossolineum.

[26] Aaron Pezem, "Zieloni czy Szarzy? Konflikt w Polskiej Partii Zielonych," *Gazeta Wyborcza*, August 8, 1989, found in AGG B II 1 1645.

Though the Polish Green Party experienced challenges, its work inspired other eastern European countries to seize the moment through networking and the founding of green parties.[27] East German activist Carlo Jordan recalled traveling to other parts of the Soviet bloc for the first time in years, specifically Lithuania, after his travel ban was lifted. He participated in a week-long peace march during which 300 to 400 peace and environmental activists traveled, paddled, and hiked through "ecological and military crisis regions," and held a rock concert at a chemical combine in Jonava.[28] During Jordan's trip to Lithuania, he met the founder of the Lithuanian Green Party, which emerged in the summer of 1989. Such meetings and shared adventures enabled activists to share information and tactics for formalizing political parties. Greenway co-founder Elizabeth Pasztor helped form the Green Party of Hungary in August 1989, and other eastern European countries followed suit.[29] Reading the political landscape, activists across eastern Europe worked with one another – and western green parties – to embrace the spirit of democratization.

Eastern European activists also quickly recognized the difficulties their countries faced in the transition, and especially critiqued a blind embrace of capitalism. With a jab at Solidarność, a *Greenway* issue argued that political and economic reforms were unavoidable but the solution should not be pure capitalism, as some in Hungary and Poland believed.[30] Greenway leaders warned that western approaches to economic problems and consumption patterns would impact their societies, nature, and environment, creating common problems for "Central and Eastern European countries."[31] They emphasized the need to work with western European activists, a tactic that Fura also employed by reaching out to West German Greens. Still, Greenway organizers recognized that post-communist states would face distinct economic and environmental concerns in the coming years. Environmental protest and activism in the crumbling Soviet bloc were not a delayed echo of earlier movements in western Europe. Activists faced economic and political impediments in addition to confronting pollution.

---

[27] Carlo Jordan, "Greenway – das osteuropäische Grüne Netzwerk (1985–1990)," in *Grünes Gedächtnis 2010: Europa Braucht Vielfalt* (Berlin: Archiv Grünes Gedächtnis, 2010), 39.

[28] Ibid., 39.   [29] Ibid., 42–43.

[30] RHG Th 12/07, "'If there is a will, there is a GREENway': The history of Greenway," *Greenway*, December 1989/January 1990, 3.

[31] RHG Th 12/07, "Greenway: First Meeting of the National Coordinators," December 15–17, 1989.

Poland's transformation predated the analogous developments in the GDR by nearly a year but foretold tensions between environmental protection, democracy, and privatization. As communism crumbled across eastern Europe, environmental issues remained important, but the rapidly changing situation also presented complications. Polish activists shifted from being part of the opposition – whether constructive or otherwise – to a marginalized party, as members of the PKE divided their loyalties between the Green Party and Solidarność. Within the bloc, though, Poland led the way in democratization and the founding of independent political parties, often leaning on western parties and activists for assistance. 1989 was a moment of optimism as activists and information flowed across the Iron Curtain at unprecedented levels. As the bloc fell apart, though, Cold War solidarity collapsed, too. New constellations of actors in a democratic system and the prioritization of privatization posed unforeseen challenges for environmental cleanup.

The Environment in the GDR's Collapse

As the GDR disintegrated, environmental issues both undermined the SED's credibility and raised questions about the future. Hints of political unrest began to emerge in the spring and summer of 1989, but it was not until autumn that East Germans openly disputed the SED's monopoly on power and the citizens' movements formed an organized opposition. Individuals from deep-rooted Church and independent networks participated in the citizens' movements, which spoke on behalf of "the people" through the fall of 1989 and the winter of 1990. The environment greatly informed these citizens' movements, becoming a centerpiece of protest that built on longstanding frustration. Along with appeals for the right to travel, transparency, and democratization, the environment and pollution abatement topped the list of nearly every citizens' movement platform.[32] Ecological conditions – and activists' protest of them – undermined the SED as it fumbled responses in a rapidly changing political climate.

The May 1989 elections foreshadowed greater troubles to come for the SED as oppositional groups contested its hegemony and used ecological critiques to demand change. Arche and others argued that significant

---

[32] For a discussion of whether 1989 was revolution, reform, "refolution," or something else entirely, see Garton Ash, *Magic Lantern* ; Gareth Dale, *The East German Revolution of 1989* (New York: Manchester University Press, 2006); Jarausch, *The Rush to German Unity*; Charles S. Maier, *Dissolution: The Crisis of Communism and the End of East Germany*, (Princeton NJ: Princeton University Press, 1997).

improvement for nature would only come through restructuring, and so they pushed for people to defy the SED with their votes.[33] Citing "environmental poisoning" among other ills, they claimed that Christians should join with the many non-Christians in the GDR who also believed in justice, freedom, and human rights to become informed about elections laws and democratize the electoral process.[34] Other groups refused to vote or participate in a corrupt system at all. They explained they would not go to the polls on May 7, because there were no alternatives that offered credible domestic, ecological, economic, and educational policies.[35] The election results revealed that the SED's hold on its people was tenuous. Official tallies acknowledged that roughly 140,000 citizens had voted *against* one-party rule, while unofficial exit polls indicated that more had gone rogue.[36] The SED likely suppressed 10 to 15 percent of abstentions and no votes, which were substantially higher in Church and university strongholds.[37] This level of engagement in an election was unprecedented and the environment featured prominently in questioning the SED's right to rule.

The controversy surrounding the elections subsided over the summer and the state went about governing – and halfheartedly handling pollution – as it had for decades. The GDR's signing of the trilateral environmental agreement with Poland and Czechoslovakia in July, which would go into effect on October 17, 1989, underscored the GDR's entrenched prioritization of the economy that hindered concrete action. The three countries promised a host of shared endeavors for the period until 1995, 2000, and 2010, apparently oblivious to developments underway in Poland and imminent in the GDR and Czechoslovakia. Though all three affirmed their commitment to reducing emissions, environmental minister Hans Reichelt quite clearly told chief economic planner Günter Mittag that the GDR's ability to reduce sulfur dioxide emissions by thirty percent was "not yet secured," nor was it likely to be.[38] The same systemic hurdles that had blocked effective environmental policies since the 1960s remained in place, eroding communism's legitimacy.

---

[33] Robert Havemann Gesellschaft (RHG) RG B 19/09, "Widerstandsrecht," 1989.

[34] RHG EP 11/01, "Ein Brief an Christen in der DDR und ihre Gemeindevertreter zu den Kommunalwahlen 1989," January 8, 1989.

[35] RHG EP 11/01, "Erklärung des Arbeitskreises Solidarische Kirche, Regionalgruppe Thüringen," March 16, 1989.

[36] "Aktueller Begriff: Die Kommunalwahlen in der DDR vom 7. Mai 1989," Wissenschaftliche Dienste, Deutscher Bundestag, www.bundestag.de/blob/276668/39aa97d8f3abe4e472ca39123e9ccod6/die_kom munalwahlen_in_der_ddr_vom_7__mai_1989-data.pdf, accessed June 15, 2015.

[37] Jarausch, *The Rush to German Unity*, 38.

[38] BArch DK 5/1991, Correspondence between Hans Reichelt and Günter Mittag, July 18, 1988.

The SED also forged ahead in terms of domestic policy, drawing up Five- and Ten-Year Plans for the economy and mass social organizations such as the GNU. In September 1989, the SED's Central Committee gave the GNU guidelines for how to proceed for the next five years. Based on the Central Committee's environmental advisory council, the GNU's goals were to "propagate appropriate forms of environmental education" and use official media to highlight its work.[39] Despite acknowledging that protecting the environment would become an even more important issue in the 1990s, the resolution did not offer any innovations. Instead, the GNU continued to rely on Landscape Days, collaboration with experts, and cooperation with other Warsaw Pact countries.[40] These were the same tired strategies that the SED had employed since the early 1970s. As communism in eastern Europe collapsed, the East German leadership attempted to ignore its way out of political unrest.

By the fall of 1989, the seemingly quiet period during the summer was over, and again, the SED faced mounting pressure. On September 4, 1989, the first of the famous Monday Demonstrations took place in Leipzig. At the end of a peaceful prayer service at the St. Nicholas Church, participants filed into the street to protest the GDR's travel bans. Although police tore posters from their hands and arrested about 100 participants, more returned the next week, and the week after that, and the week after that. By October 9, 70,000 people filled the streets of Leipzig in a peaceful demonstration, forcing the police to back down or risk the backlash of a Tiananmen Square-like situation.[41] Two weeks after that, on October 23, 320,000 East Germans packed into Leipzig's main streets, chanting "We are the people." The events in Leipzig and in other cities inspired oppositional figures to form citizens' movements to shape a new or reformed social and political system.

From the start of the citizens' movements in September 1989, critiques of pollution and calls for an ecological future were enmeshed in demands for democratization. Many citizens' movements, such as New Forum, Democracy Now, and Democratic Awakening, included prominent environmental activists among their original members. All three of those major

---

[39] Bundesarchiv (BArch) DK 5/1830, "Konzeption zur weiteren Entwicklung der umweltpolitischen Arbeit des KBs der DDR und seiner GNU," September 20, 1989.

[40] Ibid.

[41] Jarausch, *The Rush to German Unity*, 33–34. Quinn Slobodian, "China Is Not Far! Alternative Internationalism and the Tiananmen Square Massacre in East Germany's 1989," in *Alternative Globalizations: Eastern Europe and the Postcolonial World*, eds. James Mark, Artemy M. Kalinovsky, Steffi Marung (Bloomington, IN: Indiana University Press, 2020), 311.

Figure 6 "Ecology before Economy!" Poster at the Leipzig Monday
Demonstrations. October 16, 1989. (Photo by Christian Günther/ullstein bild via
Getty Images)

citizens' movements stressed the problem of environmental degradation
and ranked it among their top priorities. New Forum stated, "On the one
hand, we wish for an expansion of consumer goods and better supplies,
while on the other hand we see the social and ecological costs and plea for
a turn away from uninhibited growth." They proceeded to cite other
ecological issues, including energy policy, the estrangement of humans
from nature, the consequences of degradation, and the limiting of consumer habits for future generations.[42] Similarly, Democratic Awakening
called for the ecological restructuring of industrial society, and Democracy
Now proclaimed that the economy and ecology must be brought into
harmony.[43] The citizens' movements recognized and traded on the GDR's

[42] Neues Forum, "Gründungsaufruf: Eine politische Plattform für die ganze DDR," in *Die Opposition in der DDR: Entwürfe für einen anderen Sozialismus*, ed. Gerhard Rein (Berlin: Wichern-Verlag, 1990), 13.
[43] "Preliminary Statement of Principles," October 30, 1989, and "A Call for Intervention in Our Own Affairs," September 12, 1989, in *German Unification and its Discontents: Documents from the Peaceful Revolution*, eds. and trans. Richard T. Gray and Sabine Wilke (Seattle, WA: University of Washington Press, 1996), 9, 38.

ecological disaster to gain popularity, using it as an argument for democratization and more voices in the political process.

Because nearly every citizens' movement adopted environmental issues and long-term Stasi meddling sowed distrust among activists, a separate green party came about relatively late. The "Green Party in the GDR" was first established at the Sixth Berlin Eco-Seminar, more than two weeks after the momentous opening of the Berlin Wall on November 9. Groups from Leipzig, Dresden, Schwerin, Stendal, and Berlin who had been involved in Carlo Jordan's Arche convened to consider their environmental future while the majority of the East German population celebrated the border opening. The Green Party understood itself as a constituent part of the green movement in the GDR as well as a global ecological movement. Its primary goal was ecological transformation in the GDR, espousing a radical rejection of environmentally destructive and resource-squandering economic growth.[44] While focusing on the GDR's problems, the Green Party emphasized the interconnectedness of environmental problems across borders, which drew on Jordan's experiences and travels in other parts of the Soviet bloc.

The Green Party was Arche's political incarnation, but other activists, based on old resentments, argued its founding was undemocratic and so created a separate Green League. Like the Polish Green Party, internal fracturing hindered a coherent organization or set of policies. The Green League claimed to represent all green interests and would be an independent, non-party organization, analogous to the West German BUND, which had been crucial in the "ecologization" of conservation and the rise of a green movement in the FRG.[45] Such decisions reflected the proliferation of civil society in 1989 and the separation of associational life from political parties, often considered a precondition for democracy. They also underscored continuing distrust and rifts in the oppositional milieu out of which many of the organizers of the citizens' movements came, a lasting legacy of dictatorship and Stasi policies.[46] As in the years prior to 1989, this split over the centrality of the environment led to further challenges for the movement in the winter of 1990.

Outside of major cities, local chapters of the citizens' movement took longer to coalesce, which officials initially perceived as encouraging, but belied deep and widespread frustration. In Lusatia, district administrators

---

[44] BArch DK 5/3386, "Information über das 6. Berliner Ökologie-Seminar vom 24. bis 26. 11. 1989."

[45] Ibid. Jens Ivo Engels, *Naturpolitik in der Bundesrepublik: Ideenwelt und politische Verhaltensstile in Naturschutz und Umweltbewegung, 1950–1980* (Paderborn: Ferdinand Schöningh, 2006), 307. For more on the BUND, see Chapter 2.

[46] Jürgen Kocka, *Civil Society and Dictatorship in Modern Germany* (Hanover, NH: University Press of New England, 2010), 21.

were pleased that they did not see mass protest in their streets. By early October, though, Zittau officials felt the need to meet with a number of ministers who had started a local chapter of the New Forum.[47] Local pastor Alfred Hempel had been one of the original thirty signatories of the founding document in Berlin on September 7 and then a few weeks later publicly talked about the New Forum at a prayer service in nearby Großschönau.[48] Hempel told the audience that the New Forum was a movement of individuals "who suffer from the current conditions with us and want to change them."[49] Officials in Zittau eventually began to worry that "New Forum wants developments like in Poland and Hungary," where democratization was well underway. "This," they asserted, "we cannot permit."[50] They were optimistic that Lusatia would remain quiet in September, but by October they realized the peaceful revolutions elsewhere in the Soviet bloc were having an irreversible impact on Lusatia.

Zittau's citizens' movements inflected the national political discourse with Lusatia's specific environmental problems. Discontent revolved around the situation in the Black Triangle and the GDR's plans to expand the open-pit mining that were so central to the communist economic model. In particular, officials intended to relocate the residents of historic Zittau and level the town in order to access the coal seam that lay underneath.[51] When Hans Modrow took over leadership of the GDR in November, he explicitly rejected the destruction of Zittau in an attempt to remove this point of contention and pacify the burgeoning unrest.[52] Concessions over the fate of the city only appeased one aspect of Lusatians' dissatisfaction with the SED but did not confront the larger systemic problems that had led to the

---

[47] It should be noted that October 5 was four days before the fateful protest in Leipzig when police decided to not respond violently to mass demonstrators.

[48] Arnaud Liszka and Thomas Pilz, *Versuche in der Wahrheit zu Leben: Widerständiges Leben in der Oberlausitz, 1978–1989* (Dresden: Neisse Verlag, 2009), 67.

[49] UBG 27–8, Wolfgang Müller, "Bericht über Gespräche beim Rat des Kreises Zittau und mit den Pastorinnen und Pfarrern über das 'Neue Forum'," October 10, 1989.

[50] Ibid.

[51] Dieter Liebig, "Begleitbuch zur Ausstellung: Anspruch und Wirklichkeit: Die Energie- und Umweltpolitik in der DDR am Beispiel des Energieträgers Braunkohle" (Großhennersdorf: Umweltbibliothek Großhennersdorf, e.V., 2009), 98.

[52] Ibid., 33. Hans Modrow became the leader of the GDR on November 18, 1989, replacing Willi Stoph, who had taken over for the ailing Erich Honecker in October. Egon Krenz was voted to take over as the head of the SED on October 18, 1989 and served in that position until his resignation in December. After that, power shifted from the party to the state, and Modrow was the de facto sole leader of the GDR. Dale, *The East German Revolution of 1989*, 133.

decision to level Zittau in the first place. From Berlin to Leipzig to Lusatia, the SED was losing its monopoly on power.

Based on the citizens' movements' demands, officials and opposition convened a series of Round Tables Talks between December 1989 and March 1990. These meetings were inspired by talks that had been held between Solidarność and the PZPR a year earlier, and ultimately included the restructuring of election law, laws about the freedom of political parties and assembly, a new constitution, and economic reform.[53] In general, the Round Tables prioritized an "ecologically oriented social democracy based on justice and solidarity," in line with the citizens' movements' call for a third way between communism and capitalism.[54] The environment was essential to redefining the GDR and the future of central Europe. The January 29 meeting of the Round Table was specifically devoted to the GDR's environmental crisis, with both sides agreeing to educate politicians about environmental problems, implement stricter standards for industrial production, introduce new energy and agricultural policies, and launch environmental centers and ecological disciplines.[55] Critiques of the means of production honed in on dissatisfaction with the aging and inefficient planned economy under the SED: the pollution and its dangers to human life could not continue. The Round Table's resolutions displayed optimism about improving the environment and addressed many of the issues that delegitimized the SED in the first place.

At the conclusion of the Round Table on March 12, 1990, the participants passed a constitution that explicitly sought to tackle the GDR's environmental situation. The measures proclaimed that state policy had to protect against environmental damage and must make sparing use of nonrenewable resources and energy.[56] These statements were a clear reaction to the GDR's failed promises and policies over the last several decades. More specifically, the constitution introduced the concept of "polluter pays," claiming that "whoever is responsible for environmental

---

[53] Round Table Talks, December 7, 1989, in *Neue Chronik der DDR: Berichte, Fotos, Dokumente*, eds. Zeno and Sabine Zimmerling (Berlin: Verlag Tribüne, 1990), 140.

[54] Quoted in Hannes Bahrmann and Christoph Links, *Chronik der Wende: Die DDR zwischen 7. Oktober und 18. Dezember 1989* (Berlin: Ch. Links Verlag, 1994), 174–178. Each of the Round Table discussions had a primary topic, such as the economy or the environment. Of the sixteen discussions, the fact that one focused solely on the environment is indicative of its importance to this period.

[55] Ibid., 141–142.

[56] Preamble, "Entwurf: Verfassung der Deutschen Demokratischen Republik, Arbeitsgruppe 'Neue Verfassung der DDR' des Runden Tisches," April 1990, www.documentarchiv.de/ddr/1990/ddr-verfassungsentwurf_runder-tisch.html#prae, accessed July 14, 2015.

degradation is responsible for its restoration."[57] Up to that point, the SED had resisted using any such language, because it did not want the state to be responsible for pollution, especially transboundary issues, as in the trilateral agreement with Poland and Czechoslovakia or in German–German negotiations. As the SED's power waned and new actors gained influence, opportunities for accountability and cleanup emerged.

Despite challenges to the SED's one-party rule throughout the fall and winter of 1989 and 1990, the party attempted to counter its rapidly eroding status. The party and state attempted to adapt to the political landscape, to maintain a position of authority, and to salvage an independent GDR.[58] In October and November, key long-term party and state bosses resigned from positions of authority, most notably Erich Honecker and Willi Stoph, and a younger generation of more reform-minded SED members stepped into those roles. This turnover, however, went beyond the highest levels to include virtually all ministries and mass social organizations, such as the MUW and the GNU. Deteriorating conditions had been a catalyst for political change, which now that the system was faltering, opened up possibilities for environmental officials and enthusiasts to push through more effective policy and internationally recognized positions. Environmental leaders attempted – or were finally freed – to rectify the devastation.

Environmental minister Hans Reichelt, who had served since 1972, attempted to hold his office but was too tainted from years of feeble leadership and ultimately resigned. In a bid to retain his position, he printed and mailed postcards to members of the GNU to ask them to back a series of immediate concerns. The issues he embraced, though, represented a bare minimum, not a bold vision. In fact, they were largely ones that activists had raised for some time: investment in desulfurization equipment, the release of environmental and health data, additional energy-saving measures, importing a higher percentage of anthracite to reduce the reliance on lignite, and lead-free gasoline.[59] Though Reichelt appealed to East Germans from all regions of the country through popular and necessary improvements, his strategy was not successful. He was the face of the ministry that had withheld data and straight answers and was generally considered an ineffectual apparatchik.[60] His ploy was

---

[57] Article Thirty Three, "Entwurf: Verfassung der Deutschen Demokratischen Republik, Arbeitsgruppe 'Neue Verfassung der DDR' des Runden Tisches," April 1990, www.documentarchiv.de/ddr/1990/ddr-verfassungsentwurf_runder-tisch.html#prae, accessed July 14, 2015.

[58] Kotkin, *Uncivil Society*, 12.   [59] RHG TH 02/01, "Postkarte," undated.

[60] Joachim Radkau, *The Age of Ecology: A Global History*, trans. Patrick Camiller (Malden, MA: Polity Press, 2014), 347.

disingenuous at best, and Reichelt resigned in January 1990, when Modrow restructured the now Ministry for Nature Conservation, Environmental Protection, and Water Management.[61]

With Reichelt out, Dr. Peter Diederich began to shift environmental policies, allowing long-time experts and nature conservationists to finally implement more effective policies.[62] During the late fall and winter of 1990, citizens' movements and scientists worked to make public the extensive lands that had been dedicated to hunting reserves for the regime's elites, totaling some four percent of all GDR territory. These off-limits spaces had long been a source of contention for activists. Now, under the guidance of the recently appointed deputy minister for nature conservation, Dr. Michael Succow, they proposed reappropriating these areas, along with others, and authorizing five national parks. The GDR had avoided this step for decades, first over the question of the GDR's diplomatic status and the term "national" and then later allegedly out of concerns that increased tourism under the designation would harm preservation efforts. In February 1990, the Central Round Table passed a resolution to expand the GDR's national park program, which the Council of Ministers approved in March.[63] Through the spring, Succow and others cooperated with West German environmental minister Klaus Töpfer to create the five national parks, four biosphere reserves, and over a dozen nature parks.[64]

With the SED's grasp loosening, reports from the environmental ministry and elsewhere publicly exposed the GDR's failures and explored ways to ameliorate the pollution. Officials also began to discuss "criteria for societal development, in particular regarding economic development and the use of resources."[65] Although the formal vote for unification had not yet occurred, Diederich's ministry worked toward producing conditions that were ecological, medically humane, and responsible to market

---

[61] "Reichelt nach Kritik zurückgetreten," *Frankfurter Allgemeine Zeitung*, January 11, 1990.

[62] Karl-Hermann Steinberg replaced Diederich in April and served through the rest of the unification process. Andreas Dix and Rita Gudermann, "Naturschutz in der DDR: Idealisiert, ideologisiert, instrumentalisiert?," in *Natur und Staat. Staatlicher Naturschutz in Deutschland, 1906–2006*, eds. Hans-Werner Frohn and Friedemann Schmoll (Bonn: Bundesamt für Naturschutz, 2006), 606–607.

[63] BArch DK 5/6234, "Nationalparkprogramm der DDR als Baustein für ein europäisches Haus," March 30, 1990.

[64] Sandra Chaney and Rita Gudermann, "National Contribution to International Conservation Part II," *Environmental Policy and Law* 40, no. 4 (June 2010), 184–185.

[65] BArch DK 5/3388, "Information über die Ergebnisse der 10. Sitzung des Runden Tisches zu ökologischen Fragen sowie über die Bildung des Grünen Tisches der DDR und Vorschläge zur Ausarbeitung des langfristigen Umweltprogramms," February 5, 1990.

mechanisms. As a result, the ministry recommended increased investment in research internally as well as in the Academy of Sciences and the Academy of Agricultural Sciences.[66] Moreover, negotiations for six pilot programs, co-funded environmental projects between the FRG and the GDR, began in the winter of 1990, finally securing the necessary resources to remedy the GDR's environmental situation.[67] Under new direction and with a modified name, Diederich's ministry altered its approach to remain relevant in the swiftly evolving political atmosphere.[68]

The GNU, like other SED mass social organizations, recognized the GDR's imminent collapse and moved to situate itself in an international community. As late at September 1989, the GNU had been drafting its next Five-Year Plan, replicating the same ideas that it had been using since the 1970s.[69] By February 1990, however, the GNU's central committee broke with its SED past, renamed itself the *Bund für Natur und Umwelt* (League for Nature and the Environment, BNU), and declared independence from the Cultural League.[70] Such a move had previously been illegal. The BNU hoped to join with the West German BUND, which the independent Green League had done the previous autumn.[71] The BUND also held membership in the international organization Friends of the Earth.[72] While this decision caused friction, it reflected the desire to adapt and become more fully incorporated into internationally recognized communities. The tactic was successful in that the GNU, now the BNU, was one of the few associations originating in the Cultural League to outlast the GDR.[73] Broader

---

[66] Ibid.

[67] RHG OWK 01, "Presseerklärung: Eva Quistorp, die Grünen, Mitglied des Umweltausschusses des Europäischen Parlaments, erklärt zum Besuch der Umweltschützer aus der DDR bei Minister Töpfer am 13. Dezember 1989."

[68] The ministry went from being the "Ministry for Environmental Protection and Water Management" to being the "Ministry for Nature and Environmental Protection and Water Management" around this time. After the March elections, the name changed again, this time to the "Ministry for Environment, Nature Conservation, Energy, and Reactor Safety."

[69] BArch-Stiftungarchiv der Partei und Massenorganisationen der DDR (SAPMO) DY 27/9650, "Entwurf: Maßnahmen zur Auswertung der Präsidialratstagung des Kulturbundes vom 28.9.1989 zur Umweltpolitik und den weiteren Aufgaben der Organisation und zur Umsetzung der dazu beschlossenen Konzeption."

[70] BArch-SAPMO DY 27/6122, "Basis – Demokratische Auflösung oder zentralistisches Chaos des Kulturbundes der DDR," February 12, 1990.

[71] Hermann Behrens et al., *Wurzeln der Umweltbewegung: Die "Gesellschaft für Natur und Umwelt" (GNU) im Kulturbund der DDR* (Marburg: BdWi-Verlag, 1993), 80. Given Poland's more relaxed stance, the PKE had joined FOE earlier in the 1980s, something the SED would not have permitted.

[72] AGG B II 3 1101, "A Perspective from the East," *Airplan: Air Pollution Action Network*, no. 11, December 1987, 12.

[73] See, for example, the still-existing branch in Magdeburg "Umweltkönig," www.umweltkoenig.de /oekologie-bnu-bund-fuer-natur-und-umwelt-landesverband-sachsen-anhalt-ev-in-magdeburg-175 91, accessed July 4, 2015.

transformations allowed existing mass social organizations to reorient their work and position themselves in German–German as well as pan-European networks. While the East German state and the SED attempted to hold on to power through the fall and winter of 1989–1990, forces for political and environmental change were too great.

Working toward an Environmental Union

By the time the decision for unification was formalized in the March 1990 election, German–German cooperation in addressing pollution was already in motion. These impulses were apparent in the national parks program, in the GNU renaming itself and joining the BUND, and in joint environmental projects. With legal unification set for October 3, 1990, environmental policy for the period between the election and unification focused on how to finance and administer cleanup. The architects were not necessarily East German activists who had helped raise awareness about the crisis in the 1980s but rather those who had the money and influence to make decisions. West German bureaucrats and members of the CDU-Ost (Christian Democratic Union-East, which was technically distinct from the CDU in the FRG), which now led the East German government, led the way.[74] As such, environmental cleanup in the (former) GDR was a largely top-down process. New actors and power structures reshaped environmental concerns, introducing funds and priorities that shifted influence toward West German bureaucrats and investors while overlooking East German input.

The FRG's waxing influence over the environmental situation in the GDR began months before the election. West German Chancellor Helmut Kohl's Ten Point Plan in November 1989 already laid out environmental goals. In a broad sense, the plan swung the narrative from reform within the GDR – as citizens' movements proposed – toward unification with an emphasis on mapping out long-term objectives.[75] Kohl presented ideas on how to make the East German economy more competitive and to open it up to private enterprise, as Poland and Hungary had done.[76]

---

[74] For more on political parties in the GDR and the end of the "bloc parties," in which the CDU had been part of the National Front and subservient to the SED, see Jarausch, *Rush to German Unity*, 117–121. Lothar de Maizière was selected to lead the CDU in the fall of 1989 because he worked for the Protestant Church as a legal adviser and was not tainted by connections to the SED.

[75] Helmut Kohl (Horst Teltschik), "Ten Point Program for German Unity," November 28, 1989, http://germanhistorydocs.ghi-dc.org/sub_document.cfm?document_id=223, accessed June 23, 2015.

[76] Ibid.

Because industry had been crucial to the GDR's self-definition as a socialist state and the main source of the state's pollution, the future of the economy was critically linked to natural resources and the environment. Thus, while the GDR needed transformation just like other eastern European countries, the result – incorporation into the FRG – would be very different for (former) East Germans and for nature. West German investment pulled the GDR away from the rest of the Soviet bloc experience and toward the FRG, altering economic and environmental dynamics in central Europe.

Kohl directly confronted the fact that the GDR's pollution was a major source of concern in both Germanys and integrated abatement projects into his larger vision. Kohl drew on the greening of the FRG over the two previous decades and declared the importance of "intensifying cooperation in the field of environmental protection" in the second point of his plan.[77] Two further points recommended common German institutions based on Modrow's suggestion of a "contractual community" and a pan-European environmental council. West German attention to the environment highlighted West German federal and provincial frustration regarding the GDR's denial of the pollution in the 1980s. Improving environmental conditions in the former GDR was also an olive branch to East Germans, who would primarily benefit from the extensive financial investment. This context of environmental awareness and economic prosperity promised an era of protection in East German territory as the path to a West German-led unification became ever more apparent.

To alleviate domestic and international qualms about a single Germany in central Europe, Kohl emphasized that Germany would be part of a "pan-European" community, not an aggressor. He wanted to strengthen east–west relations and expand the European Community (EC), thereby bringing "a century that witnessed so much misery, blood, and suffering" to an end.[78] West German parliamentarians overwhelmingly backed the speech and hailed it as a historical contribution. In the GDR, the SED reacted with reservation if not outright animosity, but the general population welcomed the proposal. Placards and posters morphed from calls for "Gorbi's" help to Deutsch Marks, meaning a desire for the economic benefits unification promised.[79] This transformation signaled the end of the Cold War in Europe, German division, and the postwar order. It also reconfigured central Europe, bringing FRG funding to the Polish and

---

[77] Kohl, "Ten Point Program for German Unity."   [78] Ibid.
[79] Wolfgang Schneider, ed., *Leipziger Demo Montag Tagebuch Demontage* (Leipzig and Weimar: Gustav Kiepenheuer Verlag, 1991), 66, 79.

Czechoslovakian borders and pushing the edge of the EC eastward. Kohl reassured observers, though, that a unified Germany would act multilaterally and continue to respect the Oder–Neisse Line.[80]

Of the West German political parties, only the Greens opposed Kohl's plan to unite Germany, which they did vehemently. The Greens' resistance stemmed both from their support of East German peace, environmental, and other dissident circles turned citizens' movements as well as their self-conception as an "anti-party" party that critiqued their own system in the FRG.[81] From late 1989 through the March elections, West German Greens backed the citizens' movements in the GDR as leaders of an opposition that could turn into the leadership of a transformed state, as Solidarność had in Poland. The Green Party hoped that the people of the GDR would seriously reflect on developing their own path, define it, and find its structures, while the FRG helped to financially support the new state.[82] The Greens, along with the citizens' movements, promoted a "two state solution," in which the GDR remained independent and cultivated a third way. As early as February 1990, the Green Party feared that the opposition and the Round Tables had lost their influence, arguing that oppositional groups were no longer able to play a role "in this giant game of chess."[83]

The West German Greens proposed a divided-but-supportive approach that would improve the environment but avoid a potential resurgence of German nationalism in central Europe.[84] To their mind, a united Germany would undo the decades of peace and progress in the FRG since 1968 and become more nationalistic again. As one press release stated, "The federal government is provoking unavoidable social dangers with its *Anschluß*-policy between the Federal Republic and the GDR . . . instead of European integration it is following a nationalistic agenda."[85] The Greens recommended an action plan that emphasized ecological cooperation on a wide range of topics. They advocated for the cessation of West German and West Berlin waste exports to the GDR, the development of a new

---

[80] Jarausch, *Rush to German Unity*, 168.
[81] Belinda Davis, "A Brief Cosmology of the West German Green Party," *German Politics & Society* 33, no. 4 (Winter 2015), 53.
[82] AGG Pol 509-4, Karitas Hensel, "Der Ausschuß für 'Innerdeutsche Bezieungen' befaßte sich am 7. Februar im Rahmen eines Berichtes von Minister Seiters intensiv mit dem Artikel 23 und seinen 'Möglichkeiten'," February 9, 1990.
[83] Ibid.
[84] Jarausch, *Rush to German Unity*, 68–69. AGG Pol 509-4, Barbara Simon, "Thesen zur Deutschlandpolitik," February 7, 1990. The Anschluß comment refers to the Third Reich's annexation of Austria in 1938.
[85] AGG Pol 509-4, "Konföderation statt Eingemeindung! März 1990."

energy program, and a joint environmental commission, among other projects.[86] This notion of maintaining two distinct Germanys, in which the FRG essentially underwrote a reformed GDR, seemed unpractical and unnecessary. Unsurprisingly, it garnered little resonance on either side of the German–German border.

The elections on March 19, 1990, confirmed that the prospect of unification under the leadership of a coalition called the Alliance for Germany. Within that constellation, the CDU-Ost won forty-one percent of the vote and the other seven percent came from the citizens' movements, Democratic Awakening and the German Social Union.[87] The new, center-right government with Lothar de Maizière as prime minister took control as the GDR's only democratically elected government. The de Maizière government oversaw the East German side of the negotiations, working in close collaboration with Kohl's CDU. After March, the pace of unification accelerated toward its legal conclusion on October 3, 1990 with the dissolution of the GDR and its incorporation into the FRG.[88] The agreements ironed out in these months laid the groundwork for massive economic and environmental changes in the (former) GDR.

Through the spring and summer of 1990, the extent of the devastation, and thus the looming costs of cleanup, became a focal point of negotiations between the Germanys. The democratically elected East German government released data that officials had secretly continued to collect and analyze throughout the 1980s, adding to an already sensationalized atmosphere. In March, Diederich formally published the *Environmental Report of the GDR* in a move toward increased transparency.[89] The content reinforced activists' fears about the pollution while shocking West German audiences. The GDR's annual emissions stood at 2.2 million tons of particulate matter and 5.2 million tons of sulfur dioxide, which were the highest in Europe.[90] As a percentage of its gross domestic income, the GDR spent roughly half of what the ten most industrialized countries

---

[86] Ibid.

[87] Kowalczuk, *Endspiel*, 526–527. "18. März 1990: Erste freie Volkskammerwahl," Bundeszentrale für politische Bildung, March 17, 2010, www.bpb.de/themen/01MOVB,0,0,18_M%E4rz_1990%3A_Erste_freie_Volkskammerwahl.html, accessed July 5, 2015.

[88] The economic, cultural, and social integration, or longer-term process of unification, has taken years if not decades. For more on transformations in the 1990s, see Larissa R. Stiglich, "After Socialism: The Transformation of Everyday Life in Eisenhüttenstadt, 1975–2015" (PhD Dissertation, University of North Carolina at Chapel Hill, 2020).

[89] Peter Diederich, "Vorwort," in *Umweltbericht der DDR: Information zur Analyse der Umweltbedingungen in der DDR und zu weiteren Maßnahmen* (Berlin: Institut für Umweltschutz, 1990), 3.

[90] Ibid., 7.

in the west did on environmental protection. It also confirmed that the continued use of outdated factories and increased use of lignite had led to crisis conditions.[91]

At long last, West Germans received answers to shared environmental problems that the SED had along avoided, providing insight into the amount of cleanup that would be necessary. A July 1990 *Der Spiegel* article relied on the *Environmental Report* to expose the critical conditions facing fish and human – among other – populations tied to the Elbe River. Over seven-and-a-half-million East Germans in the Elbe's catchment area did not consistently have potable drinking water.[92] After decades of observing fish die-offs, chemical spills, and generally avoiding the Elbe's water, this information corroborated West German fears. This pollution had obviously been a source of frustration for West Germans downstream, and now they finally had the data to verify what they had suspected. The release of this information contributed to a general sense of panic and motivated citizens of both Germanys to push to get major abatement operations underway as soon as possible; projects which, of course, were only possible with significant investment from the Federal Republic.

The de Maizière government worked with West German officials to reduce pollution to West German – or German federal – standards. East Germans in the democratically elected government had worked within state-controlled institutions only months before and they seized the chance to work with West German experts. Interviews long after the fact with Klaus Töpfer and Karl-Hermann Steinberg, who succeeded Diederich as environmental minister in April, underscore a spirit of responsiveness and collaboration. Töpfer recounted having visited Merseburg, where Steinberg had lived and worked at the Leuna works in the Chemical Triangle. In the interview, Töpfer expressed appreciation for East German technical skill in the environmental fields despite the political limits in the GDR, as well as the absolute necessity of improving conditions. Excerpts from Steinberg also remembered having a good working relationship with Töpfer and being impressed with his knowledge of East German hotspots, including Espenhain, from the beginning of their interactions in December 1989.[93]

---

[91] Ibid., 7.   [92] Sebastian Knauer, "Ein Fluß geht baden," *Der Spiegel*, July 23, 1990, 39.

[93] "Karl-Hermann Steinberg berichtet von seiner ersten Begegnung mit Bundesumweltminister Klaus Töpfer im Dezember 1989 und der weiteren Zusammenarbeit beider Minister im Jahr 1990," Bundesstiftung Aufarbeitung, 2016, https://deutsche-einheit-1990.de/ministerien/muner/, accessed May 26, 2020. Steinberg had a background in chemistry, having worked at the well-known Leuna

As Steinberg looked toward an environmental union with the FRG, activists in the Church such as Hans-Peter Gensichen at the KFH advocated for multiple voices to have a say. Gensichen wrote to Steinberg in May 1990, recommending that "perspectives not represented in parliament or the government" be heard, because listening to a range of interested individuals would avoid favoring specific interests. Gensichen wished for Steinberg to form an advisory council for the reinvented environmental ministry that included the representatives from research institutes, independent environmental organizations, the media, and the Church.[94] Steinberg apparently agreed to the advisory council and began to reach out to experts and conservationists about joining the project.[95] Gensichen's initiative reflected the desire for more participation in environmental and political transformations, something many East Germans found lacking during this period. Steinberg juggled a myriad of requests from within the GDR as well as the FRG, but overwhelmingly, the influence (and money) came from western sources.[96]

Either opting out of or disregarded by national debates, East German activists continued their efforts on a local level. These activities constituted a grassroots democratic moment that was unfortunately often irrelevant at the federal level as West German bureaucrats made most of the major decisions. Still, East German activists demanded a cleaner environment and pushed policymakers from East and West to confront the egregiousness of the pollution in certain industrial areas. In the Leipzig area, groups connected to the Protestant Church, New Forum, and the local Environmental Library protested conditions while also confronting new challenges. A 1990 citizens' initiative called to end open-pit mining in Cospuden south of Leipzig, a reminder that coal dust and other pollution did not disappear just because the SED was out of power. Its signers also worried that if conditions did not get better, residents would leave.[97] Concerns about depopulation were legitimate and would become an issue later in the 1990s.

works in the 1970s and 1980s before a docent and later a professor for technical chemistry at the Karl Marx University in Leipzig. In December 1989, he joined the CDU-Ost, which put him in a position to become environmental minister. "Steinberg, Karl-Hermann," *Wer war wer in der DDR?*, www.bundesstiftung-aufarbeitung.de/de/recherche/kataloge-datenbanken/biographische-datenbanken/karl-hermann-steinberg, accessed May 26, 2020.

94   BArch DK 5/6058, Correspondence between Gensichen and Steinberg, May 20, 1990.
95   BArch DK 5/6058, Steinberg's Correspondence, June–July 1990.
96   Jarausch, *Rush to German Unity*, 148.
97   Archiv Bürgerbewegung Leipzig (ABL) 1.2, "Markleeberger Umweltinitiative," March 15, 1990.

In nearby Taucha, the local New Forum chapter worried about increased consumption and waste only weeks after the March election. Critiquing capitalism as well as the nearly defunct planned economy, the New Forum members noted an uptick in consumption with the introduction of the market economy, and correspondingly more trash. New Forum, along with the Environmental Group Taucha, started a joint campaign in May 1990 to make people more aware of the larger impact that increased consumption had on the environment. They charged residents to choose their purchases carefully and to buy conscientiously.[98] The end of socialism and rise of a market economy in the GDR presented distinct environmental threats, which activists sought to meet, even before unification was official. Thus, while having less of a presence in the highest levels of decision making, independent environmental groups continued to do what they had always done best: tackle local issues.

With the end of travel restrictions, the KFH and other activists used their new-found freedom in this transitional period to travel and network beyond the GDR. German–German meetings allowed activists from either side of the rapidly disappearing Iron Curtain to find common ground and pursue shared concerns. Of obvious interest to both sides were the matters of energy sources and consumption. Over the 1990 Pentecost holiday, East and West German Christian environmentalists came together to propose collaboration between energy experts and the Protestant Churches in both Germanys. Cloaked in the familiar language of stewardship and caring for God's creation, they also recommended practical tips on energy use. In an open appeal to parishes across the nearly unified country, Gensichen and others took the opportunity to suggest a fifty percent reduction in energy use in the churches.[99] Signers from Schwerin to Nordhausen, Berlin, and Dresden urged their home parishes to join the initiative. While policy came from state agreements, civil society organizations continued through familiar means at the local level and brought individuals with common interests together across the German–German border.

Codifying Environmental Protection and Cleanup

In the period after the March election, officials from both Germanys worked to rapidly establish not only a political and economic but also an

---

[98] ABL, Neues Forum Taucha, "Erst prüfen – dann kaufen!" May 1990.
[99] RHG Ki 18/02, "Offener Brief an Gemeinden, Gruppen, Synoden und Leitungen der Evangelischen Kirchen in der DDR," June 5, 1990.

environmental union. The two environmental ministers, Töpfer and Steinberg, had a short window in which to formulate a program for pollution reduction before rolling out agreements on how to clean up and protect the East German environment ahead of unification. The first in a series of agreements between the Germanys to form an environmental – as well as a monetary, economic and social – union was signed on May 18, 1990.[100] Then, the more comprehensive Environmental Framework Law (*Umweltrahmengesetz*, URG) followed at the beginning of July.[101] In the leadup to unification on October 3, the authors of these agreements and other officials recognized that no East German state existed to be held responsible, complicating the implementation of a "polluter pays" principle. This constellation of government and investor funds solidified that cleanup and environmental protection were top-down processes, largely in the hands of outsiders. In the GDR's long struggle to balance economy and ecology, finally the scales shifted toward the environment but with relatively little input from East Germans.

Meetings between the two Germanys regarding an environmental union had been going on since February and laid out the FRG's ambitious objectives. In the initial meeting, Töpfer declared that his intent was to eliminate the difference in environmental conditions between east and west by the year 2000. He aimed to achieve this task through economic transformation, namely the introduction of a social and ecological market economy.[102] The West German government had promised 700 million DM to six carefully selected projects, including a high temperature incinerator to abate arsenic in Dresden and a plant to deal with mercury at Buna.[103] This financial commitment grew with impending unification, and the environment proved to be an arena in which the FRG showcased the successes – and affluence – of the social market economy over the defunct communist system.

In June of 1990, weeks before the URG went into effect, officials struck a balance between economic incentive to invest in the former GDR and

---

[100] Kapitel V, Artikel 16, "Vertrag über die Schaffung einer Währungs-, Wirtschafts- und Sozialunion zwischen der Bundesrepublik Deutschland und der Deutschen Demokratischen Republik," May 18, 1990, www.gesetze-im-internet.de/wwsuvtr/BJNR205370990.html accessed May 12, 2021http://www.gesetze-im-internet.de/bundesrecht/wwsuvtr/gesamt.pdf.

[101] "Klaus Töpfer erinnert sich im Interview an die Zusammenarbeit mit seinem früheren Amtskollegen Karl-Hermann Steinberg und anderen ostdeutschen Partnern," Bundesstiftung Aufarbeitung, 2015, https://deutsche-einheit-1990.de/ministerien/muner/, accessed May 26, 2020.

[102] BArch DK 5/2849, Klaus Töpfer, "Gemeinsame Umwelt: Deutsch-deutsche Zusammenarbeit im Umweltschutz."

[103] Knauer, "Ein Fluß geht baden," 45.

environmental cleanup. East German enterprises had been owned by the state, and with the impending dissolution of the GDR, no one could be held accountable for their pollution, which was incredibly extensive. Some 15,000 contaminated sites, or brownfields, were identified as being in need of cleanup. West German or international companies, of course, did not want to foot the bill. To avoid deterring potential investors, then, *Treuhand*, the recently founded trust in charge of privatizing East German enterprises, and the German governments agreed to a "residual pollution exemption for investors" (RPEI). Federal and state governments were obligated to cover the costs rather than corporations and businesses moving into the former GDR.[104] The East German environment was thus to be improved and protected according to FRG standards with funding from the Federal Republic and, to a lesser extent, provincial governments.

The URG essentially implemented the FRG's laws, neglecting the existence of traditions and practices in the GDR that could have benefited all Germans with their inclusion.[105] Some East Germans complained that the West German Basic Law did not guarantee the right to a clean environment as the GDR's 1968 constitution had.[106] East German experts as well as official propaganda had long held the superiority of socialist environmentalism in the GDR through its inclusion in the constitution and the early creation of the MUW in 1972. By contrast, the FRG did not have a similar universal statement and only instituted an independent environmental ministry in 1986 in response to Chernobyl.[107] While the FRG already had extensive legislation before the ministry, East Germans pointed to the GDR's accomplishments to demonstrate their environmental work before 1990 and to suggest West Germans might learn something from them, too. Despite these arguments, proposed changes to existing West German law were largely discounted, reinforcing a top-down process of unification.

---

[104] Sandra Chaney, "A Chemical Landscape Transformed: Bitterfeld, Germany since 1980," *Global Environment* 10, no. 1 (March 2017), 162.

[105] BArch DK 5/2849, "Kurzbericht über die Anhörung zum Umweltrahmengesetz im Ausschuß für UNER am 13. Juni 1990, 9.00 Uhr." Michael Kloepfer, *Das Umweltrecht in der Deutschen Einigung: Zum Umweltrecht im Einigungsvertrag und zum Umweltrahmengesetz* (Berlin: Duncker & Humblot, 1991), 19.

[106] BArch DK 5/2849, Voigt, "Als Anlage wird die Beantwortung zu 1. der 'Fragen an die Ressorts zur Vorbereitung des Staatsvertrages zur Herstellung der deutschen Einheit,' vorgelegt," July 3, 1990.

[107] "Geschichte des Ministeriums," www.bmu-kids.de/ministerium/das-ministerium/geschichte-des-ministeriums/, accessed, June 8, 2020.

The FRG authorities also sidelined East German experts who had labored for the environment for decades, as well as activists who had protested pollution. The regulations reflected the West German principles of prevention, polluter pays (albeit modified to incentivize investment in the former GDR), and cooperation but did not incorporate either East German rhetoric or successful programs.[108] The difference, for example, between the East German "secondary resource acquisition" (*Sekundärrohstofferfassung*, SERO) and the "new-German 'recycling'" was actually quite small, with the implication being that there was then no need to keep SERO. Programs such as SERO had been recognized internationally in the 1970s and 1980s but were essentially ignored during unification.[109] Moreover, while the GDR did not succeed in universally ameliorating water pollution, it did implement processes to use water more efficiently, reducing consumption by ten percent between 1970 and 1988. Water purification was so effective that even the U.S. Coast Guard adopted the technology.[110] West German ideals and law were introduced in the (former) GDR, and with a triumphalist attitude, the FRG lost an opportunity to reflect on its own practices and establish the best environmental policy possible.

The East German People's Chamber passed the URG on June 29, 1990, and it went into effect two days later. The law expanded the preliminary union from May 18 and covered a wide range of issues: emissions and air quality, nuclear energy and technology, water management, waste, the chemical industry, nature and landscape conservation, and environmental impact assessment. It specified the requirements needed to obtain exemptions for old factories and the responsibilities of future owners, once many of the industries were privatized.[111] This language reflected the RPEI policies that had been created in June when the URG was finalized. All East German provisions ceased to be in force as the new laws took effect.[112] In the summer of 1990, and in response to popular and scientific demand,

---

[108] BArch DK 5/2849, "Der Rahmen für ein besseres Bild unserer Umwelt: Umweltrahmengesetz bringt bundesdeutschen Standard," undated.

[109] Ibid.

[110] Raymond Dominick, "Capitalism, Communism, and Environmental Protection: Lessons from the German Experience," *Environmental History* 3, no. 3 (July 1998), 321.

[111] Artikel 1, Absatz 4, "Altanlagen," Umweltrahmengesetz vom 29. Juni 1990, Gesetzblatt Teil I Nr. 42 – Ausgabetag: 20. Juli 1990, 653, http://deutsche-einheit-1990.de/wp-content/uploads/Gbl-URaG.pdf, accessed June 29, 2015.

[112] Artikel 8, Absatz 1, "Umweltrahmengesetz vom 29. Juni 1990," Gesetzblatt Teil I Nr. 42 – Ausgabetag: 20. Juli 1990, 653, http://deutsche-einheit-1990.de/wp-content/uploads/Gbl-URaG.pdf, accessed June 29, 2015.

the second of the GDR's two existing nuclear power plants was shut down.[113] West German regulations paved the way for healthier, brighter prospects in the former GDR but at the expense of previously existing environmental protection and the culture surrounding it.

The environment did not receive much attention in the Unification Treaty signed on October 3, 1990, but it nevertheless was an integral aspect of creating parity between east and west. The treaty promised to support a standard of living in the former GDR that was at least on par with the FRG. The social market economy was to achieve the "balance between economy and ecology" that the GDR never did through safeguarding citizens from dangers to their health and building on the agenda set out in the URG.[114] More broadly, though, the fate of the environment rested not only on real regulation but also on economic transition, social planning, and government investment in the cleanup of tens of thousands of contaminated sites. As early as October 10, 1990, Töpfer announced that the federal government would sponsor thirty-five pilot projects in the "new provinces." With some 2.4 billion German Marks devoted to cleanup, these projects identified areas of major concern, including in the chemical industry and mining.[115] The environmental ministry promptly announced another 900 million Marks for similar projects. By 1991, twenty of these projects were already under contract and the other fifteen on their way.[116] The Chemical Triangle (that included Leipzig, Bitterfeld, Halle, and Merseburg) listed in their assessment the most serious polluted and deserving of attention and resources.[117] The recovery of the East German environment over the next two decades was one of unification's greatest successes, but privatization produced more ambiguous results as people moved away and unemployment remained higher than in other parts of the country.

---

[113] BArch DK 5/6061, "Grundsteinlegung für eine Ersatzanlage zur Wärmeversorgung auf Heizölbasis in Greifswald-Lubmin," July 28, 1990.

[114] Kapitel VII, Artikel 34, Absatz 1, Vertrag zwischen der Bundesrepublik Deutschland und der Deutschen Demokratischen Republik über die Herstellung der Einheit Deutschlands (Einigungsvertrag), 31. August 1990, www.gesetze-im-internet.de/einigvtr/BJNR208890990.html, accessed May 12, 2021.

[115] AGG B II 952, Pressemitteilung der Bundesminister für Umweltschutz, Naturschutz und Reaktorsicherheit, October 10, 1990.

[116] "Bereits erfolgte Umweltentlastungen, Bundesminister für Umwelt, Naturschutz und Reaktorsicherheit, Die Umweltkrise der Modernen Gesellschaft: Konzepte und Materialien für eine praxisnahe sozialwissenschaftliche Lehrerfortbildung," 326, https://epub.ub.uni-muenchen.de /2193/1/2193.pdf, accessed September 2, 2016. https://epub.ub.uni-muenchen.de/2193/1/2193.pdf

[117] Materialien zur Deutschen Einheit und zum Aufbau in den neuen Bundesländern, Deutscher Bundestag, 12. Wahlperiode, Drucksache 12/6865, 08.02.94, 195, http://dip21.bundestag.de/dip21/ btd/12/068/1206854.pdf, accessed September 2, 2016.

The process of union brought about the prospect of much needed environmental cleanup to eastern Germany. Both East and West Germans strongly backed the efforts in the spring and summer of 1990 as experts from identified major areas of concern. In the end, though, it was largely West German laws, practices, and funds that were to abate the pollution, because the GDR had no money to do so and then ceased to exist on October 3. The resulting success brought the former GDR into a narrative of German environmentalism that many activists and experts had long desired. At the same time, this level of investment in the environment distinguished the GDR from its Soviet bloc neighbors, which did not have wealthy partner states in the west to underwrite the costs of cleanup or unemployment benefits. Nevertheless, the manner in which the cleanup happened often displaced and marginalized precisely those individuals who had pushed for such change before 1989. German unification brought significant resources for environmental protection into the former GDR, but the Federal Republic's affluence also set the "new provinces" on a different trajectory from other former Soviet bloc states, changing relationships in central Europe.

Conclusion

The tumultuous final days of communism brought about seemingly unbelievable possibilities for the environment to central and eastern Europe in short order. While economic conditions and political rights laid the foundation for dissent that ended communism, environmental pollution also crucially mobilized discontent in the period before 1989. Experts and activists from a range of backgrounds constructed a constellation of internal doubt and public frustration that helped destabilize communism. When opportunities for protest emerged, environmental devastation featured prominently, highlighting communist governments' failures to balance economy and ecology. Especially in the GDR, environmental criticism undermined the SED's promise of a clean environment, dating back to the 1968 constitution. Environmental politics were an effective means of challenging the system.

This transition to democracy and capitalism, however, created different prospects for the environment and environmental activists than under communism. New actors and considerations entered the stage as dismantling planned economies dominated the public's attention, shifting influence away from experts and activists who had had a stake before. Networks and contacts from before 1989 played an important role at the local but not necessarily at the federal level. Activists continued to advocate for improving local conditions and ecological justice as part of a tradition of protest and grassroots networking, but this made functioning at the highest levels of bureaucracy and policymaking difficult and inadvertently sidelined them. These were not skills, especially in the GDR, that had been permitted to coexist.

The major changes in power and priorities in 1989 and 1990 bewildered citizens of former communist states and often left them at a loss. Many had fumed over the environmental degradation under communism and supported cleanup, but funding for it came from outside sources, either the FRG or the EC (European Union after 1993). Policies did not come from those who had demanded it in the 1980s, making it a top-down project without much grassroots investment that led to a sense of alienation.[118] This oversight, along with high unemployment in the 1990s and into the 2000s, in many ways led to a sense of disillusionment with the once coveted concepts of democracy and capitalism. Instead of a triumphal narrative, the legacy of the 1990s is far more mixed. Borders and geopolitical blocs moved or disappeared, reconfiguring a sense of central Europe again as networks, affinities, and cooperation realigned after 1989. The collapse of communism and the introduction of new sources of funding benefited the natural environment, but those transformations presented distinct challenges to navigate for activists and residents alike.

---

[118] Barbara Jancar-Webster, "Conclusion" in *Environmental Action in Eastern Europe*, ed. Jancar-Webster, 223. A sense of alienation began in the process of unification in 1990 but became more pronounced later in the 1990s. See Peter Christ and Ralf Neubauer, *Kolonie im eigenen Land: Die Treuhand, Bonn und die Wirtschaftskatastrophe der fünf neuen Länder* (Berlin: Rowohlt, 1991), 206–207.

Conclusion

This book has argued that environmentalism in the GDR bridged the Iron Curtain and expands our understanding of the "greening" of postwar central Europe. Environmental consciousness started as a response to a variety of domestic, regional, and international impulses, and created circuits of environmental knowledge that transcended political borders to the east and west. East German environmentalisms neither simply borrowed from western, liberal democracies nor evolved in isolation from them. Moreover, environmentalisms in the GDR reacted to the Soviet-style communism in which they emerged and in relation to neighboring socialist states. The circuits of environmental knowledge that emerged thus drew on a multitude of influences, including Cold War political and economic concerns, Christian texts, Soviet rhetoric, and eastern European dissidents, to advocate for better protection. Within the GDR, commonalities and interactions between officials and Church-based or independent activists also break down the divisions between "state" and "society," revealing a more nuanced understanding of power and negotiation in the GDR. When the SED failed to fulfill its own environmental promises, critics questioned not only environmental policy but the system as a whole.

Environmental policy and protest in the GDR bring into focus the power (and limitations) of the state in twentieth-century European history. The state played a defining role in how people lived their lives, economically, politically, and socially, which in turn determined environmental conditions. The East German dictatorship had a direct impact on the quality of air its citizens breathed and the water they drank, through its industries, its regulation, and its prioritization of a Stalinist economy. More problematic for the ruling SED was its own presumption that communism could solve the GDR's pollution and promises to East Germans that it would. As a workers' state, providing for workers' well-being – physically, culturally, and otherwise – was of utmost importance.

When the SED and the state could not provide a clean environment, they set the stage for their own downfall. Of course, the environment was only one of many legitimacy deficits for the SED, but the unresolved environmental devastation was emblematic of the party's undelivered pledge. The state then hid the data that exposed the failures, turning pollution into a matter of information politics as well as of environment protection.

The opportunities to react to pollution varied significantly under a dictatorship compared to a democracy. In a democracy, the state is a separate actor distinct from economic agents, accountable to an electorate, and a protector of citizens' rights. Certainly, the West German government initially hesitated to regulate polluters – something the SED gleefully noted – but it did adapt to public opinion over time.[1] Moreover, the dissemination of information, formation of associations, and staging of protests were readily permissible in the FRG. Police interventions and the use of violence did occur in democracies, too, especially in the occupations of proposed nuclear power reactors at Wyhl and Brokdorf.[2] Still, those experiences belong in a larger, often overlooked context. The repressive character of the East German state created a distinctive form of environmentalism in the GDR. Both official and independent environmentalism evolved without guarantees of freedom of expression, assembly, or transparency. Environmental awareness and protest in the GDR expanded despite limitations that did not exist – or only existed in a much lesser form – in democratic states.

Implicit in the tension between dictatorship and democracy are lingering Cold War assumptions that environmental movements could only have been successful in a democracy. Dictatorship certainly limited opportunities for protest, and yet, despite those hardships, interest in the environment stemmed from multiple directions – in some cases from the state and party even – and posed a real challenge to the existing authorities' legitimacy. The numerous reasons ordinary East Germans engaged in environmental activities in the GDR, moreover, underscore the state's initial support for environmental protection and that it was not explicitly an oppositional issue. Rather, critics found that it was an effective weapon against the SED and the state. The resonance of the environment across different sectors of East German society helps explain its role in the collapse of communism in 1989 and suggests that the environmental movement

---

[1] Frank Uekötter, *The Greenest Nation? A New History of German Environmentalism* (Cambridge, MA: MIT Press, 2014), 86–89.

[2] Stephen Milder, *Greening Democracy: The Anti-Nuclear Movement and Political Environmentalism in West Germany and Beyond, 1968–1983* (New York: Cambridge University Press, 2017), 138–141.

simply took a different form than in a democracy. Wrapped up in a distinct set of domestic considerations, environmentalism in the GDR provides an alternative perspective of how such movements arise outside of – but not disconnected from – democracy.

The struggle to balance economy and ecology also emerges as a defining them of East German engagement with the environment. That strain exposes tensions between materialism, production, and quality of life in a competition between economic systems. The postwar period marked numerous changes that transformed consumption habits and the way people viewed themselves in a global context. These developments occurred unevenly, with the communist economies being slower to shift away from heavy industry and from coal to oil. The East German economy was intimately tied to international markets through loans, the buying and selling of technology, waste imports, and environmental pollution. Honecker consciously sought to unite economy and social policy that would raise standards of living, though it meant becoming more reliant on western aid. Intentionally and unintentionally, these decisions negatively affected public health and the East German environment.

Population growth and skyrocketing consumption in the mid-to-late twentieth century forced states and citizens to reconsider their relationship with limited natural resources. The East German leadership paid lip service to environmental policies as long as they did not interfere with the functioning of the economy. Distinct from official actions, East Germans who confronted the human toll on the environment through economic growth and consumption were at the center of global discourses in the 1970s and 1980s.[3] Because the communist state had framed its treatment of the environment and consumption in contrast to capitalism, East Germans pitched their arguments differently than environmental movements in liberal democracies. They responded to the system in which they lived. At times they embraced the SED's environmentalist claims to advocate for better protection, while at others they adopted Christian, western, or other anti-communist rhetoric to critique the SED's failures.

The GDR's position in central Europe further depicts transnational entanglements that reveal both the power and limits of borders. Despite the diplomatic and physical constraints of the Cold War, states, scientists,

---

[3] Eli Rubin and Scott Moranda, "Introduction," in *Ecologies of Socialisms: Germany, Nature, and the Left in History, Politics, and Culture*, eds. Sabine Moedersheim, Scott Moranda, and Eli Rubin (New York: Peter Lang Press, 2019), 3–7.

and activists were in communication with one another for more than two decades, creating circuits of environmental knowledge. These many actors used the networks they built to pursue their ambitions while also balancing environmental, political, and diplomatic realities. The GDR used environmental conferences to gain international recognition and normalize its status in the 1970s, but then the state also overreached, making promises it could not keep. As with the 1984 Munich Agreement on reducing sulfur dioxide levels, countries from both blocs committed to it, though the western European countries were much more likely to meet the goals. In such cases, the GDR ultimately hurt its credibility by pledging to pursue an unattainable goal, and increasingly shut out actors who might criticize East Germany's environmental record.

Activists behind the Iron Curtain intentionally looked westward for information, advice, and technology, while those in western Europe had less impetus to look east. Western Europeans generally had more responsive governments, better environmental regulation, and stronger social movements. Though asymmetrical, those interactions were crucial in supporting environmental activists in eastern Europe reacting to their own situations. Rather than simply being a delayed reaction to earlier movements in western Europe, eastern European activists applied relevant aspects of western European trends to their own situations. The emergence of an environmental consciousness was a global phenomenon in the late 1960s and early 1970s. Despite the uneven flows of information, countries on both sides were part of an international history of growing environmental movements and regulation after 1968. Moreover, though western Europeans looked eastward less than the reverse, they did pay attention to environmental hazards in eastern Europe in the 1980s, in no small part because especially West Germans felt the impact of communist pollution in their air and water.

With the collapse of communism in 1989, new political and domestic realities soon reconfigured many of the shared Cold War experiences. The wealthier FRG absorbed the GDR, which distanced the East German experience – in terms of both policy and memory – from fellow former Soviet satellite states.[4] In Poland, economic woes from privatization, inflation, and the resulting unemployment took center stage, hindering pollution abatement projects that required domestic financing. As early as 1990, the environmental ministry introduced "modernization and

---

[4] Philipp Ther, "Beyond the Nation: The Relational Basis of a Comparative History of Germany and Europe," *Central European History* 36, no. 1 (March 2003), 45–73.

restructuring measures" to curtail pollution and streamline production, merging economic and environmental goals. These efforts foundered on both counts, because they required economic sacrifice for environmental improvement, which democratic leaders viewed as impolitic.[5] Poland's accession to the European Union in 2004 again changed its relationship with Germany and Europe. Since then, both the former GDR and Poland have received significant funds to improve infrastructure, invest in newer and cleaner industries, and restore the delicate ecosystems of forests and waterways.[6] This money has largely come from top-down or external initiatives that do not necessarily engage with the policy and activism of the communist period but do reflect the ongoing ecological interconnection of central Europe.

In contrast to Poland and other eastern European countries, broad new policies quickly transformed the East German landscape with substantial funding from West German taxpayers.[7] In the 1990s, the pollution levels dropped dramatically within a matter of years. This cleanup was a combination of effective policies and deindustrialization, while federal policies simultaneously transferred wealth from east to west. Within three and a half years, ninety-two percent of East German industries had been privatized, with eighty-five percent of that being bought up by West German companies, and international investors purchased another nine percent. Moreover, unemployment topped out at nine million (out of a population of roughly seventeen million) before dropping to six million by 1997.[8] While the territory received significant relief from the federal government, the economic difficulties and resulting unemployment often overshadowed ecological recovery. In the Chemical Triangle and Lusatia, for example, these transformations brought challenges to old networks and established modes of activism. Given the new constellations, many grassroots activists of the 1980s struggled to reorient their work in the 1990s, with only a few transitioning to become politicians or public figures.

In the Chemical Triangle, local efforts continued to push for pollution abatement, but the real change came from the outside. On the southern end of the infamous region, the town of Merseburg suffered from its

[5] Curtis, ed., *Poland: A Country Study*, 63.
[6] European Commission Enlargement Directorate General, "The Enlargement Process and the three pre-accession instruments: Phare, ISPA, Sapard," February 2002, www.esiweb.org/pdf/bulgaria_phare_ispa_sapard_en.pdf, accessed March 1, 2019.
[7] Ther, "Beyond the Nation."
[8] Thomas Fleischman, "The Half-Life of State Socialism: What Radioactive Wild Boars Tell Us about the Environmental History of Reunified Germany," in *Ecologies of Socialisms*, eds. Moedersheim et al., 240–241.

unfortunate location between the chemical plants in Leuna and Buna, which synthesized ammonia and petrochemical, and Schkopau, a major plastics producer.[9] In late 1989, local New Forum members called for new ideas for cleaning up local pollution and began to organize for protection in this period of transition. During the 1990 election a few months later, Merseburg's New Forum chapter argued that "Environmental protection affects everyone, because one cannot eat money."[10] New Forum prioritized cleaner air and water, better waste disposal, renovating devastated areas, and reducing noise pollution. Students at the local technical college requested a "Center for Environmental Toxicology and Medicine" to monitor and alleviate the human consequences of the degradation.[11] The important environmental cleanup that came in the following years did not necessarily stem from New Forum's advocacy but from western investment that created new challenges for locals.

With abatement projects underway in the 1990s, images of pollution from Maron's *Flight of Ashes* faded away and economic concerns dominated the mental landscape. The largest employers in the area, the Leuna and Buna chemical works, went from each having over ten-thousand workers to not existing at all. The plants were privatized, broken up, and downsized. Large tracts of the enormous grounds fell into disuse with only much smaller chemical operations, such as Infra Leuna Gruppe, Total Raffinerie Mitteldeutschland GmbH, and Industriemontagen Merseburg GmbH, using portions of the once massive plants.[12] The largest of the new companies, Dow Olefinverbund GmbH, employed roughly 1,500 people in 2015, a small fraction of employment levels before 1990.[13] While the policies succeeded – air pollution dropped by more than a third between 1989 and 1992 – unemployment and outmigration became the town's largest concerns.[14] Despite the New Forum's 1990 quip about not being able to eat money, the rocky road to capitalism often overshadowed other achievements. Environmental regulation and the means to implement it along with less production as East German industries went bankrupt or were sold off meant that activism lost its sense of purpose and urgency.

---

[9] Schkopau was a branch of the larger Buna works.

[10] ABL 4.28.216 "Meine—Deine—Unsere Umwelt: Neues Forum Merseburg," January 1990, 2.

[11] Ibid., 8–9.

[12] Sandra Chaney, "A Chemical Landscape Transformed: Bitterfeld, Germany since 1980," *Global Environment* 10, no. 1 (March 2017), 156–157.

[13] Ibid.

[14] Materialien zur Deutschen Einheit und zum Aufbau in den neuen Bundesländern, Deutscher Bundestag, 12. Wahlperiode, Drucksache 12/6865, 08.02.94, 197, http://dip21.bundestag.de/dip21/btd/12/068/1206854.pdf, accessed September 7, 2016.

For the rural borderland of Lusatia, unification was only a partial success story, too. Activists in Zittau and other nearby towns pushed for better environmental protection in 1989–1990, reconstituting the Environmental Libraries in Zittau and Großhennersdorf as independent associations once it became possible. The library in Zittau blended the values of 1989 with the language of the preceding opposition. In the library's charter, its members expressed their commitment to "democracy in all areas of life," and reaffirmed their efforts for peace, human rights, and the preservation of nature."[15] They also collaborated with the New Forum chapter in Leipzig and the provincial organization for all of Saxony. In 1991, after the New Forum joined forces with other citizens' movements and the Greens to become Alliance 90/the Greens, they demanded a strategy to handle the "current crisis in the former GDR." They called for additional Round Table Talks to discuss privatization, to "annul the resolutions that discriminated against the former GDR in the Unification Treaty," and to express a series of environmental grievances.[16] Economic and ecological questions spanned the 1989 divide without obvious solutions.

Open-pit mining of lignite in Lusatia in the 1990s continued as before, but privatization and new federal plans to lower carbon emissions proved controversial. More effective processes in coal refining improved air quality. Western technology reduced pollution and worksite injuries, which according to the Stasi had cost roughly 100 million Marks in 1988 in one power plant alone.[17] Despite these advances, lignite was – and is – still a major contaminant. As Germany reduced its carbon dioxide emissions, Lusatians worried for the future of their most profitable industry.[18] Locals maintained positive attitudes toward open-pit mining, and the Swedish company, Vattenfall, purchased most of Lusatia's mines in the 1990s. It is among the largest employers in the area, and privatization has already cost the local population dearly. In 1990, roughly 65,000 people worked in Lusatian mines, but by 2000, that number had plummeted

---

[15] UBG 16–23, "Satzung der Umweltbibliothek – Zittau, e.V.," undated.

[16] ABL 4.28.401, Bündnis 90/Grüne Leipzig, "Sofortprogramm: zur Lösung der gegenwärtigen Krise in der ehemaligen DDR," May 1, 1991.

[17] BStU MfS HA XVIII 27513, "Hinweise: Zum Schadensgesschehen auf dem Gebiet der Volkswirtschaft der DDR im Jahr 1988." The power plant in question was Boxberg, and it tallied 669 fires, 205 other disasters, 25 explosions, 3 dead, and 33 injured. The year before there had been a larger tragedy that left 8 dead and 52 injured.

[18] Tilo Berger, "Nix für die Umwelt, nix für die Lausitz," *Die Sächsische Zeitung*, May 20, 2015.

to about 7,000.[19] Unification brought about an environmental recovery but threatened Lusatia's economic welfare.

Earlier environmental activists and dissidents also attempted to take part in the democratization of the former GDR and find a place in the political landscape. A very few, such as Matthias Platzeck of Potsdam became successful politicians on a provincial scale. A founding member of the East German Green Party, Platzeck later joined the Social Democratic Party.[20] After serving in a number of positions, he was minister president of Brandenburg from 2002 until 2013. Others, such as Carlo Jordan, made the transition to local politician. Jordan served as a representative for the Alliance 90/Greens in local Berlin in 1994–1995 but then withdrew from public office.[21] Platzeck represented more of an exception and Jordan the rule. Many of the oppositional figures did not retain the prominence they experienced in 1989–1990. A handful turned to preserving their legacy through the Robert Havemann Society and the Federal Commission for the Records of the State Security Service of the former GDR, but many more fell into obscurity, never becoming politically engaged beyond the local level after 1990.[22]

The revelation of numerous activists' work for the Stasi as unofficial informants further complicated relations within old networks after 1990. Henry Schramm from Halle, for example, became a party speaker for the East German Green Party for a short time before it merged with the Alliance 90/Green Party. Later, it was revealed that he had been an informant since 1983 and aggressively prevented a second film like *Bitteres aus Bitterfeld* that documented conditions in the Chemical Triangle from being produced and broadcast abroad.[23] Schramm had gone so far as to encourage fellow activists to rejoin the movement when they drifted away, writing to one that "I'm a little sad about your separation

---

[19] "Anzahl der Beschäftigten im Braunkohlenbergbau in der Lausitz in den Jahren von 1960 bis 2014," http://de.statista.com/statistik/daten/studie/161205/umfrage/braunkohlenbergbau-beschaeftigte-in -der-lausitz-seit-1960/, accessed June 30, 2015.

[20] Platzeck was active in both official and independent environmental circles in the GDR. He worked as the section leader of "environmental health" in the office for health inspections in the district of Potsdam between 1982 and 1990. "Minister President of Land Brandenburg Matthias Platzeck," www.bundesstiftung-aufarbeitung.de/de/recherche/kataloge-datenbanken/biographische-daten banken/matthias-platzeck, accessed May 12, 2021.

[21] "Carlo Jordan," hrsg. v. Bundeszentrale für politische Bildung und Robert-Havemann-Gesellschaft e.V., letzte Änderung September 2008, www.jugendopposition.de/index.php?id=202, accessed July 5, 2015.

[22] Tom Strohschneider, "Aus dem Schatten Gaucks," *Die Tageszeitung*, March 9, 2012, www.taz.de/! 5098809/, accessed July 5, 2015.

[23] Merrill E. Jones, "Origins of the East German Environmental Movement," *German Studies Review* 16, no. 2 (May 1993), 257.

from the environmental group, and I cannot figure out what led to it."[24] Other Stasi informants, such as Falk Zimmermann, were in Arche's inner circle to sow discord there. Zimmermann tried to remain in environmental circles after 1989, serving as a contact for Greenway in the former GDR as late as 1991, before being exposed.[25] With the opening of the Stasi files, activists learned who had previously informed on them, which deepened rifts and ended friendships.

In Berlin, confronting this past and preserving the opposition's legacy became the objective. In the early 1990s, many from the Environmental Library turned their former library on Schliemannstrasse into an archive and information center about the injustices of dictatorship.[26] Unification and the success of effective policies severed the connection between environment and opposition, at least in popular memory. The declining interest in the environment was, in large part, because the policies worked. It happened, however, in conjunction with the dissolution of East German industries and soaring unemployment. Still, the intertwining of environment, activism, and regulation that played a prominent role in the 1980s carried into the 1990s in different forms with adjusted modes of engagement.

The GDR complicates Germany's "greenest nation" narrative and forces a reconsideration of the environment and environmental policy. The GDR was a Germany, a fact that cannot be ignored even if it does not fit neatly into the supposed West German success story. Where the FRG improved environmental conditions in the 1970s and 1980s, the GDR promised to do likewise but failed. Rather than an aberration, it belongs to a much longer German history of industrialization and economic growth. Moreover, the FRG benefited from the GDR's abysmal record by shipping waste to the east and bypassing West German regulations. The FRG's strong environmental record was in part possible because of policies that exported West German pollution to its struggling communist rival. Within the GDR, too, focusing on the environment is not a monolithic story of condemnation. The environment inspired expert efforts and popular demands for improvement, demonstrating awareness and engagement even if East Germans could not substantively change policy until the

---

[24] ABL 2.2.1, Schriftwechsel 21.9.87.

[25] PKA A Kelly 3674, List of Greenway Coordinators, Bratislava, July 19, 1991. Belinda Cooper, "The Western Connection: Western Support for the East German Opposition," *German Politics & Society* 21, no. 4 (Winter 2003), 77.

[26] "Robert Havemann," www.havemann-gesellschaft.de/index.php?id=46, accessed September 7, 2016.

entire system collapsed. Commonalities, overlaps, and interactions between the two Germanys reveal more connections than appear at first glance.

The story of the GDR's environment and environmentalisms, however, is not only one of entanglement with the FRG but part of a larger central European narrative. The GDR challenges the disparate national narratives of environmental protection and protest, bringing multiple environmental influences into conversation with one another. The similarity in political and economic structure to other Soviet bloc states and physical interconnectedness of the environment makes looking eastward (in addition to westward) essential to understanding the East German case. Soviet directives to embark on environmental and cooperative projects brought East Germans into contact with Poles and Czechoslovaks, especially over transboundary pollution in the Baltic, the Black Triangle, and along the Oder–Neisse Line. Scientists and party-backed environmental groups participated in exchanges, sharing information and expertise with one another. Then in the 1980s, independent, transnational activism in eastern Europe was crucial to undermining the communist system and advocating for change. After 1985, connections with western Europe grew, too, creating a larger network of activism. The GDR's unique position on the edges of eastern and western Europe turned it into a pivot that connected the environment, people, policies, and social movements across central Europe.

The GDR and socialism more broadly complicate assumptions about human–nature relations and the rise of environmentalism during the Cold War. Communism was perceived as a threat to liberal democracies and economic prosperity, and this fear also framed western views of the environment.[27] By looking at the East German case, however, multifaceted and even conflicting approaches to the environment replace monolithic interpretations of socialist incompetence. The GDR's environmental degradation laid bare Soviet-style communism's inability to implement real solutions, but only focusing on those failures overlooks experts and activists who worked to understand and combat the devastation. Moreover, the GDR and socialist states in general raised valid if hypocritical appraisals of the limits to environmental protection in capitalist liberal democracies, just as capitalist states invoked triumphalist environmental rhetoric after the

---

[27] J.R. McNeill and Corinna R. Unger, "Introduction: The Big Picture," in *Environmental Histories of the Cold War*, eds. J.R. McNeill and Corinna R. Unger (New York: Cambridge University Press, 2010), 16–17.

collapse of communism.[28] The GDR's position at the nexus of those two systems underscores that communism and capitalism did not exist or evolve in isolation during the Cold War but rather in very close proximity. Common concerns about growth, consumption, and environmental destruction arose regardless of system and spanned the Iron Curtain in postwar Europe.

[28] Rubin and Moranda, "Introduction," 15.

Bibliography

Archival Sources

Archiv der Opposition, Robert Havemann Gesellschaft, Berlin (RHG)
Personalbestände
    Annette Beleites (AB)
    Christan Halbrock (CH)
    Hans Jürgen Tschiche (HJT)
    Hubertus Knabe (HK)
    Johannes Beleites (JB)
    Micheal Beleites (MB)
    Ralf Hirsch (RHi)
    Rüdiger Rosenthal (RR)
    Traude Chrysanthou (TC)
    Tom Sello (TS)
    Antje Wilde (Wi)
    Wolfgang Rüddenklau (WR)
    Ulrich Klotzek (UK)
Regionen
    Berlin (RG B)
    Brandenburg (RG Bra)
    Mecklenburg-Vorpommern (RG M-V)
    Sachsen (RG S)
    Sachsen-Anhalt (RG S-A)
    Thüringen (RG T)
Kirche
    Verschiedenes Gutschrift (Ki 01/02)
    Veröffentlichungen (Ki 01/12)
    Evangelische Kirche in Berlin-Brandenburg (Ki 02)
    Evangelische Kirche der Kirchenprovinz Sachsen (Ki 03)
    Evangelisch-Lutherische Landeskirche Sachsen (Ki 04)
    Evangelische Kirche des Görlitzer Kirchgebietes (Ki 05)
    Evangelisch-Lutherische Landeskirche Mecklenburgs (Ki 06)
    Evangelisch-Lutherische Landeskirche Thüringen (Ki 07)

Kirchentag (Ki 08)
Junge Gemeinde (Ki 9)
Evangelische Studentengemeinden in der DDR (Ki 10)
Stadt- und Landesjugendpfarrämter (Ki 11)
Offene (Jugend-)Arbeit/Kirche von Unten Berlin (Ki 12)
Weiteres zur Offenen Arbeit (Ki 14)
Kirchliches Forschungsheim Wittenberg (Ki 18)
Ökumenische Vollversammlung (Ki 21)
Katholische Kirche (Ki 24)
Thematische Materialsammlungen
DDR Umweltbewegung (TH 02)
Allgemein (TH 02/01)
Industrie (TH 02/02)
Kohle- und Bergbau (TH 02/03)
Energie (TH 02/04)
Atomenergie (TH 02/05)
Wald (TH 02/06)
Wasser (TH 02/07)
Luft (TH 02/08)
Müll (TH 02/09)
Stadtentwicklung (TH 02/10)
Natur- und Artenschutz (TH 02/11)
Eingaben (TH 04)
Osteuropa (TH 12)
Polen (TH 12/03)
Verschiedenes (TH 12/07)
Kirchliches Forschungsheim Wittenberg (KFH)
Arbeitskreis "Erde" (KFH 01–02)
Arbeitskreis "Landwirtschaft und Umwelt" (KFH 07–09)
Korrespondenz
Sonstiges
Ost-West Kontakte (OWK)
Berliner Ökologie Seminar (SWV 02)
Rosa-Luxemburg Affäre (EP 04)
Kommunalwahl, 89 (EP 11)
Arche – Grün-Ökologisches Netzwerk in der Evangelischen Kirche der DDR
(ÜG 03)

Archiv Grünes Gedächtnis, Robert Böll Stiftung, Berlin (AGG)
Petra-Kelly-Archiv
Bundestagsfraktion (B II 1 – B II 4)
Personalbestände
Gerhard Bächer (A Bächer)
Karitas Hensel (A Hensel)
Wilhelm Knabe (A Wilhelm Knabe)

Eva Quistorp
Deutschlandpolitik (Pol 509)

Archiv Bürgerbewegung Leipzig, e.V. (ABL)
Personalbestände
  Andreas Passarge
  Annette Bringt
  Stefan Plaszkorski
Sammlungen
  Rötha (1.7)
  Pleiße-Gedenkumzug (1.8)
  Arbeitsgruppe Umweltschutz (2.1)
  Agrar und Umwelt (4.21)
  Neues Forum/Bündnis 90 (4.28)
  SED Stadt- und Bezirksleitung Leipzig (9.1.1–9.1.133)
Bestand Markkleeberg
  Sammlung Monika Lazar
Umweltblätter
Streiflichter

Bundesarchiv (BArch) Berlin-Lichterfelde und Stiftung Archiv der Parteien und
Massenorganisationen der DDR (SAPMO) (BArch-SAPMO)
  Zentraler Runder Tisch (DA 3)
  Staatsrat der DDR (DA 5)
  Ministerratbeschlüsse (DC 20)
  Amt für Wasserwirtschaft (DK 4)
  Ministerium für Umweltschutz und Wasserwirtschaft (DK 5)
  Beirat für Umweltschutz im Ministerrat der DDR (DK 500)
  Ministerium des Innern (DO 1)
  Staatssekretär für Kirchenfragen (DO 4)
  Kulturbund der SED (DY 27)
  Parteiorganisation beim Zentralkomitee (DY 30)
  Deutscher Städte- und Gemeindetag (DZ 4)

Bundesbeauftragte für die Unterlagen des Staatssicherheitsdienstes der
ehemaligen DDR (BStU), Berlin
  Bezirksverwaltung, Auswertungs- und Kontrollgruppe, Berlin (BV AKG
    Berlin)
  Bezirksverwaltung, Abteilung Absicherung der Volkswirtschaft (BV Bln Abt
    XVIII)
  Bezirksverwaltung, Abteilung Staatsapparat, Blockparteien, Kirchen, Kultur,
    "politischer Untergrund," Berlin (BV Bln Abt XX)
  Bezirksverwaltung, Arbeitsgruppe Terrorabwehr, Berlin (BV Bln AG XXII)
  Bezirksverwaltung, Auswertungs- und Kontrollgruppe, Potsdam (BV Pdm AKG)
  Bezirksverwaltung, Kreisdienststellen, Potsdam (BV Pdm KD)

Bezirksverwaltung, Abteilung Absicherung der Volkswirtschaft, Potsdam (BV Pdm XVIII)

Internationale Verbindungen (Abt X)

Arbeitsgruppe Bereich Kommerzielle Koordinierung (AG BKK)

Spionageabwehr im Bereich Fernmelde- und Elektronische Aufklärung (Funkabwehr), grenzüberschreitende Telefonüberwachung (HA III)

Zentrale Ermittlungsabteilung (HA IX)

Absicherung der Volkswirtschaft, Sicherung der Einrichtungen der Rüstungsforschung und Rüstungsproduktion, Kontrolle der Industrie-, Landwirtschafts-, Finanz- und Handelsministerien sowie der Zollverwaltung der DDR (HA XVIII)

Verkehr, Post- und Fernmeldewesen (HA XIX)

Staatsapparat, Blockparteien, Kirchen, Kultur, "politischer Untergrund MfS" (HA XX)

Juristische Hochschule (JHS)

Rechtsstelle

Sekretariat des Ministers (SdM)

Verwaltung Rückwärtige Dienste (VRD)

Zentrale Auswertungs- und Informationsgruppe (ZAIG)

Zentrale Kontrollgruppe (ZKG)

Zentraler Medizinischer Dienst (ZMD)

Evangelisches Zentralarchiv Berlin (EZA)

EZA 101 – Ökumenischer Kirchenrat

Landeshauptarchiv Magdeburg

Baustelle Stendal

Rat des Bezirkes Magdeburg (M 1)

Kirchenfragen (P 13 IV)

Landeshauptarchiv Merseburg

Abteilung Umweltschutz und Wasserwirtschaft (IV/E)

Abteilung Bauwesen und Investitionen

Open Society Archive (OSA)

Radio Free Europe Situation Reports Czechoslovakia

Radio Free Europe Situation Reports Poland

Ossolineum Biblioteka, Wrocław

Oddział Życia Społecznego

Materiały ogólne

Międzynarodowe Prese

Ruch Wolność i Pokój

Solidarność Walcząca

Politisches Archiv des Auswärtigen Amtes (PA AA)
Außenpolitische Beziehungen bis 1979 (M 1)
Außenpolitische Beziehungen nach 1979 (M 2)
Benachbarte Länder und Ungarn (M 39)
Bundesrepublik Deutschland (M 41)
Rechtsangelegenheiten (M 50)
Zentrale Mikrofilmstelle (M 95)

Stadtarchiv Halle
Kirchenfragen
Oberbürgermeister
Stadtplako

Umweltbibliothek Großhennersdorf, e.V., Großhennersdorf (UBG)
Black Triangle Report
Personalbestände

Newspapers, Periodicals, Magazines
Bild
Frankfurter Rundschau
Gazeta Wyborcza
Neues Deutschland
Prawda: Pismo Myśli Niezależnej
Przyroda Polska
Sächsische Zeitung
Der Spiegel
Süddeutsche Zeitung
Die Tageszeitung
Die Zeit

Published Sources

Andersson, Magnus, ed. *Change and Continuity in Poland's Environmental Policy.* Dordrecht: Springer, 1999.
"National Environmental Policy in the 1980s." In *Change and Continuity in Poland's Environmental Policy*, ed. Magnus Andersson, 61–89. Dordrecht: Springer, 1999.
Arndt, Melanie. *Tschernobyl: Auswirkungen des Reaktorunfalls auf die Bundesrepublik Deutschland und die DDR.* Erfurt: Landeszentrale für politische Bildung Thüringen, 2006.
Augustine, Dolores. *Red Prometheus: Engineering and Dictatorship in East Germany, 1945–1990.* Cambridge, MA: MIT Press, 2007.
Taking on Technocracy: Nuclear Power in Germany, 1945 to the Present. New York: Berghahn Press, 2018.

Bahrmann, Hannes and Christoph Links. *Chronik der Wende: Die DDR zwischen 7. Oktober und 18. Dezember 1989*. Berlin: Ch. Links Verlag, 1994.

Bange, Oliver. "SS-20 and Pershing II: Weapons Systems and the Dynamization of East–West Relations." In *The Nuclear Crisis: The Arms Race, Cold War Anxiety, and the German Peace Movement of the 1980s*, eds. Christoph Becker-Schaum, Philipp Gassert, Martin Klimke, Wilfried Mausbach, and Marianne Zepp, 70–86. New York: Berghahn Books, 2016.

Bathrick, David. *The Powers of Speech: The Politics of Culture in the GDR*. Lincoln, NE: University of Nebraska Press, 1995.

Bayly, C.A., Sven Beckert, Matthew Connelly, Isabel Hofmyer, Wendy Kozol, and Patricia Seed, "AHR Conversation: On Transnational History; Participants: C.A. Bayly, Sven Beckert, Matthew Connelly, Isabel Hofmyer, Wendy Kozol, and Patricia Seed," *American Historical Review* III, no. 5 (December 2006): 1441–1464.

Behrens, Hermann. "Das Institut für Landesforschung und Naturschutz (ILN) und die Biologischen Stationen." In *Umweltschutz in der DDR: Analysen und Zeitzeugenberichte, Band 3: Beruflicher, ehrenamtlicher und freiwilliger Umweltschutz*, eds. Hermann Behrens and Jens Hoffmann, 69–72. Munich: Oekom, 2008.

"Umweltprobleme eines Agrarbezirks im Spiegel von 'Landschaftstagen' – Beispiel Bezirk Neubrandenburg." In *Umweltschutz in der DDR: Analysen und Zeitzeugenberichte, Band 1: Rahmenbedingungen*, eds. Hermann Behrens and Jens Hoffmann, 261–322. Munich: Oekom, 2008.

Behrens, Hermann and Jens Hoffmann, "Organisation des Umweltschutzes." In *Umweltschutz in der DDR: Analysen und Zeitzeugenberichte, Band 1: Rahmenbedingungen*, eds. Hermann Behrens and Jens Hoffmann, 41–49. Munich: Oekom, 2008.

eds. *Umweltschutz in der DDR: Analysen und Zeitzeugen, Band 1–3*. Munich: Oekom, 2008.

eds. *Umweltschutz in der DDR: Analysen und Zeitzeugenberichte, Band 1: Rahmenbedingungen*. Munich: Oekom, 2008.

eds. *Umweltschutz in der DDR: Analysen und Zeitzeugenberichte, Band 2: Mediale und sektorale Aspekte*. Munich: Oekom, 2008.

eds. *Umweltschutz in der DDR: Analysen und Zeitzeugenberichte, Band 3: Beruflicher, ehrenamtlicher und freiwilliger Umweltschutz*. Munich: Oekom, 2008.

Behrens, Hermann, et al. *Wurzeln der Umweltbewegung: Die "Gesellschaft für Natur und Umwelt" (GNU) im Kulturbund der DDR*. Marburg: BdWi-Verlag, 1993.

Beleites, Micheal. *Untergrund: Ein Konflikt mit der Stasi in der Uranprovinz*. Berlin: BasisDruck, 1991.

Berghoff, Hartmut and Uta Andrea Balbier, eds. *The East German Economy, 1945–2010*. New York: Cambridge University Press, 2013.

Betts, Paul. *Within Walls: Private Life in the German Democratic Republic*. New York: Oxford University Press, 2010.

Bjork, James E. *Neither German nor Pole: Catholicism and National Indifference in a Central European Borderland.* Ann Arbor, MI: University of Michigan Press, 2008.

Blackbourn, David. *The Conquest of Nature: Water, Landscape, and the Making of Modern Germany.* London: W. W. Norton & Company, 2006.

Blackbourn, David and James Retallack, eds. *Localism, Landscape, and the Ambiguities of Place: German-Speaking Central Europe, 1860–1930.* Toronto: University of Toronto Press, 2016.

Borejsza, Jerzy and Klaus Ziemer, eds. *Totalitarian and Authoritarian Regimes in Europe: Legacies and Lessons from the Twentieth Century.* New York: Berghahn Books, 2006.

Bösch, Frank, ed. *History Shared and Divided: East and West Germany since the 1970s.* Trans. Jennifer Walcoff Neuheiser. New York: Berghahn Books, 2018.

Bren, Paulina. *The Greengrocer and His TV: The Culture of Communism after the 1968 Prague Spring.* Ithaca, NY: Cornell University Press, 2010.

Brown, Kate. "Securing the Nuclear Nation." *Nationalities Papers* 43, no. 1 (January 2015): 8–26.

"Blinkered Science: Why We Know So Little about Chernobyl's Health Effects," *Culture, Theory, and Critique* 58, no. 4 (September 2017): 413–434.

Bruce, Gary. *The Firm: The Inside Story of the Stasi.* New York: Oxford University Press, 2010.

Brüggemeier, Franz-Josef. "Waldsterben: The Construction and Deconstruction of an Environmental Problem." In *Nature in German History*, ed. Christof Mauch, 119–131. New York: Berghahn Books, 2004.

Bunce, Valerie. *Subversive Institutions: The Design and the Destruction of Socialism and the State.* New York: Cambridge University Press, 1999.

de Certeau, Michel. *The Practice of Everyday Life*, trans. Steven Rendall. Berkeley, CA: University of California Press, 1984.

Chaney, Sandra. *Nature of the Miracle Years: Conservation in West Germany, 1945–1975.* New York: Berghahn Books, 2008.

"A Chemical Landscape Transformed: Bitterfeld, Germany since 1980," *Global Environment* 10, no. 1 (March 2017): 137–167.

and Rita Gudermann, "The East's Contribution to International Conservation Part 1," *Environmental Policy and Law* 40, no. 2–3 (April 2010): 116–124.

and Rita Gudermann, "National Contribution to International Conservation Part II," *Environmental Policy and Law* 40, no. 4 (June 2010): 179–191.

Charles, Daniel. "East German Environment Comes into the Light." *Science* 247, no. 4940 (January 19, 1990): 274–276.

Christ, Peter and Ralf Neubauer, eds. *Kolonie im eigenen Land: Die Treuhand, Bonn und die Wirtschaftskatastrophe der fünf neuen Länder.* Berlin: Rowohlt, 1991.

Cohen, Jean L, and Andrew Arato. *Civil Society and Political Theory.* Cambridge, MA: MIT Press, 1992.

Confino, Alon. *The Nation as a Local Metaphor: Württemberg, Imperial Germany, and National Memory, 1871–1918*. Chapel Hill, NC: University of North Carolina Press, 1997.

Cooper, Belinda. "The Western Connection: Western Support for the East German Opposition," *German Politics & Society* 21, no. 4 (Winter 2003): 74–92.

Curtis, Glenn E., ed. *Poland: a Country Study*. Washington, DC: Library of Congress, Federal Research Division, 1992.

DeBardeleben, Joan. *The Environment and Marxism-Leninism: The Soviet and East German Experience*. Boulder, CO: Westview Press, 1985.

Dale, Gareth. *Popular Protest in East Germany, 1945–1989*. London: Routledge, 2005.

The East German Revolution of 1989. New York: Manchester University Press, 2006.

Davis, Belinda. "A Brief Cosmology of the West German Green Party," *German Politics & Society* 33, no. 4 (Winter 2015): 53–65.

Demshuk, Andrew. *The Lost German East: Forced Migration and the Politics of Memory, 1945–1970*. New York: Cambridge University Press, 2012.

Dix, Andreas and Rita Gudermann, "Naturschutz in der DDR: Idealisiert, ideologisiert, instrumentalisiert?" In *Natur und Staat. Staatlicher Naturschutz in Deutschland, 1906–2006*, eds. Hans-Werner Frohn and Friedemann Schmoll, 535–624. Bonn: Bundesamt für Naturschutz, 2006.

Dominick, Raymond. *The Environmental Movement in Germany: Prophets & Pioneers, 1871– 1971*. Bloomington, IN: Indiana University Press, 1992.

"Capitalism, Communism, and Environmental Protection: Lessons from the German Experience." *Environmental History* 3, no. 3 (July 1998): 311–332.

Eckert, Astrid M. *West Germany and the Iron Curtain: Environment, Economy, and Culture in the Borderland*. New York: Oxford University Press, 2019.

"Geteilt aber nicht unverbunden: Grenzgewässer als deutsch-deutsches Umweltproblem." *Vierteljahrshefte für Zeitgeschichte* 62, no. 1 (January 2014): 69–99.

Ekiert, Grzegorz and Stephen E. Hanson, eds. *Capitalism and Democracy in Central and Eastern Europe: Assessing the Legacy of Communist Rule*. New York: Cambridge University Press, 2003.

Engels, Jens Ivo. *Naturpolitik in der Bundesrepublik: Ideenwelt und politische Verhaltensstile in Naturschutz und Umweltbewegung, 1950–1980*. Paderborn: Ferdinand Schöningh, 2006.

Falk, Barbara. *The Dilemmas of Dissidence in East-Central Europe: Citizen Intellectuals and Philosopher Kings*. New York: Central European University Press, 2003.

Feshbach, Murray and Alfred Friendly. *Ecocide in the USSR: Health and Nature under Siege*. New York: Basic Books, 1992.

Fink, Carole. *Cold War: An International History*. Boulder, CO: Westview Press, 2004.

Fleischman, Thomas "'A Plague of Wild Boars': A New History of Pigs and People in Late Twentieth Century Europe," *Antipode* 49, no. 2 (2017): 1015–1034.

"The Half-Life of State Socialism: What Radioactive Wild Boars Tell Us about the Environmental History of Reunified Germany." In *Ecologies of Socialisms: Germany, Nature, and the Left in History, Politics, and Culture*, eds. Sabine Moedersheim, Scott Moranda, and Eli Rubin, 227–250. New York: Peter Lang Press, 2019.

Communist Pigs: An Animal History of the East Germany's Rise and Fall. Seattle, WA: University of Washington Press, 2020.

Fleming, Michael. "The Ethno-Religious Ambitions of the Roman Catholic Church and the Ascendency of Communism in Postwar Poland (1945–1950)," *Nations and Nationalism* 16, no. 4 (October 2003): 637–656.

Frankland, Erich G. "Green Revolutions? The Role of Green Parties in Eastern Europe's Transition, 1989–1994," *Eastern Europe Quarterly* 29, no. 3 (September 1995): 315–345.

Frohn, Hans Werner and Friedemann Schmoll, eds. *Natur und Staat. Staatlicher Naturschutz in Deutschland, 1906–2006*. Bonn: Bundesamt für Naturschutz, 2006.

Fulbrook, Mary. *Anatomy of a Dictatorship: Inside the GDR, 1949–1989*. New York: Oxford University Press, 1995.

The People's State: East German Society from Hitler to Honecker. New Haven, CT: Yale University Press, 2005.

"Putting the People Back In: The Contentious State of GDR History," *German History* 24, no. 4 (October 2006): 608–620.

Garton Ash, Timothy. *In Europe's Name: Germany and the Divided Continent*. New York: Random House, 1993.

The Magic Lantern: The Revolution of '89 witnessed in Warsaw, Budapest, Berlin, and Prague. New York: Vintage Books, 1993.

Gensichen, Hans-Peter. "Die Beiträge des Wittenberger Forschungsheimes für die kritische Umweltbewegung in der DDR." In *Umweltschutz in der DDR: Analysen und Zeitzeugenberichte, Band 3: Berüflicher, ehrenamtlicher und freiwilliger Umweltschutz*, ed. Hermann Behrens and Jens Hoffmann, 149–178. Munich: Oekom, 2007.

Gieseke, Jens. *The History of the Stasi: East Germany's Secret Police, 1945–1990*. New York: Berghahn Books, 2014.

Gieseke, Jens and Andrea Bahr. *Die Staatssicherheit und die Grünen*. Berlin: Ch. Links Verlag, 2017.

Glassheim, Eagle. *Cleansing the Czechoslovak Borderlands: Migration, Environment, and Health in the Former Sudetenland*. Pittsburgh, PA: University of Pittsburgh Press, 2016.

"Ethnic Cleansing, Communism, and Environmental Devastation in Czechoslovakia's Borderlands, 1945–1989," *The Journal of Modern History* 78, no. 1 (March 2006): 65–72.

"Building a Socialist Environment: Czechoslovak Environmental Policy from the 1960s to the 1980s." In *Nature and the Iron Curtain: Environmental Policy and Social Movements in Communist and Capitalist Countries, 1945–1990*, eds. Astrid Mignon Kirchhof and J.R. McNeill, 137–150. Pittsburgh, PA: University of Pittsburgh Press, 2019.

Goldstein, Thomas W. *Writing in Red: The East German Writers Union and the Role of Literary Intellectuals*. Rochester, NY: Camden House, 2017.

Goeckel, Robert F. *The Lutheran Church and the East German State: Political Conflict and Change under Ulbricht and Honecker*. Ithaca, NY: Cornell University Press, 1990.

"The GDR Legacy and the German Protestant Church," *German Politics & Society*, 31 (Spring 1994): 84–108.

Goltz, Anna Von der. "Attraction and Aversion in Germany's '1968': Encountering the Western Revolt in East Berlin," *Journal of Contemporary History* 50, no. 3 (July 2015): 536–559.

Grady, Tim. "A Shared Environment: German–German Relations along the Border, 1945–1972," *Journal of Contemporary History* 50, no. 3 (July 2015): 660–679.

Granata, Cora. "The Cold War Politics of Cultural Minorities: Jews and Sorbs in the German Democratic Republic, 1976–1989," *German History* 27, no. 1 (January 2009): 60–83.

Gray, Richard T. and Sabine Wilke, eds. and trans. *German Unification and its Discontents: Documents from the Peaceful Revolution*. Seattle, WA: University of Washington Press, 1996.

Halbrock, Christian. "Störfaktor Jugend: Die Anfänge der unabhängigen Umweltbewegung in der DDR." In *Arche Nova: Opposition in der DDR, "Das Grün-ökologische Netzwerk Arche," 1988–90*, eds. Carlo Jordan and Hans Michael Kloth, 13–32. Berlin: BasisDruck, 1995.

"Die unabhängigen Umweltgruppen in der DDR: Forschungsstand und Überblick," *Bundeszentrale für politische Bildung*, December 15, 2011.

Halicka, Beata. *Polens Wilder Westen: Erzwungene Migration und die kulturelle Aneignung des Oderraums, 1945–1948*. Paderborn: Ferdinand Schönigh, 2013.

Hankiss, Elemér. "The 'Second Society': Is There an Alternative Social Model Emerging in Hungary?" In *Crisis and Reform in Eastern Europe*, eds. Ferenc Fehér and Andrew Arato, 303–334. New Brunswick, NJ: Transaction, 1991.

Harsch, Donna. *Revenge of the Domestic: Women, the Family, and Communism in the German Democratic Republic*. Princeton, NJ: Princeton University Press, 2007.

Hicks, Barbara E. *Environmental Politics in Poland: A Social Movement between Regime and Opposition*. New York: Columbia University Press, 1996.

Hochscherf, Tobias, Christoph Laucht, and Andrew Plowman, eds. *Divided but Not Disconnected: German Experiences in the Cold War*. New York: Berghahn Press, 2005.

Huff, Tobias. *Natur und Industrie im Sozialismus: Eine Umweltgeschichte der DDR*. Göttingen: Vandenhoeck & Ruprecht, 2015.

Hünemörder, Kai. "Environmental Crisis and Soft Politics: Détente and the Global Environment, 1968–1975." In *Environmental Histories of the Cold War*, eds. J.R. McNeill and Corinna R. Unger, 257–276. New York: Cambridge University Press, 2010.

Jancar-Webster, Barbara, ed. *Environmental Action in Eastern Europe: Responses to Crisis*. Armonk, NY: M.E. Sharpe, 1993.

"The Eastern European Environmental Movement and the Transformation of East European Society." In *Environmental Action in Eastern Europe: Responses to Crisis*, ed. Barbara Jancar-Webster, 192–219. Armonk, NY: M.E. Sharpe, 1993.

Jarausch, Konrad Hugo. *The Rush to German Unity*. New York: Oxford University Press, 1994.

ed. *Dictatorship as Experience: Towards a Socio-Cultural History of the GDR*. New York: Berghahn Books, 1999.

"Beyond Uniformity: The Challenge of Historicizing the GDR." In *Dictatorship as Experience: Towards a Socio-Cultural History of the GDR*, ed. Konrad H. Jarausch, 3–14. New York: Berghahn Books, 1999.

"Care and Coercion: The GDR as Welfare Dictatorship." In *Dictatorship as Experience: Towards a Socio-Cultural History of the GDR*, ed. Konrad H. Jarausch, 47–69. New York: Berghahn Books, 1999.

Out of Ashes: A New History of Europe in the Twentieth Century. Princeton, NJ: Princeton University Press, 2015.

Jarausch, Konrad Hugo and Volker Gransow, eds. *Uniting Germany: Documents and Debates, 1944, 1993*. New York: Berghahn Books, 1994.

Jarausch, Konrad H. and Michael Geyer. *Shattered Past: Reconstructing German Histories*. Princeton, NJ: Princeton University Press, 2003.

Jaskułowski, Tytus. *Przyjaźń, której nie było: Ministerstwo Bezpieczeństwa Państwowego NRD wobec MSW, 1974–1990*. Warsaw: Wydawnictwa Uniwersytetu Warszawskiego, 2014.

Jones, Merrill E. "Origins of the East German Environmental Movement," *German Studies Review* 16, no. 2 (May 1993): 235–264.

Jordan, Carlo. "Greenway – das osteuropäische Grüne Netzwerk (1985–1990)." In *Grünes Gedächtnis 2010: Europa Braucht Vielfalt*, 34–44. Berlin: Archiv Grünes Gedächtnis, 2010.

Jordan, Carlo and Kloth, Hans Michael, eds. *Arche Nova: Opposition in der DDR, "Das Grün-ökologische Netzwerk Arche," 1988–90*. Berlin: BasisDruck Verlag GmbH, 1995.

Josephson, Paul. "War on Nature as Part of the Cold War: The Strategic and Ideological Roots of Environmental Degradation in the Soviet Union." In *Environmental Histories of the Cold War*, eds. J.R. McNeill and Corinna R. Unger, 21–50. New York: Cambridge University Press, 2010.

Juchnowicz, Stanisław. "Słowo Wstępne." In *Ekorozwój Szansą Przetrwania Cywilizacji: Materiały z Konferencji PKE, 4–5 Czerwiec 1985*, 9. Kraków: Wydawnictwo Akademii Górniczo-Hutniczej, 1986.

ed. *Deklaracja Ideowa I Tezy Programowe Polskiego Klubu Ekologicznego*. Kraków: Nakładem Uniwersytetu Jagiellońskiego, 1989.

Judt, Tony. *Postwar: A History of Europe since 1945*. New York: Penguin, 2005.

Kabala, Stanley J. "The History of Environmental Protection in Poland and the Growth of Awareness and Activism." In *Environmental Action in Eastern Europe: Responses to Crisis*, ed. Barbara Jancar-Webster, 114–133. Armonk, NY: M.E. Sharpe, 1993.

Kaminski, Antoni Z. and Bartłowmiej Kaminski, "Road to 'People's Poland': Stalin's Conquest Revisited." In *Stalinism Revisited: The Establishment of Communist Regimes in East-Central Europe*, ed. Vladimer Tiseameanu, 195–228. New York: Central European University Press, 2009.

Karch, Brendan. *Nation and Loyalty in a German-Polish Borderland: Upper Silesia, 1848–1960*. New York: Cambridge University Press, 2018.

"Instrumental nationalism in Upper Silesia." In *National Indifference and the History of Nationalism in Modern Europe*, eds. Maarten van Ginderachter and Jon Fox, 180–203. New York: Routledge, 2019.

Karlsch, Rainer and Jochen Laufer, eds. *Sowjetische Demontagen in Deutschland, 1944–1949: Hintergründe, Ziele und Wirkungen*. Berlin: Duncker und Humblot, 2002.

Keck-Szajbel, Mark. "A Cultural Shift in the 1970s: 'Texas' Jeans, Taboos, and Transnational Tourism," *East European Politics and Societies and Cultures* 29, no. 1 (February 2015): 212–225.

Kenney, Padraic. *Rebuilding Poland: Workers and Communists, 1945–1950*. Ithaca, NY: Cornell University Press, 1997.

A Carnival of Revolution: Central Europe, 1989. Princeton, NJ: Princeton University Press, 2002.

Kirchhof, Astrid Mignon. "'For a Decent Quality of Life': Environmental Groups in East and West Berlin." *Journal of Urban History* 41, no. 4 (April 2015), 625–46.

Kirchhof, Astrid Mignon and J.R. McNeill, eds. *Nature and the Iron Curtain: Environmental Policy and Social Movements in Communist and Capitalist Countries, 1945–1990*. Pittsburgh, PA: University of Pittsburgh Press, 2019.

Kleßmann, Christoph, ed. *The Divided Past: Rewriting Post-War German History*. New York: Berghahn, 2001.

Die doppelte Staatsgründung: Deutsche Geschichte, 1945–1955. Göttingen: Vandenhoeck & Ruprecht, 1991.

Kloepfer, Michael. *Das Umweltrecht in der deutschen Einigung: Zum Umweltrecht im Einigungsvertrag und zum Umweltrahmengesetz*. Berlin: Duncker & Humblot, 1991.

Knabe, Hubertus. "Neue Soziale Bewegungen im Sozialismus. Zur Genesis alternativer politischer Orientierungen in der DDR," *Kölner Zeitschrift für Soziologie und Sozialpsychologie* 40, no. 3 (September 1988): 551–569.

Umweltkonflikte im Sozialismus: Möglichkeiten und Grenzen gesellschaftlicher Problemartikulation in sozialistischen Systemen, Eine vergleichende Analyse der Umweltdiskussion in der DDR und Ungarn. Cologne: Verlag Wissenschaft und Politik, 1993.

Kocka, Jürgen. *Civil Society and Dictatorship in Modern Germany.* Hanover, NH: University Press of New England, 2010.

Komska, Yuliya. *The Icon Curtain: The Cold War's Quiet Border.* Chicago, IL: University of Chicago Press, 2015.

Kotkin, Stephen. *Uncivil Society: 1989 and the Implosion of the Communist Establishment.* Chapel Hill, NC: University of North Carolina Press, 2009.

Kowalczuk, Ilko-Sascha. "Gegenkräfte: Opposition und Widerstand in der DDR – Begriffliche und methodische Probleme." In *Opposition der DDR von den 70er Jahren bis zum Zusammenbruch der SED-Herrschaft,* ed. Eberhard Kuhrt, 47–80. Opladen: Leske + Budrich, 1999.

Endspiel: Die Revolution von 1989 in der DDR. Munich: C.H. Beck Verlag, 2009.

Kramer, Mark. "Stalin, Soviet Policy, and the Establishment of a Communist Bloc in Eastern Europe, 1941–1949." In *Imposing, Maintaining, and Tearing Open the Iron Curtain: The Cold War and East-Central Europe, 1945–1989,* eds. Mark Kramer and Vit Smetana, 3–37. New York: Lexington Books, 2014.

Kraus, Michael, Anna M. Cienciala, Margaret K. Gnoinska, Douglas Selvage, Molly Pucci, Erik Kulavig, Constantine Pleshakov, A. Ross Johnson, Mark Kramer, and Smetana Vít, "The Cold War and East-Central Europe, 1945–1989," *Journal of Cold War Studies* 19, no. 2 (Spring 2017): 158–214.

Kubik, Jan. *The Power of Symbols against the Symbols of Power: The Rise of Solidarity and the Fall of State Socialism in Poland.* University Park, PA: Pennsylvania State University Press, 1994.

Kubow, Magdalena. "The Solidarity Movement in Poland: Its History and Meaning in Collective Memory," *The Polish Review* 58, no. 2 (2013): 3–14.

Kulesza, Michał. "Efektywność prawa i administracji w zakresie ochrony przyrody i środowiska, Fragment Raportu KOP PAN na III Kongres Nauki Polskiej." In *Problemy Ochrony Polskiej Przyrody,* eds. Romuald Olaczek and Kazimierz Zarzycki, 23–29. Warsaw: Polish Scientific Publishers, 1988.

Laakkonen, Simo, Viktor Pal, and Richard Tucker, "The Cold War and Environmental History: Complementary Fields," *Cold War History* 16, no. 4 (Fall 2016): 377–394.

Lausitzer und Mitteldeutsche Bergbau-Verwaltungsgesellschaft mbH, "10 Jahre Sanierungsbergbau mit Tagebaugroßgeräten" (2000).

Lebow, Katherine. *Unfinished Utopia: Nowa Huta, Stalinism, and Polish Society, 1949–1956.* Ithaca, NY: Cornell University Press, 2013.

Lekan, Thomas M. *Imagining the Nation in Nature: Landscape Preservation and German Identity, 1885–1945.* Cambridge, MA: Harvard University Press, 2004.

Lekan, Thomas M. and Thomas Zeller, eds. *Germany's Nature: Cultural Landscapes and Environmental History.* New Brunswick, NJ: Rutgers University Press, 2005.

Lepp, Claudia. *Tabu der Einheit? Die Ost-West-Gemeinschaft der evangelischen Christen und die deutsche Teilung (1945–1969).* Göttingen: Vandenhoeck & Ruprecht, 2005.

Liebig, Dieter. "Begleitbuch zur Ausstellung: Anspruch und Wirklichkeit: Die Energie- und Umweltpolitik in der DDR am Beispiel des Energieträgers Braunkohle." Großhennersdorf: Umweltbibliothek Großhennersdorf, e.V., 2009.

Lindenberger, Thomas, ed. *Herrschaft und Eigen-Sinn in der Diktatur: Studien zur Gesellschaftsgeschichte der DDR.* Cologne: Böhlau, 1999.

Liszka, Arnaud and Thomas Pilz, ed. *Lausitz Botin: Das Jahr 1989 in der sächsischen Provinz im Spiegel einer Zittauer Oppositionszeitschrift.* Bautzen: Lusatia Verlag, 1999.

Versuche in der Wahrheit zu Leben: Widerständiges Leben in der Oberlausitz, 1978–1989. Dresden: Neisse Verlag, 2009.

Lokatis, Siegfried and Ingrid Sonntag, eds. *Heimliche Leser in der DDR: Kontrolle und Verbreitung unerlaubter Literatur.* Berlin: Ch. Links Verlag, 2007.

Maier, Charles S. *Dissolution: The Crisis of Communism and the End of East Germany.* Princeton, NJ: Princeton University Press, 1997.

Maron, Monika. *Flight of Ashes,* trans. David Newton Marinelli. New York: Readers International, 1986.

Mauch, Christof, ed. *Nature in German History.* New York: Berghahn Books, 2004.

Mauch, Christof, Nathan Stoltzfus, and Douglas R. Weiner, eds. *Shades of Green: Environmental Activism around the Globe.* Lanham, MD: Rowman & Littlefield Publishers, 2006.

McCook, Brian Joseph. *The Borders of Integration: Polish Migrants in Germany and the United States, 1870–1924.* Athens, OH: Ohio University Press, 2011.

McNeill, J.R. and Corinna R. Unger, eds. *Environmental Histories of the Cold War.* New York: Cambridge University Press, 2010.

Meadows, Donella H., et al. *The Limits to Growth: A Report for the Club of Rome's Projection the Predicament of Mankind.* New York: Universe Books, 1972.

Metzger, Birgit. *"Erst stirbt der Wald, dann Du!" Das Waldsterben als westdeutsches Politikum (1978–1968).* Frankfurt am Main: Campus Verlag, 2015.

Meuschel, Sigrid. *Legitimation und Parteiherrschaft: Zum Paradox von Stabilität und Revolution in der DDR, 1945–1989.* Frankfurt am Main: Suhrkamp, 1992.

Mikkonen, Simon and Pia Koivunen, eds. *Beyond the Divide: Entangled Histories of Cold War Europe.* New York: Berghahn Books, 2015.

Milder, Stephen. *Greening Democracy: The Anti-Nuclear Movement and Political Environmentalism in West Germany and Beyond, 1968–1983.* New York: Cambridge University Press, 2017.

Miller, Bruce G. *Coal Energy Systems.* New York: Elsevier Academic Press, 2005.

Moedersheim, Sabine, Scott Moranda, and Eli Rubin, eds. *Ecologies of Socialisms: Germany, Nature, and the Left in History, Politics, and Culture.* New York: Peter Lang Press, 2019.

Möller, Christian. *Umwelt und Herrschaft in der DDR: Politik, Protest und die Grenzen der Partizipation in der Diktatur.* Göttingen: Vanderhoeck & Ruprecht, 2020.

"Zwischen Gestaltungseuphorie, Versagen und Ohnmach: Umwelt, Staat und volkseigene Wirtschaft in der DDR," *Zeitschrift für Unternehmensgeschichte* 60, no. 2 (October 2015): 141–167.

Moranda, Scott. *The People's Own Landscape: Nature, Tourism, and Dictatorship in East Germany.* Ann Arbor, MI: University of Michigan Press, 2014.

Murdock, Caitlin. *Changing Places: Society, Culture, and Territory in the Saxon-Bohemian Borderlands, 1870–1946.* Ann Arbor, MI: University of Michigan Press, 2010.

Mühlberg, Felix. *Bürger, Bitten und Behörden: Geschichte der Eingabe in der DDR.* Berlin: Karl Dietz Verlag, 2004.

Naimark, Norman. *The Russians in Germany: A History of the Soviet Zone of Occupation, 1945–1949.* Cambridge, MA: Harvard University Press, 1995.

Neubert, Ehrhart. *Geschichte der Opposition in der DDR, 1949–1989.* Berlin: Ch. Links Verlag, 1997.

Neumann, Ulrich. "Was war, war wenig und viel: die Anfänge der Arche." In *Arche Nova: Opposition in der DDR, "Das Grün-ökologische Netzwerk Arche," 1988–90,* eds. Carlo Jordan and Hans Michael Kloth, 81–98. Berlin: BasisDruck, 1995.

Nohara -Schnabel, Ilka. "Zur Entwicklung der Umweltpolitik in der DDR." *Deutschland Archiv* 9 (1976): 809–829.

Oberkrome, Willi. *"Deutsche Heimat": Nationale Konzeption und regionale Praxis von Naturschutz, Landschaftsgestaltung und Kulturpolitik in Westfalen-Lippe und Thüringen (1900–1960).* Paderborn: Ferdinand Schöningh, 2004.

Olaczek, Romuald. "Konserwatorska Ochrona Przyrody w Polsce – Osiągnięcia, rozczarowania, oczekiwania." in *Problemy Ochrony Polskie Przyrody,* eds. Romuald Olaczek and Kazimierz Zarzycki, 87–107. Warsaw: Polish Scientific Publishers, 1988.

Olaczek, Romuald and Kazimierz Zarzycki, eds. *Problemy Ochrony Polskiej Przyrody.* Warsaw: Polish Scientific Publishers, 1988.

Oschlies, Wolf. *Bald ist Polen doch Verloren: Umweltzerstörung hinter Oder und Neisse.* Cologne: Böhlau, 1987.

Palmowski, Jan. *Inventing a Socialist Nation: Heimat and the Politics of Everyday Life in the GDR, 1945–1990.* New York: Cambridge University Press, 2009.

Paucke, Horst and Adolf Bauer. *Umweltprobleme: Herausforderung der Menschheit.* Berlin: Dietz Verlag, 1979.

Pavlínek, Petr and John Pickles. *Environmental Transitions: Transformation and Ecological Defence in Central and Eastern Europe.* New York: Routledge, 2000.

Pearson, Benjamin. "Faith and Democracy: Political Transformations at the German Protestant *Kirchentag*, 1949–1969." PhD Dissertation, University of North Carolina at Chapel Hill, 2007.

Peperkamp, Esther and Małgorzata Rajtar, eds. *Religion and the Secular in Eastern Germany, 1945 to the Present*. Boston, MA: Brill, 2010.

Pence, Katherine and Paul Betts, eds. *Socialist Modern: East German Everyday Culture and Politics*. Ann Arbor, MI: University of Michigan Press, 2008.

Penn, Shana. *Solidarity's Secret: The Women Who Defeated Communism in Poland*. Ann Arbor, IN: University of Michigan Press, 2005.

Pfaff, Steven. "The Politics of Peace in the GDR: The Independent Peace Movement, the Church, and the Origins of the East German Opposition," *Peace & Change* 26, no. 3 (July 2001): 280–300.

Polak-Springer, Peter. *Recovered Territory: A German–Polish Conflict over Land and Culture, 1919–1989*. New York: Berghahn Books, 2015.

Pollack, Detlef. *Politischer Protest: Politisch alternative Gruppen in der DDR*. Opladen: Leske Budrich, 2000.

Port, Andrew I., *Conflict and Stability in the German Democratic Republic*. New York: Cambridge University Press, 2007.

Port, Andrew I. and Mary Fulbrook, eds. *Becoming East German: Socialist Structures and Sensibilities after Hitler*. New York: Berghahn Books, 2013.

Porter-Szücs, Brian. *Poland in the Modern World: Beyond Martyrdom*. Malden, MA: Wiley-Blackwell, 2014.

Quint, Peter E. *The Imperfect Union: Constitutional Structures of German Unification*. Princeton, NJ: Princeton University Press, 1997.

Radecki, Wojciech. *Prawnokarna ochrona środowiska naturalnego w PRL*. Wrocław: Zakład Narodowy im. Ossolińskich, 1981.

Radkau, Joachim. *Nature and Power: A Global History of the Environment*. New York: Cambridge University Press, 2008.

The Age of Ecology: A Global History. Trans. Patrick Camiller. Malden, MA: Polity Press, 2014.

Reaves, John Andrew. "The Development of an Ecologically Critical Sorbian Literature as a Consequence of the German Democratic Republic's Dependence on Soft Coal as an Energy Source." PhD Dissertation, University of Wisconsin at Madison, 1996.

Rein, Gerhard, ed. *Die Opposition in der DDR: Entwürfe für einen anderen Sozialismus*. Berlin: Wichern-Verlag, 1990.

Richardson-Little, Ned. "Dictatorship and Dissent: Human Rights in East Germany in the 1970s." In *The Breakthrough: Human Rights in the 1970s*, eds. Jan Eckel and Samuel Moyn, 49–67. Philadelphia, PA: University of Pennsylvania Press, 2013.

The Human Rights Dictatorship: Socialism, Global Solidarity, and Revolution in East Germany. New York: Cambridge University Press, 2020.

Richter, Michael. *Die friedliche Revolution: Aufbruch zur Demokratie in Sachsen 1989/90*. Göttingen: Vandenhoeck & Ruprecht, 2009.

Rink, Dieter. "Environmental Policy and the Environmental Movement in East Germany," *Capitalism, Nature, Socialism* 13, no. 3 (September 2002): 73–91.

Rosenbladt, Sabine. *Der Osten ist grün? Ökoreportagen aus der DDR, Sowjetunion, Tschechoslowakei, Polen, Ungarn.* Hamburg: Rasch und Röhring Verlag, 1988.

Roth, Roland and Dieter Rucht, eds. *Die sozialen Bewegungen in Deutschland seit 1945: Ein Handbuch.* Frankfurt: Campus, 2008.

Roth, Roland and Detlef Murphy, "From Competing Factions to the Rise of the Realos." In *The German Greens: Paradox between Movement and Party*, eds. Margit Mayer and John Ely, 49–71. Philadelphia, PA: Temple University Press, 1998.

Rüddenklau, Wolfgang, ed. *Störenfried: DDR-Opposition 1986–1989: mit Texten aus den "Umweltblättern."* Berlin: BasisDruck, 1992.

Rubin, Eli. *Synthetic Socialism: Plastics and Dictatorship in the German Democratic Republic.* Chapel Hill, NC: University of North Carolina Press, 2008.

"Amnesiopolis: From Mietskaserne to Wohnungsbauserie 70 in East Berlin's Northeast," *Central European History* 47, no. 2 (June 2014): 334–374.

Rucht, Dieter. *Die sozialen Bewegungen in Deutshcland seit 1945: Ein Handbuch.* Frankfurt am Main: Campus Verlag, 2008.

Rupprecht, Tobias. "Socialist High Modernity and Global Stagnation: A Shared History of Brazil and the Soviet Union during the Cold War," *Journal of Global History* 6, no. 3 (November 2011): 505–28.

Sabrow, Martin, ed. *1989 Und Die Rolle Der Gewalt.* Göttingen: Wallstein, 2012.

Schaefer, Bernd. *The East German State and the Catholic Church, 1945–1989.* New York: Berghahn Books, 2010.

Schama, Simon. *Landscape and Memory.* New York: Alfred A. Knopf, 1995.

Schneider, Wolfgang, ed. *Leipziger Demo Montag Tagebuch Demontage.* Leipzig and Weimar: Gustav Kiepenheuer Verlag, 1991.

Schroeder, Klaus. *Der SED-Staat: Geschichte und Strukturen der DDR, 1949–1969.* Cologne: Böhlau, 2013.

Schubert, Dirk. "Path Dependencies Managing the River Elbe and the Requirements of Hamburg's Open Tidal Seaport." In *Rivers Lost, Rivers Regained: Rethinking City–River Relations*, eds. Martin Knoll, Uwe Lübken, and Dieter Schott, 156–176. Pittsburgh, PA: University of Pittsburgh Press, 2017.

Schüring, Michael. *"Bekennen gegen den Atomstaat": Die evangelischen Kirchen in der Bundesrepublik Deutschlnd und die Konflikte um die Atomenergie, 1970–1990.* Göttingen: Wallstein Verlag, 2015.

Scott, James C. *Seeing Like a State: How Certain Schemes to Improve the Human Condition Have Failed.* New Haven, CT: Yale University Press, 1998.

Sheffer, Edith. *Burned Bridge: How East and West Germans Made the Iron Curtain .* New York: Oxford University Press, 2011.

Silomon, Anke. *"Schwerter zu Pflugscharen" und die DDR: Die Friedensarbeit der evangelischen Kirchen in der DDR im Rahmen der Friedensdekaden 1980 bis 1982.* Göttingen: Vandenhoeck & Ruprecht, 1999.

Slobodian, Quinn. "China Is Not Far! Alternative Internationalism and the Tiananmen Square Massacre in East Germany's 1989." In *Alternative*

Globalizations: Eastern Europe and the Postcolonial World, eds. James Mark, Artemy M. Kalinovsky, Steffi Marung, 311–327. Bloomington, IN: Indiana University Press, 2020.

Snajder, Edward. *Nature Protests: The End of Ecology in Slovakia*. Seattle, WA: University of Washington Press, 2008.

Steinbach, Walter Christian. *Eine Mark für Espenhain: Vom Christlichen Umweltseminar Rötha*. Leipzig: Evangelische Verlagsanstalt, 2018.

Steiner, André. *The Plans that Failed: An economic History of the GDR*. New York: Berghahn Books, 2010.

Stief, Martin. *"Stellt die Bürger ruhig": Staatssicherheit und Umweltzerstörung im Chemierevier Halle-Bitterfeld*. Göttingen: Vanderhoeck & Ruprecht, 2019.

Stiglich, Larissa R. "After Socialism: The Transformation of Everyday Life in Eisenhüttenstadt, 1975–2015." PhD Dissertation, University of North Carolina at Chapel Hill, 2020.

Stokes, Raymond. "From Schadenfreude to Going-Out-of-Business Sale: East Germany and the Oil Crises of the 1970s." In *The East German Economy, 1945–2010: Falling Behind or Catching Up?*, eds. Hartmut Berghoff and Uta Andrea Balbier, 131–144. New York: Cambridge University Press, 2013.

Stola, Dariusz. "Opening a Non-Exit State: The Passport Policy of Communist Poland, 1949–1980," *East European Politics and Societies and Cultures* 29, no. 1 (February 2015): 96–119.

Stoler, Ann Laura, ed. *Haunted by Empire: Geographies of Intimacy in North American History*. Durham, NC: Duke University Press, 2006.

Stoltzfus, Nathan. "Public Space and the Dynamics of Environmental Action: Green Protest in the GDR," *Archiv für Sozialgeschichte* 43 (2003): 385–403.

Ther, Philipp. "Beyond the Nation: The Relational Basis of a Comparative History of Germany and Europe," *Central European History* 36, no. 1 (March 2003): 45–73.

Tiseameanu, Vladimer, ed. *Stalinism Revisited: The Establishment of Communist Regimes in East-Central Europe*. New York: Central European University Press, 2009.

Tompkins, Andrew S. *Better Active than Radioactive! Anti-Nuclear Protest in 1970s France and West Germany*. New York: Oxford University Press, 2016.

"Grassroots Transnationalism(s): Franco-German Opposition to Nuclear Energy in the 1970s," *Contemporary European History* 25, no. 1 (February 2016): 117–142.

Trutkowski, Dominik. *Der geteilte Ostblock: die Grenzen der SBZ/DDR zu Polen und der Tschechoslowakei*. Cologne: Böhlau Verlag, 2011.

Umweltbericht der DDR: Information zur Analyse der Umweltbedingungen in der DDR und zu weiteren Maßnahmen. West Berlin: Institut für Umweltschutz, 1990.

Uekötter, Frank. "Entangled Ecologies: Outlines of a Green History of Two or More Germanys." In *History Shared and Divided: East and West Germany since the 1970s*, ed. Frank Bösch, trans. Jennifer Walcoff Neuheiser, 147–190. New York: Berghahn Books, 2018.

The Greenest Nation? A New History of German Environmentalism. Cambridge, MA: MIT Press, 2014.

The Green and the Brown: A History of Conservation in Nazi Germany. New York: Cambridge University Press, 2006.

Weiner, Douglas R. *A Little Corner of Freedom: Russian Nature Protection from Stalin to Gorbachev.* Berkeley and Los Angeles, CA: University of California Press, 1999.

Models of Nature: Ecology, Conservation and Cultural Revolution in Soviet Russia. Pittsburgh, PA: University of Pittsburgh Press, 2000.

Wensierski, Peter. *Beton ist Beton: Zivilisationskritik aus der DDR.* Hattingen: Scandica-Verlag, 1981.

Null Bock auf DDR: Aussteigerjugend im anderen Deutschland. Reinbek bei Hamburg: Rowohlt, 1984.

Von oben nach unten wächst gar nichts: Umweltzerstörung und Protest in der DDR. Frankfurt: Fischer Verlag, 1986.

Wentker, Hermann. *Außenpolitik in engen Grenzen: Die DDR im internationalen System, 1949–1989.* Munich: Oldenbourg, 2007.

White Jr., Lynn. "The Historical Roots of Our Ecologic Crisis," *Science* 155 (March 1967): 1203–1207.

Williams, John Alexander. *Turning to Nature in Germany: Hiking, Nudism and Conservation, 1900–1940.* Stanford, CA: Stanford University Press, 2007.

Würth, Gerhard. *Umweltschutz und Umweltzerstörung in der DDR.* Frankfurt/Main: Peter Lang Verlag, 1985.

Zahra, Tara. *Kidnapped Souls: National Indifference and the Battle for Children in the Bohemian Lands, 1900–1948.* Ithaca, NY: Cornell University Press, 2008.

Zimmerling, Zeno and Sabine Zimmerling, eds. *Neue Chronik der DDR: Berichte, Fotos, Dokumente.* Berlin: Verlag Tribüne, 1990.

Zuppke, Uwe. "Aus der Tätigkeit des Zentrums für Umweltgestaltung." In *Umweltschutz in der DDR: Analysen und Zeitzeugenberichte, Band 3: Berüflicher, ehrenamtlicher und freiwilliger Umweltschutz,* eds. Hermann Behrens and Jens Hoffmann, 273–282. Munich: Oekom, 2008.

Zuzowski, Robert. *Political Dissent and Opposition in Poland: The Workers' Defense Committee "KOR."* Westport, CT: Praeger, 1992.

Index